P9-DNE-497

ALSO BY RICHARD WHITTLE

The Dream Machine:
The Untold History of the Notorious V-22 Osprey

PREDATOR

PREDATOR

THE SECRET ORIGINS OF
THE DRONE REVOLUTION

RICHARD WHITTLE

HENRY HOLT AND COMPANY

NEW YORK

Henry Holt and Company, LLC
Publishers since 1866
175 Fifth Avenue
New York, New York 10010
www.henryholt.com

Henry Holt® and 🅷® are registered trademarks of
Henry Holt and Company, LLC.

Portions of chapters 1, 3, and 4 were previously published in different form
in "The Drone Started Here" in *Air & Space Smithsonian* (May 2013).
Portions of chapters 5 through 10 were previously published in different form
in "Predator's Big Safari," Mitchell Institute for Airpower Studies,
Mitchell Paper 7 (August 2011).

Library of Congress Cataloging-in-Publication Data
Whittle, Richard.
Predator : the secret origins of the drone revolution / Richard Whittle.
    pages cm
Includes bibliographical references and index.
ISBN 978-0-8050-9964-5 (hardback)—ISBN 978-0-8050-9965-2 (ebook)   1. Drone
aircraft—United States—History.   2. Drone aircraft—United States—Design and
construction.   3. Karem, Abraham, 1937–   4. Aerospace industries—California,
Southern—History.   I. Title.
    UG1242.D7W57 2014
    623.74'69—dc23   2014014070

First Edition 2014

Designed by Kelly S. Too

Printed in the United States of America

1   3   5   7   9   10   8   6   4   2

For Faye

There is, perhaps, in every thing of any consequence, a secret history which it would be amusing to know, could we have it authentically communicated.

—James Boswell, The Life of Samuel Johnson, LL.D.

CONTENTS

PREDATOR

PROLOGUE

Late in the afternoon of Wednesday, July 12, 2000, a bus carrying about a dozen "high political rollers," as thirty-six-year-old Air Force Captain Scott Swanson viewed them, pulled up at Indian Springs Air Force Auxiliary Field, a broiling desert outpost northwest of Las Vegas. The visitors included the National Security Council's deputy counterterrorism chief, a senior official from the CIA's Counterterrorist Center, officials from other intelligence and military agencies, and the director of a shadowy Air Force technology shop known as Big Safari. Indian Springs was home to the 11th and 15th Reconnaissance Squadrons, units assigned to fly a relatively new unmanned, remote-control aircraft. Though the drone was equipped with nothing deadlier than daylight and infrared video cameras, it bore a menacing name: Predator.

Swanson, a former special operations helicopter pilot, had flown Predators for the past two years, mostly in regular intelligence, surveillance, and reconnaissance missions over the Balkans. But soon he was to join Big Safari as that outfit's sole Predator pilot, which was why he had received a phone call from the Pentagon a few days earlier asking him to organize a show-and-tell session for those on the bus.

"There's going to be a bunch of people in suits," Swanson was told. "Can you do a briefing on Predator and show them some capabilities in flight, but keep it quiet?"

On the other end of the call was Air Force Colonel James G. Clark, whose official title was technical director, simulation and integration, Office of the Assistant Vice Chief of Staff, Headquarters, U.S. Air Force. In reality, Clark worked for the service's two top leaders, the four-star chief of staff and the civilian secretary of the Air Force. He was their favorite fixer, an inside operator who was canny about how to bypass bureaucracy and who relished getting things done, as he liked to put it, "quick and dirty." This was partly why Clark encouraged everyone to call him by his nickname, Snake—or, if regulations required they salute him, Colonel Snake. He consciously cultivated the image of a shrewd and slippery operator who might be dangerous if stepped on, a reputation he found useful in intimidating real or potential opponents. For the past three years, the Predator had been Snake Clark's pet project, and for the past two years, Big Safari's as well.

On the phone, Clark told Swanson the suits were coming to Indian Springs to get a better understanding of what they might expect from the Predator if it were used "in a rugged part of the world." Clark slithered around the obvious question of what precise mission the government had in mind, but Swanson got the message. He read daily intelligence briefs and worked with intelligence officers, and he could guess which rugged part of the world, and even which country, was of such keen interest to these particular visitors.

From their air-conditioned bus, the delegation climbed down into the shimmering desert heat at Indian Springs and filtered into an air-conditioned briefing room, where Swanson gave them a PowerPoint presentation on the Predator and what it could do. Introduced six years earlier under a new type of rapid Pentagon procurement program, the Predator was the military's first Medium Altitude Endurance Unmanned Aerial Vehicle—a drone that could linger in the air well beyond twenty-four hours, pointing cameras at the earth and transmitting live video images back to its operators. The little aircraft owed its phenomenal endurance to its unique configuration, a design informed by its inventor's childhood hobby. The Predator had thin, tapered wings stretching forty-nine feet from tip to tip and a slender fuselage just under half that long, eight feet shorter than a Piper Cub's. Fashioned from lightweight composite materials, the fuselage was flat on the bottom, rounded on top, and bulged into a dome at the nose. With its flimsy wings and skin, the craft resembled a weekend hobbyist's glider and couldn't fly much faster. Powered by a four-cylinder engine akin to those used on snowmobiles, the small propeller on the plane's tail could push it through the air at a sluggish top speed of just over eighty miles an hour.

Another reason the Predator could stay airborne for so long was that there was no pilot inside. Instead of a cockpit, the dome at the aircraft's nose housed a satellite dish; its two-member flight crew remained on the ground. Seated before an array of computers and color video screens in a metal box resembling a freight container, they flew the drone by remote control, using a satellite data link. As they did, one of the two crew members, designated the sensor operator, aimed and manipulated a turret under the Predator's chin that held two video cameras—one to shoot color images in daylight, the other able to produce infrared images by detecting variations in temperature, whether by day or by night.

As Swanson briefed them on the basics, his visitors interrupted with questions. Some wanted to know specifics about the Predator's speed, range, and endurance. Some wanted to know if the video from the Predator's cameras was sharp enough to identify an individual, and from what altitudes. Some wanted to know whether people on the ground could see the Predator or hear its engine. The visitors also wanted to know what tactics he would use to find a specific person and how hard that might be to do.

Swanson's responses almost all began with "It depends." But in order to better answer some of their questions, he invited his guests to follow him back out into the heat and down the Indian Springs flight line, where they could examine one of the faux freight containers the Air Force used to fly its small fleet of Predators.

To tour the twenty-four-foot-long, eight-foot-wide, eight-foot-tall ground control station, known to insiders as a GCS, the members of the party had to take turns, entering two at a time. Before taking anyone inside, Swanson suggested that while his visitors waited, they might try to spot or hear a Predator; one was orbiting a mile or two from the airfield, he assured them, launched a bit earlier by a crew inside the GCS.

The sky was clear and it was quiet around the desert airfield, but no one would detect the drone.

Two by two, Swanson's guests entered the GCS through one of two large, meat-locker-style doors on one side of the container that were opened by swinging a big lever handle. It was chilly inside the dark compartment, where constant air-conditioning was necessary to keep the electronic equipment from overheating. Even in the desert, some of the Air Force people working in the GCS wore jackets.

To their right as the visitors entered was the Predator's equivalent of a cockpit, a pair of identical consoles flush against the front wall, each faced by a brown, mock-leather chair for the flight crew that looked more comfortable than it was. In front of each chair was a keyboard; on a metal rack above the keyboard at each console were two nine-inch screens side by side that displayed data about the aircraft. Above the nine-inch screens were two nineteen-inch monitors for each console, one stacked above the other. The lower monitor normally displayed imagery, the upper one a moving map, although what they showed could be changed.

Each console also featured controls much like those of a normal airplane—or a video game. To the right of the keyboard at each console was a joystick with several buttons on it. To the keyboard's left was a lever that moved forward and back. The joystick on the left console normally governed the Predator's control surfaces; that console's lever was the aircraft's throttle. The joystick and lever on the right console normally served as the controls for the Predator's cameras—the stick was used to aim them, the lever to zoom their view in or out. Below the two consoles were pedals that moved the drone's inverted-V tail like a rudder to help change the Predator's direction in flight. When the drone was on the ground, the pedals worked as brakes.

Either console could be used to fly the Predator, but only one controlled the drone's flight at any given time. Normally that was the left console, and the Predator's pilot would sit in the left-hand chair; the right console was usually used to control the cameras, and the drone's sensor operator would sit in the right-hand chair. But with the push of a red button, the functions of the two consoles could be switched so that two pilots could sit at the flight consoles, the second officer serving as copilot to assist during takeoff or landing.

Behind the flight crew were work stations holding computers, other electronic gear, and telephones used by intelligence analysts who typically worked in the GCS. Along the walls—which were covered with thin synthetic paneling of the sort often seen in mobile homes—were fold-down vinyl seats similar to the canvas ones in military transport planes, but without seat belts or shoulder harnesses. Toward the back of the container was a second meat-locker-type door, which, like the first, had to be opened and closed gently to avoid making noise that might distract those working inside.

As each pair of guests stood behind the flight console chairs watching the Predator's video, the crew showed them the view through the color TV camera, useful only in daylight, then switched to the black-and-white infrared camera's view. The sensor operator also toggled the infrared sensor between its two modes, "white hot" and "black hot," in which warmer objects looked either white or black in contrast to cooler objects. The crew focused and zoomed in on vehicles driving around the airfield, on individuals walking from place to place—and then on the visitors standing just outside the door, waiting to enter the GCS. Swanson got the feeling the delegation was impressed; there were hushed conversations, whispers back and forth, and a lot of notes taken.

Not long after the guests left, Swanson learned that his guess about their reaction to the demonstration must have been correct, as was his hunch about the mission they had in mind. The Predator was going to play hide-and-seek in Afghanistan with one of the world's most wanted men: the elusive leader of the Islamic fundamentalist terrorist group Al Qaeda, Osama bin Laden. And when it did, Scott Swanson would be the chief pilot.

Life with Big Safari was getting interesting in a hurry.

This is the story of the first armed drone ever to be flown by intercontinental remote control and used to kill human beings on the other side of the globe. The military has long had an interest in unmanned aircraft, but before the Predator, drones were at best a niche technology. The Predator itself was widely ignored at first, until a series of iconoclastic visionaries began transforming it from a simple eye in the sky into an exotic new weapon. Once the Predator became capable of firing laser-guided missiles at enemies half a world away, military and industry attitudes toward such unmanned aerial vehicles changed nearly overnight. The drone revolution began.

How and why that happened is a tale previously told only in dribs and drabs, and often inaccurately. This account is based on five years of reporting and hundreds of interviews with the insiders who made the Predator what it became—an invention that not only changed the military, the CIA, and warfare itself, but also led the way into a new technological age. Drones of all kinds are now poised to transform civilian aviation, law enforcement, agriculture, and dozens of other human endeavors.

This is the drone revolution's book of genesis, and like another creation story it opens near the confluence of the rivers Tigris and Euphrates. It begins with a boy in Baghdad.

1

THE GENIUS OF THE GENESIS

He was a born engineer. From the time Abraham Karem was a toddler, he was always drawing things and making things and taking things apart to see how they worked. At age two he pulled the back off a large standing radio, the sort owned by every middle-class Jewish family in Baghdad in 1939, and pulled out the big glass vacuum tubes one by one, looking for the talking man inside. Abe cried when a technician came and put the tubes back. Not long afterward, he became intrigued by the magic of electrical switches—*click*, the light went on; *click,* the light went off! One day he climbed on his uncle Ezra's bed, found a round, brown light switch on a cord beneath the pillow, and took it apart, getting a 220-volt sting he seemed to regard as more interesting than painful.

When not engaged in this sort of basic research, little Abe was usually building a toy of his own design out of cardboard, or drawing something with a pencil or crayon on a piece of paper. His parents proudly encouraged their little prodigy. When Abe was eight, they gave him and his oldest brother, Isaac, each a set of Meccano, a British construction kit much like the Erector sets popular in America. Meccano provided perforated strips and plates of sheet metal; miniature girders of different sizes; wheels, pulleys, gears, axles, nuts, bolts; and instructions for using the parts and pieces to make models of all sorts. You could put together little buildings—or ships, bridges, cars, and trucks—or you could design and construct your own creations. In 1937, the year Abe was born, Meccano offered eleven different sets, numbered 0 through 10, according to rising levels of difficulty. Their parents got Abe a No. 2 and Isaac, who was seven years older, a No. 7, but Isaac quickly grew frustrated and abandoned his kit. Before long, Abe appropriated the No. 7 and combined it with his No. 2 to create toys as complex as those in Meccano No. 10.

By the time he got the Meccano kit, Abe was sure he was going to be a mechanical engineer. But as a teenager, he acquired a new ambition. His family had immigrated to Israel in 1951 as part of an exodus of roughly 120,000 Jews from Iraq, which, with other Arab League nations, had tried three years earlier to wipe the newly declared Jewish state off the map before it could take root. Abe's father, a prosperous textile merchant named Moshe Kiflawi, already owned land in Israel. He had taken his wife, Flora, and their boys to Jerusalem during World War II, when the British still governed what was then Palestine, seeking a safe haven for his family after a June 1941 pogrom in Iraq that left 130 Jews dead and hundreds injured. Forced by the British to return to Iraq at war's end, the family was relieved to get out again, even at the cost of forfeiting all their Iraqi property to the regime in Baghdad.

Once back in Jerusalem, Abe—who as an adult would change his surname from Kiflawi to the Hebrew for "vineyard," to make it sound Israeli—was eager to fit in. Already fluent in Hebrew, he found schoolwork easy and had plenty of time for the nonprofit youth clubs that abounded in newborn Israel, which was heavily influenced by socialist attitudes of collectivism. Diminutive, intellectual, and cursed with flat feet that made it painful to run, Abe initially joined a chess club and an "electrotechnical" club. Then he discovered the Aero Club of Israel, where a young adult counselor was teaching members to make model gliders that could fly. When Abe built his first glider and saw it rise into the air, his heart soared with it. Within a year, he was flying models in competitions. Within two, he was the instructor for his Aero Club chapter. He also now knew what he was *truly* going to do with his life. Mechanical engineering wasn't it after all. He was going to be an aeronautical engineer. He was going to spend his life designing aircraft.

On October 26, 1973, a Friday, Abe Karem was clearing his desk for the weekend when an unexpected visitor burst into his office at Israel Aircraft Industries, whose manufacturing and modification facilities lay on the north side of Lod International Airport, near Tel Aviv. Colonel Ezra "Beban" Dotan didn't need to introduce himself, and not because he was a famous fighter pilot. He and Abe had known each other for years, first as Aero Club members, then working together as young majors in the Israeli Air Force. They had a lot in common, and they were entirely different.

Now a small, pale, baby-faced thirty-six-year-old, Karem had made his mark in the Air Force by leading teams of engineers in quick-reaction fighter plane modifications that three times won the Israel Defense Prize, the military's highest honor for technical achievement. Joining the Air Force in 1961 after earning his aeronautical engineering degree at Technion, the Israel Institute of Technology at Haifa, Karem served until 1969. He rose quickly to the rank of major and was so respected as an engineer he could get the Air Force commander in chief on the phone—a privilege that may have spoiled the young genius, who later in life, preferring to deal with those at the top, developed a hazardous habit of going over other people's heads.

At government-owned Israel Aircraft Industries, the most important aerospace company in the country, Karem was director of preliminary design—IAI's director of innovation, in effect. He was known as a brilliant engineer, but he was also known for *knowing* he was a brilliant engineer—and for being impatient with those who weren't also above average. Precocious subordinates often became acolytes. Those who weren't, or who just weren't team players, often found themselves quickly out the door. Abe Karem simply refused to work with anyone he didn't respect. He also didn't mind telling subordinates exactly what he thought of them, and he could let them go with as little apparent regret as Beban Dotan downing an enemy in a dogfight.

Physically, Dotan dwarfed Karem. He was big, muscular, tanned, and known not only as an audacious fighter pilot but also, within the Air Force, as a congenial commander. Nicknamed Mr. Skyhawk, from the moniker of the U.S.-made Douglas A-4 fighter planes he flew, Dotan was celebrated for downing five Syrian MiGs—including two in a single May 12, 1970, air battle in which he killed one MiG-17 by the unorthodox means of firing an antitank version of the unguided Zuni rocket. He was also a fan of Karem's, for Dotan appreciated his friend Abe's brilliance as an engineer; indeed, that was why he had come to see him this Sabbath eve.

Dotan dispensed with pleasantries.

"Abe, why don't you give me a Zuni rocket with a dihedral wing?" he demanded without even sitting down.

"Ezra," Karem softly scolded, motioning to a chair in front of his desk, "don't tell me what I need to give you. Tell me how you'll use it."

"I want to fire it from my aircraft so they'll turn the radars on and shoot missiles at it," Dotan said.

He didn't need to explain further why he wanted to add a wing that was dihedral, a common shape on airplanes, to a Zuni, a tubelike munition just five inches in diameter. Nor did he need to explain why he was in a hurry to get it. For the past twenty days, and for the third time since the creation of the Jewish state twenty-five years earlier, Israel had been at war with its neighbors Egypt and Syria, but with a frightening difference. Israel's Air Force, which six years earlier had dominated the skies and been a key to victory in the so-called Six-Day War, had been rendered nearly impotent this time by surprising new enemy air defenses.

The Egyptians and Syrians had invaded from two sides on October 6, choosing the most important holiday in Judaism, Yom Kippur, to launch their surprise attack. Egyptian tanks and troops flooded across the Suez Canal. Syrian forces joined by Iraqi and Jordanian troops pushed Israeli forces back to the edge of the Golan Heights, which Israel had captured from Syria in the Six-Day War. After initial setbacks, the ground troops of the Israel Defense Forces repelled the invaders, establishing a bridgehead on the Egyptian side of the Suez and holding the Golan Heights. Under pressure from their respective superpower allies, the United States and the Soviet Union, Israel and its foes had signed cease-fire agreements two days before Dotan came to Karem. Whether or not those bargains held, though, the Israeli Air Force was going to need a way to counter those Arab air defenses in the future.

In the four short weeks of what history would dub the Yom Kippur War, Israeli air losses had been devastating. Mobile batteries of Soviet-built SA-2, SA-3, and SA-6 surface-to-air missiles, or SAMs—supplied to Egypt and Syria by Moscow, operated with the help of Soviet advisers, and supplemented by thousands of advanced antiaircraft guns—had cost Israel not just one hundred warplanes but also its far more precious pilots. The SAMs had also inflicted untold Israeli casualties on the ground by making it difficult for the Air Force to provide Israeli ground troops effective close air support with attacks on enemy land forces. Using the Soviet-led Warsaw Pact's tactics and equipment, the Arabs had erected a five-layered air defense umbrella consisting of long-range radars and missiles, short-range radars and missiles, and fighter aircraft. The long-range radars, positioned beyond Israel's reach, would "paint" an Israeli fighter as it approached Arab forces and transmit the aircraft's position to a short-range SAM battery lying in ambush. The short-range battery would then turn its radar on just long enough to target the Israeli plane and fire a SAM. Within seconds, a missile traveling nearly three times the speed of sound would be homing in on the Israeli aircraft from a short and deadly range. As its missile flew, the SAM battery would douse its radar and scurry away to avoid being targeted by Israeli planes armed with missiles that homed in on radiation.

Dotan had just spent days flying risky observation missions over the battle lines in a desperate search for ideas on countering the enemy tactics, which was why he was in Karem's office that evening. What Israel needed, Dotan told Karem, was a decoy to fool those SAM radars, and the radar image of a Zuni rocket with a dihedral wing ought to look enough like an airplane to do the trick. As an Israeli fighter jet neared the enemy air defense umbrella, its pilot could launch a winged Zuni. The enemy's long-range radar would see the rocket as a manned aircraft and signal a short-range SAM battery to attack it. When the SAM battery turned its radar on to target the Zuni, Israeli planes with antiradar missiles would detect the SAM radar and fire at the enemy missile battery while the SAM battery pointlessly fired on the decoy.

Karem silently pondered Dotan's idea for a moment, the roar and whine of jets on the runways outside the only noise in the room. Then he waved his friend off.

"You don't need a rocket and you can't afford the dihedral," Karem said. "You do need a decoy, but it can't be a Zuni." Karem knew the Zuni's radar signature was too small to mimic that of a fighter plane. "Invite me for lunch tomorrow," he told Dotan. By then, Karem promised, he'd have a solution.

After Dotan left, Karem called his wife, Dina, to tell her he wouldn't be home for dinner that evening after all, news she was used to after seven years of marriage. Karem stayed at the office through the night, feverishly working the engineering challenge Dotan had given him. The next day, promptly at noon, he was on the doorstep of Dotan's home in a suburb north of Tel Aviv. Under his arm was a set of drawings produced during his all-nighter: a design for a winged decoy about the size of a small target drone, but with special radar-reflecting spheres on its sides to make it look big to SAM radars. Light enough to hang under a manned jet's wing, Karem's decoy would be unpowered but aerodynamically shaped so that when released at thirty thousand feet it would glide at a plausible fighter plane speed of Mach 0.85—about 575 miles an hour at that altitude—into the enemy air-defense umbrella.

The next morning, Dotan took Karem's glide decoy idea to the commander in chief of the Israeli Air Force, Major General Benjamin "Benny" Peled. By midday, IAI had Air Force approval to build some prototypes as a quick-reaction project. The ranks of IAI's engineers had been thinned by the war, as many were reservists called up by the military, but Karem assembled a small team from those available and started work immediately, pushing his group to keep at it nearly around the clock.

A week into the project, someone came back from a trip abroad with a copy of a magazine article describing a new U.S. Air Force radar decoy with folding wings that had just been flight-tested successfully. Karem urged the Israeli Air Force to consider trying to get the U.S. decoy instead of having IAI produce his, but he was instructed to carry on with his work. Four weeks later, his decoy made its first test flight. Over three more weeks, seven further tests were flown. Not all were successful, but the prototypes flew well enough that Karem's preliminary design work was largely done, which allowed him to turn his attention to other things.

Soon after his work on the decoy, Karem decided to take a major gamble with his career. For most of his decade and a half as an aeronautical engineer, he had focused on the problems and possibilities of manned fighter planes and transports. But for the last couple of months, he had spent twenty hours a day thinking about what amounted to an aircraft with no pilot inside. There was nothing new about pilotless planes; inventors had designed them in a cornucopia of configurations since the First World War. By the 1970s, Jane's, the authoritative military publishing company, listed 120 separate types of pilotless planes in a *Robot Aircraft Today* pocket guide to what experts of the day usually called remotely piloted vehicles, or RPVs. Yet except for radio-controlled target drones, few unmanned aircraft had been adopted by the world's militaries, in large part due to poor reliability. As Karem knew, aircraft without pilots on board tended to crash a lot more than those with pilots inside them. But this decoy project had taken him down a novel mental path, and before long that path would lead him on a journey of discovery, a pioneering exploration of an aviation frontier.

Only two months after finishing work on the decoy for the Israeli Air Force, Karem stunned his bosses and most of his coworkers at IAI by quitting his job as director of preliminary design. He left to start his own company, a move he had been mulling over since before the Yom Kippur War. After only three years at IAI, Karem had become deeply disillusioned with the way things were done at the massive aerospace company. All IAI's stock was held by the Israeli government, and in Karem's view government officials and many IAI executives treated the company more like a jobs program than a corporation. They hired far more people than necessary; the way Karem saw it, IAI's employees did less work in more time at higher cost to the taxpayers than was warranted. He believed in his bones that in most fields, especially aeronautics, the best work and the best ideas were produced not by large organizations—especially those influenced by politics—but by small teams of talented people working hand in hand toward common goals.

Karem's belief in teams stemmed from his youth, when Israel was still a vibrant work in progress, a magnet for Jewish idealists, and a dynamic dream coming true for Jews the world over. He fondly remembered how, in those days, younger members of the fresh and still fragile Jewish state teemed with plans and hopes for building a new society, a fundamentally good civilization, and a sanctuary for the Jewish people after centuries of persecution and a Holocaust whose extent was still being revealed. His high school home room teacher for four years, a tail gunner in a British bomber during World War II, preached that the Jews would survive and secure their freedom only if they lived one for all and all for one. The young counselor who advised Abe's chapter of the Aero Club stressed the importance of members helping one another with their designs. At IAI, Karem had been a rapidly rising star, but after proving several times that he could do major work faster and better with fewer people and save the taxpayers money at the same time, he found his efficiency rewarded mainly by resistance. One executive even reproached and threatened him for telling the Air Force that the modification of a particular fighter plane could be done in one year instead of the three IAI had estimated, saving two million out of the three million man-hours of labor the company was planning to commit to the project.

By January 1974, Karem was fed up, and after running the idea past friends in the Air Force he announced that he was leaving IAI in May to start his own company. After he invited a handful of his favorite engineers to come along, an IAI vice president called Karem into his office.

"Abe, we all love you," the man said. "We owe you a lot. But we had a meeting about you forming your own company, and we decided we are going to crush you. So don't do it."

"Why?" Karem asked. "You are seventeen thousand people, and I'm going to be what, five hundred?" At the time, Karem hoped to build a company that would be about that size.

Size didn't matter, the vice president said, but "every time we're going to propose something, they will say, 'But Abe will do it faster and cheaper,' and we're not going to have that."

As Karem later learned, the warning was friendly, but the threat wasn't idle.

———————

The clash between Karem's brash ways and the realities of IAI kindled his decision to leave the company, but something else was at work as well. The task of designing that radar-tricking glide decoy had led Karem to look at things in a new light. When he did, he had an epiphany.

The decoy he designed for IAI was primitive; in fact, it would have been less capable than the remote-control target drones used since the 1930s to train fighter pilots and antiaircraft units. But while thinking about the problem the decoy was meant to solve, Karem realized that an unmanned aircraft with the right capabilities could do far more than merely trick SAM batteries into revealing their locations. A remotely controlled drone armed with antitank missiles and designed to loiter in the sky for hours at a time could be one way to defeat—or, better yet, deter—another invasion of Israel.

Geography had forced Egypt's tanks to mass as they funneled through holes blasted in defensive embankments to cross the Suez Canal and enter the Sinai Peninsula. "Looking at that," Karem recalled years later, "I said, if we are right on top of this high concentration of forces, you can throw some missiles at them. They will say, 'This is not a good day,' and back off, and we are not killing that many people. You let them spread, they throw their armor against your armor, their air force against your air force, and all of a sudden you have thousands and tens of thousands of casualties."

Pilots add weight to an aircraft, and more weight requires carrying more fuel; besides, pilots need to land every few hours to rest. But a fleet of pilotless aircraft such as Karem was imagining would have the persistence—the flight endurance—to provide an air-to-ground defensive missile system guarding Israel's borders day and night. Moreover, if the enemy shot one down, no pilot would be lost. Achieving the necessary flight endurance would be one of the hardest parts of his challenge, but Karem was sure he could design such a drone. For one thing, he believed himself not only the best engineer in aeronautics but probably the best engineer of any kind in all of Israel. Beyond that, he had been a model aircraft hobbyist since his teens, and as a modeler his specialty was a type of aircraft whose sole objective was endurance.

Thrown or towed into the air like a kite on a fifty-meter-long string and then released, free-flight gliders are the oldest form of model aircraft and among the trickiest to build. A schoolchild's paper airplane technically fits the definition, but in competitions the models are far larger—wingspans of six feet are common—and more sophisticated. Model gliders are built of lightweight material, such as balsa and tissue, and usually weigh a pound or less. The goal is to make a plane that is capable of staying airborne long after its launch or its release from the tow line, but without any remote or automated controls to help keep it aloft.

Like the materials used to build it, a tow-line glider's flight characteristics are the opposite of a jet fighter's. A model glider typically floats through the air at two or three miles an hour or less, gently circling until aerodynamic drag and the law of gravity return the aircraft to earth. In international competitions, the winning aircraft is the one that accumulates the most flight time over a series of launches within a strict limit of three to three and a half minutes per flight. The time limit and multiple rounds prevent winning or losing by the luck of the wind, though catching a thermal of the sort birds often ride is a favorite technique for success.

A good free-flight glider is rugged enough to withstand turbulence and return to stable flight or take a hard landing, yet light and aerodynamic enough to fly as close to three minutes as possible even in calm air. Most carry a dethermalizer, a device operated by a timer or activated by radio signal, which moves a control surface to put the plane into a "deep stall"—a sudden dive—and bring it to a gentle landing. Deep stall is used after a round's maximum flight time has been achieved, or to escape a thermal that threatens to carry the model away.

The best free-flight modelers employ all sorts of tricks and techniques to improve endurance, and Karem was a world-class free-flight modeler. Free-flight gliders were what Abe had learned to build in the Aero Club, and he pursued the hobby into adulthood. In August 1963, as a twenty-six-year-old Air Force officer, he placed tenth in his category representing Israel at the free-flight World Championships in Wiener Neustadt, Austria.

Two years later, Abe met Dina Schleiffer, a petite, lively, smart conscript who showed up one day in the Air Force engineering spaces, assigned to fulfill her obligatory two years of military service drafting technical drawings for engineers. Only eighteen, she was ten years younger than Abe, but he found her much more mature and confident than older girls he knew. They started dating, and soon Dina was traveling with Abe to free-flight competitions. She loved the little planes he designed, especially one he put together just as a spare and called his "ugly duckling." She loved helping him launch his gliders when he competed. Most of all, Dina loved Abe, and in 1966 they married. For the rest of their lives, she would some-times accuse him of tilting at windmills, but she always helped him in his work and backed him when he took major risks.

A month or two after leaving IAI, Karem set up a company of his own called Matos (Hebrew for "aircraft") and began work on his idea for an armed drone to patrol Israel's borders. Friends in the Air Force counseled him to be less ambitious in his design; he should just make a reconnais-sance drone with a TV camera that would send imagery to forward air controllers (officers on the ground who direct air strikes) rather than arm the RPV itself. The Air Force commander, Benny Peled, himself an aero-nautical engineer, was even less encouraging. Peled told Karem that he wouldn't buy such a drone for the Air Force because its mission was fun-damentally an Army job. Appalled, Karem pointed out that if he created a pilotless aircraft for the Army, it would have to be a helicopter, so that it could operate from wherever the Army was stationed. But a helicopter flies on a column of thrust created by rotors whose blades turn hundreds of revolutions per minute to keep the craft airborne, a fuel-thirsty and violent way to fly compared to airplanes. As Karem reminded Peled, heli-copters shake like hell and have lousy endurance. Karem was also aware that others had taken on this challenge with unsatisfying results. In the late 1950s, the U.S. Navy built and deployed an unmanned helicopter to carry antisubmarine torpedoes; in the 1960s, the Navy added a TV cam-era and various weapons, and used the aircraft in Vietnam for reconnais-sance and attacking enemy convoys moving at night. But in 1971 the Navy cancelled the program after half of the 810 unmanned helicopters that had been built crashed. Most of those that remained were used as target drones.

Unhappy with Peled's response, Karem told the Air Force commander that designing a drone helicopter for the mission he envisioned would be excruciatingly difficult.

"That's why you're Abe!" Peled cheerfully replied.

Karem came up with a preliminary design, but the Army declined to buy it. So Karem went back to his drawing board, as he would do nine times more over the next three years, without ever making a sale. He ultimately concluded that because of IAI's political influence, the Israeli military was never going to buy anything from his new company. Former colleagues confirmed that IAI was indeed out to kill his company; his friends, meanwhile, told him he might as well go to the United States. If he did, no one could accuse him of betraying Israel by leaving—not after all he'd done for the country.

Deeply frustrated, Karem decided that emigrate was what he would do. He would take his talents to the United States, where opportunities for entrepreneurs were far greater and the aerospace industry far larger. Dina and Abe's three brothers—Jacob, Isaac, and Joseph—all supported his decision.

Karem quickly decided that he and Dina should live in the Los Angeles Basin. With some of the finest flying weather in the United States, the area was home to aviation companies large and small, multitudes of engineers, skilled technicians, and subcontractors galore. An inventor could find just about any kind of help or parts he needed in order to design and build aircraft there, and Karem already had contacts in the area.

Which was why, one sunny Sunday in 1978, he and Dina were driving around the L.A. suburbs looking for a house to buy. As they considered and rejected one house after another, it quickly became clear that their priorities were very different. Finally Dina put her finger on the problem.

"I'm looking for a house with a garage attached. You're looking for a garage with a house attached," she teased.

They laughed, but Abe knew she was right. Dina cared about buying a house that would suit their needs, but Abe wanted a roomy garage that would serve as a laboratory where he could do his research and development.

In the end Abe found a garage he liked, and it happened to be attached to the front of a Spanish-style house Dina liked, on a tall, pleasant hill in

Hacienda Heights, an affluent suburb east of the city. Built to hold three cars, the garage had six hundred square feet of floor space and an equally spacious attic. Before long, both would be crammed with tools; raw materials; handmade molds to fabricate small wings and other aircraft parts from plywood, urethane foam, and fiberglass; and a four-by-eight-foot granite-topped table flat and true enough to serve as an assembly bench. Karem liked to remind himself that Orville and Wilbur Wright had invented their first aircraft in a bicycle shop. Why couldn't a garage become part of aviation history, too?

The epiphany Karem experienced while working on his antiradar decoy for the Israeli Air Force was the primary reason he turned his attention to drones, but it was not the only one. In the late 1970s, Karem believed that RPVs were one type of aircraft a lone inventor could still develop in a garage; he was also convinced that he could build something infinitely better than the RPVs created by the big aerospace companies. Big aerospace companies didn't build many pilotless aircraft because their primary customer, the military, remained largely uninterested in RPVs other than as target drones. If military commanders thought about unmanned aircraft at all, they usually thought of them as fragile toys. Drones were a niche technology, and always had been.

The U.S. military first tried to build pilotless aircraft during World War I, when the Army experimented with a couple of "aerial torpedoes." The one that came closest to being produced was the Kettering Bug, a tiny biplane designed to take off from rails and deliver a two-hundred-pound warhead fifty miles away, guided by a complicated autopilot system that involved a barometer and a gyroscope. The Bug never really worked as planned, until a test a few days before November 11, 1918, the day World War I ended. On Armistice Day, the War Department cancelled the project. For a few years afterward, the Army and Navy funded research into radio control of aircraft, but absent a war both services quickly lost interest.

In the 1930s, the idea of using radio signals to fly airplanes remotely was pursued by Hollywood actor Reginald Denny. The British-born

Denny, who had served as a Royal Flying Corps aerial gunner in World War I, was a pilot and model aircraft enthusiast who owned a hobby shop on Hollywood Boulevard. Denny first created a company to produce radio-controlled model aircraft, then expanded into producing slightly larger monoplanes as radio-controlled target drones for the U.S. Army, which used them to train antiaircraft gunners. During World War II, the Army bought more than fifteen thousand of these balsa-and-plywood target drones from Denny's Radioplane Company, a fact Denny touted to an actor friend whose Army Air Forces job was to publicize Hollywood's contributions to the war effort. When future U.S. president Captain Ronald Reagan sent Private David Connor to the Radioplane Company to photograph its drone assembly line for the Army's *Yank* magazine, Connor discovered a girl so fetching he returned later to take more photos of her. Eventually he showed the photos to movie studio contacts, and after the war Norma Jean Dougherty left Radioplane for a legendary Hollywood career as Marilyn Monroe.

Another World War II attempt to use radio-controlled aircraft ended far less happily, and probably changed U.S. political history. In 1944 the Army Air Forces undertook a secret plan to attack sites in occupied France and Holland that the Germans were using to launch V-1 "buzz bombs" and V-2 ballistic missiles, weapons that were terrorizing London and inflicting heavy civilian casualties. Under the Army's Project Aphrodite, twenty thousand pounds of high explosives were packed into much-used B-17 bombers, which were rigged to be flown by remote control, then crashed into targets by a "mother ship" flying much higher. Getting such a flying bomb airborne by radio was problematical, so a crew of two airmen was needed to take off in the modified bomber, designated a BQ-7, to arm the explosives and engage an autopilot to turn control over to the accompanying mother ship, then bail out over England. On August 4, 1944, four BQ-7s were launched. One exploded and killed its crew before reaching the English Channel; none of the others reached its target.

Eight days later, under the code name Project Anvil, the U.S. Navy tried the same technique to attack a site at Mimoyecques, France, near Calais, where the Germans were building guns to bombard England with giant shells. The Navy's explosives-packed PB4Y-1 Liberator, a B-24 modified for radio control, exploded shortly after takeoff, eight miles southeast of Halesworth Airfield, in Suffolk. No trace was ever found of the radio control expert on board, Lieutenant Wilford John Willy, nor of the pilot, Lieutenant Joseph P. Kennedy Jr., older brother of John F. Kennedy and the son who had long been groomed by their father to run for president. Kennedy and Willy were posthumously awarded the Navy Cross.

Radioplane continued to sell the Army its propeller-driven remote-control target drones after the war, and in 1955 the company added a film camera to one, creating the world's first unmanned reconnaissance aircraft. The Army bought hundreds. The Air Force, however, was generally uninterested in planes without pilots inside—until May 1, 1960, when the Soviet Union shot down a high-altitude U-2 reconnaissance jet flown over its territory by CIA pilot Francis Gary Powers.

Eight days after Powers was downed and captured, the Air Force secretly awarded a contract to Ryan Aeronautical Company to adapt its jet-powered Q-2 Firebee target drones for photo reconnaissance. The project was blocked a few weeks later, just as flight tests were being conducted, by Pentagon bureaucrats with other priorities and Air Force leaders more eager to spend their reconnaissance money on a sexy new manned spy plane called the SR-71. The SR-71 was going to fly at Mach 3—three times the speed of sound—and at altitudes no Soviet missiles could reach. The Air Force got interested in Ryan's reconnaissance drone again, though, when, on October 27, 1962, one day before the end of what became known as the Cuban Missile Crisis, another U-2 was shot down over Cuba and its pilot killed.

Two years later, the United States sent troops to South Vietnam to fight Communist insurgents, and over the next eight years the Air Force modified and deployed more than twenty derivatives of Ryan's jet-powered target drones for photo reconnaissance. The drones were also used as decoys to fool North Vietnamese air defenses, to drop propaganda leaflets, and to carry sensors able to eavesdrop on enemy communications. These Firebees, Fireflys, and Lightning Bugs, as they were variously designated, flew 3,435 missions over eight years.

The technology was hardly convenient, however: the miniature jets could neither take off nor land like regular aircraft. They had to be launched from under the wing of a C-130 transport plane to fly their missions while being remotely controlled from a ground station transmitting radio signals susceptible to interference from other radio traffic. Early versions deployed a parachute to land over South Vietnam—sometimes in a rice paddy, sometimes in the jungle, sometimes in the ocean off Da Nang, sometimes in hostile territory. To avoid damage from hard landings, saltwater contamination, or just losing a drone, later versions were plucked from midair by a beefy CH-3C helicopter after their parachute opened. Manipulating two twenty-foot-long hydraulically operated poles and an array of three hooks, the helicopter crew would snag the parachute's cords and, with a winch that fed a thousand feet of steel cable out a reinforced hole in the chopper's floor, reel the two-thousand-pound drone into a position about twenty feet underneath the helicopter for delivery to a recovery zone. The drone's still-photo film cartridge then had to be flown out of Vietnam for development and analysis, with photos of interest flown back later, a process that sometimes took days. Often there was no recovery to perform and no film to develop. On average, such drones flew fewer than four missions apiece. More than half of these RPVs, 544, were shot down or crashed.

Despite these experiments, no large constituency for drones ever developed within the military. The reasons were largely cultural. The pilots who ran the Air Force usually didn't pay much attention to aircraft that flew without a member of their proud fraternity inside. The Army, committed to helicopters after Vietnam, wasn't particularly interested in any sort of airplane, so there was no natural home for drones in that service. The Navy experimented with its helicopter RPV and some Ryan drones during Vietnam, but ship captains never liked the idea of aircraft with flammable gas that flew without a pilot inside to handle an emergency landing on their decks. Besides, once the Vietnam War ended and defense spending plunged, there were more pressing and promising uses for available funds. Throughout this period, the only sectors of the government that remained truly interested in drones were the CIA and a super-secret intelligence agency called the National Reconnaissance Office, which used some exotic RPVs to spy on the Soviet Union and

China during the Cold War. But even their interest blew hot and cold; among the cloak-and-dagger set and their politician bosses, spy satellites were seen as more promising.

When Karem arrived in America, he saw a vast new frontier beckoning. As he surveyed it, he was sure he could make his mark in his new country, and maybe a fortune as well. First, though, he had to invent a better drone, and find a customer willing to buy it.

From the time he joined the Aero Club in Israel as a boy, Karem had read every book, magazine and newspaper article, and every scholarly paper he could find that had to do with flight. For nearly every airplane or helicopter ever built anywhere in the world, he could reel off from memory not just the numerical designations and names but also figures and facts, including who had designed the aircraft. He had also studied the myriad methods of flight found in nature, whose aerial creatures employ an amazing array of airfoils (wing shapes) to travel through the fluid known as air. They do so in a wide variety of ways. Songbirds flap and flit on wings that taper sharply. Hummingbirds hover and dart by beating their tiny wings dozens of times a second. The housefly's flat, wide wings are less airfoil than paddle, leading some scientists to conclude that, given a fly's typical weight of twelve milligrams or less, the air is so viscous that the insect less flies in it than swims.

Nature's best soarer is the fish-eating albatross, a seagoing bird that glides over the ocean for hours at a time, floating on outstretched wings whose span is roughly twenty times longer than their chord, meaning their width front to back. This "high-aspect-ratio wing" is the shape favored by free-flight modelers. When Karem set out to build his better drone, he took the albatross as his model. More schooled in ornithology than in eighteenth-century English poetry—the language was his fourth, after all—Karem called his new drone the Albatross. At the time, he was unaware that in English the name had been synonymous with "burden" ever since 1798, when Samuel Taylor Coleridge published his epic poem "The Rime of the Ancient Mariner." Karem's Albatross, however, would prove to be not a burden but a boon.

Thoroughly schooled in the hapless history of unmanned aircraft, Karem believed RPVs had largely failed to catch on for two reasons: most could fly for only a couple of hours at a time and most fell out of the sky at rates that would raise alarms if anyone were inside them. He blamed those flaws on the fact that most RPVs had been developed either by modelers accustomed to making toys that were cheap to build and replace or by aerospace corporations whose best people worked on more lucrative products and whose unmanned aircraft were designed, like target drones, to be expendable, not least because their customers, the military, expected no better.

Karem took an entirely different approach. At IAI, he had always encouraged his staff to be innovative because, as he liked to say, "The customer doesn't really know what he wants." What Karem meant was that military officers couldn't possibly know enough about the latest technologies to understand what was feasible. At weekly meetings, he had instructed his IAI engineers to figure out what the customer wanted, then try to design something providing three to five times as much capability. Now working out of his garage in Los Angeles, Karem was determined to design his Albatross well enough to show potential customers that a drone could stay airborne not just for hours but for days at a time. He was also convinced that he could build his RPVs with the same rigor and reliability required of the fighter planes he worked on in Israel.

By a stroke of good fortune, one of the first people to befriend Karem in Los Angeles was Ira Kuhn, a physicist consultant to the Defense Advanced Research Projects Agency, known by the acronym DARPA. Then, as now, DARPA existed to fund farsighted and even far-fetched ideas to help the military stay on the cutting edge of technology. Kuhn and Karem met at a tiny Santa Monica company called Developmental Sciences Inc., where Karem had gone to work in 1977 to gain a foothold in the U.S. aerospace industry. Karem was helping the two engineer owners develop a couple of RPVs, including one for DARPA whose progress Kuhn was monitoring for the agency. When Karem quit Developmental Sciences in 1980—storming out one day after the owners refused to make him a full partner—and went to work full-time in his Hacienda Heights garage, Kuhn persuaded DARPA to fund development of Karem's Albatross. Fearing Defense Department auditors would object to funding an aircraft being developed in a garage, however, DARPA gave Kuhn's consulting company a $350,000 contract to finance Karem's work. "We were DARPA's conduit to get it to him," Kuhn explained years later. Karem's work in Israel had such a good reputation that, even if Karem *was* working out of a garage, DARPA Director Robert Fossum figured his Albatross project was a good bet.

The Albatross wasn't meant to be an operational RPV, just a technology demonstrator. It wasn't much bigger than a model, and was made mostly of mahogany plywood, spruce, urethane foam, and fiberglass shaped in molds Karem had fabricated himself. The diameter of the fuselage's bullet-shaped nose measured 300 millimeters, or 11.8 inches, the same as the unvarying chord of its 15-foot wing. The wing sat atop the fuselage, midway between the nose and tail; at its rear end, a small vertical stabilizer 18 inches tall and half as wide pointed straight up. Two larger tail fins, or horizontal stabilizers, extended down in an inverted V, a configuration Karem chose so those appendages could serve as skids and keep the pusher propeller on the tail from hitting the ground during runway landings. The propeller, meanwhile, was powered by a two-stroke, single-cylinder McCulloch 101 go-kart engine. Radio-controlled, the Albatross could take off and land like a regular airplane using detachable landing gear and a nose wheel. It also had a parachute for emergency landings. Most notably, Karem's little drone weighed 105 pounds when totally empty but could carry 95 pounds of fuel, an uncommonly high "fuel fraction" of 47.5 percent—a key feature of aircraft endurance.

To build the Albatross, Karem hired just two helpers. The first was Jim Machin, a premed student and free-flight modeler recommended by a mutual friend when Karem was looking for someone to help him film a deep stall demonstration. Even as he developed the Albatross, Karem was talking to DARPA about creating a larger drone for the Navy, an aircraft configured in much the same way but whose wings and stabilizers would fold into its fuselage so it could be launched into the air with a booster rocket from a shipboard canister. This larger RPV would be recovered by putting it into a nose-up deep stall, then catching it in a net on the ship's deck after a retrorocket slowed its descent. A DARPA official who heard Karem describe his concept couldn't believe it was possible to put an aircraft into such a stall without crashing it. One day, as Dina and Abe drove home from a morning spent with Machin filming deep stalls performed by one of Karem's free-flight gliders, Dina asked Abe, "Didn't you want somebody to help you in the garage?" Soon the college student was in Abe's garage four hours a day, making composite parts, helping Karem put his prototype together, and ultimately abandoning his own plans to go to medical school.

Karem's second hire was Jack Hertenstein, a UCLA-educated electronics engineer he had met at Developmental Sciences. Though endowed with a wry sense of humor, Hertenstein showed little interest in other humans and had a number of unique habits. His lunch each day consisted of a can of beans and a can of tuna, eaten directly out of their containers with a wooden tongue depressor and followed religiously by a banana and a Snickers bar. He was equally addicted to remote-control aircraft. Born in 1937, the same year as Karem, Hertenstein was twenty-eight and a well-paid engineer at a big aerospace company when he abruptly stopped his new Austin Healey sports car along a country road on a Sunday afternoon. Seeing some people using handheld radio control systems to fly little airplanes, he decided to watch and was smitten. The next morning, Hertenstein was waiting at the door when his local hobby shop opened. He bought one of every radio control model airplane in stock, thinking to himself as a bemused clerk tallied the substantial bill, "This just has to be done, and it's going to be done, and we've got a lot of money, so just go ahead and do it."

Seventeen years later, Hertenstein was an expert in every aspect of radio control and in avionics (a contraction of "aviation electronics"), which happened to be one of the few aspects of aircraft technology in which Karem had limited expertise. Karem hired Hertenstein in October 1982 to design and build reliable electronic devices to operate the Albatross's control surfaces and internal machinery, to put together its radio control system and autopilot, and to be its primary operator. By this time, Karem was acutely aware he needed help with avionics, for a year earlier a first prototype built using electronics bought from a subcontractor had crashed on its maiden flight at a federal test range in Utah. The pyrotechnics used to deploy its parachute had been miswired. DARPA had scheduled another Albatross test flight for the following summer, but as Karem watched the Utah test range technicians fail to get tracking equipment and other gear needed for the demonstration working properly, his patience ran out. He packed up the Albatross, left without letting the technicians fly it, and hired Hertenstein a few weeks later.

A little before noon on November 30, 1983, Jack Hertenstein and two Air Force engineers sent by DARPA were standing on a dry lakebed at El Mirage, near Adelanto, California, under clear skies, watching a new Albatross lazily orbit a two-mile aerial course about a thousand feet overhead. The Albatross would continue to orbit above the three men for an hour, and then another hour, and then another hour.

Over the past two years, Karem and his two-man team had not only built a better prototype but also improved nearly every piece of equipment needed to operate it, from an analog autopilot Hertenstein designed that measured air pressure at the wingtips and stabilized the plane as it flew, to a data link that beamed to the ground information such as speed, altitude, and climb rate. With Hertenstein standing ready to take over with a radio control box if necessary, Karem and Machin were taking turns piloting the Albatross from inside a nearby camping trailer. They had converted the trailer to a ground control station for the Albatross by removing the air conditioner to make space and installing a small control panel with a couple of TV monitors and joysticks. For this DARPA test flight, which had begun with a rolling takeoff at 11:39 a.m., they had also installed a special device in the Albatross to measure how much fuel the drone was burning each minute it flew.

At two hundred minutes, Hertenstein told Karem they should land because the sun would soon be setting and it would be unsafe to fly with no lights on the Albatross. Using his radio control box, Hertenstein took over the flying—and had to break off his first attempt to conclude the flight when a dirt biker who appeared from out of nowhere zipped directly across the drone's landing path. On the next try, Hertenstein brought the Albatross in smoothly, flaring the nose upward to slow its final approach speed from about sixty-three to fifty-five miles per hour as it touched down. The wheels hit the lakebed at 3:14 p.m., bringing the test's total flight time to three hours, thirty-five minutes. The fuel monitor showed that, at the rate at which its go-kart engine had been consuming gas, the Albatross could have remained airborne an astonishing forty-eight hours or more—five to ten times as long as any RPV ever flown.

The DARPA official in charge of Karem's project, Robert M. Williams, was gratified to hear the test results, and not only because the data confirmed his own calculations. When Williams had told some Air Force experts that Karem was developing a drone able to carry close to its own weight in fuel and fly for two days and maybe more, they assured him that no one could design such an aircraft, that physics made it impossible. Abe Karem had proved them wrong. But when he looked upon what he had made, he knew it was just a beginning.

2

THE BLUES

They called it the *Yale Daily News* Asian Expedition, a rather grandiose appellation, perhaps, for four college students on a road trip. But even in his twentieth year, Neal Blue liked to think big, and the concept had been his. The plan was to spend the summer of 1955 driving a car from Paris to Calcutta, skirting the Iron Curtain to learn how people on the edge of the Soviet Bloc lived and how their economies functioned. Even in his second year at Yale University, Blue was keenly interested in such matters.

Medium in height, modest in weight, chiseled in his features, sophisticated beyond his years, he was the eldest son of hardworking Denver, Colorado, Realtors James E. and Virginia Neal Blue, politically active Republicans whose pro-business, anticommunist views were passed on to their offspring. Having bought and sold used cars during his high school years because he could make a lot more money that way than by mowing lawns, Neal already knew he would be an entrepreneur after he finished Yale. He was a pure-blooded—and often enough in later years a cold-blooded—capitalist, a shrewd deal maker with a nose for opportunity and a knack for planning and finance. "He always had a plan," his high school friend Norman Augustine would remember decades later. "To make some money or win an election or write an article or give a speech or what have you." Moreover, as the audacious expedition he put together before his twenty-first birthday proved, and as he would demonstrate repeatedly later in life, Neal Blue knew not only how to *make* big plans, but also how to *execute* them, a crucial step that eludes most big thinkers. In time, his abilities would make him uncommonly wealthy. They would also make him a founding father of the drone revolution.

A photo taken on June 3, 1955, shows Blue with three Yale classmates who had decided to join him and spend the summer between their sophomore and junior years on a ten-week, seventeen-country, two-continent odyssey—an undertaking more daring than it might sound in these days of cell phones and the Internet. The four young Americans were going to cross merciless deserts and rugged mountains in lands where the roads were poor and the inhabitants could be hostile—lonely places where the bad luck of a breakdown or an encounter with armed brigands could mean serious trouble, even death.

The well-scrubbed young faces of Blue and his upper-crust Class of '57 partners, Henry G. von Maur, Charles W. Trippe, and G. Morgan Browne Jr., betrayed no trepidation as they posed for a news photographer at New York Harbor on the eve of their departure. Standing dockside next to the red-and-white Dodge Sierra that would carry them on their trek, wearing suits and ties and short haircuts, they were clearly trying hard to look serious while seeming to scrutinize an invisible spot on the station wagon's hood. Berthed in the background was the luxurious and historic SS *Ile de France*. The grand ocean liner—which had crossed the Atlantic regularly a few years earlier to convoy GIs to Europe to fight World War II—would now convey the Dodge Sierra to the continent for an exploit the Yale men would document in dispatches to the *New York Times*.

"They will sail tomorrow for France," the photo caption inaccurately reported. Trippe's father was Pan American World Airways founder Juan Trippe, so while the car would sail, the young men would fly to Europe via Pan Am. Several weeks earlier, Trippe Sr. had also secured them a meeting with the publisher of the *Times*, Arthur Hays Sulzberger, during which the four classmates would pitch their proposal that the paper pay them for regular reports on their expedition as it unfolded. Blue figured they needed to prove that they were serious about their undertaking, so before going to see Sulzberger at the newspaper's Times Square headquarters, he and his friends put together a slick brochure describing their "Global Goodwill Tour." The publisher agreed to buy a weekly article with photos, so their next stop was the Chrysler Building, a few blocks east, on Forty-Second Street. There, the promise of coverage in the *Times* got the students not only free use of the Dodge Sierra but also modifications to toughen it for the rigors of Third World roads. "Dodge engineers have equipped the car with heavy duty springs, a heavy duty cooling system, battery and generator as well as tinted glass to cut down on heat," the dockside photo's caption noted. "The car is also equipped with a special engine that will operate on low octane gas."

Their itinerary would take the four young men from France to Germany to Austria; then south through Communist but independent Yugoslavia and on to Greece; then east through Turkey, Lebanon, Syria, Iraq, Iran, Afghanistan, Pakistan, and finally to India. From Calcutta, they would fly home. "U.S. Students Find Contrasts on Balkan Tour," read the headline on the first article they filed, which noted that jagged rocks in a rutted, unpaved road in the Yugoslav province of Macedonia had dented the Dodge's gas tank and "smashed" the exhaust pipe. A July 22 article reported a "rough, three-day drive" across the Iraqi desert from Syria to Baghdad. Eight days later, they were in Kabul, Afghanistan: "4 Yale Men Greeted by Afghans with Free Tea and Free Shave," the headline said. "The Afghans are not far from Stone Age culture in some places," the Yale men reported. "Their standard of living is the lowest the expedition has seen. But they have a pride and independence that command respect." Three weeks later, *Times* readers learned that "Driving through the Khyber Pass into Pakistan was like moving into a new world, or at least a different age." Once out of the pass, which cut through Pakistan's ungoverned North West Frontier Province, the Yale men saw that "an amazing number of areas were set aside for specialized military training." Even in Peshawar, a relatively modern city, "the tribesmen stroll through the streets carrying rifles," they reported. "A glance at their long knives and war axes made it easy to believe their reputation as among the fiercest warriors in the world."

The expedition was a great success, and it only whetted Neal's appetite for adventure. A few days before Christmas that same year, his parents were startled to get a long-distance call from Neal and his brother, Linden, who was one year younger and one year behind Neal at Yale, saying they were on their way home to Denver for the holidays but were spending the night in Pittsburgh. They would also need to spend a night or two elsewhere along the way, they added, for they were flying themselves home in the Yale Aviation Club's two-seat Aeronca Chief airplane, which with a 65-horsepower engine didn't fly very fast. In fact, following the Pennsylvania Turnpike across the state as a navigation aid on that dreary winter day, Neal and Linden had seen cars below moving faster than their plane.

Their parents were flabbergasted. *Flying yourselves?* That was when their sons explained how they had each taken forty hours of flying lessons at four dollars an hour that fall. Linden had gotten his pilot's license the day before they left New Haven. Neal would get his license only after the holidays, but they were already pretty proficient pilots. Otherwise, the Yale Aviation Club wouldn't have entrusted them with its Aeronca. It was all part of a marvelous idea Neal had for a trip even more audacious than the *Yale Daily News* Asian Expedition, but they would explain that part when they got home.

Four days later, safe and sound in Denver, Neal and Linden told their parents they wanted to buy a small plane of their own and spend the next summer flying through Latin America. They would start in Denver, hop to Mexico, and then fly through Central America to Panama, over the water to Colombia, and then weave down the jagged Cordillera de los Andes mountain chain on the west side of the South American continent to Santiago, Chile. Turning east, they would fly to Argentina, then head north through Uruguay, Brazil, Venezuela, and across the Caribbean before landing in Miami. They planned to conclude their journey back in New Haven as the fall semester at Yale began.

Originally Neal had wanted to spend the summer flying across the Soviet Union to see what lay behind the Iron Curtain, but the Soviet embassy in Washington never got the brothers the necessary permission from Moscow. Since both Neal and Linden had studied Spanish at Yale, they had decided instead to explore Latin America and look for a business opportunity to pursue after college. "Presented with a fait accompli," as a newspaper article later recounted, "their parents became resigned and then enthusiastic about their summer plans."

The trip to Latin America would be more expensive than the *Yale Daily News* expedition, and Neal decided they should finance this one by putting together a "syndicate" of newspapers to buy articles and photos. To establish the syndicate, they spent their 1956 spring vacation flying across the United States, pitching their proposal to city editors at major papers. Before each stop, they would send the next newspaper on their list a "night letter" (a reduced-rate telegram transmitted after office hours for delivery the next morning) requesting an appointment. Then, without awaiting a reply, they would fly in and show up in person to describe their plan. For a package fee of $1,500, they offered fifteen hundred words of copy and four glossy photos a week.

Their syndication plan succeeded splendidly. They signed up major papers coast to coast, including the *Boston Globe*, *New York Herald Tribune*, *New Orleans Times-Picayune*, *Houston Post*, *San Diego Union*, and their hometown *Denver Post*. The papers paid the brothers a combined $3,000 in advance, more than covering the $1,350 they had paid for the used 1946 Piper Super Cruiser they had purchased to fly across the country while putting the syndicate together. Buoyed by that success, and realizing they needed an aircraft with more power, speed, and range for the expedition to Latin America, the Blues now elevated their aim. On a trip to New York, they visited *Life* magazine and negotiated another good deal. *Life* would provide them all the film they needed for the trip and consider buying their story when they got back. Armed with that commitment, the Blues next contacted the New York public relations agency for Piper Aircraft, whose director liked the idea of the free publicity the young men were promising if the company loaned them a better plane than their Super Cruiser. An agreement was quickly struck there, too, and the Blues delivered as promised.

Their trip in the *Blue Bird*—as they dubbed the brand-new, four-seat, fabric-covered Tri-Pacer plane Piper loaned them—included a number of adventures. In Ecuador, they visited with headhunters who showed them "the apple-sized and goateed head of a German prospector the Indians had captured 25 years ago." In Chile, they skied the Andes in springtime and had to make ad hoc repairs to their landing gear after a wheel rolled into a deep rut during a takeoff from frozen Lago de los Incas. In Brazil they got lost over some flatlands, ran low on fuel, and had to make a forced landing on a country road, bashing their plane's wings into fence posts as they bounced to a stop. While Neal flew home to arrange repairs for the *Blue Bird*, Linden spent two weeks in Brazil, putting his time to good use by interviewing the country's president, Juscelino Kubitschek, for their newspaper syndicate and sunbathing on a Rio de Janeiro beach with a pretty girl he met there.

Ultimately their aerial expedition included forty-four stops in one hundred and ten days and nine crossings of the Andes. *Life* bought their story and photos for eight thousand dollars, a princely sum in the 1950s, and then featured Neal and Linden on the cover of its April 8, 1957, issue, under the headline "The Flying Blue Brothers." Shown in the cockpit of the *Blue Bird* wearing gleeful grins, the two dashing young men looked for all the world as if they were capable of anything.

Neal and Linden Blue found the investment opportunity they were looking for during one of the first stops on their tour. In Managua, Nicaragua, a letter of introduction from some friends of their mother's got them an interview with the president, Anastasio Somoza García, who had been the country's dictator and a reliable U.S. ally for two decades. Their talk with "Tacho" Somoza in July 1956 was not intended as grist for their articles for *Life* or the newspapers; instead, it was meant to be a discussion of investment ideas between a couple of ambitious young Americans endowed with pioneering spirit and a head of state eager to explore new financial opportunities. Tacho liked wealth himself—he generally used patronage rather than violence to maintain power—and couldn't have been more charmed by his young visitors. When Neal told him that some agronomists the brothers had met in Guatemala thought they might find it profitable to grow cacao, the basis for chocolate and other foods, Somoza was all for it.

"Why don't you guys come down and go into business?" asked the president, who had spent his teenage years in Philadelphia and gone to college at a small business school there.

A year later, using some of their *Life* and newspaper fees to buy a plane of their own, the Blues flew back to Managua. But this time they would not be meeting with Tacho Somoza: he was dead, shot on September 21, 1956, by an assassin who was himself killed on the spot. Tacho's eldest son, Luis, was now president, and Neal and Linden visited the new ruler. They also renewed acquaintances with Luis's younger brother, Anastasio Somoza Debayle, a Class of '46 West Point graduate known as Tachito, who served as a senior official in the National Guard and helped his brother rule Nicaragua. When the Blues explained that they were interested in starting a cacao plantation on the country's agriculturally underdeveloped east coast, they found Tachito just as welcoming as his father had been.

"Well, happy to have you here," Tachito replied. "That would go well here in Nicaragua, and furthermore, we have some land that we'll invest in your company for an equity position. So come to Nicaragua!"

By 1958, Neal and Linden, ages twenty-three and twenty-two respectively, had graduated from Yale and become the principal owners of a three-thousand-acre cacao and banana plantation carved out of the jungle along Nicaragua's northeast coast. The Somoza family owned 17 percent of the venture, which was financed by the Nicaraguan Development Bank. Before long, the plantation had five hundred employees, its own airstrip, and a house designed by Neal that the Blue brothers shared. They often flew a plane across the country to Managua, where they rented another house, this one up in the cool hills outside the capital, and socialized with Tachito and, more often, his brother Luis. The Blues also had a standing invitation to the presidential palace, and though seeing Luis could require waiting for hours in an ornate anteroom, over the next couple of years they found many reasons to stay in close touch with both the Somoza brothers.

On March 24, 1961, Neal passed some anxious hours waiting in the tower of Managua's airport, trying to get word over air traffic control radio of Linden, who was overdue on a return trip from the United States. To save a stop for fuel and a day's transit time, Linden had planned to fly in the brothers' Beechcraft Twin Bonanza from Key West to Nicaragua via Cuba, using an international airway over the island nation's capital, Havana. Tensions between the United States and Cuba were running high: two years earlier, Cuba's pro-U.S. dictator had been overthrown in a revolution led by belligerent, blustery Fidel Castro, and the country had immediately become a close ally of the Soviet Union. As Castro suspected, the CIA was now trying to help Cuban exiles overthrow his Communist regime; years later, it would be revealed that the CIA was also plotting to assassinate the island nation's new leader.

Linden was well aware that he'd chosen a touchy moment to be flying through Cuba's air space. "There were some clouds I didn't want to get into," he recalled years later. "I was talking to air traffic control Havana. As I approached the coast, I asked them for a change in altitude. They said, 'Stand by,' and then when they came back on, they said, 'Your flight over the international airway has been cancelled. You're to land in Havana.' And I said, 'Well, I don't really want to do that. I think I'll return to Key West.' And they said, 'No, you're going into Havana, and we have two jets being vectored on you to make sure that you do.'"

As Linden dutifully descended, he assured a passenger he had with him, Gerber baby food executive Don Swenson, that the Cubans would probably search the plane for contraband and, finding none, let them go. All they had aboard was a banana puree machine the Blues had bought as part of a proposal to sell pureed bananas to Gerber for baby food. Swenson had been on his way to Mexico City when Linden persuaded him to fly to Nicaragua with him for the weekend to see the brothers' plantation and show workers there how to use the puree machine.

When their plane came to a stop on the tarmac in Havana, Linden instantly saw that he had been naïve to assume their stay would be brief. Bearded men carrying submachine guns rushed to surround the plane, and Linden and Swenson were whisked to the government's intelligence headquarters for an interrogation that lasted until eleven o'clock that night. The interrogator had them watch as he signed a transcript, adding beneath his signature with a flourish, "Death to the invaders!" Then the two men were taken down a hallway; as a door opened, they felt a blast of heat on their faces before they were shoved into a cramped, smelly room containing nearly forty sweat-soaked prisoners. All were Cubans.

For the next twelve days, the two Americans were held by the government and given no opportunity to communicate with anyone. Every time the door opened, Linden tensed, waiting for his name to be called and wondering if hearing it would mean he was on his way to freedom or to execution. He also wondered if anyone at home knew where he was.

They did—and his parents were working feverishly to get him and Don Swenson freed. Their friend U.S. Senator Gordon Allott, a Colorado Republican, made calls to the State Department and elsewhere on their behalf, trying to work behind the scenes. Another friend, Peter Dominick, a Republican serving his first term in the U.S. House of Representatives that year, counseled them to make Linden's captivity public and speak about it as loudly as possible so the Cubans couldn't deny they were holding him. After several days of intense negotiations, Cuba finally released the two Americans. A photograph accompanying an April 6 *New York Times* story about tensions with Cuba showed Swenson and Linden after their arrival in Miami on a Pan Am flight, both looking gaunt and a bit in shock. Linden also looked a little angry, and for good reason: as he and Swenson were being marched under guard to the airliner in Havana, Linden had seen his Beechcraft across the ramp. When he protested that he wanted to fly his *own* plane home, he felt the business end of a submachine gun in his ribs. "¡Camine!" was the reply. "Walk!"

Thirteen days after Linden and Swenson were released, CIA-backed exiles invaded Cuba at the Bay of Pigs, staging their operation from the northeast coast of Nicaragua. For reasons that included President John F. Kennedy cancelling a key air strike the exiles had planned to mount on Castro's air force using old World War II B-26 bombers provided by the CIA, the invaders were repulsed, and nearly all 1,511 of them killed. Linden was convinced he and Swenson had narrowly escaped death themselves, for as he later learned most of their fellow prisoners were taken out and shot after the invasion. Had he and Swenson been held only a little longer, their captors might well have assumed that the two Americans they had captured flying over Cuba two weeks before the invasion were complicit and executed them, too.

The abrupt and frightening confinement by Cuban authorities was a formative experience for Linden. Suddenly, through no misdeed of his own, he had lost his freedom to the whim of a regime with the absolute power to decide whether he lived or died, a regime that might have killed him just on the suspicion—false, he insisted years later—that he was in league with the CIA and Castro's enemies. Linden and Neal Blue had always been anticommunists; now they were anticommunists with a grievance.

The Blues left Nicaragua the next year. The brothers had joined Air Force ROTC while in college, and now the Air Force was demanding that they serve the three years they had signed up for. Commissioned second lieutenants upon graduation from Yale, they had managed to delay their service by enrolling at an agricultural university in Managua and thereby receiving graduate student deferments. By 1962, though, they could put off their obligation no longer. Besides, it was clear by now that they weren't going to get rich growing cacao and bananas. Before returning to the United States, they left the plantation to the Nicaraguan Development Bank and the Somozas.

Linden reported for duty first; Neal followed six months later. Though they were avid fliers—Neal had once aimed to fly fighter planes—neither signed up to become an Air Force pilot. That would have meant extending their service beyond three years, which wasn't part of their plan. They were going to be entrepreneurs.

In 1963, the year after the Blues left Nicaragua, a leftist rebel movement funded by Cuba and the Soviet Union began working to overthrow the Somozas. Taking their name from 1920s rebel leader Augusto César Sandino, the insurgents called themselves the Sandinista National Liberation Front, or more simply Sandinistas. As the years went on, the Blue brothers watched the rise of the Sandinistas with much interest and concern—and they never forgot their friends in Nicaragua.

Two decades after leaving Nicaragua, Neal and Linden Blue were the owners of Cordillera Corporation, a private Denver company whose substantial holdings included local commercial real estate, construction businesses and ranches, oil and gas interests in Canada, aviation facilities, and 880 acres of the valley at Telluride, the Colorado ski resort—land they bought in 1983, to much local consternation, for a mere six million dollars. Neal Blue, the driving force in their investment company, had a reputation for bare-knuckle bargaining and hard-nosed tactics that would result in more than one lawsuit against the Blues and their companies over the years. Linden, widely regarded as the kinder and gentler of the two, was his older brother's partner but had also served a term on the Denver city council in the early 1970s, attended Harvard Business School, and held top jobs at Gates Learjet Corporation and Beech Aircraft Corporation, where in 1982 he became president and chief executive officer. Along the way, Linden became an expert in, and ardent advocate of, using advanced composite materials such as carbon epoxy—a new technology in those days—to build aircraft.

Politically, the Blue brothers were dedicated to helping President Ronald Reagan win the Cold War, which in the early 1980s appeared increasingly likely to get hot. The Soviet Union and its chief allies in Latin America, Castro and the Sandinistas, had been growing bellicose in recent years, a factor that in 1980 helped Republican Reagan make Democrat Jimmy Carter a one-term president. The year before, the Soviets had invaded Afghanistan, Castro had celebrated his twentieth year in power, and the Sandinistas had forced Neal and Linden Blue's former business partner—and more recently dictator in his own right—Anastasio Somoza Debayle to flee Nicaragua. Somoza's overthrow was hastened by international outrage over human rights violations by his National Guard, whose atrocities were brought into clear focus when one of its soldiers was filmed murdering American TV newsman Bill Stewart in cold blood on June 20, 1979. President Carter refused to let Somoza settle in the United States; just over a year later, the exiled caudillo was assassinated in spectacular fashion in Asunción, Paraguay. Somoza died in a hail of bazooka and machine-gun fire that shredded him and his yellow Mercedes as it drove by a house that hid his ambushers.

Three years after Somoza's assassination, the CIA began supporting Nicaraguan rebels whose goal was to overthrow the Sandinistas, who had established a dictatorship of their own, leftist brand. The CIA-backed insurgents, mostly ex–National Guardsmen, became known as the Contras, from *counterrevolutionaries*. On September 1, 1983, the same year the Contras were organized, a Soviet fighter plane shot down a South Korean airliner over the Sea of Japan, killing all 269 passengers and crew on board. An outraged President Reagan went on national television to denounce the Soviets for the plane's downing and to announce stiff sanctions against Moscow. A couple of weeks later, the White House further announced that, to help pilots avoid Soviet airspace, the president would allow all nations free use of a revolutionary new constellation of navigation satellites the U.S. military was launching.

The still-incomplete array would consist of twenty-four satellites circling the earth every twelve hours in six orbital planes while emitting continuous radio signals. Read by the right kind of receiver, these radio signals would tell users their location, velocity, and the time of day with unprecedented precision. For the first time in history, humans or machines would be able to know where they were within a few yards, how fast they were traveling down to fractions of a mile per hour, and what time it was within a millionth of a second. Navigation Signal Timing and Ranging Global Positioning System was the name of this new technology; initially referred to by the acronym NAVSTAR, it later became known as GPS.

Interested in technology since he was a youngster, and familiar since his *Blue Bird* days with the difficulties of aerial navigation, Neal Blue found his imagination fired by the coming availability of GPS. He began following the system's development avidly, and when he heard of a Silicon Valley company named Trimble Navigation Ltd. that was already making products based on GPS applications, he flew to California to meet the firm's founder. He came back with a new idea: theoretically, an unmanned aircraft equipped with a GPS receiver connected to an autopilot could be flown with great accuracy to any point on the globe that its aerodynamics and fuel capacity would enable it to reach. If such a drone also had a couple of hundred pounds of TNT in its nose, and was built cheaply enough, it could be a poor man's cruise missile.

Neal had been following the turmoil in Nicaragua closely, and now it occurred to him that the Contras—or a covert ally of theirs, perhaps— might use a weaponized drone to destroy Managua's military aviation fuel supplies and thereby ground a fleet of attack helicopters the Soviets had given the Sandinistas in 1984. The heavily armed Soviet choppers had been chewing up the CIA-backed Contras. Well aware of the domestic and international pressure to stop supporting the Contras, Neal reasoned that the GPS-guided flying bombs might be just the covert weapon the Reagan administration needed. "You could launch them from behind the line of sight, so you would have total deniability," Neal explained some years later.

Neal also believed that if the GPS-guided drones were inexpensive enough, the U.S. military could use them to stop the swarms of Soviet tanks that analysts expected to pour through the Fulda Gap, lowlands on the border between West and East Germany, if Moscow decided to invade Western Europe. The risk of a Soviet invasion of West Germany had preoccupied Neal for a long time, partly because his wife was an East German by birth. Anne Prause's father had smuggled his family out of the Communist German Democratic Republic before the Berlin Wall was built in 1961. For Neal, meeting Anne was one of the highlights of the *Yale Daily News* Asian Expedition—she had been a stewardess on his Pan Am flight to Europe—and they married in 1962. Over the years, they had talked a lot about the need to stop the Communists, and about the horrors of indiscriminate Allied bombing of Germany during World War II, which Anne and her family had witnessed. The precision of GPS-guided drones, Neal reasoned, could prevent such tragedies.

By the early 1980s, then, Neal Blue felt certain he had perceived the need for a unique new weapon. Brash as ever, he concluded that he and his brother, Linden, should look for the right opportunity to add the development of an armed, inexpensive, GPS-guided drone to their eclectic business portfolio.

One day in the summer of 1985, Neal read a report in the *Wall Street Journal* that Chevron Corporation, which the previous year had bought

Gulf Oil for $13.3 billion in a deal financed largely by borrowing, was "circulating an informational packet among prospective buyers 'identifying assets that might be for sale.'" Among the former Gulf properties Chevron wanted to spin off was GA Technologies Inc., a nuclear energy and defense research company in La Jolla, California, a palmy suburb of San Diego where Neal happened to own a house already. Neal and Linden's company, Cordillera Corporation, had just finished its annual planning meeting, and afterward Neal had decided that Cordillera should shift 50 percent of its business portfolio into high-technology products and companies. When Neal heard about GA Technologies, he thought, *My God, this fits perfectly.*

Founded in 1955, GA Technologies was originally General Atomic, a division of nuclear submarine builder General Dynamics Corporation formed to explore peaceful uses of atomic energy. Renamed after it was acquired by Gulf, GA Technologies now had a staff of fifteen hundred—many of them scientists and engineers—and revenue of $170 million in fiscal year 1984. The company's businesses included building nuclear research reactors, experimenting with nuclear fusion, and doing research under Pentagon contracts for President Reagan's new Strategic Defense Initiative, the "Star Wars" program to create exotic ground- and space-based weapons able to shoot down incoming ballistic missiles. Neal had been interested in nuclear power since 1947, when experts first began saying that atomic energy would one day provide a clean form of power too cheap to measure, and GA Technologies was just the sort of high-tech enterprise he wanted to own.

In August 1986, the *Wall Street Journal* reported that Denver businessmen Neal and Linden Blue were buying GA Technologies for "more than $50 million." (The price was closer to $55 million, Neal revealed years later, with more than $20 million in cash from their Canadian oil and gas holdings going into the purchase; the rest was borrowed.) GA Technologies had expanded into defense work earlier in the 1980s, when its president was Harold Agnew, a physicist who worked on the Manhattan Project during World War II. Now Neal Blue decided to expand the company's defense work into an entirely different undertaking: unmanned aircraft.

———

As his new employees pondered how to get into the drone business, Blue found someone to lead the way, an aviator who knew a lot not only about airplanes but also about the military, the Pentagon, and Congress. He also happened to be looking for a job.

Thomas J. Cassidy Jr., fifty-four years old when a banker friend introduced him to Neal, was a retired U.S. Navy rear admiral who had been one of that service's hottest fighter pilots for three decades. Born and raised in the Bronx, big in every dimension, Cassidy was brassy and gruff, and he could cuss like the sailor he had been his entire adult life. He could also employ Irish altar boy charm when it suited him. He loved to fly, and he liked to say he enjoyed it because it was complicated, which made it satisfying, and you could do it sitting down. A "good stick" in the cockpit, Cassidy left college after two years to become a naval aviation cadet, winning his wings in 1953 and finishing his academic degree later.

Cassidy started out in propeller-driven World War II F6F Hellcats and went on to pilot every type of jet fighter the Navy possessed and several Air Force planes to boot, flying all over the world. During the Vietnam War, when better-turning Russian-built MiG fighters were besting American pilots in aerial duels, Cassidy was selected to fly MiG-17s and MiG-21s, acquired through third-party nations, in secret mock dogfights conducted to develop new U.S. tactics. He later commanded Miramar Naval Air Station, home of the famous Navy Fighter Weapons School just outside San Diego known as "Top Gun." When Hollywood director Tony Scott came to Miramar to film the eponymous 1986 hit movie starring Tom Cruise, Cassidy not only played himself in a cameo as base commander, but also flew an F-5 Tiger the script called the "black MiG-28."

In all, Cassidy logged about six thousand hours in the cockpit over the course of his thirty-four-year Navy career. He also did several tours behind a desk in the Pentagon, including one year as an "action officer" and a second stint as director of the Navy's Aircraft Weapons Requirements Branch, followed by three years running the Tactical Readiness Division for the chief of naval operations. Cassidy knew how the sausage was made in the military-industrial complex—how defense equipment got marketed, sold, developed, tested, and put into service. He knew what aircraft the armed services owned, what aircraft they wanted, how they decided what they needed for the future, and how hard it was to get a new program started.

Privately, Cassidy thought Neal Blue's flying bomb drone idea was dumb, though naturally he didn't say so in his initial conversations with Blue about working for him. He knew about target drones and the parachute-recovery remotely piloted vehicles used in Vietnam to little effect; and as a fighter pilot, he knew you couldn't go after heavily armored Russian tanks with little GPS-guided drones. He also knew there was no demand for such a weapon within the armed services. Furthermore, even if the military decided it wanted a drone like the one Blue had in mind, Pentagon regulations would require that the services first write a formal Operational Requirements Document saying what the aircraft had to be able to do, then hold a big competition for a contract to build it—a competition in which a relatively small company like General Atomics would be presented with criteria it likely couldn't meet. Once Blue hired him, though, Cassidy learned that his new boss wasn't just daydreaming, and he wasn't going to be happy until his company was building GPS-guided drones. After all, Neal Blue had made several fortunes in his life by investing where others saw no opportunity. As Blue liked to say, "My golden rule is to always buy straw hats in the winter." So Cassidy got busy.

One thing he and Blue quickly agreed on was that the newly renamed General Atomics would develop a drone on its own, without government involvement, adopting the "build it and they will come" principle. Blue's high school friend Norman Augustine, a highly successful and much-admired aerospace executive, had published a popular book in 1983 about the defense acquisition system containing pithy observations he called Augustine's Laws. One law addressed the inexorable rise in the cost of developing aerospace technology: "In the year 2054, the entire defense budget will purchase just one aircraft." The Air Force, Navy, and Marines, Augustine added, would have to share the plane. The last thing Blue wanted to do was get tied up in the "defense acquisition system" his friend Augustine had lampooned, a sclerotic bureaucracy that could mangle the execution of even the most elegant technological ideas.

Not long after joining General Atomics, Cassidy met Bill Sadler, an aviation entrepreneur in Scottsdale, Arizona, who had designed and was selling a single-seat "ultralight" plane that Cassidy thought had possibilities. Built for sport, the aluminum monoplane had an open pod cockpit made of fiberglass and Kevlar, a pusher propeller in back of that, and twin booms leading back to a horizontal stabilizer. The configuration resembled a 1950s British fighter jet called the Vampire, so its designer called it the Sadler Vampire.

Sadler, an electrical engineer with a master's degree from the Massachusetts Institute of Technology, was intrigued by the idea of turning his sport plane into an "attack drone" so inexpensive that thousands could be sold. After a meeting in June 1987 with the Blues and Cassidy at General Atomics' headquarters, he signed a time-and-materials contract to convert his Sadler Vampire into a drone with a computerized autopilot whose guidance would come from a GPS receiver. Sadler took one of his ultralights, shortened the wingspan from thirty to eighteen feet, gave it a smaller tail, and then installed a Trimble Navigation GPS receiver and connected it to the autopilot.

Soon Cassidy was flying from San Diego up to Phoenix about once a month to meet with Sadler and gauge his progress. They would rendezvous at Sadler's house in Scottsdale before sunrise and drive to Gila River Memorial Field, an abandoned single-runway airstrip on a dusty Native American reservation fourteen miles south of Phoenix. Sadler would haul the prototype down from his shop in Scottsdale on a trailer, folding its wings up into a triangle to fit. The two men had to launch early to catch the signals from the only four GPS satellites the military had deployed so far, and one of the men had to be in the cockpit to take off and land and make sure the plane flew properly. Cassidy could fly anything, but he was too big to fit into the little pod cockpit, so Sadler served as safety pilot during the tests, getting the plane airborne and remaining ready to take over when necessary. With each passing month, the autopilot did more of the flying. The goal was to get the plane to the point where its autopilot alone could fly it to waypoints using GPS signals to navigate. Part of the challenge was to program the autopilot so that it wouldn't put the plane into a stall or otherwise cause it to go out of control.

Neal Blue wanted to call his pet project the Birdie, because "birdies go cheep, cheep, cheep." Potential military and international customers, he was sure, would get the pun and appreciate the point that this was going to be a very inexpensive weapon. After Cassidy finished rolling his eyes, he started collecting alternative suggestions, and soon a blackboard in his office was cluttered with a couple of hundred possible names. The former Navy admiral pondered them for a while, then chose one he thought conveyed the right image for their product. Early one morning, as Sadler was getting ready to climb into the cockpit for a flight test, Cassidy told him, "Oh, by the way, we have a name for the airplane now." Then he walked to the tail and smoothed on a sticker bearing the new appellation. Later, Cassidy and the Blue brothers would insist it was pure coincidence that an Arnold Schwarzenegger movie set in Central America and released within days of their first meeting with Bill Sadler was also called *Predator*.

3

A STRAW HAT IN WINTER

Since 1909, with breaks only for wars, the world's largest and most important aviation exposition and air show has been held in Paris, France. First staged in the city's magnificent Grand Palais des Beaux-Arts as L'Exposition Internationale de la Locomotion Aérienne, since 1953 the renamed Salon International de l'Aéronautique et de l'Espace has been held four miles north of Paris, at Le Bourget, the city's first airport, where on May 21, 1927, ecstatic crowds swarmed the *Spirit of St. Louis* as exhausted American pilot Charles Lindbergh completed the first nonstop transatlantic flight. Now held only in odd-numbered years, the Paris Air Show, as it's commonly known, attracts aircraft manufacturers, aviation vendors, airline executives, military officers, political leaders, media representatives, and passionate fans of flying from around the globe. Major manufacturers and military powers show off their aircraft in daily aerial displays for the paying public and official attendees. Rich companies rent air-conditioned "chalets" along the runways, where invited guests can drink and dine as they watch, or talk business in private rooms. Major aviation deals are kept secret for weeks or months so they can be announced in Paris, where news-hungry aerospace reporters from every continent are sure to flock for the biennial two-week extravaganza.

No aviation exhibition has ever matched the Paris Air Show. From

May 13–23, 1988, though, a small band of politicians and businessmen in San Diego, California, tried. At Brown Field, an old U.S. Navy training base ten miles south of downtown San Diego and a mile and a half north of the Mexican border, they staged "Air/Space America 88," touted as the first in a biennial series of exhibitions that would rival the Paris Air Show. *Aviation Week & Space Technology* described the ambitious event as "the latest attempt to establish an all-encompassing international aerospace exhibition in the U.S."

The show's opening day featured a visit from Vice President George H. W. Bush and was followed by two weekends of aerial displays open to the ticket-buying public. The Air Force Thunderbirds flew patriotically painted F-16 fighter jets in heart-stopping formation aerobatics. Army paratroopers floated down to targeted spots on the field with remarkable exactitude. For $985, spectators could circle out over the nearby Pacific Ocean at Mach 2—twice the speed of sound—in an Air France Concorde supersonic transport. Kids of all ages loved the show. More than two hundred thousand people attended. No one would have guessed that the organizers would wind up owing the City of San Diego and other creditors more than four million dollars, bankrupting the Air/Space America organization and making its first edition its last. The show was a critical success but a financial belly flop.

The hidebound mentality of the military-industrial complex was responsible for the failure. Sandwiched between the weekends of aerial wonders were five professional trade days devoid of flying, during which aviation industry executives and marketers hawked their wares to potential military and commercial customers. Four massive white tents arrayed in a quadrant along Brown Field's 7,972-foot main runway served as pavilions for 350 exhibitors. To the disappointment of the organizers, however, only one major airframe manufacturer, F-16-builder General Dynamics Corporation, exhibited, which was seen as "reflecting industry reluctance to get involved in still another major air show," *Aviation Week* commented. Most exhibitors were makers of small aircraft components or service companies, with two prominent exceptions. "Soviet officials were active throughout the show in promoting their products and capabilities," *Aviation Week* noted, and "two remotely piloted vehicles were displayed for the first time."

Looming over Booth 500, a prominently situated space just inside the west entrance to one of the pavilions, was the new General Atomics "Predator" prototype. Painted in green, brown, and beige jungle camouflage, the stubby-winged aluminum monoplane was mounted on a pedestal as if making a diving turn onto a target. Bill Sadler had designed the display and even built the pedestal himself. He and Tom Cassidy were in the booth for much of the show, telling potential customers and reporters how the 340-pound Predator would be capable of carrying 300 pounds of explosives in its nose and flying autonomously for as far as 300 miles at speeds of up to 120 miles an hour to attack out of the blue and with precision. *Aviation Week* reported that General Atomics "plans to market the vehicle to the Defense Dept. and ultimately to foreign countries as an unmanned, low-cost weapon system to strike enemy targets with guided munitions, cluster weapons or a high explosive warhead." So far, though, the Predator had been flight-tested for only sixty hours, and never without a safety pilot aboard.

At the southwest end of a pavilion next door was another booth displaying a drone, this one made by an Irvine, California, company called Leading Systems Inc. Neal Blue had heard of Leading Systems, and he knew that its much different RPV, the "Amber," was funded by DARPA, which meant it must have real potential. But Blue didn't know much more about Leading Systems or its RPV, so when the youngest of his two sons, freshly minted Cornell University graduate Karsten, said he and a college friend would like to go to the air show, Neal told them to get passes from Cassidy and see what they could find out about the competition while they were there.

The next day, Karsten and his friend Mike Melnick, wearing badges identifying them as "Neal Blue" and "Linden Blue," turned up at the Leading Systems booth, whose Amber display was impossible to miss. An orange-and-white, full-scale model of the drone's slender fuselage—a mere seventeen inches in diameter—was standing on its tail, with its nose rising nearly to the top of the two-story tent in a pose one Leading Systems wag called "a gigantic phallic symbol." The display was all the more striking because, as featured photos showed, the fuselage lacked the real Amber's willowy wings, pusher propeller, and inverted-V tail.

But both the model and the photos showed that the fuselage's nose had an odd downward bulge.

Manning the booth was a short, bald, middle-aged man with a gentle smile who spoke with a distinctly foreign accent. Seeming happy to meet Karsten Blue and his friend, the man asked if he could scan their badges with a business card reader to store their contact information. He had heard of General Atomics and its Predator, he told them, and would like to know more about their aircraft.

Karsten and Mike Melnick could see that the man was disappointed when they couldn't provide answers to his detailed questions about the Predator. Moreover, when Karsten tried to change the subject to the Amber, the man turned suspicious. Amber was a government project, he explained, and there were limits to what he could tell them. After all, he added gravely, "For all I know, you are Russian spies." Then he grinned, but Karsten couldn't tell if he was teasing.

Karsten chuckled at the suggestion, but he could see that it was time to move on. As he and his friend left, Karsten picked up a company brochure. He also took a closer look at the Leading Systems man's badge so he could tell his father about him. The badge read, "Abraham Karem, President."

There was much Abe Karem could have told his young visitors that spring of 1988, for over the past four and a half years he had been moving rapidly to capitalize on the success of the Albatross technology demonstrator he had built in his garage for DARPA. Within weeks of the November 1983 flight that proved the Albatross's phenomenal endurance, Karem's DARPA ally Bob Williams told him to put together a detailed proposal to develop a larger "endurance RPV" that would be able to carry enough weight to perform military missions. Williams said they would call the new drone Amber, and their aim would be to give the military a revolutionary, days-long aerial reconnaissance capability. DARPA's leaders would never invest much money in such a project, Williams knew, for the agency's mission was to advance military science, not procure defense equipment. But he was confident his bosses would put at least a few million dollars into the project as seed money, if he could get the armed services to invest as well.

Persuading the services to adopt the cutting-edge technologies DARPA fostered was never a requirement, but it was always a goal, and Williams knew he had a good argument to take to them. After all, Karem had practically defied the laws of physics by designing a plane that weighed 105 pounds empty, 200 pounds fully fueled, and could stay aloft two days on 15.2 gallons of gas. Rather than having to fly dull and sometimes dangerous reconnaissance missions with manned aircraft whose crews had to land after a few hours and risked being shot down over hostile territory, what if the military could just hang an RPV over a target area for days at a time and have it send back imagery of what was happening on the ground below? Williams thought that would be great.

Getting the armed services to change their ways was a Herculean task, but Williams knew the timing for selling such a project to the military was the best in years. In 1984, for the first time since the end of the Vietnam War, senior leaders of the Department of the Navy and the Army were taking a serious interest in reconnaissance drones. So was the Central Intelligence Agency. Each had its own reasons.

Early that year, the Navy Department's aggressive young secretary, John F. Lehman Jr., had become interested enough in drones to instruct subordinates to buy the Marine Corps an Israeli "mini-RPV" called the Mastiff, and to get U.S. industry involved in developing something like it for both the Marines and the Navy. Lehman had seen the Mastiff fly in Israel in January, during a trip whose purpose was to look for equipment and weapons for the Navy and Marine Corps, which operates under the Navy Department. Lehman scheduled his visit after the most traumatic event in recent Marine Corps history: a terrorist bombing in Beirut, Lebanon, on October 23, 1983, that killed 241 U.S. servicemen, mostly marines. The marines were in Lebanon as part of an international peacekeeping force sent to help tamp down a long-running sectarian civil war. A Muslim terrorist had driven an explosives-laden truck into their barracks, and by the time Lehman landed in Israel, Marine Corps leaders were determined to find better ways to conduct "tactical reconnaissance," such as detecting enemies before they attack fixed positions.

Lehman saw the Mastiff fly at an Israeli air base in the Negev Desert. At first glance, the drone looked like little more than a big model airplane, but its boxy fuselage had a television camera inside, and Lehman was impressed when his hosts took him into a control van to see live images that the Mastiff was beaming back to a monitor. As a pilot in the van flew the Mastiff by remote control over a practice bombing range a few miles distant, Lehman could see defunct tanks and other vehicles used for target practice by Israeli fighter plane pilots. When the drone circled back to the base, Lehman could look at the monitor and identify the types of aircraft parked on the tarmac. The Mastiff could stay airborne at most four hours, and at relatively low altitude, but Lehman decided the marines could use such a capability, and the drone and its control van were small enough for ground troops to transport.

The Navy secretary was even more excited by the possibility of developing a mini-drone like the Mastiff to spot targets for four World War II battleships he had persuaded President Ronald Reagan and Congress to bring out of mothballs. Each of the four dreadnoughts bristled with nine sixteen-inch guns that could fire man-size shells the weight of an economy car twenty-three miles. But because the munitions came to earth at over-the-horizon distances, the ship's gunners usually had no way to see where their shells were landing, unless a manned aircraft were sent to observe the target, which was both inefficient and dangerous. Critics derided Lehman's battleships as far too vulnerable and their guns as far too inaccurate in the guided-missile age, but Lehman saw their sixteen-inch batteries as a terrific standoff weapon and a magnificent reminder of the American might Reagan was reasserting around the globe. To make them more effective and fend off critics, though, he wanted to give their gunners a better way to spot targets. After seeing the Mastiff, he believed reconnaissance drones could be the answer.

DARPA's Bob Williams thought Army leaders might be interested in the Amber for a different reason. The Army had been trying for more than a decade to develop a Cold War–inspired mini-RPV of its own that could carry a TV camera and a laser designator, a device to shine a laser beam on a target and guide special artillery shells to their mark. The Army's drone was named Aquila, Latin for "eagle," but by 1984 this Aquila was proving to be a turkey.

Powered by a propeller about two feet in diameter that was housed in a big, round duct at the drone's tail, the Aquila had a short, fat fuselage and broad but stubby swept wings. The Army's operational requirements called for the Aquila to stay airborne just three hours at a time, but that proved to be a challenge. In 1984 alone, after more than a decade of development, ten of sixty-six Aquila test flights ended in crashes or had to be aborted with an emergency parachute landing. The Aquila's several Army managers, analysts would later find, had steadily added requirements that caused cost increases and schedule delays and drove the little drone's weight up to crippling levels. By 1984, the Army was estimating that it would cost more than two billion dollars to develop and procure 543 Aquilas and their ground stations. That was four times as much money for about two-thirds the number of Aquilas originally planned—and the drone was still years from being ready for service.

By mid-1985, Williams had persuaded the Navy, Marine Corps, and Army all to help DARPA develop the Amber, with the Navy taking the lead. The Navy Department agreed in December 1984 to a "remote control vehicle joint program" aimed at creating a drone able to fly twenty-four hours or more at altitudes of up to thirty thousand feet. DARPA would award Leading Systems a five-million-dollar contract to get under way and manage the project until the company built and demonstrated an Amber prototype. The Navy would invest twenty-five million dollars and take charge once the prototype proved the basic design was sound. Under Navy supervision, Leading Systems would develop different Amber versions able to carry various payloads, from daylight and infrared video cameras to special radars and sensors able to intercept electronic communications. Eventually, the company might also develop an Amber with a warhead in its nose.

In July 1985, the Army joined the program, raising the total Amber budget to forty million dollars. Two months later, Karem met with Melvyn R. Paisley, an assistant secretary of the Navy, and came away believing that the Pentagon would hire Leading Systems to produce up to two hundred Ambers a year once he proved the technology. The CIA was also interested in the drone, though in just what way and to what extent still remained a secret that participants in the program were forbidden by law to reveal three decades later.

The Amber project commenced during a memorable period in Karem's life. On March 16, 1984, seven years after arriving in America from Israel, he and his wife, Dina, at last became U.S. citizens. Hearts swelling, they took the oath of allegiance along with hundreds of others in a naturalization ceremony held under the glittering chandeliers of the Dorothy Chandler Pavilion, a Los Angeles venue that hosted the Academy Awards that year as well. Karem's new country also seemed to be recognizing that its new citizen was an aviation pioneer and an invaluable resource: a couple of weeks after his naturalization, Karem got a Top Secret clearance from the Defense Department. Following what a friend later described as his "wilderness years" in the garage, Karem was sure his vision was at last about to be realized.

From the moment Williams gave him the green light, Karem was a man in motion, doing a thousand things at once to get Leading Systems out of his garage and Amber into the air. He was designing, calculating, negotiating, researching, budgeting, buying, leasing, hiring—seemingly every day, seemingly all at once. Some nights he got by on only two hours of sleep. Weekends were workdays. He was going full throttle because at last he was living his dream. He was determined to build a company—a team, to be precise—that would defy the norms of the military-industrial complex, whose bloated bureaucracy, corporate mentality, and corrupting politics had made cost overruns, schedule delays, and outright failure in defense programs commonplace since World War II. Above all, Karem dreamed of leading the way into a new era of unmanned aviation the way pioneers of the early twentieth century led the way into the air—people such as Glenn Curtiss, Donald Douglas, Jack Northrop, Igor Sikorsky. These aviation greats—"people who should make us humble," in Karem's words—worked aeronautical wonders with small but talented teams of collaborators. They produced aircraft that pilots and passengers could rely on and nations could use to deliver the mail, expand commerce, and win wars. That was how Karem wanted to make drones.

Knowing government money was on its way, he tapped his savings and borrowed cash from his mother, brothers, and other family members. He leased an industrial building in Irvine, thirty miles south of his Los Angeles home, figuring a town in coastal Orange County would be more attractive to the kind of people he wanted to hire. With eighteen thousand square feet of floor space, the structure had more than enough room for offices and the various shops needed to create prototypes. Karem also planned to use the facility to refine and produce a less capable drone called the Gnat. He and his first employee, Jim Machin, had created the Gnat in Abe's garage, intending to sell it as a target drone and a trainer for RPV pilots. The Gnat was smaller than the Amber, and its wing attached at the bottom of its fuselage, rather than at the top as with both the Amber and the Albatross. The family resemblance among the three drones, though, was clear. All three had a high-aspect-ratio wing, a pusher propeller, and inverted-V tail fins.

By the time Air/Space America 88 came along, Karem was in his fifth year of developing the Amber. A company brochure boasted that Leading Systems had "a team of 95 exclusively devoted to development, production and flight operations" of UAVs, or unmanned aerial vehicles. The term UAV was becoming more fashionable than RPV because of the increasing autonomy in air vehicles made possible by the rapid evolution of computer technology. Small as it was, Leading Systems now had six engineering departments, five manufacturing departments, and two test groups. Among the company's key players was Frank Pace, a software engineer with degrees in math and computer science whom Karem had hired to help run the company. Pace had come from Brunswick Company's defense division, and his talent for writing software would be crucial to making a digital flight control system for the Amber. Only four such systems had been built at the time, including one Brunswick had done for a decoy drone.

Karem remained his company's chief designer, and the Amber was his creation. The prototype of the new drone weighed nearly five times as much as the Albatross, held three times as much fuel, and could carry video cameras, radar, or other payloads weighing up to a hundred pounds. Karem designed and constructed one version that would take off and land from a runway conventionally; DARPA wanted this version built first to prove the drone's endurance and test its flight characteristics. He also designed a model with features he and Williams assumed the Navy would need. This "Amber I" lacked landing gear, and its wings, fins, and propeller were meant to fold against the fuselage so it could be launched at sea from a torpedo tube or a canister. The drone's appendages would unfold after launch, blossoming into their functional positions after the UAV was blasted into the air by a booster rocket, which would fall away after doing its job. Upon returning to a ship or sub, this version would go into a deep stall—much like the free-flight models Karem had flown years before—then fire a retro-rocket downward to ease its descent into a shipboard net. Ever inventive, Karem had even designed this version so it could be launched straight out of its transport box by ground troops or put into flight from under the wing of a manned aircraft.

Karem's creativity didn't stop there. The Cold War had been heating up in recent years, as President Reagan challenged the Soviets rhetorically and beefed up the military to deter and, if necessary, fight the Warsaw Pact in Europe or other Moscow allies elsewhere. Karem imagined a range of possible missions for the Amber, so for added versatility he designed three different fuselages. One had a nose shaped like a snake's head to house both a TV camera and a small radar. The nose of the second bulged downward to accommodate a "moving target indicator" radar, which could distinguish objects in motion from ground clutter. A third Amber design had a missile-shaped nose to carry a warhead. Karem wanted his potential military customers to see all the possibilities.

In mid-1986, Karem moved his company to a two-story, 180,000-square-foot building in Irvine that was far too large for his team but provided enough space for the sizeable manufacturing orders he anticipated from the Navy and Army. He also leased, with an option to buy, a small airfield near El Mirage, California, a dry lake bed in the desert about ninety miles north of Irvine. He wanted his own airfield where flight testing could be done, pilots could train, and the Gnat could be used to evaluate software and technologies developed for the Amber.

Besides doing all its own testing, Leading Systems built nearly every component of its drones in house, from composite structures to the "actuators" that move aircraft control surfaces; from flight control and ground station electronics and computers to gearboxes, alternators, and even propellers. The company's machine shop fabricated mechanical parts of all kinds, right down to the landing gear. After hiring more than a dozen engineers and technicians with Formula One and other race car experience, Karem even set out to build the first engine expressly designed for UAVs.

On the surface, Leading Systems certainly seemed to be a success. Two weeks after the Air/Space America show ended in May 1988, visitors to Karem's booth at yet another trade fair in San Diego, the Fifteenth Annual Association of Unmanned Vehicle Systems Technical Symposium and Exhibit, could see just how extraordinary his new drone was. At 7:48 a.m. on June 6, minutes after the show opened, an Amber took off from Karem's airfield at El Mirage. Simultaneously, a digital electronic display at his booth in the trade fair began tallying the Amber's flight time. The display added minutes all that Monday. It added minutes all that night and throughout the next day. It added them into Tuesday night. At 10:10 p.m. on June 7, Karem's team finally landed the Amber—a phenomenal thirty-eight hours and twenty-two minutes after takeoff, an unofficial record for a UAV. The Amber had stayed aloft several hours longer than any other drone ever demonstrated.

That stunning performance wasn't the only reason outsiders might assume Leading Systems was a success. Nearly a year before the Amber set its endurance record, the officer running the Navy's unmanned air vehicle office, Captain Penn E. "Pete" Mullowney, had told *Aviation Week* that his service was "working to procure a total of 96 Amber vehicles capable of ship and ground launch," and that they "could be fielded with the Marine Corps and Navy units in early 1990." A year later, Mullowney gave *Aviation Week* another rosy prognosis for the Amber. To all outward appearances, then, the Navy was happy with the Amber, and in May 1988 the drone was apparently on a steady course toward putting its unprecedented capabilities to work helping defend America. But, as Karem learned the hard way, appearances can be deceptive in the byzantine world of military procurement, where politics and personalities can be more decisive than performance in determining what ultimately is purchased.

As early as August 1987, in fact, Karem had begged DARPA to hold off on transferring his project to the Navy. A seismic shift in the politics of military drone programs was taking place, and Karem feared that his project might get buried in the legislative avalanche that followed. The trigger was the boondoggle known as Aquila, which earlier that year had attained the status of public scandal. In tests at Fort Hood, Texas, between November 1986 and March 1987, the Army UAV performed correctly on a mere 7 of 105 flights—after the service had spent fourteen years and $1.2 billion developing the artillery-spotting drone. Outraged, defense experts in Congress took a closer look at all drone programs. Finding "excessive redundancy" in the few drones the armed services were developing, they decided radical surgery was needed. The fiscal 1988 defense appropriations bill directed the Pentagon to consolidate drone research and development under a new multiservice Unmanned Air Vehicle Joint Program Office—the JPO, as insiders called it, pronouncing it "JAY-poe." The bill also scrapped all funding for the Aquila, and to "encourage" the JPO to eliminate duplication, Congress slashed the year's budget for drone research and development in half—from $103 million to $52.6 million. For good measure, the legislation froze all spending on drones until the Pentagon produced an "improved RPV master plan."

A few months later, the Pentagon designated the Navy to run the JPO, and now Karem knew his project was in trouble. From the time the Navy created his RPV office in 1985, Captain Pete Mullowney's top priority had been to bring into the fleet a smaller short-range drone like the one Navy Secretary Lehman had seen in Israel, the Mastiff. Mullowney's office was developing a mini-RPV similar to the Mastiff, called Pioneer, and the Pioneer was being built by a joint U.S.-Israeli team of contractors with considerable political clout. With the Pentagon budget for drones cut in half, Karem felt all but certain that if push came to shove in a contest for dollars between the Pioneer and the Amber, Leading Systems would get pushed and the Amber would get shoved.

To make matters worse, Karem and his JPO overseer were constantly at odds. Mullowney had assigned the Amber program to Lieutenant Colonel Joseph G. Thomas, a Marine Corps aviator and a recent graduate of the Program Managers Course at the Defense Systems Management College, whose core curriculum was bureaucracy. Cultural and temperamental opposites, Thomas and Karem clashed over the marine's focus on process and the inventor's focus on performance, the bureaucrat's imperative to manage the Amber and freeze its design for production and the inventor's impulse to improve his creation as much as possible before production began. Karem was terrified that too much government regulation would turn his Amber into another Aquila.

Karem and his overseers also battled over the government's money, which Thomas thought Karem spent far too freely. "I could not control Abe Karem," Thomas complained years later. "I couldn't control Abe's burn rate, and I was running out of money." His time overseeing Karem's project, Thomas mused, was "my most notorious failure of any kind as a manager."

Karem bridled at what he saw as inept or political interference by the government. His relationship with his Navy overseers wasn't helped by his tendency to display disdain for those who either failed to appreciate his insights or offered ideas he deemed wrong. Ronald Murphy, who oversaw the Amber for DARPA before the Navy took charge of it, later admitted that he had been as worried as Karem about what would happen when the JPO took charge of the project. "My concern was it would be cancelled fairly quickly, because nobody would put up with Abe, and he no longer had an intermediary," Murphy said. "You can only tell people they're stupid for so long."

In 1988, under the new JPO, under the austere new budget for UAVs, and under the jaundiced eye of Lieutenant Colonel Thomas, Karem feared that his Amber, revolutionary as it was, might go into a deep political stall. If that happened, he planned to keep Leading Systems alive by designing a new drone to sell to foreign militaries. This larger, heavier aircraft would be less capable than the Amber, a requirement for getting

State Department licenses to export it, but it would combine some of the Amber's best features with some from his little Gnat trainer. The chord of the new drone's wing at the root (its width from front to back, where the wing met the fuselage) measured 750 millimeters, so Karem named his new product the Gnat 750.

General Atomics had attracted some favorable attention at the Air/Space America 88 show, but Tom Cassidy, like Abe Karem, was getting no joy from his attempts to sell unmanned aerial vehicles to the armed services. In late 1988, the former admiral persuaded a bevy of Army and Navy officers to meet him and the Blue brothers at dawn on a chilly Army test range near Yuma, Arizona, to witness a demonstration of the prototype Predator, the kit plane Bill Sadler was trying to turn into a UAV. Among those attending was the director of plans, policy, and doctrine for the U.S. Joint Special Operations Command, Rear Admiral Cathal Flynn—an impressive "get." Sadler was in the cockpit of the little plane and flew it during takeoff and landing, but he let the Predator's GPS-guided flight control system fly the semi-drone through a programmed, U-shaped, thirty-five-mile course of tethered weather balloons. The Predator navigated to within ten to twenty yards of three balloons designated as mock targets.

"This system illustrates a new family of weapons which will outdate more expensive weapon systems," Neal Blue told a *San Diego Union* reporter invited to observe. "It's a fire-and-forget system. Once you fire it, you can walk away."

Cassidy also spoke to the reporter and told him that the Predator would be able to slam into targets at ranges of three hundred miles while carrying three hundred pounds of explosives or a small nuclear warhead, yet each plane would cost just thirty thousand dollars.

The reporter noted in his article that General Atomics had exhibited but not flown its Predator at the air show the previous May, and that the company had been getting "calls from U.S. allies in Europe and the Middle East, but not from the Pentagon." The article contained no comments or reaction from Admiral Flynn or any of the other military officers present.

After the demonstration of the prototype in Arizona, Cassidy and his boss hoped their contacts in the military would call back expressing interest. What they got was silence. As Neal Blue put it years later, "They came. They saw. They left."

Even as Karem continued to clash with his handlers at the JPO, DARPA remained impressed with the Amber's growing capability. In the February 1989 issue of *Aerospace America*, a magazine published by the American Institute of Aeronautics and Astronautics, the agency's Ronald Murphy noted that the Amber's "order of magnitude increase" in flight time over previous drones had already led the Joint Chiefs of Staff to establish a new "endurance" category in the RPV master plan demanded by Congress. But in a separate article in the same issue, a DARPA deputy director provided a reality check. Despite support in Congress, an "unquestioned need" for such a drone "on the battlefield," and the technology's demonstrated capability, "DARPA's decision to turn Amber over to the services could prove fatal to the program," Robert A. Moore wrote. "The services are having difficulty finding adequate funding for field evaluation of Amber while simultaneously meeting the expense of fielding Pioneer."

When Karem read the article, his heart sank: Moore might as well have invited the Navy to cancel the Amber. But Abe Karem wasn't a quitter. Getting a shock from the light switch on his uncle Ezra's bed hadn't stopped him from taking things apart when he was a toddler. Seeing his drone proposals undermined by his former colleagues in Israel hadn't stopped him from pursuing his aviation dreams. Nor did giving up occur to Karem now. Instead, he became a man possessed.

For the next two years, Karem spent nearly every waking moment trying to save the Amber and Leading Systems. In early 1989, the JPO invited contractors to compete for a contract to produce a UAV for the Army and Marine Corps, asking for a drone that could loiter over an area as much as ninety miles from its base for five to twelve hours. Karem offered the Amber, and Leading Systems was one of three bidders. Mullowney's office announced that two bidders would be selected to compete for the final award—a potential billion-dollar deal. The winner would be commissioned to build an expected four hundred drones and fifty systems needed to fly them (ground control stations and related gear) within five years.

The Amber clearly could perform the mission, but the JPO also made it clear that the finalists would have to prove they had the experience, facilities, manpower, and "organizational structure" to produce aircraft in significant numbers, and provide parts and supplies to the services later on. Karem's deputy, Frank Pace, told his boss that Leading Systems needed to team with a much bigger company to have a chance, but Karem was reluctant.

"He didn't really want to team," Pace mused years later. "He didn't want anybody to tell him what to do."

For months, Karem dithered. In the end, though, he had no choice—Leading Systems was running out of cash. In August 1989, he signed a teaming agreement with Hughes Aircraft Company, a far larger and richer defense contractor with extensive manufacturing experience. Hughes agreed to help produce the short-range UAV if Leading Systems and its Amber were chosen, and to take charge when the program reached full production. Hughes also agreed to help Karem pursue export sales of his Gnat 750, mainly by guaranteeing bank loans to Leading Systems. Hughes would guarantee up to five million dollars initially and as much as twenty-five million if their team won the short-range UAV contract. The collateral for the loans would be Karem's company—lock, stock, and barrel. If Leading Systems later proved unable to repay its borrowings, Hughes could foreclose and take ownership of all physical and intellectual property that didn't belong to the government.

Karem sent the JPO a copy of the teaming agreement on August 17, 1989, the day he and Hughes signed it. Less than a month later, the JPO narrowed the competition for the short-range UAV contracts to the other two competitors.

Stymied once again by the JPO, Karem pinned his hopes on the Gnat 750. Within days of losing the short-range competition, he was in Turkey, then Germany, then Washington, talking with possible export agents and foreign manufacturing partners. A planned Gnat 750 flight in Kuwait on

October 20 "was cancelled by the Kuwaitis when they were told I am an ex-Israeli," Karem reported to a Hughes official. But he also expressed hope that he could find a Turkish manufacturing partner, and he said that Pakistan, another Muslim nation, had shown some interest in the Gnat 750. He was optimistic that Israel might buy some Gnats as well.

As Karem scrambled to rescue his dreams, Leadings Systems dutifully transferred ownership of his company's six Ambers to the JPO as required—seven had been built, but one had crashed due to engine failure. Then, knowing the JPO would put the Ambers in storage and forget them, Karem tried to get someone in the armed forces to use them and keep the project alive. With help from his old DARPA sponsor Bob Williams, now an adviser to the U.S. Southern Command in Tampa, Florida, Karem and Hughes proposed that SOCOM, as the command is known, use the Ambers to search out drug traffickers in the jungles of South America. On March 30, 1990, a Hughes official briefed the SOCOM commander and described the idea.

But time was running out. The very same day, the Defense Contract Audit Agency refused to honor a Leading Systems invoice for $1,340,000—a devastating financial blow for Karem, who was near the end of his line of credit. By September 14, Leading Systems owed Hughes almost $5 million and couldn't pay an overdue phone bill of $1.81. In October, Leading Systems filed for bankruptcy. In November the JPO ordered Leading Systems to send the six Ambers it had to Naval Air Weapons Station China Lake, in the western Mojave Desert, to be warehoused. Later that month, the JPO officially terminated the Amber program.

"They didn't really want our airplane around, and Abe was actually told his airplanes wouldn't see the light of day after that," Pace recalled sadly years later. "And true to their word, they took our airplanes and sealed them up, shipped them to China Lake . . . They had six perfectly flyable airplanes. They closed down our support contract and drove us out of business."

Ira Kuhn, the physicist and advanced technologies consultant who had served as a conduit for DARPA to fund the Albatross when Karem was working in his garage, wanted to help Abe, and not just for friendship's sake. Kuhn had never taken money from Karem, nor had a financial interest in his projects, and he never would. But after more than a decade of association, Kuhn firmly believed, as he was fond of telling others, that Karem was a "national asset," a genius whose work could be invaluable to America's defense. During the Amber's deep political stall, Abe had leaned on Ira heavily for advice, sending him drafts of his plans, proposals, and letters and calling Kuhn almost daily on the phone. Now, with the Amber dead and buried, Kuhn wanted to help Karem salvage what he could of Leading Systems.

Hughes foreclosed in late 1990, taking legal possession of all Leading Systems' property. At first, the big defense company told the bankruptcy court it might establish a UAV subsidiary and hire Karem as a consultant, but that plan fell through when Karem's chief supporter at Hughes was struck down by a sudden illness. By January 1991, Hughes was trying to sell the assets of Leading Systems, and Karem was trying to help find a buyer—ideally someone with money who would appreciate the value of what he had accomplished, take possession of all his physical and intellectual property from Hughes, and then bankroll Karem and the core of his team in a fresh start, with the Gnat 750 as their base. Kuhn made some calls, talked to some friends, and came up with an idea: what about the Blue brothers, Neal and Linden, the owners of General Atomics?

With Karem's encouragement, Kuhn called Linden, the brother Kuhn knew best, and told him about Karem—his brilliance, his team, and the promise of his drones. "You guys have been wanting to get into the unmanned vehicle business," Kuhn told Linden. "Why don't you get serious and go up and buy the remains of Leading Systems? I'll try to talk Abe into bringing the residual team down to your company and continuing this thing."

Kuhn's timing was excellent. Only a few weeks back, Linden had told Neal that they really needed to move on from their prototype Predator and develop a serious aircraft. The modified aluminum kit plane was proving the concept of using GPS to guide a drone, all right, but otherwise they were at a dead end. A year after the flight demonstration the company staged for the military at Yuma, Sadler still hadn't been able to automate the Predator sufficiently to fly without him in the cockpit. Besides, in Linden's view, the aluminum Predator couldn't hit the performance marks that would be required of a real military UAV.

If General Atomics wanted to get into the UAV business in a serious way, Linden argued, the company needed to build a drone made of composites, materials such as carbon epoxy, that could be baked into rigid forms to serve as lightweight but sturdy aircraft parts and structures and be less visible to radar than aluminum. As a top executive at Gates Learjet from 1975 to 1980, Linden had overseen experiments that used composites to make aircraft parts, and he knew a lot about the still-emerging technology. He also told Neal they needed to develop a UAV with a high-aspect-ratio wing, which would be essential to creating a drone with exceptional range and endurance. In other words, General Atomics needed to build the kind of drone Abe Karem had already designed.

Neal listened. By now it was clear that the military had no interest in using UAVs as cheap cruise missiles; moreover, the potential targets that had inspired his interest in the concept were gone. In Nicaragua the Sandinistas were out of power; in Europe, the Berlin Wall had fallen; the Soviet Union was collapsing. In the foreseeable future, at least, no Russian tanks would be pouring into Western Europe.

The Blue brothers began a series of conversations with Karem, and on Valentine's Day 1991 Karem faxed Kuhn copies of a "first-cut" proposal he had sent General Atomics and a counteroffer he had gotten back. Karem's proposal envisioned General Atomics buying his assets from Hughes, then investing nearly four million dollars over the next two years in a "separate entity" to build UAVs. General Atomics would put Karem, Pace, and other members of his core team on salary; in addition, the company would pay Karem and Pace royalties on all sales of Gnat 750s. Karem would be in charge of the entity, but "new faces" would market the product to the Defense Department and thus "shield Abe."

The General Atomics counteroffer was straightforward and hard-nosed, reflecting Neal Blue's style and Karem's utter lack of negotiating leverage. General Atomics would settle with Hughes on a price for the assets of Leading Systems, and then hire Karem and his core team as regular employees. The team would report to Tom Cassidy in the General

Atomics Advanced Technologies Group. "Abe will be chairman of this group as well as Chief Engineer. Operations of the activity will be under the direction of Frank Page [*sic*] as General Manager," the counteroffer stipulated, misspelling Pace's name.

Hughes bowed to expediency and Karem to reality. Both accepted the offer from General Atomics almost overnight. In March, the company put Karem, Pace, Jim Machin, Jack Hertenstein, and seven other Leading Systems engineers and pilots on salary, reporting to Cassidy. With the exception of the El Mirage airfield, which Karem and his family had bought but still owed money on, the Blues bought all the assets of Leading Systems for a price negotiated solely with Hughes. They got a warehouse full of office furniture, several small Gnat trainers, a couple of Gnat 750s, some digital ground control stations, and a long list of other expensive aviation equipment. They also got all the intellectual property Leading Systems had created from 1980, when Karem incorporated the company, through 1990. As a court document catalogued it, this included all "patents, trademarks and trade names," all copyrights, all "proprietary information, trade secrets, know-how," all Karem's inventions, all export licenses approved by the State Department, all licenses to use intellectual property belonging to others, all "documentation, disks, tapes, computer software, blueprints, drawings, sketches, recordings, film, photographs or other tangible medium" used in "research, design, development, manufacturing, test, evaluation, operation, maintenance, training of personnel, repair or overhaul of products." For all those assets, the Blues paid $1,850,000—about one-tenth the value of the physical property alone.

Inexpensive as the investment was, the wisdom of making it was debatable at the time, considering how indifferent the military was to drones. Karem had offered an ingenious new technology that was revolutionary, but politics and personality had trumped performance, and what little interest the armed services had in other such machines was fading as fast as the Soviet Union. In 1989, with the Cold War over, the Democrats controlling Congress had demanded a "peace dividend," and newly elected President George H. W. Bush had agreed to cut sixty-four billion dollars in defense spending within five years. Prized programs such as the Navy's F-14 Tomcat fighter plane, the Marine Corps' V-22 Osprey tiltrotor transport, and the Air Force's F-15 Eagle fighter were on the chopping block, and the Army was shrinking significantly.

In 1990 the market for drones was nearly nonexistent. Neal Blue, though, had faith in his golden rule of investing: always buy straw hats in winter.

4

PREDATOR REBORN

One Monday in March 1993, Abe Karem was sitting at his desk at the Adelanto, California, offices of work-starved General Atomics Aeronautical Systems Inc., a company Neal and Linden Blue had created after buying Leading Systems. Just before noon, someone came by and said, "Get in the car. We're going to El Mirage."

A twenty-minute drive away, El Mirage was the Mojave Desert airfield Karem had bought for Leading Systems as a place to fly Ambers and Gnats within Federal Aviation Administration rules for drones. Karem had lost the property as part of his company's bankruptcy, but General Atomics now leased a hangar from the airfield's new owner and kept ten Gnat 750s there. In 1992, Turkey had finally agreed to buy six of those drones and a ground control station for about fourteen million dollars, a deal whose seeds Karem had sown back when he was trying to save Leading Systems. So far, however, that was the only drone sale General Atomics had made, though a couple of smaller deals for demonstrations and studies had provided work enough to keep Tom Cassidy's aeronautics enterprise going.

On the drive to El Mirage that March Monday, Karem learned that another Gnat 750 sale was in the works. The Central Intelligence Agency had sent some senior officers to see the Gnat 750 fly, discuss buying a couple for a secret operation, and at all events get a photo of Karem at the airfield. The new CIA director, Jim Woolsey, was about to initiate an operation whose scope was modest but whose effect on the future of drones would be momentous, and if the agency was going to buy Gnats, Woolsey wanted to know that his friend Abe Karem was involved.

At age fifty-one, bald, bespectacled R. James Woolsey Jr. was an old Washington hand. A native of Oklahoma, Woolsey had arrived in the nation's capital in the latter part of 1968 as a young Army officer who also happened to be a Phi Beta Kappa alumnus of Stanford University, a Rhodes scholar, and a Yale Law School graduate. At Yale earlier that year, Woolsey had led a student campaign to secure the Democratic presidential nomination for Vietnam War opponent Eugene McCarthy, who lost the prize to U.S. Senator Hubert H. Humphrey of Minnesota. After the campaign, Woolsey reported for active duty in the Army to fulfill a Reserve Officer Training Corps obligation from his years at Stanford, where joining ROTC had gotten him an exemption from the draft. Assigned to staff jobs at the Pentagon and the National Security Council, Woolsey finished his Army service, spent three years as general counsel of the Senate Armed Services Committee, then served as undersecretary of the Navy under President Jimmy Carter. In 1981 the Reagan administration named him to a high-level commission studying how to base MX nuclear missiles.

The so-called Townes Commission's challenge was to figure out how a sufficient number of MX missiles could be based so as to ensure their survival in a theoretical Soviet first strike, and thus deter such an attack in the first place. Among the ideas considered was a design for a low-flying, long-soaring unmanned aircraft able to carry one ninety-plus-ton MX and stay aloft nearly seven days. The aircraft's designer was Abe Karem, who had come up with the idea after discussing the MX survival challenge at length with science consultant Ira Kuhn. Karem completed his drawings in a week, working at his customary frenzied pace when seized with an idea, and Kuhn dubbed it "Big Bird."

Defense Secretary Caspar Weinberger and President Reagan were both interested, and Karem's concept got front-page coverage in the

Washington Post. Air Force opposition, however, killed it. But Woolsey thought Big Bird brilliant—he liked unconventional thinking—and became a lifelong Abe Karem advocate. In the late 1980s, Woolsey even tried to intercede at top levels of the Pentagon to prevent the Navy-run JPO from killing Karem's revolutionary Amber—a favor that backfired badly when word of the intrusion filtered down to the JPO.

Two years after Karem's bankruptcy, President Bill Clinton nominated Woolsey to head the CIA. The director-designate was a lifelong Democrat but often described as a neoconservative, a label he found every bit as annoying as the media found it handy. The term generally described someone liberal on domestic and social issues but who also favored muscular military and foreign policies and was reliably pro-Israel. Clinton's nomination of Woolsey was widely seen as payback to neoconservatives for their election support of his candidacy, and Woolsey was quickly confirmed by the Senate. He was sworn in on February 5; the next day he called relevant CIA officials to his office to talk about one of his new boss's top intelligence priorities: Bosnia.

Bosnia-Herzegovina was a multiethnic republic of the former Yugoslavia, whose post–Cold War breakup in 1992 unleashed decades of repressed hostility among Croats, Muslims, Serbs, and smaller ethnic groups. The result was a civil war that marked the worst conflict in Europe since 1945 and led to demands for intervention to stop it. Western triumphalism was in the air—political scientist Francis Fukuyama had just published his book *The End of History*, predicting the rise of global liberal democracy—and most of America's leaders felt inclined or even obliged to use U.S. military power for world peace, especially now that the Soviet Union's history really *had* ended and Moscow wasn't going to interfere. Seven months before Clinton's election, his predecessor, President George H. W. Bush, had joined the European Union in recognizing the independence of the Yugoslav provinces of Croatia, Slovenia, and Bosnia.

The leaders of once-dominant Yugoslav province Serbia responded with violence. In league with ethnic Serb insurgents eager to carve their own republic out of Bosnian territory, Serbia's military laid siege to Bosnia's capital in 1992; by early 1993 they had been shelling Sarajevo's citizenry with all manner of weaponry for months. The siege led the United Nations to send peacekeeping troops to the Sarajevo airport, declare a "no-fly zone" over Bosnia, and begin airlifting aid to the beleaguered population. Undeterred, the Serbs began firing on UN troops as well.

Clinton wanted to break the Serb blockade, and he was both shocked and chagrined to find out how little his military and intelligence agencies could tell him about what was actually happening on the ground around Sarajevo. Chronic cloud cover over Bosnia, a territory as large and mountainous as West Virginia, was making it impossible to track Serb artillery. Spy satellites and manned U-2 reconnaissance jets were proving inadequate to the task. Their still-photo cameras were unable to penetrate the clouds, U-2 flights were limited—in part to reduce the risk of their pilots being shot down—and orbiting satellites overflew the region only a few minutes a day. Serbs, moreover, knew when the satellites were going to pass overhead. They hid their weapons in barns and wooded valleys before the satellites arrived, brought them out and fired when no satellite was scheduled, and moved their big guns at night. Clearly, what the military and the CIA needed was a way to get cameras or other sensors below the clouds and conduct surveillance for long periods. The White House wanted ideas on how to do that—in a hurry.

What about UAVs? was Woolsey's first thought. He posed that question at the February 6 meeting in his CIA headquarters office; a couple of weeks later, he got answers from agency experts, including a woman he and others would later refer to only by the alias Jane. Described in a CIA-approved magazine article as a "young, talented, multiengine-rated pilot and engineer," Jane, along with a team of experts, had been experimenting even before Woolsey's arrival with flying drones at extended ranges by relaying their remote-control and sensor signals through a manned aircraft. As Jane briefed Woolsey on their work, the director saw a photo of a Gnat 750 and recognized it immediately. "Hey, that's Abe's design," Woolsey said. Then he wondered, "Where *is* Abe these days?"

To find out, Woolsey called their mutual friend Ira Kuhn, who explained that Abe now worked at General Atomics for Neal and Linden Blue. By happenstance, Woolsey also knew Linden Blue. They had met years earlier, at the Hudson Institute, a conservative Washington think tank where Linden was a board member and Woolsey a frequent conference participant. Woolsey's next call was to Linden, who told him, "Jim, we'll give you whatever you need. We'll make it happen."

Waiting for Karem when he arrived at the sun-bleached El Mirage airfield in March 1993 was Thomas A. Twetten, CIA deputy director for operations, chief of the spy agency's clandestine branch. With Twetten was the chief of the air branch of the agency's Special Activities Division—the covert action arm of Twetten's directorate—and a couple of subordinates. By the time Karem arrived, the CIA party had already watched a Gnat 750 fly. Shielding his eyes against the desert sun as the drone passed by at what he guessed was two thousand feet in altitude, Twetten was shocked at how noisy the aircraft was. The Gnat's engine buzzed like a lawn mower, and one in need of a tune-up at that.

"This is a non-starter unless you can put a silencer on it," Twetten told Karem. "I mean, that thing's got to be really quiet."

Karem assured him that noise would be no problem because "this is just a temporary, developmental engine."

"Can this thing loiter for twenty-four hours?" Twetten asked.

Karem assured him it could. On a full load of fuel, the Gnat 750 could stay in the air for as long as forty hours—depending on altitude, wind conditions, and weather—while carrying about 130 pounds of cameras, radars, or other sensors. The drone's greatest intrinsic limitation was range, for the Gnat 750's remote controls operated on the "C-band" radio frequency, whose characteristics required that the antennas of both the drone and its ground control station stay within "line of sight" of each other. A Gnat 750 could fly as far as 130 or even 150 miles from its ground station, but their antennas had to communicate on a direct path—no mountains or tall buildings in between, no flying over the horizon. The Gnat 750's range might be improved, however, by relaying its signals through a manned aircraft to provide a line of sight to the drone at higher altitudes—exactly the concept that Jane and the CIA's covert air operations branch already had been studying.

As the two men finished their discussion, someone with a camera snapped a photo of Karem and Twetten in front of the General Atomics hangar, their faces turned toward the bright sun. Twetten, in slacks and a dress shirt, sleeves rolled up to the elbows of his crossed arms, is hatless and white-haired in the picture. Wearing sunglasses and smiling broadly, he looks down at the shorter Karem. Standing to Twetten's left, Karem wears blue jeans and a long-sleeve shirt. A pair of sunglasses dangles from his left hand, and he squints directly at the camera. He smiles a bit wanly, perhaps because of the large, stiff baseball cap on his head. The cap bears the logo of General Atomics and seems a poor fit.

General Colin Powell, chairman of the Joint Chiefs of Staff, was as eager as Woolsey to provide President Clinton with better information about Serb artillery and other military movements in Bosnia. Returning to the Pentagon from a White House meeting on the subject in early 1993, the nation's top military officer summoned the director for intelligence of the Joint Chiefs of Staff, Rear Admiral Michael W. Cramer, and briefed him on the meeting. Powell gave Cramer two orders. First, go find a system of some kind that will "get us ground truth." Second, go see Jim Woolsey and discuss why the United States needs better technology to track mobile weapons, whether in Bosnia or elsewhere. The same challenge had marred the military's otherwise sterling performance two years earlier, during Operation Desert Storm, the six-week shooting war in which U.S. and allied troops evicted Iraqi dictator Saddam Hussein's invading army from Kuwait. The Iraqis were able to hide most of their Scud ballistic missiles from U.S. forces—despite concerted Air Force attempts to locate and strike them—by moving the tractor-trailer-size weapons under highway overpasses and into desert wadis or by camouflaging them. In all, the Iraqis fired eighty-eight Scuds into Israel, Bahrain, and Saudi Arabia, killing and wounding civilians and, in one single dumb-luck hit, dozens of U.S. troops.

Cramer left Powell's office, returned to his own, and called in Navy Commander Steve Jayjock, an intelligence officer the admiral knew had worked on classified UAV programs at DARPA in the 1980s. Cramer told

Jayjock what Powell wanted and directed him to research what was possible. A week or two later, the two were standing at a whiteboard in Cramer's office, jotting down ideas about the capabilities a drone would need in order to produce the intelligence Clinton wanted. How high and far must it fly? How long must it loiter? What sensors must it carry? How much could it cost without stirring up fatal resistance from the armed services or Congress, especially at a time of post–Cold War "peace dividend" cuts in defense spending? Above all, how could they quickly get the drone they needed from an acquisition bureaucracy that generally needed a dozen years or more to design, develop, test, and field any new type of airplane?

The first thing Cramer and Jayjock agreed was that whatever they proposed had to be COTS, a government acronym (pronounced the way it looks) meaning "commercial, off-the-shelf." In other words, the drone couldn't just be a concept; it had to exist already, at least in basic form. Then they decided that, to preclude objections about the cost of losing such a drone to air defenses or accidents, the price per aircraft should be no more than $2.5 million—precisely the cost of each of the forty-two cruise missiles the Navy had fired a month earlier at a nuclear fabrication facility in Iraq after UN inspectors looking for weapons of mass destruction were obstructed by Iraqis.

The next requirement Cramer and Jayjock scribbled on the whiteboard was that the drone must carry sensors that could detect what was happening on the ground—at night, through clouds, no matter the weather. In addition to a daylight camera, its payloads should include a temperature-sensitive infrared camera and a "synthetic aperture radar," a computerized radar whose software uses the motion of the vehicle it rides on to electronically produce returns equivalent to that which would be transmitted by an antenna hundreds of yards in diameter.

The wish list grew still longer. The two men decided that everything on the drone should be unclassified, thus allowing the imagery gathered to be shared widely within the military. This requirement would also prevent enemies from gaining secret knowledge if they recovered a UAV that crashed or was shot down. They also wanted the drone to be able to fly over a target that was as many as five hundred miles from the UAV's ground control station and stay there for at least twenty-four hours. This meant it not only would have to remain airborne far longer than a day to get to the target and back, but also would have to be able to communicate with its ground station "beyond line-of-sight," or over the horizon. To do that, both the craft and its ground station would have to be equipped with satellite communications antennas.

When the brainstorming session finally ended, Cramer directed Jayjock to conduct an industry survey and find out what the half dozen or so companies that had built drones could offer to match their initial list of requirements. He told him to report back within six weeks.

The day Clinton named Woolsey to lead the CIA, Navy Captain Allan Rutherford was in his native California, visiting the San Diego offices of General Atomics during a "get-acquainted tour" of companies that made drones. Rutherford, an electrical engineer, had spent much of his twenty-two years in the Navy at sea and loved navigation, but of late his career had led him into shore billet jobs that involved buying weapons and equipment. By 1993 there was more electrical engineer than sailor in Rutherford's appearance. He had an office worker's tan, wavy black hair, and a trim black mustache, and he wore reading glasses. As a newly promoted four-striper, he now worked in the Defense Department's UAV Joint Program Office, and it was his job to make sure Pentagon drones used as many common parts and systems as possible. Rutherford needed to know potential suppliers, which was what had brought him to General Atomics, where he met Tom Cassidy and Frank Pace. That day, in a loose-leaf calendar Rutherford used as a work diary, he noted only that General Atomics owned software that Leading Systems had created for the Amber.

Three weeks after his drop-by at General Atomics, Rutherford got a call from Admiral Cramer, who had been advised by a retired Navy man to get Rutherford's help on the UAV project. Soon Rutherford found himself meeting with Cramer and Jayjock in the admiral's Pentagon office to talk about the drone that the chairman of the Joint Chiefs wanted. Cramer ticked through the wish list he and Jayjock had created, and then told Rutherford that he wanted him to manage the drone project. Cramer also gave him an ambitious target to hit: he wanted the new UAV fielded within two years. Given the usual pace of new product development at the Defense Department, this would require something akin to a miracle. At the very least, a lot of stars would have to align.

Another star presently did. On April 7 the Pentagon acquired a new undersecretary of defense for acquisitions and technology—a new "procurement czar," in media argot. John M. Deutch—longtime professor of chemistry at the Massachusetts Institute of Technology, former senior Energy Department official, defense technology expert—had a résumé larded with degrees and honors and service on federal commissions. He also had a reputation for being imperious, and his new job gave him great, if not total, power to decide what the military would buy and how the purchases would be made.

Among other convictions, Deutch believed that the armed forces needed far more drones. Given the miniaturization of computers and the proliferation of digital technologies, from cameras to satellite communication, Deutch thought the military was woefully behind the curve in developing and using unmanned aircraft. In his view, drones were a potentially lifesaving reconnaissance technology that would have been operational by now if the armed services weren't so myopic or the acquisition system such a mire. A drone able to fly high, for example, could replace manned U-2 flights along North Korea's border, doing the job at far less cost and at no risk of losing a pilot. Deutch realized that this notion was heresy in the Air Force, which loved its U-2s and their daring pilots, but he wasn't about to let that stop him.

As soon as he took office, Deutch began talking regularly with Jim Woolsey, whom he had known for years from his work in defense circles. When Woolsey discovered that Deutch shared his interest in UAVs, the CIA director enthusiastically described his initiative to have the spy agency buy Gnat 750s from General Atomics.

That spring, Deutch called CIA operations director Twetten and invited him to his office for a chat. When Twetten arrived, he was surprised to find Deutch's conference table ringed with three-star officers from each armed service. After discoursing on why UAVs were a "thing of the future," Deutch declared that the military needed to think more about which service or office should be responsible for UAVs once they became numerous, as they inevitably would. Then he turned to Twetten, who was wondering why he was there, and said, "Tell these fellows what you're up to in the drone program."

Perhaps out of habit, career clandestine officer Twetten kept his remarks brief and vague. "We're working on a small drone that we think might be operational within a year or so," Twetten told the officers. "At this point it looks like it'll be primarily available for imagery, and if one of you has the need for it—well, it's pretty low-tech, understand. We're not talking about flying it over a sophisticated antiaircraft environment." After uttering "low-tech," Twetten could see the military men's eyes glaze over. For the military, Twetten knew, "high-tech" was sexy, "low-tech" a yawner.

Deutch was equally unsurprised by their reaction. He had hoped to stimulate their competitive juices by letting the officers know that the CIA was buying a new drone. But the new procurement czar knew he would have to push hard to change military attitudes about UAVs, for most aviators in the Air Force and Navy seemed to regard drones as a threat, the Marine Corps lacked enough money to develop them on its own, and most Army leaders viewed the technology warily after the billion-dollar snake bite the Aquila had inflicted on their service. But if there seemed to be no natural home for drones in the military, Deutch was determined to find one or create one. Somehow, he would find a way to shoehorn UAVs into the system.

Not long after Twetten's visit to his office, Deutch invited the principal owner of General Atomics to pay him a visit. Neal Blue arrived assuming the new undersecretary of defense, being a former Energy Department official, might want to talk about a special nuclear reactor General Atomics had developed. Instead, Blue found half a dozen senior military officers in the room and Deutch wanting to discuss UAVs. Noting that the CIA was buying Gnat 750s from Blue's company, Deutch talked a bit about why UAVs were a potentially "enabling technology" that the military needed as well. "You've got a capability of doing this," Deutch said to Blue. "How soon can you deliver something?"

"Six months" was what came out of Blue's mouth. What went through his mind was *Manna from heaven*. Buying straw hats in winter was about to pay off once again.

Soon Tom Cassidy was calling Steve Jayjock so often that Jayjock got a second phone installed on his Pentagon desk so he wouldn't miss other calls. In the wake of Deutch's conversations with Woolsey, Jayjock had been assigned to work with the CIA on its drone project and keep those in the Pentagon informed. The CIA and Pentagon drone initiatives weren't being merged, but they were being coordinated.

In April, Jayjock accompanied a CIA officer to Israel to see that country's "Scout," a mini-RPV in use since the early 1980s that was a possible alternative to the Gnat 750. Jayjock viewed the trip as a waste of time. Having become familiar with the predecessor Amber when he was assigned to DARPA years earlier, Jayjock was sure the CIA was right to buy the Gnat 750, and he thought the Pentagon should just give General Atomics a sole-source contract to provide the UAV that the Joint Chiefs wanted, too. General Atomics owned the software Karem had developed for his Amber, which had flown more hours without crashing than any drone ever built; in Jayjock's view, Karem's software was the key to success. But Jayjock understood that for several reasons—including pressure from other companies and the Israelis to give them a chance at the contract—the Pentagon was going to have to hold a competition to choose its new drone.

On May 17, Allan Rutherford outlined in his work diary what had been settled in the six weeks since Deutch's arrival at the Pentagon. The CIA would take five million dollars from other agency programs to buy two Gnat 750s from General Atomics and fly them over Bosnia as an "operational demonstration." What the CIA learned would be shared with Rutherford's office, which would put together a separate program to get the military a similar but better drone, one more rugged than the Gnat 750, equipped to operate "beyond line-of-sight" via satellite, and

able to meet the other basic requirements Cramer, Jayjock, and Rutherford had come up with. The CIA would deploy the Gnat 750s first
because Woolsey had more discretion to shift money within his budget
than the military did. Money for the Pentagon's drone would have to be
obtained through regular channels: by creating a "program of record"
and getting Congress to authorize and appropriate funds for it.

Things were moving quickly. Rutherford didn't yet have a drone ready
for Bosnia, but stars were aligning.

The Pentagon project gained yet more momentum on July 12, 1993, when
Deutch signed a two-page memo that Rutherford had drafted weeks earlier titled "Endurance Unmanned Aerial Vehicle (UAV) Program." The
first page directed Rutherford's office to "expeditiously contract for an
endurance UAV" to provide "urgently needed, critical, worldwide,
releasable near real time intelligence information on mobile targets."
The second page listed the drone's technical requirements, and they
were nearly identical to those Cramer and Jayjock had sketched out on a
whiteboard earlier in the year. Deutch's memo also imposed a tough
deadline: the drone must make its first flight within six months of a contract being awarded.

The memo said nothing about how Rutherford was to navigate the
bureaucratic maze so he could meet that deadline, but a little more than
a week after Deutch signed the UAV memo yet another star came into
alignment. Larry Lynn, an expert in radar and surveillance technology
who had been deputy director of DARPA from 1981 to 1985, arrived as
Deutch's deputy on July 21—personally recruited by Deutch to help
prune some of the bureaucratic bramble out of defense procurement.
Within weeks, Lynn came up with an idea. He and Deutch would create
a new category of projects: instead of developing equipment from scratch,
the Pentagon would buy "mature" technology—a weapon or a piece of
equipment that was ready or near ready to use—in small batches and let
military users try it out. If the users liked the product, more could be
bought under normal procurement rules. If not, little time or money
would be lost. These Advanced Concept Technology Demonstrations, as

Lynn called them, would essentially allow the military to take new products for a test drive. Lynn and Deutch decided the new endurance UAV would be the first such project.

On November 17, Lynn signed a memo much like Deutch's of July 12, except that Lynn's directed Rutherford's office to award a contract for an endurance UAV "within 40 days after money is appropriated." Money was appropriated a few days later, and not by coincidence. Rutherford and others working on the drone project had briefed key congressional aides even before Deutch officially created the project. They also arranged for Deutch, Joint Staff intelligence director Cramer, and other senior officers to meet with key members of Congress about the new UAV.

Perhaps no meeting proved more important than the one Jayjock arranged for Cramer with Representative Jerry Lewis, a conservative Republican from Southern California with big hair and a toothy smile who was serving his eighth two-year term. Lewis was a power in the House, especially on defense spending. Edwards Air Force Base and Fort Irwin, the Army's largest training center, were located in his district, and as a senior member of the House Appropriations Committee and its powerful Defense Subcommittee Lewis had a lot to say about which Pentagon programs got funded and at what levels. His district also happened to include El Mirage, and Lewis was delighted to hear that General Atomics was providing a UAV to the CIA and might build one for the Pentagon, too. Soon one of his top aides, Letitia White, was hearing from Tom Cassidy almost as often as Jayjock was. That fall, as House and Senate committees wrote the next year's defense bills, Lewis made sure twenty million dollars was added for an endurance UAV.

Five days before Congress finished its work on the defense bill, Rutherford's office sent "draft solicitations" to contractors asking for bids on the new drone. General Atomics and three other contractor teams responded, and on November 29 a competition officially began. Exactly forty days later, on January 7, 1994, the UAV JPO awarded the contract to General Atomics. Within six months, the company would have to demonstrate a UAV that met the requirements in Deutch's memo. Within thirty months, it would have to deliver ten drones and three ground control stations for use in military exercises or actual deployments. General Atomics agreed to do all that for the relatively modest sum of $31.7 million.

A month after the award, Rutherford's commanding officer got a seething letter from an executive of TRW, a major defense contractor, which had teamed with Israel Aircraft Industries to bid on the contract. TRW Vice President Robert J. Kohler charged that the award to General Atomics was "of questionable legality." The "40 day rush," he complained, gave contractors too little time to form good teams and created "the perception that the government really wanted to go sole source to General Atomics." Holding the competition "over the Christmas holiday made it even tougher" and "gave a huge advantage to General Atomics," he wrote. Kohler conceded that TRW and IAI had bid sixty million dollars more than the winner—three times as much—but he confidently declared that "this job cannot be done for the contract value awarded to General Atomics."

Rear Admiral George Wagner, Rutherford's commander, replied by letter that every point in Kohler's letter was "incorrect," and he offered to "debrief" the TRW-IAI team to explain why. But after Wagner's reply, Rutherford never heard another word about Kohler's protest. Years later, Rutherford insisted that no one directed or induced him to award the contract to General Atomics. His office, he said, simply picked the best design for what was by far the cheapest price.

Not long after Neal Blue's company won the Predator contract, a small team of CIA and General Atomics personnel began flying a Gnat 750 over Bosnia. They launched the drone from a military air base in western Albania called Gjader, located on the inland side of some foothills on the coast of the Adriatic Sea. The team's footprint was small; members lived on a military-style patrol boat docked at a nearby port. Line-of-sight communication to the skies above Sarajevo, roughly 140 miles distant, was possible, but a nearby range of mountains required the CIA team to relay its ground station's signals to the Gnat 750 through a manned aircraft, a small, quiet "motor glider" known as a Schweizer RG-8. Operational flights were limited to a mere two hours by the

Schweizer, whose crew of two needed six of the craft's eight hours of endurance to get to and from an orbit area over the Adriatic Sea.

Despite this limitation, the Gnats gave U.S. forces exactly the sort of intelligence President Clinton wanted. Flying at six thousand feet or lower, but apparently undetected, the Gnat 750 carried sensors that allowed its operators to distinguish real artillery from decoy, find surface-to-air missile sites, and spot tanks and gun movements. The experiment wasn't entirely successful, however: the video relayed by the Gnats was often degraded by interference at Gjader from unshielded power cables and fluorescent lights, and bad weather and problems with data links—the signals sending video and other imagery back to the ground station—also caused problems. After a couple of months, the CIA halted the flights but, overall, the operation was considered worthwhile. Later in the year, the agency's two Gnat 750s flew again, from an island off the coast of Croatia, and *Aviation Week* reported that the CIA might buy three of the six Gnat 750s that Turkey had ordered and outfit two of them to serve the relay role played by the manned Schweizer. To those involved in the drone project, though, it was clear that the relay system was no better than a stop-gap solution. Ultimately, the drone's designers would have to come up with something better.

Meager though the results of the missions were, Woolsey would later recall with great satisfaction seeing Gnat 750 video of pedestrians crossing a bridge in Mostar, Bosnia. He was proud of the fact that the CIA's modest program helped spur the Pentagon to get its own endurance UAV—one that would turn the history of drones upside down.

Contract in hand, the General Atomics team had just six months to build a prototype of the new drone, and redesigning the Gnat 750 to carry the satellite dish the Pentagon wanted, plus up to 500 pounds of payload instead of 130, would require a superhuman effort. To add the satellite dish, Karem gave the Gnat a serious nose job, adding a large upward bulge to house the round antenna, whose diameter was thirty inches. To carry the additional weight of the satellite antenna and a synthetic aperture radar, the drone had to grow in every dimension. The wing on this new UAV would be 1,100 millimeters at the root, not 750; its fuselage would be 9 feet longer than the Gnat's 17.5 feet; and its wingspan would be more than a third longer than the Gnat's wingtip-to-wingtip length of 35 feet. All this would require fabricating a lot of new parts, engineering and testing how those inside the fuselage fit together, and writing new flight control and other software. Because it would be so different, the plane clearly needed a new name.

Rutherford and others in government had been calling the aircraft Tier II because Deutch and Lynn had decided the Pentagon should build UAVs for different altitudes, starting with a low-altitude Tier I and going up to a high-altitude Tier III. That, at least, was the official story: in fact, Tier I was a cover for the CIA's Gnat 750 purchase, which was secret until *Aviation Week* revealed it in September 1993. Two months later, the magazine reported that one of the CIA's Gnat 750s had crashed near El Mirage, brought down by an apparent software malfunction, which forced the agency to lease a third Gnat 750 from General Atomics. As the engineers at General Atomics were putting together the first prototype Tier II for the Pentagon, Cassidy told Rutherford he had a name for the new UAV. They would call it, Cassidy declared, the Predator.

Rutherford cringed. Tier II was just a surveillance and reconnaissance drone, an eye in the sky. "Predator" sounded like a weapon. Nobody had suggested arming the new drone, though some in Congress were talking about equipping it with a laser designator so the UAV could guide bombs and missiles dropped by manned aircraft to targets. If Tier II began looking like a weapon, Rutherford feared the Air Force might try to kill the project. The fighter pilots who ran that service seemed instinctively hostile to the idea of unmanned combat planes. But when Rutherford tried to resist, Cassidy kept repeating "Predator" over and over, and finally it stuck.

No one ever mentioned that General Atomics had used the name before.

As aircraft go, the new Predator's name was the sexiest thing about it. Constructed of graphite epoxy composites and lighter than an economy car, it was powered by a four-cylinder Rotax 912 piston engine, an Austrian motor used in ultralight sport aircraft that buzzed like a big mosquito. The drone's top speed was just over a hundred miles an hour, and its cruising speed in a windless sky would be somewhere between eighty and ninety—about the velocity of a professional baseball pitcher's changeup. Like its Karem-designed forebears—the Albatross, the Amber, and the Gnat—the new Predator's appearance resembled a glider more than a powered aircraft. Its thin wings stretched almost forty-nine feet from tip to tip—nearly twice the length of its fuselage. The fuselage, while much longer than the Gnat 750's, was eight feet shorter than a Piper Cub's. Those wispy wings would help the Predator stay airborne more than a day and a night without guzzling fuel.

Another Karem feature familiar from the Albatross, the Amber, and the Gnat was the Predator's tail. It sported two rectangular stabilizers jutting down in an inverted V—a configuration that added aerodynamic stability but also, in a rough landing, allowed the stabilizers to serve as skids, preventing the drone's propeller blades from shattering on the runway and slinging dangerous debris across an airfield. Perhaps the most striking aspect of the reborn Predator, though, was the bulge Karem had given it forward of the wings. That aerodynamically sculpted hump, situated about where a manned aircraft's cockpit might be, would hold the satellite dish. Directly beneath that hump and protruding from the bottom of the fuselage was another prominent feature: a "chin turret," holding daylight and infrared video cameras.

The ground control station, where operators would sit to fly the new Predator and aim its sensors, would be housed in the same boxy brand of three-axle trailer NASCAR teams used to haul stock cars from race to race. The GCS, as insiders called it, was thirty-six feet long, eight feet wide, and eight feet tall. At one end of the interior was a console holding an array of computer screens and controls. There, one pilot and one "sensor operator" would sit in faux leather chairs, manipulating control sticks like those of a conventional airplane to fly the drone and aim its sensors. Their computer screens would display flight information such as altitude, airspeed, and other vital data. Two other screens would show video from the Predator's cameras, and the console would hold keyboards and communications gear, including a radio the pilot could use to talk to air traffic control towers.

On July 3, 1994, four days before the contract's six-month deadline for a demonstration, program manager Rutherford traveled to El Mirage to witness the Predator's first flight, an event planned for just after sunrise, when the desert winds would be calmest. The dress code that summer Sunday morning was casual—Frank Pace was in tennis shorts—and the mood optimistic but nervous. To meet their extraordinarily tight deadline, the members of the General Atomics team had put in twelve to fourteen hours a day, six days a week, since Christmas.

Tim Just, a champion model aircraft pilot Karem had hired at Leading Systems to fly the Amber, would operate the Predator on its maiden flight. At about 6:30 a.m., Rutherford, Cassidy, Pace, and other observers watched the demonstration from a spot near where the CIA's Twetten had posed with Karem fifteen months earlier, roughly two hundred feet from the El Mirage runway and a third of the way down its three-thousand-foot length. A technician turned a switch on the drone's fuselage, then darted to safety as the Rotax engine grumbled to life and the Predator's pusher propeller began buzzing. Pace, a born-again Christian, whispered a hurried prayer.

Soon pilot Just added power, and the Predator began rolling down the runway. A moment later, the drone eased into the air, nose tilted upward about five degrees. The takeoff was going beautifully—until the Predator's engine choked and sputtered just as it passed the audience. Pace nearly choked himself, panic replacing the tingle of nervous excitement he'd enjoyed earlier as he waited for the flight to start.

Inside the GCS, Just saw the engine's revolutions per minute plunge on his control panel and made a snap decision. He turned the ignition off and then, as gently as he could, maneuvered the Predator's broad nose downward. The sleek, long-winged little bird wanted to keep flying, but Just set the drone back down on its spindly tricycle landing gear as quickly as he could. Then he desperately applied the brakes, nearly standing on his rudder pedals as the Predator rapidly rolled down the last thousand feet of runway. It stopped with barely two feet left.

Wheels up to wheels down, the Predator's maiden flight had reached an altitude of about fifteen feet and lasted, by Pace's count, fourteen seconds.

"First flight!" Rutherford cried gleefully, declaring the program's six-months-to-fly deadline met.

As those on the tarmac watched, a technician ran out and shut off the drone's battery. When he did, the loss of voltage triggered a small explosive charge used to deploy an emergency parachute General Atomics had insisted the plane carry, and which the technician should have disarmed before killing the battery. Startled by the loud "pow!" the technician ducked and covered his head as the orange-and-white parachute puffed out, then settled gently over him. Rutherford was annoyed to learn that the company's only parachute packer was away that day, so there could be no second flight. Others were relieved.

As in most flight tests, the prototype was rigged with telemetry that beamed data about its mechanical and other systems to recorders nearby. A study of the results showed there had been a sharp drop in fuel flow as the aircraft took off, and the engineers quickly saw why. To make the Predator as light as possible, and avoid the risk of a big explosion if it crashed, the General Atomics team had put just enough fuel in the tank to orbit the airfield a time or two and land. As the drone's nose had risen during takeoff, almost all its fuel sloshed out of the engine feeds in the bottom of the Predator's two fuel tanks, starving its motor of gas.

Abe Karem wasn't present that day at El Mirage. Had he been, he might have caught such a simple mistake, for he was meticulous about testing. In the days leading up to test flights, he would always ask his teams one question over and over: "How can we fail?"

But a month earlier, just before the Predator was finally ready to fly, Karem had quit General Atomics. His job had never been a good fit. Tom Cassidy was one reason; the retired admiral couldn't seem to construct a sentence without four-letter words, and though Karem had heard those words long before he knew Cassidy, he didn't enjoy hearing them again, or so often. Cassidy's temper bothered him as well: he would never forget how Cassidy had once grabbed Karem's briefing papers after a presentation, tore them in half, and threw them in a trash can to show how violently he disagreed with him. Karem also had little financial incentive to stay at General Atomics. Neal Blue was poised to reap the rewards of an invention Karem had devoted more than two decades of his life to developing, yet he was paying Karem nothing beyond his salary.

Those were probably reasons enough to leave, yet they weren't the main impetus. In truth, Karem decided to part ways with General Atomics for the same underlying reason he had quit IAI in 1974 and started designing drones in the first place. At heart, Karem was an inventor, pure and simple. To be happy, he simply *had* to be working on something new—and he had to be doing it *his* way. As he put it himself, "I am not a guy who can stay in standing water with high nitrogen and frogs jumping around the water lilies. I am a salmon, and a salmon needs oxygen—fast streams with a lot of oxygen."

After leaving General Atomics, Karem set out on his own to compete for the next big UAV contract the Pentagon was going to award. This one was "Tier II Plus," a surveillance drone able to fly at altitudes of sixty thousand feet and ranges up to three thousand miles. Karem already had a design, an unmanned flying wing he called the W570. He also already had a new company, Frontier Systems Inc., a legal entity he had created in 1991, right after Leading Systems went out of existence.

Frontier Systems didn't win the Tier II Plus contract, which ultimately produced a drone by Northrop Grumman Corporation called the Global Hawk. But not long after Karem lost that bid, he called his former DARPA ally Bob Williams, who had given him his contract for the Albatross UAV demonstrator in 1984, and Williams, now a special adviser to the general in charge of the U.S. military's Southern Command, offered some thoughts. Over the next few years, on contracts provided by DARPA, Frontier Systems developed the A160 Hummingbird, a small, lightweight, unmanned helicopter whose rotor changed its speed in flight to turn at the most efficient number of revolutions per minute. The revolutionary design brought Karem full circle: in 1974, Israeli Air Force commander Benny Peled had urged him to design a drone helicopter, and though Karem had done so, he'd never found a buyer for it. This time he did. In May 2004, Boeing acquired Frontier Systems and its A160 for a price never officially announced but rumored to be as much as sixty-five million dollars. Just over a month shy of his sixty-seventh birthday, Abe Karem had finally turned a profit on one of his dreams, and a handsome one.

Yet he couldn't bring himself to retire. Ten years after the Frontier Systems sale, Karem was still at it, working in a small industrial building in Lake Forest, California, where he and the thirteen employees of Karem Aircraft Inc. were attempting to make his newest dream a reality. This time Karem wanted to build a manned aircraft he called the Aerotrain. A tiltrotor, the craft would swivel the rotors on its wings upward to take off like a helicopter, and forward to fly like an airplane. The Aerotrain would be the size of a Boeing 737 jetliner and use Karem's patented optimum-speed rotor design. By eliminating the 737's need for runways, Karem was sure his tiltrotor would revolutionize both regional air travel and military operations. Just like the pioneers of the early twentieth century who led the way into the air—people such as Glenn Curtiss, Donald Douglas, Jack Northrop, and Igor Sikorsky—the boy from Baghdad still wanted to change the world.

On August 31, 1994, two months after the Predator's first flight, and after the prototype had been flown enough to prove itself airworthy, General Atomics staged an official rollout at El Mirage.

"General Atomics said its new Predator unmanned aerial vehicle had a successful 45-minute demonstration flight yesterday at the company's El Mirage test facility," the *San Diego Union-Tribune* reported the following morning. "The craft, one of 10 on order from the Pentagon, performed various maneuvers and collected reconnaissance photos for an audience of about 200 people, the company said."

The audience of two hundred consisted of General Atomics employees, government officials, and invited guests, including spouses and children. Seated in rows of folding chairs under a large white canopy to shield them from the piercing desert sun, they watched the Predator perform flawlessly. Then they heard speeches by Tom Cassidy, Allan Rutherford, and Congressman Jerry Lewis, who praised the new drone as a sensible use of scarce defense dollars. Cassidy and Rutherford were pleased to see Lewis there. Given the rocky history of UAVs, both knew they would need all the help they could get to sell the military on the Predator.

After the successful rollout at El Mirage, Rutherford started selling. He carefully cultivated reporters he felt he could trust—primarily at *Aviation Week* but also elsewhere—to generate stories about the Predator. Others were also encouraging favorable coverage of the program, and that fall the campaign to sell the Predator enjoyed its biggest payoff so far. Tom Brokaw, host of NBC's *Nightly News*, aired a report on what the anchorman described as a new "high-tech spy plane." In his introduction to a piece about the Predator by reporter Ed Rabel, Brokaw said, "It looks like a toy but is being called a breakthrough."

One day soon, that description would be proven accurate beyond any doubt.

5

PREDATOR'S PROGRESS

The shiny wood table was V-shaped, long on both sides, and situated so that the person seated at its apex faced a large screen on the opposite wall. Designed for video teleconferences, the theater-size room was part of what is purportedly one of the most secure facilities in the world: a war room complex in the bowels of the Pentagon called the National Military Command Center. Early on the morning of January 11, 1995, military officers of junior rank, mostly lieutenants and captains, began filtering in, some stifling yawns, some with coffee cups in hand, and took seats at the wide end of the massive table. Soon they were joined by majors, lieutenant colonels, and on up the ranks, until the seat at the head of the table was the only one unoccupied. Then that seat was taken by Army Major General Patrick M. Hughes, who six months earlier had replaced Rear Admiral Michael W. Cramer as director of intelligence for the Joint Chiefs of Staff, or, in military parlance, the J-2.

Moments after Hughes took his seat, the screen on the opposite wall came alive, silently showing a five-ton Army truck from above, in living color, as it slowly rolled down a paved road cut through the prickly scrub brush and parched sand of Fort Huachuca, a dusty, desolate Army base located in the southeast corner of Arizona. Headquarters of the U.S. Army Intelligence Center, Fort Huachuca was fifteen miles north of the Mexican border, in Cochise County, named for the Apache war chief and home to Tombstone, where the famous Gunfight at the O.K. Corral played out between the Earps and the Clantons and their allies in 1881. Fort Huachuca was also the location chosen for initial testing of the Predator, partly because drones could be flown in restricted military airspace without Federal Aviation Administration permission.

Military test drives were the next stage of the Predator's development, and the test driving was being done by a small detachment of troops from the Army's Military Intelligence Battalion (Low Intensity), the MI BN LI, as the Army abbreviated the unit's name. The commander of the MI BN LI—insiders dropped the *N* and called it the Mibli, pronounced "MIB-lee"—had jumped at the chance to help Navy Captain Allan Rutherford's office with the Predator. Based in Orlando, Florida, the Mibli had been formed in the 1980s to provide reconnaissance over Central America by flying small propeller planes equipped with sensors in sometimes dangerous low-level missions. With the Cold War over and democracy breaking out in Central America, the battalion was shrinking—whole companies were disbanding as their planes grew obsolete—and its commanders were eager for new missions to help the unit survive. Some Mibli pilots turned up their noses at the idea of flying a UAV, but volunteers were learning to operate the Predator from the safety of its ground control station, where small teams of soldiers flew the drone, manipulated its cameras, and sat at work stations equipped with computers and other equipment needed to record and analyze the UAV's video.

On this January morning, Mibli soldiers were also driving the truck the Predator's camera was following, for the benefit of Major General Hughes and the rest of the Pentagon audience. Mibli troops would also play roles as "enemy" troops in scenarios performed to demonstrate for the new J-2 what the drone could do. Four years earlier, during the 1991 Gulf War, so-called gun camera videotape, which showed precision strikes on Iraqi tanks, bridges, and other targets by manned aircraft dropping laser-guided bombs, had been a staple of military news briefings, helping sell the allied campaign to astonished television viewers. More recently, the captivating power of aerial video shown live had been demonstrated on June 17, 1994, two weeks before the Predator's first flight, when a fleet of TV news helicopters equipped with cameras followed a white Ford Bronco around Los Angeles for five hours. Former pro football star and accused double murderer O. J. Simpson was a passenger in the Bronco, whose driver led authorities on a low-speed chase while Simpson decided between surrender and suicide, mesmerizing a national TV audience. Between Gulf War gun cameras and Simpson's dramatic ride, CNN and other networks were now hooked on aerial video. For the military, though, using live aerial video was something exotic and entirely new—especially live aerial video shot from a drone. General Hughes wanted to experience it.

As the Predator's camera tailed the green Army truck around Fort Huachuca, Predator manager Rutherford stood up in the Pentagon war room and welcomed the J-2, taking care not to get cute. By nature, Rutherford was an ebullient sort, but he knew that Hughes had a reputation for being a no-nonsense, "show-me" intelligence officer who was not fond of irony, sarcasm, or cynicism in a briefing. After crisply explaining how the Predator had come about, why this was the first Advanced Concept Technology Demonstration, and what that meant, Rutherford introduced his deputy, civilian Jay Stratakes, a career Naval Air Systems Command aeronautical engineer. As the video rolled on, Stratakes called up on a separate screen the first of a dozen or so slides to go with a detailed briefing on what the Pentagon called the Medium Altitude Endurance UAV Predator. His title slide bore a logo that Stratakes had devised and drawn himself, an emblem (later discarded for fear of copyright violation) depicting the insect-faced, human-hunting alien title character in the 1987 Arnold Schwarzenegger thriller *Predator*.

As Stratakes narrated slides showing the new Predator drone's development schedule and describing its sensors, ground control station, and other equipment in detail, the video from Fort Huachuca rolled on. During the presentation, some in the war room couldn't resist commenting on the video feed, especially after one officer wondered aloud, "What was that vehicle? I wish we could see that again," at which point the drone's camera slewed back and zoomed in for a closer look. "It's like they're reading our minds," someone muttered. Only then did Rutherford explain, a bit sheepishly, that the operators in the GCS in Arizona could hear what those in the war room audience were saying, and even see them sitting at the V-shaped table—not by design, but because the Predator's video was being piped into the room through the National Military Command Center's video teleconferencing system. No one working in the GCS intended to eavesdrop; the two-way sound and video was simply a by-product of the jury-rigged method by which the Predator's imagery was entering the Pentagon.

However the moving pictures were reaching them, the officers in the war room seemed astounded by what they were watching. For decades, photo reconnaissance had consisted solely of black-and-white still shots taken by manned aircraft—usually flying fast and at either low or high altitude to avoid getting shot down—or by satellites orbiting the earth and thus able to make only brief passes over target areas. In either case, the still photos had to be developed on the ground, then examined and analyzed by trained imagery analysts to produce so-called actionable intelligence. Previously that work required at least several hours; often it took days. Now, all of a sudden, a general at the Pentagon was watching live video of things happening on the ground in Arizona, more than two thousand miles away; if he wanted to, he could even talk to the crew flying the plane shooting the imagery. The Gnat 750's video from Bosnia had appeared live on a tiny screen at CIA headquarters in 1994, arriving by transatlantic fiber-optic cable. But in 1995, piping video from a drone into a Pentagon conference room was a challenge far more complex than simply bouncing a signal off a satellite, as TV networks had done for years. Streaming video would soon be routine throughout the military, but for the moment it was unheard of—a veritable magic trick.

The magician who prepared the Predator program's prestidigitation that day was a man of extraordinary intellect. An expert on nuclear weapons, computer networks, and satellites, he was fluent in both the electromagnetic spectrum and multiple European languages. He held a multiengine-rated commercial aircraft pilot's license, was a skilled mariner, and could quickly use, repair, or quite often improve nearly any new machine or technology put before him. This remarkable technoscientist, who had joined the Pentagon's Predator project when it began in 1993, would be responsible for a long string of innovations in the imagery and communications systems of the new endurance UAV, devising improvements that—combined with the aeronautical genius of Abe Karem's legacy airframe design—would transform the nature of drones much as the mouse, the Internet, and wireless digital communication transformed the personal computer. His ideas and work would turn what was at first merely an interesting technology into a pivotal one. Werner, an alias, is how he must be identified in this account—not because he is a covert operative, for he never was, but because he prefers to remain anonymous.

Nicknamed the Man with Two Brains by one Pentagon official and the Thousand-Pound Head by a military officer who worked with him, Werner came to Rutherford's team while under contract as an "imagery scientist" for the National Exploitation Laboratory of the National Photographic Interpretation Center, which no longer exists by that name but at the time was a component of the CIA's Directorate of Science and Technology. The mission of the National Exploitation Laboratory (known as the Nell, from its acronym, NEL) was to figure out how best to get the most out of imagery gathered by collection devices and sensors of all types, which might include enhancing the images artificially. When the team responsible for the fledgling Predator program needed help improving what were at first grainy video feeds from its cameras, the Nell sent Werner to Rutherford.

Werner quickly became fascinated with the new UAV. He saw its video as the perfect reconnaissance medium for military officers of the CNN Generation, as he called them, who he thought tended to feel more informed by live-motion imagery than by still photos. But as the Predator began its twenty-four-month demonstration period, Werner realized that getting intelligence officers and an imagery interpretation bureaucracy accustomed to still photos to even *look* at the drone's video would be the first major hurdle. Video imagery was streamed back to the controllers by the Navy's Vietnam-era drone helicopter and the service's little Pioneer UAV in tactical operations. Werner knew, though, that a common conceit among imagery analysts was that only still photos could be parsed sufficiently to reveal things an enemy was trying to hide. In fact, most imagery analysts preferred to work with black-and-white instead of color photos. They were used to poring over snapshots, not watching events unfold in real time, when they could be harder to interpret. Many intelligence analysts dismissed color video as a toy.

Given this cultural attitude, no infrastructure for distributing reconnaissance video to those who might use it even existed. At the time, the only way anyone could see the Predator's video was to be inside the ground control station as the aircraft flew, or to watch a videotape after the fact. The drone's bulbous nose held a satellite dish, but the first dish installed was merely a placeholder, a UHF (ultra-high-frequency) antenna with too little bandwidth to handle the amount of data required both to control the aircraft and to stream video. The UHF antenna was soon to be replaced with one still being developed that would offer far greater bandwidth and data flow by operating on what is called the Ku-band radio frequency. For now, though, the Predator could send streaming video to the GCS only through the drone's C-band radio antenna. This was the same line-of-sight device whose limits had led the CIA to relay signals to and from the Gnat 750 through another aircraft as it flew over Bosnia the previous year, an inconvenient and unsatisfactory fix.

Rutherford, eager to generate military interest in his project, had contracted with a private firm to turn raw tapes of Predator video into packaged presentations and deliver them every few weeks, beginning in September 1994, to military leaders, civilian Pentagon officials, members of Congress, and congressional aides. Set to music ranging from operatic classical to instrumental rock and roll, the tapes were essentially commercials for the Predator, and they proved to be an effective way of keeping those who would help decide the drone's future apprised of its progress. But Werner, Rutherford's imagery adviser, had a more ambitious goal: he wanted to make it possible for leaders in the Pentagon to see Predator video *live*. Only then, he believed, could they grasp the drone's revolutionary potential.

Rutherford was all for a live video feed, and Werner was sure he could figure out technically how to get the Predator's streaming images into the Pentagon. But Werner also knew that getting Defense Department bureaucrats to approve such a thing would require far more clout than either he or Rutherford had. Then, in late 1994, Werner learned that the new J-2, Major General Hughes, had been forced to cancel a planned visit to Fort Huachuca to watch Predator video live in the GCS. Suddenly he saw an opportunity to get the Predator's video into the Pentagon. *If the general can't go to the video,* Werner thought, *the video must come to him.* Werner figured that all he needed was for the general to lend his authority to such a scheme, and in December Hughes did.

Armed with a letter signed by Hughes explaining that the bearer was on a special mission for the two-star general and should be granted any cooperation he needed, Werner spent several days at the Pentagon that month talking to people who knew how video and other communications media were brought into the Building, as insiders call the nation's military headquarters. In short order, he had a plan.

Werner's first step was to persuade an electronics vendor to lend him a thirty-six-thousand-dollar digital video compressor, a machine made by Compression Labs Inc. and known as a Rembrandt codec, short for "coder/decoder." Assured that the loan could result in substantial sales of such machines to the military, the supplier was happy to provide the Rembrandt, a light gray box resembling a large window air conditioner. In the first week of January, Werner had the eighty-seven-pound Rembrandt shipped to Fort Huachuca.

Next Werner implemented step two of his plan, which required adding an ad hoc feature to the Predator's ground control station. Under the initial design, the Predator's video was never meant to leave the GCS. When it arrived from the drone, the video was seen live by the pilot, the sensor operator, and a couple of intelligence analysts sitting a few feet behind them at two computer work stations. The analysts would record the imagery on eight-millimeter videotape as it came in and select individual frames or sequences of frames—shot by the Predator's camera at thirty frames a second—for closer examination. After copying the selected frames into a computer as individual screen grabs, the analysts would "exploit" the images, meaning study them for militarily relevant information, annotating and highlighting what they found. Important objects in the image would be circled. Arrows and lines that directed the eye would be superimposed. Little text boxes would be added.

The annotated screen grabs would then be saved as separate computer files—one image per file—and transmitted to a U.S. military data storage center at Royal Air Force Station Molesworth, in the east of England, an airfield used by American planes in World War II. Since 1991 the base also housed Joint Analysis Center Molesworth, an intelligence facility abbreviated JAC Molesworth and called Jack Molesworth, or simply, the Jack. Big computer servers at the Jack stored intelligence imagery at different levels of classification, which users with the appropriate clearances could call up remotely. This was the system long used to store satellite images, and out of custom and habit the Predator was being treated like a low-flying satellite. In fact, the equipment at the Jack couldn't even handle video.

Predator screen grabs had yet to be sent anywhere, but by the end of 1994 the capability for transmitting them was in place. Parked near the drone's GCS in Arizona was the Trojan Spirit II, a mobile satellite system housed in two large, green Army transport trucks. One of the trucks in the system carried a satellite earth terminal with a dish 5.5 meters in diameter; the other truck carried an earth terminal whose dish measured 2.4 meters across. The larger antenna was intended to receive signals from the Predator once the Ku-band satellite dish being developed was installed in the drone's bulbous nose. The smaller mobile earth terminal was meant to send screen grabs to a Trojan Spirit hub at Fort Belvoir, a base in northern Virginia, for relay to JAC Molesworth. At Fort Huachuca, though, both satellite trucks were sitting unused.

When Werner arrived at Fort Huachuca in early January 1995, he had with him a fanny-pack-size, jungle-green camouflage tool bag filled with electrical, computer, and video connectors of various types and sizes. He got some Mibli soldiers to put the Rembrandt video compressor on a table in a tent between the Predator ground control station and the satellite dish with the 2.4-meter antenna. He used a coaxial cable to feed the Predator's analog video signal into the Rembrandt, which could digitize and compress the video for satellite transmission, then ran a data cable from the Rembrandt to the satellite terminal. Satisfied with this setup, Werner flew back to Washington.

Again carrying the letter from Major General Hughes in his pocket, Werner then drove half an hour south to Fort Belvoir. At Belvoir, he took a borrowed technician with him into a long, air-conditioned room filled with rows and rows of floor-to-ceiling metal racks stacked with electronic equipment. One rack contained a patch panel—a switchboard, essentially—that was used to route signals to and from mobile Trojan Spirit satellite terminals around the world. As Werner had recently learned, the other side of the same room held equipment used to connect participants in military video teleconferences, wherever they might be. Werner had the technician run a cable under the room's raised floor from the Trojan Spirit hub patch panel to the video teleconferencing system switch. Now Predator video could flow via satellite from the Trojan Spirit at Fort Huachuca to Fort Belvoir, then into the video teleconferencing hub, then into the ultra-secure National Military Command Center. No one had explicitly authorized Werner to make this connection, but he was confident it would work.

On January 11, Werner was back at Fort Huachuca, up at three in the morning and in the ground control station. The two-way video feed worked perfectly: Werner watched Hughes and his officers at the V-shaped table in the Pentagon war room, while the officers watched the Predator video streaming live from Arizona. Werner savored the moment. Allan Rutherford thought it magic.

Eight days later, the Predator set a new UAV endurance record, flying at Fort Huachuca for forty hours and seventeen minutes—nearly two hours more than the 1988 record set by its ancestor the Amber. Over the next few months, Rutherford staged many more video demonstrations in the Pentagon war room. For many who saw them, the demos were mesmerizing. Rutherford marveled at how generals unused to video reconnaissance would stare at the screen as if in a trance while the Predator flew at a crawl over barren desert, beaming back meaningless shots of sand and Joshua trees. Meanwhile, Rutherford's small team and the Mibli took the new drone on the road. During February and March 1995, some of the six Predator drones built by General Atomics were used in a counterdrug exercise along the southwest border with Mexico. In April and May, the Mibli flew Predators from Fort Sumner, New Mexico, in the U.S. military's largest annual air and missile defense exercise, Roving Sands.

Roving Sands '95 would be the Predator's military debut, and a major step toward acceptance. That year, more than seventeen thousand troops from all four armed services and those of several U.S. allies conducted maneuvers that sprawled across New Mexico and into Arizona. The Predator provided reconnaissance for troops and used its cameras to search out mock Scud missiles (plywood replicas on five-ton Army trucks) hidden amid cacti, beneath trees, or under highway culverts. In only eighteen missions, the Predator logged 173 hours in the air and found 50 percent of all plywood Scuds "killed" in the exercise.

The success at Roving Sands led the Joint Special Operations Command to invite the Mibli to fly the Predator in June with special operations forces conducting a classified exercise in the Everglades of Florida, an event that brought the vice chairman of the Joint Chiefs of Staff to the Pentagon war room for a live video demonstration. The show for Admiral William A. Owens that day didn't go as Rutherford hoped it might. As the nation's second-ranking military officer ate lunch and listened to Rutherford's briefing, live Predator video appeared on the screen, but it was impossible to recognize what the imagery was showing. After a considerable silence as those in the room waited in vain for the image to come into focus, Rutherford quipped, "Admiral, as you can see, we're very closely monitoring the green blob that's eating the Everglades." To Rutherford's relief, Owens laughed. As it turned out, the problem was just a loose cable. After it was fixed, the admiral declared that he liked what he saw.

Encouraged, Rutherford flew to Stuttgart to brief officers of the U.S. European Command on the Predator, hoping to get permission to test the drone in actual military operations. He quickly won approval to operate it over Bosnia, the former Yugoslav republic whose ethnic war had been a catalyst for developing the drone in the first place. Things were reaching a boiling point in the Balkans, where UN peacekeeping troops had been deployed since 1992. NATO warplanes had been enforcing a no-fly zone over Bosnia since 1993, and tensions had escalated considerably over the following two years. When Rutherford came calling, commanders in Germany were happy to try tracking Serb weapons and activities with an unmanned drone. They were happier still to have the unmanned Predator after June 2, when a Serb missile shot down U.S. Air Force pilot Captain Scott O'Grady's F-16C during a patrol over Bosnia. O'Grady parachuted safely, but U.S. forces took five days to find him and send a Marine Corps helicopter into Bosnia to get him out.

Rutherford was ecstatic. Less than a year after its first flight, the Predator would get a chance to prove itself in combat.

In the summer of 1995 Tom Cassidy flew to the Balkans to see how his company's new Predator was doing in its first combat deployment. The former fighter pilot and Navy rear admiral arrived with great expectations: he believed he would find the military taking full advantage of the revolutionary new form of reconnaissance his company had given them—full-motion video, as it was known—and hungering for more. He also assumed the good news about the Predator would be spreading quickly; since the system wasn't classified, its video could be shared with just about anyone in uniform. Instead, Cassidy found intelligence analysts sitting at work stations in a covered truck trailer that was parked behind a barbed-wire barrier and a sign reading "Restricted Area." Inside, the analysts were turning the Predator's video into still photos. Cassidy couldn't believe it. They weren't *watching* the video—they were turning it into *still photos*.

"Why?" an astonished Cassidy asked one of the Army people.

"We're used to having eight-by-ten glossies, so that's what we want," the analyst replied.

Recalling his trip to Bosnia years later, Cassidy felt exasperated all over again. "They would take the video stream, which is eighteen hundred frames per minute, and freeze-frame every single one of them—you can imagine on a thirty-hour mission how many frames you have—and *print* them! Then they had this Army three-star running around the Pentagon telling everybody, 'Predator video's no good. Look at these out-of-focus freeze frames!'"

The reality wasn't quite that bad. Cassidy didn't realize that the imagery analysts weren't freezing every video frame, just those that seemed
to show something of interest, usually no more than a dozen or so at a
time. But the point was the same: they weren't watching the video for its
own sake.

The Predator's first combat deployment also got off to a slow start in
other respects. It began on July 8, when a half dozen chunky C-130
cargo aircraft touched down at the same airfield in Albania the CIA
had used to fly the Gnat 750 over Bosnia in 1994. Inside the holds of
the C-130s were three disassembled Predators in tan polyester-plastic
crates. The C-130s also brought a ground control station, two small
Trojan Spirit II satellite earth terminals with 2.4-meter dish antennas, a
UHF satellite antenna, and roughly fifty-five military and civilian personnel. Only five were military pilots—three Army, one Navy, one
Marine Corps—but General Atomics had sent its chief pilot, Tim Just,
to help out. The Air Force had sent no pilots, but some of its civil engineers had arrived in advance to set up a tent city.

After decades of Albania's peculiar brand of isolationist commu-
nism, followed by widespread looting after the system's collapse, Gjader
air base was largely just a concrete runway with concrete aprons. The
base's most interesting feature was a tunnel dug into a nearby mountain
to the southwest; reached by a very long taxiway, the tunnel still served
as a bomb-proof hangar for some old MiG fighter jets. At the base itself,
there was no electricity, no running water, no toilets, and not a single
building the Americans could use. The Air Force engineers had set up a
portable clamshell hangar for the three Predators, and an array of tents
to shelter, feed, and provide other needs for the multiservice detachment
sent to fly the drones. Next to the ground control station, they set up an
improvised work station consisting of two big "expando vans"—five-ton
trucks with boxlike shelters on their trailers—parked with their rear
ends facing each other and connected by wooden steps and a platform.
One truck was the Predator unit's operations center, the other a "Rapid
Exploitation and Dissemination Cell." This RED Cell—the scene of Cassidy's rude awakening—had been added so that more intelligence analysts could be present to exploit the Predator's video, print screen grabs,

annotate the resulting still photos, and transmit them to JAC Moles-worth in England.

Before the deployment, imagery scientist Werner had been asked to figure out how the unit could stream the Predator's video almost five hundred miles up the coast of the Balkan Peninsula and across the Adriatic Sea to the Combined Air Operations Center at Vicenza, Italy, a NATO command center known by the acronym CAOC. The CAOC (pronounced "KAY-ock") was a collection of trailers where U.S. and allied command-ers ran and monitored air operations over the Balkans. For the Preda-tor's first deployment to succeed, the CAOC's planners would have to see the value of the intelligence the UAV produced and get accustomed to including the drone in their plans. Werner and the Predator's other advocates also wanted to transmit the UAV's video to the CAOC to spread the word about this new reconnaissance tool to as many commanders as possible.

Getting the ground control station connected to the CAOC took some creative thinking, since the Predator's satellite uplink was the Tro-jan Spirit, whose mobile terminals could transmit only to their hub at Fort Belvoir, Virginia. After consulting with the CAOC, Werner devised a double bank shot. First he set up one of the two Trojan Spirit earth terminals at Gjader to send the Predator's video by satellite to Fort Bel-voir; then he arranged to have the video signal brought back across the Atlantic to NATO's southern headquarters in Naples and to the CAOC in Vicenza through an existing Defense Department fiber-optic cable laid across the ocean floor. The signal would travel roughly 54,000 miles—25,000 up to the satellite, 25,000 down to Fort Belvoir, and about 4,000 from Belvoir to Italy—to cover the 476 miles from Gjader to the CAOC. Still, since radio waves travel at the speed of light, the video would arrive at the CAOC with less than a second's delay.

Tom Cassidy did his part to make sure people watched Predator TV, though the military's lack of video dissemination technology limited that opportunity. After visiting the Predator base in Albania, Cassidy went to Naples to see Admiral Leighton W. "Snuffy" Smith Jr., commander in chief of U.S. and NATO forces in the Balkans, and told him that the intelligence analysts at Gjader were converting video into printed freeze frames. "I said, 'We built this thing so you could watch the war on television. You've got to get with it and do that,'" Cassidy recalled. "Fortunately I knew the guy, so he agreed."

At first, however, there was no Predator video to watch, and except for an accident of geography there might have been none at all. The Predators sent to Albania that July were equipped only with the placeholder UHF satellite antenna. The broader-bandwidth satellite antenna, which would transmit and receive frequencies in the Ku band, was still being manufactured. From Gjader, pilots could fly the Predator up the Adriatic coast and turn east over Croatia to reach Bosnia using the line-of-sight C-band antenna, which offered bandwidth enough to both control the plane and stream its video back to the GCS. But once the Predator flew behind a range of mountains between Bosnia and Gjader, the C-band signal was blocked and the flight crew had to rely on the beyond-line-of-sight UHF satellite antenna to communicate with the drone.

Crews hated this patchwork solution, for the UHF antenna offered so little bandwidth that streaming video with it was impossible. The UHF antenna sent video at about 19 kilobits per second, which meant the video came back at a rate of one frame per *minute* instead of thirty frames a second. Worse, the single frames that came in were random and intermittent. The flood of data captured by the Predator completely overwhelmed the UHF antenna; in effect, all the Predator could do via UHF was take a useless still photo every one to five minutes. The Predator detachment could only hope that the Ku-band system would arrive before their deployment ended. Otherwise, the impression the drone made on commanders elsewhere might be embarrassing, if not disastrous.

One night, however, someone realized that the valley in which Gjader lay was oriented at a northwest angle pointing directly toward Sarajevo, scene of most of Bosnia's fighting. Better still, there was a gap in the mountains between Gjader and the Bosnian capital. Sarajevo was 157 miles away, far too distant for those at Gjader actually to see the Predator, even with binoculars. But for radio waves, Sarajevo was in Gjader's line of sight. The Predator's C-band antenna was guaranteed to operate at distances only up to 115 miles, but when Werner was told about the quirk in the geography between Gjader and Sarajevo, he advised the young commander of the operation, Army Captain Scott Sanborn, to try flying over Sarajevo within a certain altitude and zone. If his calculations were correct, Werner explained, the GCS antenna would find the Predator's C-band antenna if the drone loitered in that spot.

At the end of a regular mission, and with every bit of transmit-and-receive hardware in the system torqued to highest capacity, a crew flew the Predator to Sarajevo. To no one's surprise, Werner was right. As the drone reached the city at the altitude he had suggested, crisp color video of the Bosnian capital began pouring into the GCS; more important, the same images began appearing on Predator screens at NATO's regional headquarters in Naples and at the CAOC in Vicenza. Soon the phone in the Predator operations center was ringing constantly, as officers in Naples and Vicenza called with requests from commanders, who had long lists of "targets" they wanted the Predator to fly over, locations where the Serbs might be hiding tanks, artillery, or surface-to-air missile batteries.

Suddenly the Predator wasn't just a trifle anymore. Seventeen years after Abe Karem first began designing drones in his Los Angeles garage, the latest version of his invention was much in demand.

By August, the Mibli was flying missions so regularly the Serbs began to realize that when they heard something like a loud mosquito buzzing overhead they were being watched. Soon they began gunning for the Predator. While its small size and white composite skin made the drone hard to spot with the naked eye, and its slow speed was below velocities usually targeted by military radars looking for combat planes, Serb troops finally bagged one on August 11, 1995.

Chief Warrant Officer 3 Greg Foscue, a Mibli pilot, was in the ground control station at Gjader that overcast Friday, taking turns with Tim Just of General Atomics in flying the first mission using a Predator with a Ku-band satellite dish. They were tracking a convoy of Serb military vehicles traveling west on a highway out of Brčko, a town in northern Bosnia, as Air Force Brigadier General–select Glen W. "Wally" Moorhead III, chief of staff for the NATO task force, monitored the mission from Naples. Army Captain Sanborn, the commander at Gjader, was nervous about the mission. Sanborn had asked for a three-day "stand-down" of flights so his crews could train with the new Ku-band aircraft, which had arrived only a couple of days earlier. He had been granted a stand-down lasting a single day. Keeping tabs on whether the Serbs were moving heavy weapons in violation of UN resolutions was a top priority, he was told, and his commanders were relying on the Predator to help them accomplish that for their civilian bosses.

Moorhead himself was relaying instructions to the Predator unit through Captain Greg Gordy, an Air Force intelligence officer, as they sat at either end of a long wooden table in a secure conference room at NATO headquarters in Naples. They were watching the Predator's video on a twenty-seven-inch cathode ray tube TV usually used for video teleconferencing. Gordy was communicating live with Sanborn, who was in the RED Cell in Albania, through a secure computer chat room when Moorhead said he wanted the Predator to fly lower over the convoy so they could see what the Serb trucks were carrying. Sanborn balked. The Predator crew was already flying the drone only about seven thousand feet above the ground because its sensor operators had so little practice focusing the camera over the Ku-band satellite link, which created a lag of approximately half a second between the GCS and the aircraft. Sanborn feared that the Predator was already within earshot, eyesight, and antiaircraft gun range of the Serbs below.

"Are you sure you want us to do this?" Sanborn messaged Gordy.

"Yes," Gordy messaged back. "I've got the general sitting here, and that's what he wants to do and he understands the risks."

"Roger that," Sanborn replied.

As General Atomics pilot Tim Just took the Predator lower, Sanborn grew even more anxious. "We're at risk of getting shot down," he messaged Gordy.

Undeterred, Moorhead ordered another pass, this time even lower. As Just put the Predator into a descent, the video screens in the GCS, the conference room in Naples, and the CAOC suddenly froze on a frame showing the road and a blurry vehicle of some kind. No one knew for sure what had happened, but Sanborn could guess.

On the chance that the drone had simply "lost link," pilots Just and

Foscue and other crew members spent several hours monitoring the GCS screens. Later, others scanned the skies above Gjader, hoping to see the Predator automatically flying back home. It never arrived.

That evening, in the group tent the Predator unit shared, Sanborn was sitting on his cot when the phone next to it rang. Sanborn answered, then listened silently for a bit as Tim Just, whose cot was next to Sanborn's, sat watching and munching on a snack.

"Yes, I do," Sanborn said into the phone. "He's sitting right next to me, eating a bag of Cheetos."

After Sanborn explained the call, he and Just had a good laugh. The caller had been an officer with a combat search and rescue unit assigned to the CAOC who was gearing up to launch a mission. The officer wanted to know if Sanborn had any idea where they ought to look for the lost Predator's pilot. Sanborn politely explained that since the Predator was unmanned, the rescue unit could stand down.

The next day, the Belgrade news agency Tanjug reported that Serbian forces had shot down a UAV that Friday. Whether by mistake or for propaganda, Tanjug called the UAV "Croatian," but Serb TV later aired video of Serb troops standing on the Predator's wing.

Three days later, on August 14, Sanborn flew to Naples on the Mibli's twin-engine C-12 King Air supply plane to discuss with Moorhead and others at NATO why the Predator had been shot down. Just as Sanborn was headed into Moorhead's office, he was handed a message to call the Mibli in Albania—urgently. The unit's operations officer, Captain Mark Radtke, needed to talk.

"I don't have good news for you," Radtke said when Sanborn reached him. "We lost another one."

"You're kidding me," Sanborn said. "What happened?"

As Sanborn was on his way to Naples, Tim Just had been flying a second Ku-band Predator whose engine simply quit over Bosnia. Like the seagoing albatross that inspired its basic design, the Predator soared easily, and the aircraft continued to glide. Even so, Just quickly calculated that there was no way to reach the coast and ditch the Predator in the sea, his preferred course of action. He knew from having flown these routes every day, though, that there was a big mountain nearby, a place where no one was likely to be or go, so he simply turned the drone left, put the aircraft into the steepest, fastest dive it could make without falling apart, and plowed the Predator into that isolated peak, trying to smash it into bits too small to matter if the Serbs found them.

The next day, the *Washington Post* reported on the Predator losses, which it described as "crippling an experimental intelligence-gathering effort begun only last month."

Defense Secretary William Perry asked the Joint Chiefs of Staff to conduct an investigation into the Predator losses, and a team from U.S. European Command was sent to Naples to make inquiries. The Mibli was ordered to stop flying, and did for several days, until Admiral Smith himself intervened. The Predator was a work in progress, Smith told the Joint Chiefs, but it was already proving valuable. He had accepted the risk of flying the experimental drone over Bosnia, and would continue to accept it. The reward was worth the risk.

Smith and other commanders liked what they were getting out of this new drone. The deployment to Albania was supposed to last just sixty days, but the Predator's stay was extended after Serb forces mortared a Sarajevo market on August 28, 1995, leading NATO to mount a major air campaign called Operation Deliberate Force. The air campaign's goal was to force the Serbs to agree to peace talks, and after five days of intense attacks on their surface-to-air missile sites, artillery, tanks, and troops in the Sarajevo area, allied commanders called a halt to see if Belgrade was ready to negotiate. When the Predator detected the Serbs moving heavy weapons into place for more attacks on Sarajevo, the allies resumed the air strikes. Two weeks later, Serb military leader General Ratko Mladic agreed to a cease-fire, and abided by it.

The Predator's deployment to Albania ended on October 26, after the Serbs agreed to negotiate with Bosnia and Croatia at Wright-Patterson Air Force Base in Dayton, Ohio, with U.S. and NATO diplomats and military leaders serving as mediators. Shaky as its start had been, the new drone had made a big and positive impression. Commanders weren't terribly concerned about the two Predators lost, which would cost only

$1.5 million apiece to replace—less than a tenth the price of Scott O'Grady's downed F-16C. When the drones went down, moreover, no rescue force had to be sent to save pilots whose training cost millions and whose lives were priceless. And the cost had clearly been worth it: by spotting Serb artillery movements, the Predator played a key role in the success of Operation Deliberate Force. That November, U.S. and NATO commander Admiral Smith sent the Predator team a "Bravo Zulu" message, the naval signal for "Well Done."

"You proved the inherent value of UAVs is the ability to fly in areas where putting manned vehicles would be unacceptable due to risk or operational considerations," Smith wrote. He then congratulated the Predator team for "extended surveillance of heavy weapons withdrawal from the Sarajevo area, reconnaissance operations during Deliberate Force, and confirmation of warring factions' compliance with UN mandates."

Smith wasn't the only senior military leader paying attention. Even before the Navy's Rutherford arranged for the Army's Mibli to fly the Predator over Bosnia from Albania, the Air Force's highest-ranking officer was maneuvering to take over the drone for his service, and he was making no secret of the fact. "U.S. Air Force Chief of Staff Ronald Fogleman is turning out to be a big supporter of unmanned aerial vehicles," *Aerospace Daily* reported on June 19, 1995. At the National Defense University in Washington three days earlier, Fogleman had vowed that "the U.S. Air Force on my watch is going to aggressively embrace the UAV concept." A month later, the director of Air Force operational requirements told *Aerospace Daily* that Fogleman's service wanted every Predator that was made.

Fogleman's attitude toward UAVs represented a dramatic shift. Like nine of the fifteen Air Force chiefs of staff before him, Fogleman was a fighter pilot, and among that white scarf fraternity disdain for drones was usually Pavlovian. But Fogleman was also a member of another elite group. Four years after graduating from the U.S. Air Force Academy in 1963, he had piloted F-100F Super Sabre jets at treetop level and supersonic speed over the jungles of Vietnam as a Misty Fast FAC, the letters an acronym—pronounced "fack"—meaning "forward air controller," military terminology for a target spotter. "Misty" was the radio call sign used by the volunteer pilots of this top-secret Operation Commando Sabre; "Fast" was the way they flew. A Misty Fast FAC's mission was to bird-dog enemy movements and lead fighter-bombers to targets on the Ho Chi Minh Trail, the rugged logistics route Communist North Vietnam used to funnel men and materiel through Laos and Cambodia to Viet Cong insurgents fighting the U.S.-backed government of South Vietnam.

By today's standards, Misty Fast FAC missions were primitive in technology and nearly suicidal in technique. Navigation and reconnaissance devices available in the 1950s-vintage Super Sabre were almost laughably limited: Misty Fast FAC pilots carried paper maps in the cockpit and usually used handheld 35-millimeter single-lens reflex cameras to take reconnaissance photos. On some missions, though, the Super Sabres served as bait, escorting RF-4C Phantom II jets that had cameras in their noses and flying low to flush out photo targets for the Phantoms. Few aerial missions in Vietnam were more dangerous. Fogleman was the eighty-sixth Misty Fast FAC pilot, and 28 before him were downed by enemy fire. Of 157 pilots who became Misty Fast FACs, 34—nearly a quarter—were ultimately shot down. Most were rescued, but 7 were killed and 3 became prisoners of war.

On a second Vietnam tour, Fogleman flew the RF-4C Phantom II himself, so airborne reconnaissance—using aircraft, as opposed to satellites, to gather intelligence from above—was in his blood. When he assumed command of the Air Force on October 26, 1994—a week after NBC's Tom Brokaw called the Predator a "breakthrough"—airborne reconnaissance was one of his top priorities. Fogleman saw a worrisome gap looming in the nation's ability to conduct such reconnaissance. The last regular Air Force RF-4C flight had occurred earlier in 1994. Congress had just voted to reactivate the SR-71 Blackbird, a Mach 3 spy plane the Air Force had retired in 1990, but reviving the exotic jet would take a couple of years and be costly. With defense spending still declining after the Soviet Union's collapse, some in the Pentagon argued that satellites could fill the reconnaissance void, but Fogleman was unpersuaded.

To him, the Predator and the high-altitude UAVs being developed under the Tier programs created by Pentagon procurement czar John Deutch looked like a better solution.

Fogleman also thought the Army was the wrong service to fly and manage UAVs, given the Army's abysmal history with the Aquila and its limited use of airplanes. He was convinced the Army would treat a drone like a truck, not an aircraft, but the Predator was a far different breed from the Aquila, the Pioneer, and other UAVs the military had developed. The Predator was a real airplane, far different in appearance from a Piper Cub but not dissimilar in size. Abroad, the Predator would need to share runways with Air Force planes. In operations, the drone would have to be integrated into the daily Air Tasking Order, the overall plan for coordinating military aircraft.

Even as the Army was taking the Predator to Albania, Fogleman created a new unit to fly drones. He named it the 11th Reconnaissance Squadron, revivifying a decommissioned RF-4C outfit he had flown with on Misty Fast FAC missions in Vietnam. The 11th RS, as the new squadron was known in the Air Force, opened its doors on July 28, 1995, at Indian Springs Air Force Auxiliary Field, a small, remote facility forty-five miles northwest of Nellis Air Force Base in Nevada. In the beginning, most pilots who were sent there figured their careers were over.

On November 22, 1995, after three weeks of cloistered negotiation at Wright-Patterson Air Force Base, representatives of Bosnia, Croatia, and Serbia reached an agreement to end their vicious ethnic wars. Soon twenty thousand American troops and forty thousand from other countries were on their way to the Balkans to enforce the new Dayton Peace Accords. U.S. commanders were quick to decide they wanted the Predator there with them. The Mibli, General Atomics, and Rutherford's team moved rapidly to get ready for the new deployment. They would take three air vehicles equipped with both synthetic aperture radar and a Ku-band satellite antenna. This time, though, the Predator would fly from a military air base called Taszár, in southern Hungary, a former Warsaw Pact nation now applying for membership in NATO. Hungary's government was eager to help keep the peace in former Yugoslavia, whose civil strife had sent refugees flooding across its border.

The Dayton Accords were formally signed in Paris on December 14. Two days later, a top Pentagon panel chaired by Admiral Owens, the vice chairman of the Joint Chiefs, decided the Air Force should become "service lead" for Predator operations. A Joint Chiefs committee recommended that the Air Force take over when the Predator's two-year test-drive period under the Advanced Concept Technology Demonstration ended that coming July.

Four months later, in April 1996, Defense Secretary William Perry agreed to give the Predator to the Air Force, but with a caveat. In a nod to "jointness," the ever popular idea that the armed services should cooperate and share hardware, Perry decreed that while the Air Force would operate the Predator, the Navy would keep developing the drone and procuring its various elements. And as a practical matter, the Army's Mibli would continue operating the Predator in Bosnia for a few more months while the Air Force trained some of its own pilots to fly an aircraft by remote control.

With the Air Force scheduled to take charge of the Predator that summer, Navy program manager Rutherford was asked to go to Langley Air Force Base, in southeast Virginia, on June 13 to take part in a review of the Predator program at Air Combat Command (known as ACC, with each letter pronounced individually). ACC was operational headquarters for the Air Force's warplanes; as such, it was the Predator's future owner. Navy Commander Steve Jayjock, the intelligence officer who had coordinated between the CIA and the Defense Department as their respective Gnat 750 and Predator programs began in 1994, went to ACC with Rutherford and another briefer, Army Colonel Tim Fulcher. Jayjock was appalled at how the three were treated.

Four-star general Richard Hawley, a fighter pilot who had taken command of ACC on April 5, chaired the Langley event, which was held in a huge conference room. Hawley greeted Rutherford, Jayjock, and Fulcher in front of about sixty of his officers by announcing that he, Hawley, was the new owner of the Predator—even if the Navy was still its program office—because the Air Force chief of staff wanted it that

way. With defense budgets declining and many pilots already leaving
the service, the Air Force couldn't simply ask for volunteers to fly the
Predator, as the Army had done. Instead, Air Force pilots would have to
be ordered to report for this duty—and Hawley made it plain that, in his
opinion, any pilot involuntarily assigned to fly this stupid thing would
hate to trade soaring through the sky for sitting in a frigid van for hours.
Hawley did nothing to hide the fact that he felt like a car salesman pitching a lemon.

The other officers in the room followed their leader's cue. As Rutherford took the dais and showed his first slide, ACC fighter, bomber, and
U-2 pilots openly showed their contempt—especially two young majors
wearing U-2 patches. Scoffing laughs greeted a photo of the Predator.
Wisecracks and snorts were audible as Rutherford described the Predator's speed and range, its capabilities and limitations. Questions were
hostile. One of the U-2 pilots even accused Army officer Fulcher of lying
about the Predator's accomplishments in Bosnia. Fulcher was furious,
and Jayjock squirmed as he watched, his own blood pressure rising. To
Rutherford's shock, Hawley did nothing to tamp down the hostility during the three-hour verbal slugfest. Still, Rutherford did his best to parry
the verbal blows; smiling, he calmly reminded the ACC officers that it
hadn't been his idea to assign them the Predator. Jayjock would always
admire how cool and professional Rutherford was that day.

Afterward, upon returning to his Naval Air Systems Command office,
Rutherford felt heartsick. He had spent the last two years trying to make
the Predator a reality, and he hated the idea of handing it over to the Air
Force. Maybe Fogleman really wanted the Predator, but maybe Air Force
leaders just wanted to keep another service from having it. Ever since the
Air Force's separation from the Army in 1947, the two had waged an
unending political battle over which should control aircraft whose main
mission was to support ground forces. Rutherford couldn't help wondering how long the Predator would last once the Air Force got hold of it.
The white scarf wearers at Air Combat Command obviously wanted to
shoot it down.

———

On Halloween Day 1996, twenty-three years after he entered the Air Force, James G. "Snake" Clark, age forty-four, was promoted to colonel. Three months after he pinned on the silver eagles denoting his new rank, Clark got a phone call from General Ron Fogleman.

"Snake, what do you know about Predator?" the chief of staff asked.

"Arnold Schwarzenegger—great movie," Clark cracked.

Fogleman ignored the joke. "Good," the general said. "I want you to go over there and tell me what the hell is going on."

Clark knew "over there" was Taszár. On September 2, the Air Force's 11th Reconnaissance Squadron had officially taken over Predator operations from the Army's Mibli, which had been flying the drone over Bosnia by remote control from Hungary since March 14. One day short of a month after the Air Force assumed control, one of the three 11th RS pilots at Taszár crashed one of the three Predators based there. The pilot was blameless; as with the Predator over Bosnia the previous August, the drone's engine failed.

In the three months since that accident, Fogleman had been getting a stream of complaints about the Predator from Army leaders enforcing the Dayton Accords. On January 29, 1997, the vice chief of staff of the Army, General Ronald Griffith, had gone so far as to send a "message to the field" saying, "Predator support to the 1st Armored Division was less than satisfactory" in Bosnia. Army commanders said the Predator wasn't in the air often enough to do them much good. Air Combat Command claimed weather was the problem; the Predator's wispy wings were too prone to icing, and ACC's recommendation was that the unit simply be brought home for the winter and sent back in summer. Others suggested that the pilots the Air Force had assigned to fly the Predator just weren't very good. Everyone knew that commanders of manned aircraft units weren't sending their best when told to give up pilots for the new drone squadron.

Fogleman wasn't sure what to believe. "I want someone who's going to tell me the truth," the chief told Clark.

Despite Clark's nickname, Fogleman implicitly trusted him—relied on him, in fact, to do things even the chief of staff couldn't get done through regular channels. Fogleman would give Snake Clark a task or money or just an idea, say, "Go do it," and then provide top cover for him when others protested. Irreverent, sassy, and unafraid to step on toes, Clark was an acquired taste. He spoke in a preening patter—its flavor was slightly acidic and reminiscent of W. C. Fields—but his wise guy bite was tempered by hints of self-deprecation. He was a disciple of Colonel Richard "Moody" Suter, a charismatic and revered Air Force figure. As a major in the 1970s, Suter stepped on a lot of toes, too, but he maneuvered the service into creating an innovative annual fighter pilot exercise called Red Flag. Based on lessons learned in Vietnam and credited with helping U.S. forces own the air in every conflict since, Red Flag taught American and allied fighter pilots how to win by pitting them against mock enemy air and ground forces in simulated but realistic battles.

Clark, who had been a pallbearer at Suter's funeral the previous January, enjoyed working on special projects for Fogleman, and he loved playing what he called Pentagon Poker—"I'll see your three-star and raise you a four-star"—when someone got in his way. He made the most of his nickname; Clark figured being known as Snake helped deter bureaucratic foes. But the nickname actually predated his service in the Air Force. Sigma Pi Delta fraternity brothers at Catholic University in Washington, impressed with the way Clark sweet-talked a coed into revealing the location of a statue stolen as a sorority prank, dubbed him Snake in 1970. Clark had Irish charm as well as Irish blood—the New Jersey native wore a black armband every St. Patrick's Day—and those who relied on his special talents or reported to him often found him charismatic. Even the two wives who divorced Clark before he married a third time remained friends with him. Not surprisingly, many of those he trumped at Pentagon Poker resented him, but Clark worried little about them. He did worry about his bosses, though, and shortly after Fogleman's call Snake Clark began arranging a trip to Taszár.

Fogleman was getting complaints about the Predator partly because senior military leaders were becoming addicted to its video. For the deployment to Taszár, the U.S. European Command had created a new video dissemination system that sent the drone's imagery via satellite not only to NATO headquarters in Naples and the CAOC in Vicenza, but also to Supreme Headquarters Allied Powers Europe, in Mons, Belgium; to other military commands around Europe; to the Pentagon; and to various points in Washington—forty locations in all. Werner liked to say the system was created after he "infected" the military with a craving for video by piping it into the Pentagon.

The Predator's video was usually screened on office televisions; compared to the imagery seen in the ground control station, the video was grainy, for it arrived after being digitized, compressed, decompressed, and converted back to analog format. Even so, many viewers were captivated by their newfound ability to watch images live and in color as the drone's cameras found Serb checkpoints, searched for mass graves, or monitored cantonments where the warring parties had agreed to store military vehicles. Commanders all around Europe and Washington took to phoning the Predator ground control station in Hungary to ask questions about what they were seeing or to make special requests. *What was that vehicle? Which road is that? Can you go back and take another look behind that barn?* Predator crew members, all relatively low in rank, were at first startled to get direct calls from generals and admirals, some of them with four stars on their shoulders. But soon such calls became so routine that the crews started joking about "Predator crack" and "Predator porn" addicts. When the Air Force took over and the Predator video channel largely went blank, the addicts grew agitated.

A shortage of pilots was one problem. Standard practice required that two pilots be at the controls when the Predator took off and landed; Air Force pilots were also supposed to get twelve hours of rest between flights. With only three pilots assigned to it, the 11th RS detachment at Taszár could fly only one twelve-hour mission a day throughout October and November 1996. In early December, four new pilots arrived, as well as one from General Atomics, but the previous three Air Force pilots went home, and the weather over the Balkans, which was often cloudy, rainy, or snowy, became a hindrance. Under a rule adopted after another near crash that fall, believed to have been caused by icing, the 11th RS didn't fly its Predators in wet weather, or even through clouds.

The second Air Force detachment sent to fly the Predator arrived at

Taszár on December 4, led by Major Jon Box, a former aerial refueling tanker pilot from Texas who was two months shy of his fortieth birthday. Box and the three other 11th RS pilots who came with him flew the drone only six days that December, logging nine flights in all. But only four were reconnaissance missions—the rest were tests and check flights—and two of the missions over Bosnia had to be aborted because of weather. From December 28, 1996, to January 26, 1997, the four pilots didn't fly their Predators at all; they were prevented from doing so by the Air Force weather rules, which banned them from taking off when there was any "visible moisture" or if visibility was below minimums.

Every day, a launch crew of two pilots and three or four sensor operators would show up on time, get briefed on the day's planned mission over Bosnia, go through preflight checks of the GCS and the aircraft, and then sit and wait for permission to take off. Every day, the base weather forecaster would tell Box he saw visible moisture near the airfield, or that visibility was too poor for the drone to fly. Box would put the crew on hold for hours, sometimes all day, waiting for the weather to lift, but then the CAOC would cancel the mission. Every night, Box and his pilots and sensor operators would gather in their tent, shove the same videotape into a VCR, and watch the same movie for the umpteenth time. The movie perfectly reflected their situation: it was *Groundhog Day*, the 1993 comedy starring Bill Murray, in which a TV weatherman covering a Groundhog Day celebration in Punxsutawney, Pennsylvania, gets caught in a time loop that makes him relive the same day again and again.

After the movie, at precisely ten o'clock each night, one of Box's pilots, Major Ray Miller, would go outside, face the side of the sprawling, muddy tent city at Taszár where two thousand Army troops lived, and scream at the top of his lungs, "I . . . LOVE . . . IT . . . HERE!" Box played dumb when the Army "mayor" at Taszár demanded to know who was screaming every night.

Nearly every night, Box, Miller, and others in their group would go outside and sing a little song Box and Miller had made up based on the 11th RS's official nickname, the Black Owls, a moniker represented on shoulder patches depicting a black owl diving with talons bared. Soulfully sung to the tune of the chorus of the venerable "Whiffenpoof

Song"—"We're little black sheep who have gone astray. Baa, baa, baa"—
the Black Owls song reflected the Predator pilots' view of the way the
Air Force felt about them: "We are the black owls who've lost our way.
Hoo . . . hoo . . . hoo . . . ."

Toward the end of January, Box and some of his Predator team finally
studied tapes of the near crash the previous fall and decided that it hadn't
been caused by icing but by the pilot taking the Predator's nose up too
high at takeoff, creating an aerodynamic stall. As a result of their study,
the restrictions on taking off with visible moisture in the air were loos-
ened and the detachment flew nearly every day in February.

On February 24, ACC commander General Hawley arrived with six
colonels to inspect the Black Owl squadron's Predator operation. He left
without telling Box what he thought. Three days later, Box learned that
Snake Clark would be arriving in mid-March on behalf of the chief of
staff, accompanied by another colonel who was ACC's operations director, plus two lieutenant colonels and a major; their assignment was to
investigate the squadron's operation.

On March 17, Clark and his party flew into Taszár after official stops
in Germany and Italy. The delegation stayed two days. On the third day
of Clark's visit, Box was told to report to the office of the Air Force colonel in charge of the Taszár airfield. The colonel was a reservist Major Box
had clashed with after Box had set up an unauthorized tent so field representatives from General Atomics could live more comfortably. Box had
also irritated the colonel by handing out parking passes for the Air Force
side of the field to transportation and other personnel whose help he
needed.

When Box entered the room, Clark was sitting at the colonel's desk
and the colonel was standing up—crying. Clark asked the colonel
whether it was true that he had reprimanded Box for setting up the tent
and giving out the parking passes. The colonel acknowledged that he
had. As Box watched, wide-eyed, Clark chewed out his fellow Air Force
colonel some more.

"Don't you realize that you're the senior Air Force officer here and
you're supposed to be protecting those guys and doing whatever they
need to go do their mission?" Clark demanded. "And you've been fighting

him. This is what I heard you said about Jon Box at an Army staff meeting. You got up on the stage and you said, 'I'm really proud of how the Army and the Air Force have been working together—except for one pompous ass major.'"

Things got better for Box and the Black Owls after that.

After visiting Taszár, Clark decided that while the Predator was still technologically a work in progress, the biggest flaw in the program was interservice rivalry. "Clearly Predator's biggest problem is political," Clark wrote in a report to Fogleman. "The Army is still mad that they lost the program after the ACTD. Their possible agenda is to prove that the USAF cannot properly support their ground commanders and to regain control of the Predator program or restore funding to their Hunter program." Army officers, Clark wrote, were keeping a "daily detailed record" of when the Predators flew or didn't, and sending it to higher headquarters. "The USAF has no control over it's [sic] own destiny with Predator as long as the Navy is in charge of the program office running the JPO," Clark argued. "There needs to be a single USAF office to run the entire program."

After he read Clark's memo, Fogleman started quietly campaigning to get the Air Force total, not just operational, control over the Predator.

"After my report was done," Clark wrote years later, "I was convinced that the Predator and I would go our own separate ways."

He was wrong.

6

WILD PREDATOR

Visitors to the 645th Aeronautical Systems Group at Wright-Patterson Air Force Base in Dayton, Ohio, must find their way to Building 557, the second of three modern, parallelogram-shaped office structures on Loop Road West. Once there, they must register at a reception window in the lobby. Photo ID must be shown. Cameras are not allowed. Cell phones or other electronic devices must be deposited in a bank of lockboxes built into a nearby wall. Proceeding past the lobby requires an escort, who must punch a code into a keypad to enter the first-floor hallway. After walking a ways down the hall, the escort will turn left, then punch another code into another keypad to open another door on the right. Upon closing that door, the escort will cross a ten-foot vestibule to a sturdy vault door, where a square black button that rings a buzzer must be pressed to gain entry.

Hung on the vestibule's left wall are signed 1980s-vintage photographs of President Ronald Reagan, President George H. W. Bush, and British Prime Minister Margaret Thatcher, each bearing a handwritten note of thanks for unspecified achievements by the unit headquartered behind the vault door. Hung on the vestibule's right wall is a color photo—taken by the gun camera of a Soviet MiG-17 fighter jet—showing a C-130AII aircraft in flames and plunging toward earth during the hottest days of the Cold War. Seventeen crew members, including eleven

Russian linguists and intelligence analysts, died in that special reconnaissance aircraft, which four MiGs attacked without warning on September 2, 1958, after it inadvertently flew from a base in Turkey into
denied airspace over Armenia. The vaulted door framed by these photographs bears a sign embossed on metal and mounted on walnut that
declares, "Those who say it cannot be done should not get in the way of
those doing it." Above the sign is a striking emblem that depicts an African shield with two crossed spears. This insignia speaks to the fact that,
no matter which of several official names the 645th Aeronautical Systems
Group has borne during its six-decade history, this obscure Air Force
unit has always been known to the few who are aware that it exists as Big
Safari.

Created during the Cold War to help the Air Force, the CIA, and
other agencies keep an eye on the Soviet Union and its Cold War allies,
Big Safari quickly evolved into a real-world echo—though far less
zany—of Q Branch, the fictional British Secret Service technology shop
in the James Bond movies. Big Safari didn't rig attaché cases to spew tear
gas or fit snazzy sports cars with machine guns and ejection seats but,
like 007's Q Branch, Big Safari was staffed with clever engineers and
technicians whose mission was to devise and field often exotic gear quickly.
Big Safari was just more specialized: beginning with its first assignment
in December 1952—installing the largest aerial camera ever on a huge
C-97 Stratofreighter cargo plane, a project code-named Pie Face—Big
Safari's game was tricking out "special purpose aircraft," often with aerial
reconnaissance devices, usually in a hurry, and expressly for special missions. Big Safari and its contractor partners also serviced and tweaked
their products to keep them useful.

Big Safari was small. In the 1990s, the unit had only twenty-one people at its Wright-Patterson headquarters and a few dozen more in small
detachments and "operating locations" housed at contractor facilities in
California and Texas, where most of the hands-on work was done.
Wherever they were and whatever the project, Big Safari operators
prided themselves on being creative, sly, and largely anonymous. Until
the Internet came along, the organization itself was so deep in the shadows that even four-star generals who became chief of staff were often

taken by surprise to learn that Big Safari existed—a fact usually conveyed in a few whispered words. Big Safari operated in the "black world" because its innovations often needed to remain secret to succeed. Beginning with Pie Face, the organization cloaked its work in opaque code names such as Lulu Belle, Hot Pepper, Purple Passion, Speed Light, Cobra Eye, and a series of projects whose sobriquets began with "Rivet."

By law, Big Safari had "rapid acquisition authority," which allowed it to bypass much of the bureaucratic molasses that bogs down most military procurement. By dispensing with what its leaders disdained as "administrivia," and by working hand-in-glove with defense contractors and the operators of its aircraft, Big Safari could get innovative new gear into action within months, weeks, and sometimes even days, rather than the years it routinely takes to develop and field most military technology. Big Safari's philosophy was expressed in mottoes, catchphrases, and admonitions such as "Minimum but adequate," "Off-the-shelf," "Need to know," "Modify, don't develop," and "Provide the necessary, not the nice to have."

When General Ron Fogleman decided in 1997 that it would be nice for the Air Force to have total control of the Predator, Big Safari's director was William D. W. Grimes, who had run the semisecret technology shop for the past eleven years. A Baptist minister's son raised in Danvers, Massachusetts, Bill Grimes found his vocation in the Air Force. He entered the service upon receiving his bachelor's degree in experimental psychology from Brown University, which he attended on an ROTC scholarship. Grimes graduated in 1959—or, as he liked to put it, before the Ivy League school "got wacky" by making course grades optional and banning ROTC from its Providence, Rhode Island, campus.

In the Air Force, Grimes was trained as a navigator, then became an electronic warfare officer with the 348th Bombardment Squadron at Westover Air Force Base, in south central Massachusetts. His unit's mission was straight out of Dr. Strangelove, Stanley Kubrick's 1964 satire of Cold War logic. Under the Strategic Air Command's massive retaliation strategy, Grimes and his fellow B-52 Stratofortress long-range nuclear bomber crew members remained on twenty-four-hour alert for a week at a time. Their aircraft, fueled and ready, sat on a nearby runway, while they lived underground in a shelter nicknamed the Mole Hole, ready to fly off and nuke the Soviet Union at a moment's notice if so ordered. Now and then they scrambled into the air for practice.

Grimes found such exercises exciting. But in 1966 he got involved in an actual contest with the Soviets—aerial cat and mouse—by requesting and receiving a "green door assignment," as highly classified intelligence postings were called. For the next seven years, stationed at Eielson Air Force Base, Alaska, he used his electronic warfare skills aboard a sensor-packed Big Safari aircraft code-named Wanda Belle. Technically an RC-135S, Wanda Belle's mission was to sit on strip alert on Shemya Island, all but the last western link in the Aleutians chain, and rush into the sky to track and record data on Soviet missile tests when a launch was detected. Flying in those northern reaches was hazardous. Wanda Belle's sister ship, code-named Rivet Amber, disappeared over the Bering Sea without a trace on June 5, 1969, just six months after Wanda Belle hydroplaned off the runway during a landing at Shemya and was wrecked. Grimes wasn't aboard that day, and unlike the Rivet Amber's crew his Wanda Belle mates were lucky and suffered only minor injuries. Transferred to Texas to help equip a replacement aircraft, Grimes himself was invited to join Big Safari in 1973. Thirteen years later he became its commander, then stayed on as its civilian director upon retiring from the Air Force as a colonel in 1990.

As a career airborne reconnaissance practitioner, Grimes was intimately familiar with UAVs, as was Big Safari. In the 1960s, Big Safari converted the first Q-2C jet target drones into Firefly reconnaissance UAVs, flight-tested the various configurations used in Vietnam, and trained the crews who flew them. During the run-up to the 1991 Gulf War, Big Safari added GPS navigation and special metal spheres to forty target drones and turned them into decoys that Iraqi radars saw as F-15 and F-16 fighter planes. Of forty U.S. aircraft the Iraqis claimed to have shot down in the opening hours of the war, thirty-seven were Big Safari decoys. Around the same time, Big Safari studied Abe Karem's Amber, the Predator's genealogical forebear, when U.S. Southern Command was looking for a better way than manned aircraft to sniff out illicit drug laboratories in the jungles of Latin America.

More recently, UAVs had been a significant drain on Big Safari's budget. Defense Department officials had taken badly needed RC-135 re-engining money to help fund Advanced Concept Technology Demonstrations of two high-altitude drones, the so-called Tier II Plus Global Hawk and the Tier III Minus DarkStar. No one at Big Safari liked this shift in focus, especially after the DarkStar crashed and was destroyed during its second flight on April 22, 1996. But Grimes had been impressed with the Predator, and he thought its ability to fly into far more dangerous airspace and stay there far longer than a manned plane could offer enormous potential for the military. He was also sure Big Safari could exploit the Predator's possibilities—and he didn't think the regular Air Force would appreciate, much less fully develop, the drone's potential.

Neither did Mike Meermans, a retired chief master sergeant who joined the staff of the House Permanent Select Committee on Intelligence in 1995 after a twenty-two-year career in Air Force intelligence. Meermans had come to know Big Safari's work well during his tenure in the Air Force, and he was a big fan of Bill Grimes, whom he deemed a "national treasure." Meermans had flown during his Air Force career as a crew member on Big Safari aircraft from Rivet Joint to Compass Call, a communications-jamming version of the C-130. He later became an Air Force Compass Call program officer, then finished his career as chief of airborne reconnaissance operations at Air Force headquarters in the Pentagon from 1990 to 1995. When Meermans went to work for the House Intelligence Committee, its vice chairman was Representative Jerry Lewis, the California Republican who was emerging as the nascent Predator's chief promoter in Congress. In June 1996, Lewis sent Meermans to observe an exercise at Key West, Florida, that included the Predator. Meermans came back infatuated.

"Mr. Lewis, this little guy is going to be a winner!" Meermans assured his boss.

Lewis and his aide Letitia White, who had worked closely with Tom Cassidy of General Atomics and Navy Captain Allan Rutherford to get the Predator off the ground, feared the Air Force didn't share Meermans's view of the Predator. Rutherford's rough reception at Air Combat

Command the previous year had made clear what most Air Force pilots thought about the slow little drone, and there was little reason to think the service's acquisition arm would feel differently. The Air Force's top priority was the fantastically capable but also fantastically costly F-22 Raptor, a supersonic stealth fighter plane then expected to cost an average $166 million per aircraft. Pentagon officials and defense experts in Congress, meanwhile, were arguing over reconnaissance aircraft far more exotic and expensive than the Predator, from the manned SR-71— cancelled for cost by the Air Force in 1989 but revived by Congress in 1994—to the DarkStar and Global Hawk high-altitude drone projects. When Lewis asked Meermans what he thought they could do to help the far less sexy Predator not just survive but thrive, Meermans knew right away. In the course of his intelligence committee job, Meermans talked regularly with his old friend Bill Grimes, and he knew the Big Safari director was itching to take the Predator under his wing.

In the spring of 1997, Meermans brought Grimes to one of the most secure locations in Washington, the House Intelligence Committee hearing room, a curved, wood-paneled chamber tucked into the dome of the Capitol that was both soundproof and regularly swept for listening devices. Soon Meermans and Grimes were joined by Congressman Lewis, Letitia White, and recently elected Representative James A. Gibbons, a Nevada Republican who was both a new intelligence committee member and an old Air Force RF-4C pilot. Neither Grimes nor Meermans had let the Air Force legislative liaison office know that the Big Safari director was in town to meet Lewis—a breach of protocol that might provoke a flap if discovered. If they were found out, Meermans told Grimes, they could just explain that he had asked Grimes to educate Lewis and Gibbons about Big Safari. But everyone present knew the real agenda.

After introductions, the members and aides took seats on the bottom row of the room's two-tiered, twenty-seat dais and Grimes launched into what he called the "dollar version" of his Big Safari 101 briefing: What is Big Safari? How does it function? What programs come under it? The briefing was illustrated with viewgraphs—PowerPoint wasn't yet ubiquitous in 1997—shown with a projector Grimes set up on the faux-leather surface of the room's six-foot-long wooden witness table. There was nothing in the briefing about the Predator. But after the briefing ended, Grimes gladly answered questions posed by the congressmen and their aides about what he saw as the drone's potential and how Big Safari would develop the Predator if given the chance.

As Meermans had anticipated, Lewis and Gibbons were impressed, and a few weeks later Lewis sent the Air Force a message the way members of Congress frequently do. The House Intelligence Committee's report on its annual intelligence authorization act noted that the underlying bill would transfer to the Air Force all authority over the Predator still held by the Navy, as also directed by that year's defense authorization bill. But the committee's report added that the panel "has been keenly interested in the rapid, flexible, and innovative acquisition approaches that hallmark Big Safari, and it strongly urges" the Air Force to let Big Safari manage further development of the Predator.

On October 1, 1997, the Air Force assumed full control of the Predator, as required by the defense bill. As required by good political sense, the Air Force made Big Safari the Predator's System Program Office, thus assigning it to work with General Atomics and other contractors to improve the Predator and increase its capabilities. One of the first things Grimes did was give a consulting contract to Werner, the imagery scientist who first figured out how to pipe the Predator's video into the Pentagon, then how to get it from Albania to command posts around Europe. Grimes, too, wanted to turn this interesting technology into something important.

Eight months later, the Air Force version of Q Branch would start doing exactly that.

Air Force Captain Scott Swanson had thought that by 1998 he would be piloting the V-22 Osprey, a futuristic aircraft the Marine Corps and his service were developing that could take off and land like a helicopter but fly with the speed of a fixed-wing airplane. As an Air Force Special Operations Command helicopter pilot with a Gulf War combat tour and two years of dicey search-and-rescue missions over the stormy North Atlantic under his belt, Swanson was ready for a new challenge. The

Osprey was supposed to be a revolution in aviation, and the Air Force was going to use it for special operations. But the Osprey wasn't ready when Swanson was. By 1998, the V-22 was a decade late; a poster child for what was ailing Pentagon procurement, the new tiltrotor wasn't slated to go into service until 2001. So as Swanson's tour at the 56th Rescue Squadron in Iceland neared its end, he started looking for an assignment to tide him over until the Air Force needed Osprey pilots.

One day Swanson was perusing potential billets on an Air Force electronic bulletin board when an odd one caught his eye. The 11th Reconnaissance Squadron, a three-year-old unit at Indian Springs Air Force Auxiliary Field near Las Vegas, was looking for pilots willing to fly a UAV called the Predator, though in this case "fly" wouldn't mean actually leaving the ground. Not a seductive thought for most Air Force aviators, who generally sign up to experience the thrill of defying the law of gravity. In fact, the 11th RS announcement made it clear that the Air Force was having trouble filling the squadron's pilot billets; the offer promised that after a two-year Predator tour volunteers would be guaranteed the assignment of their choice.

Ordinarily, flying UAVs wouldn't have interested Swanson. The red-haired, freckle-faced Minnesota native suffered from none of the preening egotism common among fighter pilots, but even as a kid in the Minneapolis suburb of Minnetonka, Scott Swanson knew that when he grew up he wanted to join the Air Force and fly. A subscriber to *Aviation Week & Space Technology* magazine at age thirteen, he got his private pilot's license the same week the aptly named Lindbergh High School gave him his diploma. Swanson went to the University of Minnesota on an Air Force ROTC scholarship and left in 1986 with a degree in aviation management. For him, being a pilot was a calling, and he was good at it. His aerospace studies professor at U Minn was so impressed with Swanson's skills that he planned to recommend him for the prestigious Euro-NATO Joint Jet Pilot Training program, which turns out fighter pilots for the United States and its European allies. The professor was stunned when Swanson said thanks but no thanks; he only wanted to fly search-and-rescue helicopters, an idea he had been fixated on since he was a boy.

"Are you crazy?" his professor sputtered. In the Air Force, he warned, being a helicopter pilot was a career killer.

"I don't care," Swanson told him. "I'm just looking forward to flying and having a good time."

That was what Swanson had done ever since, pretty much, and his professor had been right about the effect that flying helicopters would have on his career. After twelve years in the Air Force, Swanson should have been a major. Instead, he was still just a captain; worse yet, he had been passed over for promotion, a sign he might never make higher rank. Even so, Swanson was happy in the Air Force, and he knew he would be happy with another assignment flying helicopters, if he could find one. But he also had another keen interest, one that even predated his fascination with flight and made the idea of operating the Predator more appealing to him than it would be to most pilots: Swanson was a computer geek.

Thanks to an innovative program created in 1968 by suburban Minneapolis school districts and the University of Minnesota College of Education, with help from IBM and other big information technology companies, Swanson had been fascinated by computers since first grade. Under what became the Minnesota Educational Computing Consortium, students at his elementary school were among those allowed to use teleprinters and phone modems to do dial-up time-sharing on a Hewlett Packard computer so they could learn the rudiments of programming. They could also play primitive computer games. Scott's favorite was *Lunar Lander,* in which he had to fly a spacecraft he couldn't see—computer display screens were still in the future—and land the vehicle on the moon. A player flew the Lunar Lander by reading its altitude and speed on a teleprinter and changing the space vehicle's position by typing commands on a keyboard, which sent code to the computer. Scott also liked a game called *The Oregon Trail,* which required a player to drive a Conestoga wagon across the frontier by typing in commands such as "cross the river." As they traversed the frontier, players had to "hunt" and "kill" wild game for food, in an early version of the game, by typing in words such as "Bang" or "Pow," and in a later edition by using a mouse to put crosshairs on images of wild animals.

Steering a craft he wasn't inside, therefore, was not a novel concept to Swanson; he was always interested in innovative technologies. Besides, after two years of flying helicopters in rough weather out of Reykjavík, including in two frigid Iceland winters, and with the promise that he could choose his own assignment after a tour with the 11th RS, the Predator job sounded appealing on a lot of levels.

Single guy living in Vegas? New and interesting technology? Yeah, Swanson thought, *I could go do this.* So he volunteered.

Three weeks into April 1999, Swanson was chatting with Major Bob Monroe in the 11th Reconnaissance Squadron operations director's Indian Springs airfield office when the telephone rang. Monroe didn't ask Swanson to leave; since joining the Predator squadron nine months earlier, the former helicopter pilot had earned Monroe's trust.

Swanson had transferred in from Iceland the previous June and, after twelve weeks of Predator training, deployed with a small 11th RS detachment to Taszár, Hungary, to fly surveillance missions over Bosnia. The unit was getting ready to come home for the winter in October 1998 when the Serb military and rebellious ethnic Albanians in Kosovo started a new round in what had become a chronic series of clashes between the two. The fighting stopped after the UN Security Council called for a ceasefire and threatened military action to make both sides comply, but the Predator deployment was extended to monitor what was happening in Kosovo and to help NATO prepare for another possible air campaign against the Serbs. U.S. commanders also began discussing whether to move the Predator's base south to Tuzla, Bosnia, to be closer to Kosovo.

From Hungary, the Predator needed eight hours of flight time just to *get* to Kosovo, flying south over Croatia, down the Adriatic, and across Albania to reach the Serb province. Swanson found that both his years in cockpits and his old *Lunar Lander* skills came in handy during such missions. A Predator pilot could see where his aircraft was going only by looking at a video screen, and even then his view was limited to a nose camera that peered straight out the drone's nose, supplemented by the view provided by sweeping the sky with its surveillance camera. Predator pilots couldn't feel the aircraft's motion, hear its engine, smell a fuel leak, or see what was in the air around their machine. Many of their commands to the aircraft, moreover, weren't made by moving the control stick and throttle on their console or the rudder pedals at their feet, but by typing on a keyboard.

Swanson proved adept at flying with only one of his five senses able to help. Beyond that, his ability to conceptualize, plan, and execute intricate missions—skills he had learned flying helicopters for Air Force Special Operations Command—gave him a leg up on many of his fellow Predator pilots. He excelled at flying missions out of Taszár, and when winter weather forced the detachment to return to Indian Springs around Christmas 1998, Swanson's superiors at the 11th RS immediately made him both a pilot instructor and the squadron's weapons and tactics officer—which was why Swanson was sitting in Monroe's office in April 1999 when the operations director's telephone rang.

"Wow," Monroe said quietly as he hung up. "They're gonna throw a laser designator on the Predator."

"Do you know what they're going to use?" Swanson asked.

"An AN/AAS-44(V)," Monroe replied, reciting the first five letters individually but finishing up with "forty-four Victor."

Swanson wasn't familiar with that particular laser designator, a device that pulses a laser beam at a target to mark it for bombs or missiles, which then home in on the reflected light, or "sparkle," bouncing off the target. As a special operations pilot, though, he had learned to use a different laser designator.

As Monroe explained, the phone call was from Big Safari, which on April 14 had been directed to install laser designators on four Predators, the number of drones that usually accompanied a ground control station. Equipped with such a device, the Predator should be able to "buddy-lase"— that is, shine its laser beam on targets that higher-flying fighter planes couldn't see and thus guide their bombs or missiles to those targets. The order to install the laser designator, approved by the Air Force chief of staff, gave Big Safari a tight deadline: three weeks. Monroe had been called, he told Swanson, because Big Safari would need a pilot to fly the Predator in tests of the device once it was installed, and perhaps in combat missions.

Swanson's inner geek was aroused. After his conversation with Monroe, he went straight to the 11th RS's "vault," a room where classified information could be stored or accessed by computer, and downloaded and printed the manual for what insiders called the Forty-Four ball. The device, he learned, was actually a turret containing both a laser designator and an infrared camera to find targets. Raytheon Corporation had developed it for the Navy's Sikorsky SH-60 and HH-60 Seahawk helicopters—birds of a feather with the Sikorsky MH-60 that Swanson had flown as a special operations pilot.

"Whoever's going will need to read this," Swanson told Monroe, plopping the manual for the Forty-Four ball down on the major's desk.

Monroe looked up and grinned. "You just volunteered," he said.

A few days later, Swanson was working for Big Safari. At the time, he thought it was a temporary assignment.

Swanson and Monroe knew exactly what combat need had generated the laser designator order. A month earlier, the United States and its NATO allies had launched a new air campaign against Serbia's military; the seething conflict in Kosovo had boiled over again that winter despite the UN ceasefire imposed the previous fall. So far, Operation Allied Force had been less effective than hoped. When Serb troops perpetrated further atrocities against ethnic Albanians, NATO was willing to respond, but only with air strikes, for no member nation wanted to send troops and risk casualties in a quasi-civil war. The desire to avoid casualties extended to aircraft and their crews as well, and Air Force leaders were wary of Serbia's formidable, mostly Soviet-made antiaircraft defenses. "These guys are very good," Chief of Staff General Michael E. Ryan testified to Congress before the operation began, warning that Allied air losses were "a distinct possibility." The risk was confirmed on March 27, the fourth day of the air strikes, when a Serbian surface-to-air missile battery brought down a U.S. F-117 stealth fighter, whose pilot safely ejected and was rescued. Even before that, the NATO air commander, Air Force Lieutenant General Michael Short, imposed a fifteen-thousand-foot "hard deck" on how low Alliance planes could fly over Yugoslavia, a floor designed to keep crews out of antiaircraft gun and shoulder-fired SAM range. But from fifteen thousand feet or higher, and with mountainous Kosovo frequently blanketed by fog and clouds, pilots were soon having trouble finding mobile military targets or verifying that they could hit them without harming civilians. U.S. commanders were still groping for ways to adapt.

To some, the Predator seemed an obvious solution. With no one aboard, a Predator could fly beneath the hard deck with no risk of casualties, and its camera could zoom in on objects miles away. In theory, Predator video would make it much easier to find and validate targets; it would also help reduce civilian casualties. A handful of Predators—the same ones Swanson's detachment had flown from Hungary the year before— had deployed to Tuzla just a few days before Operation Allied Force, and the CAOC in Vicenza immediately tried to use them to guide pilots to targets. The controllers in Vicenza quickly learned, though, that doing so wasn't as simple in practice as in theory.

Predator video could be seen live on screens at NATO's southern headquarters in Naples, at the CAOC, at the U.S. European Command in Stuttgart, Germany, at the "Jack" in England, even on a nineteen-inch television on a table in the Mons, Belgium, office of U.S. Army General Wesley Clark, the Supreme Allied Commander. Clark even had a TV that could receive Predator video at his official residence in Mons, a Flemish-style mansion called Château Gendebien, whose grounds covered twenty-three acres. Predator video could also be seen in certain offices at the Pentagon and in the Situation Room at the White House. But pilots flying strike missions over Yugoslavia had no Predator screens in their cockpits, and their controllers at Vicenza found it nearly impossible to talk pilots onto targets they could see on Predator screens at the CAOC. Even a flier who could spot a Predator in the air had no way of knowing exactly what the cameras housed in drone's sensor ball were seeing or even what direction the lens was pointing. Part of the problem was the "soda straw" view offered by the drone's cameras; part of the problem was the homogeneity of houses and roads in that part of the world. Air controllers might tell a pilot to look for a tank or armored car hiding behind "that house with the orange roof in the cul-de-sac," but lots of neighborhoods had cul-de-sacs and nearly every house had an orange tile roof.

The Allied air commander himself, Lieutenant General Short, had experienced this problem firsthand. Short was in his Vicenza office about 5:00 p.m. one day when the red phone on his desk rang. That meant someone senior to him was calling—in this case, General Clark, who was peering at a Predator screen and "trying to figure out why the system wasn't working," as Clark put it years later.

"Mike, I'm . . . looking at live Predator video," Clark told Short.

As Short recollected it later, his immediate response was to think: *Don't you have something better to do? Isn't there a president or a prime minister or somebody you ought to be talking to?* But then Clark said he had just seen three Serb tanks on a road outside Kosovo's capital, Pristina, and he told Short that it was "imperative" that those tanks be destroyed before dark.

"Sir, I'm not normally in the business of getting involved in attacks on individual tanks, but I'll certainly go down and take a look," the air commander responded.

When he got to the CAOC, Short found a young major with a Predator screen tracking the tanks Clark had seen. By radio, the major was trying to help an A-10 Warthog fighter pilot find and attack the tanks. But the A-10 pilot couldn't find what the Predator was seeing even when given geographical coordinates for the target; the Warthog's inertial navigation system lacked GPS and tended to drift into imprecision after a couple of hours in the air. The young captain in the cockpit and the major in the CAOC were getting ever more frustrated and testy—especially after Short arrived and told the major that General Clark "wants those three tanks killed."

"A lot of interest in killing those tanks, four twenty-one," the major told the pilot. "I'd like you to work on it."

"Roger," the young pilot replied, but after another couple of minutes, he still couldn't find the tanks.

"ComAirSouth and SACEUR are real interested in killing those tanks," the major pressed, referring to Short and Clark by the acronyms for their titles. "Have you got them yet?"

"Negative," responded the pilot.

Short embellished the story at an Air Force Association meeting the following winter, telling the gathering that after the major told the A-10 pilot that "General Short really wants those tanks killed," the pilot finally grew so exasperated that he sputtered over the radio, "God damn it, Dad, I can't see the fucking tanks!" Years later, after that tale had been repeated as gospel in books and doctoral dissertations, Short admitted that the A-10 pilot was not, in fact, his son. But the incident occurred and the point was the same. The high altitude/low collateral damage imperative frustrated pilots over Kosovo that spring and was a major hindrance for NATO. Especially after the phone call from General Clark, Mike Short and other commanders knew they had a problem to solve, and they were in the market for creative solutions.

One Friday afternoon in early April 1999, Colonel Snake Clark was trying to wrap up work in his Pentagon office and head home for the weekend when his phone rang. Clark's caller that day was General Mike Ryan, who had succeeded General Ron Fogleman as Air Force chief of staff in October 1997. Before Fogleman retired, he and Ryan had a conversation about staff, and Fogleman told his successor, "You don't know Snake Clark, but you need to get to know him, because he can do things for you. But he will piss people off, so you've got to provide some top cover for this guy." Fogleman explained to Ryan that Snake Clark was the sort of person who knew how to accomplish things the Air Force as an institution had "antibodies against." Ryan took Fogleman's advice and soon came to depend on Clark much as Fogleman had done.

Ryan told Clark that NATO air commander Short was "real concerned" that the Predator lacked the necessary technology to provide Allied pilots with an accurate position of a target spotted by the drone's camera.

"I know," Clark replied. "It doesn't exist."

"Invent it," Ryan ordered.

Short had discussed the problem with the commander of U.S. Air Forces Europe, General John P. Jumper, a fighter pilot with a knack for innovation. Jumper had in turn called Ryan and suggested several ideas.

Clark started arranging to fly to Vicenza immediately to discuss the problem with the staff at the CAOC. Then he phoned Werner, now under contract to Big Safari. As Clark knew, the technoscientist had been working off and on for three years with software engineers from General Atomics on an improvement to the Predator's video system that might ease General Short's problem, if not entirely solve it. Werner's idea was to embed metadata—information about an image that can't actually be seen in the image, such as geographic coordinates—in the Predator's video. Formatted so a computer could read it, the embedded metadata could be extracted and used to generate a moving digital terrain map with a graphic overlay, shown on a separate screen. The graphics consisted of a trapezoid showing the precise spot on the ground being viewed by the Predator's sensors, plus a symbol representing the location of the Predator itself, both overlays generated in real time. To generate this exploitation support data, as Werner named it, all the operators needed was a laptop computer, two devices to encode and decode data in video images, and a few cables. And Werner knew the system worked: he had had it installed in a Predator ground control station and tested it three times before Operation Allied Force kicked off. Because no official requirement for such a system existed, though, Air Combat Command had made Werner uninstall the experiment within thirty days each time he tested it.

Before Clark left for Vicenza, he also called Bill Grimes, who had another idea for a way to help allied aircraft see and strike mobile targets in the Balkans. "We could put a laser designator on this thing," the Big Safari director told Clark.

Equipping a drone with a laser designator wasn't a new idea. The Army's ill-fated Aquila, cancelled in 1987, was supposed to carry a laser designator to guide artillery shells to targets. More recently, some in Congress had proposed putting laser designators and even weapons on drones, including the Predator. Obvious as the idea might be, however, adding such a device to an existing aircraft was no simple matter, which made the order to do so more than daunting when Grimes gave it to Captain Brian Raduenz and added, "You've got to find something you can put on in two weeks."

Raduenz (pronounced "RUH-deens") was an eleven-year Air Force veteran who had just turned thirty-three. A native of Eveleth, Minnesota, home of the U.S. Hockey Hall of Fame, Raduenz had ranked second academically out of 105 students in his 1984 graduating class at Eveleth High School but won an appointment to the Air Force Academy primarily to play hockey. The academy's hockey coaches at the time, who recruited him, were also from Eveleth. Raduenz graduated from the academy in 1988 and four years later earned a master's degree in electrical engineering at the Air Force Institute of Technology, located near Big Safari's headquarters at Wright-Patterson Air Force Base. More brainy than brawny for a hockey player, Raduenz was also unusual for an engineer: gregarious, cheerful, and endowed with a puckish sense of humor. His 110-page master's thesis bore the technically severe title "Digital Signal Processing Using Lapped Transforms with Variable Parameter Windows and Orthonormal Bases." The paper's preface, however, ended with this sentence: "Finally, I must thank my wonderful parents, whose love and devotion made me the great guy that I am today."

Assigned to work on the Compass Call program at Wright-Patterson after finishing his master's, Raduenz joined Big Safari in 1994, his first green door assignment, and was sent to Detachment 2 at an airfield in Greenville, Texas, where secret modifications to RC-135s of various configurations were done. As in hockey, an aptitude for creative, unselfish teamwork was an asset in Big Safari, and Raduenz thrived there. Raduenz's work in Greenville led Grimes to take him along to Saudi Arabia in May 1997 to talk to officials in Riyadh about a version of Rivet Joint the Saudis were to buy from the United States, and their first stop was Bahrain. They arrived on May 9 and, after checking in at the Bahrain Hilton, met in the hotel's swanky bar for drinks and dinner. After they'd both had a couple of cocktails, Raduenz seized the opportunity to talk to the boss about his future—and got a welcome surprise.

After more than four years with Big Safari, Raduenz told Grimes, he was due to be reassigned to a regular Air Force job unless he could line up another green door assignment, which was what he wanted. Raduenz didn't say so, but sitting in Bahrain in a sport jacket and open-collar shirt having drinks with Bill Grimes, whose wispy gray beard and wrinkled khaki trousers were good camouflage for a mind crammed with important secrets, was a hell of a lot more fun than sitting in uniform behind a desk in an office building at some dreary Air Force base or in the Pentagon.

The bar was nearly empty, but Grimes cast a conspiratorial glance to either side, then leaned toward Raduenz and told him in a low voice, "I have something I've been working on. I briefed Congress on how we would do it, and I told them I could run it with a captain and a couple of good enlisted guys, and if that happens, I want you to go head that up."

Raduenz felt a tingle go up his spine.

"I can't talk about it right now in any detail, but it's a UAV program," Grimes added, prompting Raduenz to give him a quizzical look. UAVs were supposed to be anathema in Big Safari after the way DarkStar and Global Hawk had siphoned off money in recent years.

"This one's different," Grimes said, as if reading Raduenz's mind. "This one actually works."

"You mean the Predator?" Raduenz whispered eagerly.

Now Grimes gave Raduenz a look. "That's the one," he said, "but you can't breathe a word of this to anybody. If it gets out what's going on, it could kill the whole thing. Nobody knows I went up there and briefed Congress on how we would do this. If they find out, it could really mess things up."

No one found out, and in August 1998 Raduenz and five other engineers and technicians—"I cherry-picked them," Grimes said years later— opened what Big Safari called its Operating Location Detachment 4 in a corner of the General Atomics manufacturing plant at Rancho Bernardo, California. Now, a mere eight months later, Raduenz's tiny team had been given two weeks to put a laser designator on the Predator. There wouldn't be a moment to spare.

On Saturday April 17, three days after Raduenz and his team got under way, four Raytheon engineers arrived at the General Atomics facility in Rancho Bernardo with their company's AN/AAS-44(V), a gray device that vaguely resembled the head of some disembodied *Star Wars* robot. Unlike the smooth, round, white Wescam Model 14, the standard camera-carrying "sensor ball" beneath and just behind the Predator's bulbous nose, Raytheon's Forty-Four ball was a rugged sphere with sliding surfaces and two round and two rectangular apertures in its aluminum skin. The round apertures were very different in size, and instead of allowing light to enter a camera, the smaller aperture allowed the Forty-Four ball to shine a laser designator's beam at a target. After propping the Forty-Four ball up on a stand atop a conference room table, the four Raytheon engineers gave a small group of General Atomics engineers and the Big Safari team a tutorial on how the ball's infrared camera and laser designator worked.

A laser—the word is actually an acronym for "light amplification by stimulated emission of radiation"—emits a stream of electromagnetic pulses in a fashion similar to radar but on a far shorter wave length. A laser designator beam is pencil-thin, allowing it to be aimed, rather than broadcast like a radio signal, but the beam is a narrow cone that expands as it travels, and when it hits an object the light scatters in every direction. A bomb or missile carrying a seeker tuned to the same wave length and programmed to recognize a code embedded in the designator's beam picks up this so-called sparkle and follows it to the target. It's a highly accurate way to guide a weapon, and both beam and sparkle are invisible to the naked eye.

An officer at Big Safari's headquarters in Dayton had discovered the Forty-Four ball in a phone call to Raytheon after rejecting other possibilities from conventional Air Force sources. The Forty-Four was bigger and heavier than the Predator's normal Wescam sensor ball, but its laser designator was cutting edge. There were only two drawbacks. First, the Raytheon ball lacked a daylight camera, so Predators carrying it would lose their color video capability. Second, although Raytheon was manufacturing seventy of the balls, the Navy owned them all and was installing them on antisubmarine warfare helicopters.

Breaking into a service bureaucracy's schedule to borrow or buy even a few laser balls was a tall order, but after some high-level phone calls the Navy agreed to sell the Air Force four Forty-Four balls—at a premium of roughly 40 percent. For the engineers, meanwhile, there was a lot to do. The Forty-Four needed a slightly different tray to sit on inside the

Predator's fuselage to accommodate its greater weight and keep its laser and infrared beams steady as the drone flew. Electrical and other connections between the ball and the aircraft and the aircraft and its ground control station had to be altered. A small cadre of company and Air Force pilots and sensor operators had to learn to use the laser ball. Mechanics had to be shown how to service and repair it.

Like many of the others, Raduenz was at work every morning by seven and knocked off at midnight, day in and day out, for the next five weeks. There were no Saturdays, no Sundays. Sometimes he didn't even know what day it was. He was running on adrenaline. He was working harder than ever before. He was also having the time of his life.

Raduenz and the other engineers creatively noodled their way through a thicket of software and electrical dilemmas. The General Atomics facility was too small to test the ball's infrared sensor, so Raduenz and Jeff Hettick, a senior company software engineer, put the ball on a cart, wheeled it back against a wall, opened a door on the other side of the lab, and aimed the infrared camera at the side of a distant building. By six days into the project, the team had installed the ball on a Predator and shipped it to El Mirage to test its aerodynamics. After a General Atomics crew flew a Predator carrying the new ball on a test flight there, the project moved to Indian Springs in Nevada, where Captain Scott Swanson and a couple of Air Force sensor operators would fly tests.

Big Safari had to borrow Swanson, Major Scott Hill, and the sensor operators because Air Combat Command, the Predator's putative operator, wanted nothing to do with this "hobby shop" project, as Grimes heard one of ACC's people disdainfully call it. Big Safari and ACC had long been butting heads over their utterly opposite philosophies. Big Safari was about innovation; ACC was about regimentation. When Big Safari and General Atomics proposed gluing two-inch-by-two-inch blocks of half-inch-thick plywood inside the wheel wells of early model Predators to stop the landing gear wheels from chafing the fuselage's composite walls, ACC took four months to approve the "modification." ACC approved it, moreover, only after Big Safari and General Atomics wrote a technical order specifying how many tenths of an inch of plywood must rub away before mechanics replaced the wood patches. Now the 11th RS commander refused to let his crews in Tuzla fly the Predators with laser designators because the modification lacked an Air Force manual to guide operators and mechanics—all the crews had was a Navy manual. Grimes was still fuming about the incident more than a decade later. "You're at war and you won't fly a new capability?" he said. "That's not my kind of warrior."

On May 4, 1999, just one day shy of three weeks after Big Safari got the assignment, General Atomics pilot Edwin Kimzey flew the first Predator carrying a Forty-Four ball from Indian Springs over a Nellis Air Force Base test range, where an Air Force sensor operator lased mock targets for F-15E and A-10 ground attack aircraft. No bombs were dropped, but an A-10's laser tracker verified that the Predator's laser spot was on target. The Big Safari and contractor teams were elated—until the Predator landed.

When it did, the drone's spidery front landing gear collapsed. Raduenz watched in horror as the Predator's nose and the Raytheon ball smacked onto the concrete, bounced three times, then skittered down the runway as the aircraft rolled to a stop. The only Forty-Four ball they had was intact but damaged beyond immediate repair—a serious setback. When the team later watched video recorded by the Predator's nose camera during the accident, the view began straight ahead, suddenly fell to the ground, shook as the drone's nose bounced, then showed a steady but jittery image of concrete while the Predator rolled to a stop. The camera kept recording for a bit, showing nothing but a small square of concrete, until an out-of-focus bug of some kind crawled through the picture, an oblivious and unharmed passerby.

The room roared with laughter.

The accident delayed the project eight days, but on May 13 the team flew a different Predator with a new Forty-Four ball under its nose on a second test at Nellis, this time lasing targets for actual bomb drops by F-15Es. Three of four bombs hit their targets. The fourth missed because of a weapon malfunction.

Ten days later, a massive C-17 Globemaster transport plane landed at Tuzla Air Base carrying three Predators, three Forty-Four balls, a ground control station modified to control the laser designator, four crews of operators trained to use it, including three General Atomics pilots, and a handful of Air Force maintainers. The C-17, put under Colonel Snake Clark's direction for this special mission, had flown the more than six thousand miles from Nellis to Tuzla nonstop, refueling in midair to get the modified Predators into the war in Bosnia quickly. They were met at Tuzla by Clark, who scoffed when Lieutenant Colonel Dana Richards, the 11th Reconnaissance Squadron commander and one of those on board the C-17, told him they needed to fly to Rhein-Main Air Base at Frank-furt, Germany, before unloading their cargo. Regulations required any-one reporting for duty at Tuzla to get personal weapons, chemical warfare gear, and mandatory training in spotting land mines and other hazards in Bosnia before assuming their duties, Richards pointed out.

"We don't need any of that crap," Clark said, and loudly ordered Richards off the plane. "If it comes down to these seventeen Predator guys with nine millimeter sidearms holding off the Serbian hordes at the gate, I think the party's over."

Earlier, the Air National Guard colonel in charge of the base had argued the same point with Clark. "They'll get their training, they'll get their weapons, but these guys are here at the direction of the chief of staff of the Air Force," Clark had assured his nominal peer. Then the master Pentagon Poker player pulled out his cell phone and asked if the colonel wanted to discuss it with the chief of staff. "I could arrange that phone call," Clark said.

The base commander folded.

The arrival of the new team fit neatly under a rubric for the laser desig-nator project thought up by Big Safari's first, and at that point only, Preda-tor sensor operator, a crusty master sergeant from Maine named Jeff A. Guay. "Gunny" Guay, thirty-nine, had spent most of his twenty-two years in the Air Force as an imagery analyst, plying his trade in part on Big Safari aircraft. He was just the kind of guy Grimes loved: a renegade who was innovative, resourceful, and not afraid to stir things up. By the time the Big Safari team got to Tuzla, Guay had dubbed their mission Project WILD Predator.

WILD, Guay explained, stood for "Wartime Integrated Laser Desig-nator." He liked the acronym. It described the ride they were on.

_____

In late April, Werner arrived in Tuzla and installed his exploitation support data mapping system in a ground control station being used by the
11th RS. That allowed controllers at the CAOC to see precisely where the
Predator's camera was looking in real time and thus give pilots better
directions, though it could still be hard to talk them onto targets. Snake
Clark used his pull at Air Force headquarters to make sure ACC declared
Werner's invention a standard element of the Predator system.

Using the WILD Predators was less simple. Mechanical and other
"haste makes waste" problems kept the Big Safari team from flying a
CAOC-directed operational mission with the WILD Predators for the
first ten days they were at Tuzla. Instead, they tested the laser designator
in a couple of training flights by using it to point out mock targets to
planes, which allowed the fighter pilots to confirm that their laser gear
could see the Forty-Four ball's laser spot.

Only on June 2 were Swanson and Guay directed to buddy-lase a target in Kosovo for an A-10 Warthog attack plane controlled by the CAOC
in Vicenza, a mission that would be reported as operational but was in
fact more a test than an act of war. Swanson circled the Predator while
Guay put the crosshairs of the laser designator on a derelict shed they
were told was the target. When the A-10 arrived, Guay shone the Forty-
Four ball's laser beam on the shed so the A-10's laser tracker, called a Pave
Penny, could pick it up. Swanson and Guay listened through their green
headsets as the CAOC and the pilot talked. The only noise in the ground
control station was the hum of its air-conditioning and the whirring of
the many fans keeping computers and other electronic equipment cool.

"What's your code?" the pilot asked the controller, referring to a four-
digit number needed to connect the Pave Penny to the Predator's laser
beam. The answer came back, and the pilot punched the code into a keyboard in the cockpit. "I've got your spot," the pilot said, then released a
laser-guided five-hundred-pound bomb. Swanson, Guay, and the others in the ground control station kept their eyes on the shed. Something
suddenly streaked across the screen, and the building disappeared in a
blinding burst of white.

"Woo hoo!" Guay shouted as the screen momentarily whited out. Then he traded high fives with Swanson and some other officers who had been watching over their shoulders in the ground control station.

The WILD Predator never got closer to combat—by coincidence, Serbia agreed to peace terms the day after the successful test. By July 2 the three Predators and their Forty-Four balls were on their way back to El Mirage. On October 1, Captain Brian Raduenz was promoted to major. In a ceremony at General Atomics, Bill Grimes donned his old colonel's uniform and ceremoniously pinned a major's golden oak leaves onto his protégé's collar. In photos of the event, Grimes beams like a proud father.

In truth, the laser designator experiment was more educational than effective, though the team's rapid work would garner medals for some. The WILD Predator unit's daily maintenance report for June, however, said that "all sorties with the AN/AAS-44 installed experienced high occurrences of Ku lost link failures." Electromagnetic interference between the laser ball and the Ku-band satellite dish in the Predator's nose was suspected. Shortly after Operation Allied Force ended, Big Safari was directed by Air Combat Command headquarters to take the Forty-Four balls off the three WILD Predators, put the laser balls in a warehouse, and reinstall standard Wescam balls. The laser designator had been a wartime expedient, the directive noted, not a modification approved through normal channels.

Though short-lived and unwelcome in some quarters, the WILD Predator opened eyes. To those paying attention, it was now clear that this drone could do more than carry sensors and watch a war. Properly equipped, the Predator might become lethal.

7

THE SUMMER PROJECT

After forty years at the CIA, Charles E. Allen was already a legend when he became assistant director of central intelligence for collection on June 2, 1998. Allen had survived a bit part in the 1986–87 Iran-Contra Affair; he had also famously predicted Saddam Hussein's 1990 invasion of Kuwait. Now Allen was in charge of coordinating all secret intelligence gathering by the CIA and by more than a dozen other agencies of the U.S. government.

Sixty-six days after he took on that sweeping responsibility, the big, bearish, bullheaded workaholic acquired an obsession. On August 7, Al Qaeda terrorists smashed suicide truck bombs into the U.S. embassies in Dar es Salaam, Tanzania, and Nairobi, Kenya, killing 213 people and wounding more than 4,500. Among the dead were a dozen Americans, including two CIA employees. Seven months earlier, Osama bin Laden had declared war on the United States in the name of Islam for the second time since 1996. Bin Laden and Al Qaeda had long been on the CIA's threat list, but from the day of the embassy bombings on, Charlie Allen's chief goal in life was to destroy Al Qaeda—and see as many of its leaders as possible captured or killed, beginning with the elusive Osama bin Laden.

Success was equally elusive. After the embassy bombings, Allen held a daily meeting on bin Laden in the soundproof conference room of his sixth-floor office at CIA headquarters, where representatives of various intelligence agencies and other offices discussed how to anticipate or discover Al Qaeda's plans and find the terrorist group's leaders. Officers from the CIA's Counterterrorist Center, known as the CTC, participated, as did the agency's special bin Laden desk, designated Alec Station after the son of the unit's first director. Also taking part were members of the CIA's Directorate of Operations—the agency's cloak-and-dagger arm—and officials and experts from the National Security Agency, the Defense Intelligence Agency, the military's Joint Staff, and the National Imagery and Mapping Agency. Allen found the sessions a useful way to prep for more exclusive daily meetings with the CIA's executive director on the same topic, and for "deep dive" meetings on Al Qaeda convened by Director George Tenet once or twice a week.

Despite all this deliberation, concrete information and good ideas were hard to come by, and President Bill Clinton's initial response to the embassy bombings disappointed Allen and many others. On August 20, Clinton ordered cruise missile strikes in retaliation. Thirteen missiles were aimed at a pharmaceutical plant in Khartoum, Sudan, suspected of being used to produce the nerve gas VX for Al Qaeda. Sixty-six cruise missiles hit an Al Qaeda training camp near Khost, Afghanistan, where intelligence indicated bin Laden might be that day. Both targets were destroyed—and both strikes proved an embarrassment to the United States. No evidence of chemical weapons was found at the plant in Khartoum, whose destruction put about three hundred people out of work, killed a night watchman, and obliterated the source of more than half of Sudan's legitimate drugs. The strikes in Afghanistan killed twenty to thirty people, according to CIA estimates, but neither bin Laden nor any other Al Qaeda leader was among them.

That same month, Clinton signed a Memorandum of Notification authorizing the CIA to use tribal proxy forces to capture bin Laden or his associates. The Navy, meanwhile, was ordered to keep submarines able to fire cruise missiles within range of Afghanistan, ready to attack if bin Laden was spotted. Five days before Christmas, the Agency learned that bin Laden was to spend the night at the governor's house in Kandahar, the spiritual home of his Taliban allies. But after the military argued that a cruise missile blast might kill too many innocent people in the urban setting, those running a major White House meeting on what to do decided against a strike.

In February and again in May 1999, HUMINT (for "human intelligence," meaning spies or other people) reported bin Laden's presence at locations that cruise missiles might strike without risk of "collateral damage." The CIA and the military, however, were unable to verify that the Al Qaeda leader was there. Satellites could take photos of locations and buildings where bin Laden might be, but the images came in hours later, providing no certainty of success if used as the basis for a missile strike. Clinton administration officials were wary of launching another strike that might backfire, especially after faulty intelligence led U.S. forces to mistakenly bomb the Chinese embassy in Belgrade, Yugoslavia, in May of that year during the air campaign in Kosovo.

By early 2000, eighteen months after the embassy bombings in Africa, the CIA's Afghan agents and allies had reported several sightings of bin Laden and claimed to have made unsuccessful attempts of their own to assassinate him, leaving Allen and others increasingly frustrated. In early April, the National Security Council's top counterterrorism official, Richard Clarke, wrote a strongly worded memo to his old friend Charlie Allen requesting a detailed report on everything being done to find bin Laden and demanding suggestions for new initiatives. As far back as 1996, Clarke had argued that the CIA should be authorized to kill terrorists who wanted to kill Americans—a view regarded as radical in those days—and he thought the CIA now had that authority under Clinton's August 1998 Memorandum of Notification. Clarke also urged Allen to meet with Vice Admiral Scott Fry, director of operations for the military's Joint Staff, who had complained to the NSC that keeping a submarine "in the basket," as the Navy called it, in the hope of attacking bin Laden was a waste of expensive resources.

Not long afterward, Allen met with Fry at the three-star admiral's office in the Pentagon. "I think we might have a game changer," Fry said, explaining that he wanted to tell Allen about it "because no one else seems interested." Then they walked down the hall to see one of Fry's subordinates, Air Force Brigadier General Scott Gration, the Joint Staff's deputy director for operations. Earlier that year, Gration had asked Fry to let him come up with innovative ways to pinpoint bin Laden's where-abouts and produce the "actionable intelligence" President Clinton wanted before he would order a strike against the Al Qaeda leader.

The military, Gration told Allen, had an extraordinarily powerful telescope able to beam images back to a control station by satellite. If the CIA could sneak the device into Afghanistan and set it up on a moun-taintop, providing a wide-angle view of a place bin Laden or his senior lieutenants were known to frequent, it might be possible to spot him. Once the telescope found him, the Air Force could fly a Predator over-head to keep the terrorist leader in sight long enough for action of some sort to be taken, whether that meant a snatch operation or a cruise mis-sile attack. Whatever was done, using the Predator to keep him in sight would dramatically increase the chances of success. The aircraft might take a few hours to get to the area from its launch point, but it would be able to loiter overhead for twenty-four hours or more, keeping bin Laden in view, or even following him if he departed. With the "persistent dwell" provided by its endurance, the Predator just might make the dif-ference in what so far had been an exasperating exercise.

Allen agreed. The idea was damned exciting, he told Gration.

Allen already knew more than a little about drones. In one of his previous assignments, Allen had worked a bit with General Atomics when the company sold the CIA the Gnat 750s the Agency flew over Bosnia from Albania in 1994. Until the spring of 2000, though, Allen hadn't thought of using a UAV to help solve the problem that had vexed him for almost two years: how to take out bin Laden and learn enough about Al Qaeda to disrupt and if possible defeat the terrorist network.

When he got back to Langley and drafted the report Clarke had requested, Allen included both the telescope and the Predator in his list of new options. He also started talking about those ideas informally with Cofer Black, the head of the CIA's Counterterrorist Center. Black liked the idea, but his boss, James Pavitt, was the CIA's deputy director for operations, and, as Allen would soon learn, Pavitt, who outranked him, was adamantly opposed to both the telescope and the Predator. Planting the telescope was too risky, Pavitt argued, and flying a surveil-lance drone over Afghanistan wouldn't significantly improve their

As a twenty-six-year-old air force officer, Abe Karem placed tenth in his category while representing Israel at the free-flight model World Championships in Austria. Free-flight modeling inspired Karem and schooled him in designing drones with uncommon flight endurance.

By the time Karem was in his early thirties, he was director of preliminary design for Israel Aircraft Industries—and a determined dreamer.

Designing a decoy to fool Egyptian and Syrian defenses that devastated Israel's air force in the 1973 Yom Kippur War led Karem to an epiphany: a remote-control drone armed with antitank missiles might defeat—or, better yet, deter—another invasion of Israel.

Yale students Neal (left) and Linden Blue learned to fly so they could tour Latin America in search of postcollege business opportunities during the summer of 1956. Their daring journey in the *Blue Bird* led the young entrepreneurs into partnership in a banana and cacao plantation in Nicaragua partly owned by the ruling Somoza family.

In August 1986, the *Wall Street Journal* reported that Denver businessmen Neal and Linden Blue were buying Chevron spinoff GA Technologies, a nuclear power company. Neal (far left) decided their renamed General Atomics should expand into unmanned aircraft.

Inspired by the advent of GPS and his desire to help NATO deter a Soviet invasion of Western Europe, Neal Blue decided General Atomics should develop a kamikaze drone. Displayed at a 1988 air show before the company abandoned it and hired bankrupt Abe Karem, this "poor man's cruise missile" was the first Predator.

When President Bill Clinton complained in 1993 that neither the military nor intelligence agencies could find Serb artillery pounding civilians in Bosnia, CIA Director James Woolsey decided a drone could solve the problem. Woolsey also immediately thought of an aeronautical engineer he considered a genius: Abe Karem.

The chief of the CIA's clandestine branch, Thomas A. Twetten (left), visited the General Atomics hangar at El Mirage, California, in March 1993 to see about buying some of the company's drones for spy missions over Bosnia. Satisfied that General Atomics could deliver what the agency wanted, Twetten posed for a photo with the drone's designer, Abe Karem.

Conservative rules during initial Air Force Predator operations in the Balkans in late 1996 left flight crews at the drone's base in Hungary feeling like characters in the movie *Groundhog Day*. On a later deployment, Major Jon Box (center, in flight suit, between man and woman in camouflage) and his detachment were a lot happier.

In May 1999, the first test flight of a Predator rigged to guide bombs to targets ended with the drone nose down on the runway. It wasn't funny at the time, but Colonel Snake Clark (left) and Big Safari Director Bill Grimes (right) later shared a laugh with Air Force Secretary F. Whitten Peters when Clark was presented with a model memorializing the accident.

Special operations helicopter pilot and lifelong computer geek Captain Scott Swanson became Big Safari's first Predator pilot. Swanson was at the drone's controls when the Predator's cameras spotted Osama bin Laden in Afghanistan in September 2000.

Master Sergeant Jeff A. "Gunny" Guay, Big Safari's first Predator sensor operator, was an innovative, resourceful renegade who was never afraid to stir things up. Guay would aim the laser beam that guided the Predator's first lethal missile strike.

As a cocky fighter pilot in Southeast Asia in 1970, Captain Johnny Jumper (third from right) learned to love laser-guided weapons, which hit targets accurately from much safer altitudes for fliers.

As commander of Air Combat Command, General John Jumper decided in 2000 to arm the Predator with laser-guided Hellfire missiles, a project he sped up after some senior officials at the CIA and National Security Council grew interested in using the drone to kill Osama bin Laden.

NSC counterterrorism chief Richard Clarke believed that President Clinton had given the CIA all the authority it needed to kill Osama bin Laden following the Al Qaeda terrorist bombings of two U.S. embassies in Africa in 1998. In the months before 9/11, Clarke was particularly eager to send the armed Predator to kill the terrorist leader before Al Qaeda killed Americans again.

In January 2001, Predator 3034 was chained by its landing gear struts to a concrete pad on a test range at China Lake Naval Weapons Station for a "static ground launch" of a Hellfire to see whether a missile rocketing off its wing would rip the aircraft apart.

Master Sergeant Leo Glovka (left) and Captain Curt Hawes stand triumphantly over the target tank they hit on February 21, 2001, with one of the first Hellfires ever launched from an airborne Predator.

Predator 3034 was initially painted white and bore the marking "WA"—the two-letter base code for Nellis Air Force Base, where the first Hellfire tests were conducted. When 3034 launched the first-ever lethal drone strike, in Afghanistan, the aircraft was painted air superiority grey and bore no markings at all.

In the spring of 2001, the CIA hired a contractor to build a residence typical of Afghanistan as a test target for Predator-launched Hellfire missiles. The adobe building constructed at China Lake bore so little resemblance to an Afghan villa that test participants dubbed it "Taco Bell" and hung up a mock sign advertising "Hellfire Tacos, 3/99¢."

To help the CIA determine whether a Predator-launched Hellfire could kill Osama bin Laden indoors, plywood silhouettes and air pressure and temperature gauges were placed inside the Taco Bell for test shots fired in May and June 2001.

After one Hellfire shot in June, the test team inspecting the interior of the Taco Bell found bits of brick and metal a bit larger than BBs in the plywood silhouettes. They also found multiple holes in the rinds of watermelons, which, to save time and money, had been substituted for the manikins usually used to measure a weapon's lethality.

CIA Director George Tenet, with the NSC's Richard Clarke sitting behind him, watched President Bush address the nation on the evening of September 11, 2001, from the White House bunker. Before that day, Tenet and Clarke were at odds about whether to use the armed Predator to try to kill Osama bin Laden. Afterward, Tenet became a Predator disciple.

Air commander General Chuck Wald, styrofoam cup in hand to catch sunflower seed shells, watches live CIA Predator video with subordinates at an air base in Saudi Arabia as the war in Afghanistan begins. "Who is in control?" Wald fumed to a fellow general after being surprised by the Predator's first missile launch. "I'm ready to fold up and come home."

A special Air Force team launched the first intercontinental drone strikes from a complex on the CIA campus that became known as the Trailer Park. Later, those involved created a memento—a coin embossed with a mobile home built around an armed Predator and bearing a motto reflecting the CIA's shift to ordering Hellfire strikes independently: "Never Mind . . . We'll Do It Ourselves."

chances of doing anything about bin Laden if he were found. Pavitt also made it clear that he did not want money taken out of his budget to pay for such operations.

After getting Allen's report, Clarke called a meeting of the Counter-terrorism Security Group, a committee composed of the head of each federal agency's counterterrorism or security office, to talk about the tele-scope and Predator schemes. When Black described Pavitt's objections, Clarke exploded. The CIA's beloved HUMINT had produced nothing for years, he scoffed. "I want to try something else."

Black coolly replied, "I will take the message back."

Charlie Allen was equally respected and resented at Langley for his aggressive impatience and a tendency to go around people to get his way. He was also renowned for calling 6:30 a.m. meetings, working in his office until 9:00 or later each evening, and spending several hours there every Saturday and most Sundays and holidays. It was surprising, then, that the CIA's deputy director, Air Force General John A. Gordon, found Allen at home when he telephoned him there on Memorial Day 2000. But the general wasn't calling to trade pleasantries. Gordon had planned to spend the holiday at a picnic on a wealthy friend's Baltimore estate. Instead, largely thanks to Allen, the deputy director was on his way to Langley—and he was boiling mad.

Since asking his old friend for a report on new ways to hunt bin Laden, Richard Clarke and Allen had had several back-channel conversations about the Al Qaeda leader and the Predator. On April 25, Clarke had sent a memo to members of the Counterterrorism Security Group titled "Afghan Eyes." In it, he advocated having the CIA fly the Predator to search for bin Laden. Formally, the Agency had yet to respond. Told by Clarke that the CIA was dragging its feet, President Clinton's national security adviser, Sandy Berger, chose Memorial Day to send a message demanding to know the Agency's position on the issue.

When Gordon got Allen on the phone early that Monday morning, he wasted little time. "Get in here!" he shouted.

"Yes, sir," Allen replied.

When the meeting in the director's seventh-floor conference room began, Cofer Black and others from the CTC were at the table. So was their boss, James Pavitt; like Gordon, Pavitt was clearly not happy to be there.

"What the hell is all this about?" Gordon asked Allen.

"Well, we want to change the situation in Afghanistan," Allen said. Then he explained how a covert Predator operation might work. To fly and take care of the Predators they used, the CIA could borrow Air Force crews and hire General Atomics technicians. After taking off and landing in a country neighboring Afghanistan, the Predator could circle over an area for hours, sending its video back to Washington, just as it had done for the military from Bosnia.

"Why would we want to do this?" Pavitt demanded.

The cost would be minimal, and the payoff potentially large, Allen replied. Allen then explained the high-powered telescope's role in the operation. His staff had thought through where to put it and how to get it there. One good spot might be a mountain near Darunta, where one of bin Laden's associates, Abu Khabab, was said by Afghan sources to be holed up in a camp known to the CIA, experimenting with chemical and maybe biological weapons by killing dogs and videotaping their death throes. Maybe some followers of Northern Alliance leader and U.S. ally Ahmad Shah Massoud, the Taliban's chief indigenous foe, would help a CIA paramilitary team carry the telescope over the mountains from Pakistan and set it up overlooking the area.

Pavitt dismissed that scheme. "We're not going to risk our people humping all this equipment over all these mountains and putting it up," he declared.

"The biggest thing, of course, is to fly the Predator, which has both infrared and electro-optical capabilities," Allen continued. With the Predator, the CIA could look for bin Laden night and day, and increase its knowledge of Al Qaeda and the Taliban in the bargain.

The debate lasted three hours, from about 10:00 a.m. until 1:00 p.m., with neither Allen nor Pavitt giving ground, but both frequently raising their voices. Allen sensed that Gordon, wearing blue jeans and clearly still hoping to make it to his Baltimore picnic, was only getting angrier as the discussion wore on. It was a "very ugly scene," Allen recalled years later. "I still smart over it." It also ended in a stalemate.

The next day, CIA Director George Tenet was briefed on the Memorial Day meeting. When he and Allen discussed the matter, Tenet asked, "Why do I care whether I have an image of a guy, whether he's six feet four or six feet?"

"Because we need to find and identify this individual," Allen said. "We need to be able to locate him, know where he is, track him, geolocate him, and take whatever action's required."

Four weeks later, on June 25, Richard Clarke sent Tenet a memo saying that other agencies in the Counterterrorism Security Group "are unanimous that the Predator project is our highest near-term priority and that funding should be shifted to it." The CIA had been resisting the idea partly because the project was expected to cost three to four million dollars, a relative pittance by Pentagon standards but serious money for the CIA. Four days after Tenet received Clarke's memo, the so-called Small Group, a special interagency committee of top officials cleared to see the most sensitive information concerning bin Laden, approved Clarke's Afghan Eyes plan. Under an arrangement imposed by the White House, the Defense Department and CIA would share the costs.

As part of this compromise, the operation would be considered a mere test of the idea that a Predator could find Osama bin Laden. The CIA and the Air Force would try using the drone to hunt the terrorist leader. What came next would depend on how well the experiment worked.

Several days after the Afghan Eyes decision, Snake Clark phoned Captain Scott Swanson at Indian Springs Air Force Auxiliary Field in Nevada. Scraped out of the desert forty-five miles northwest of Las Vegas after the Japanese attack on Pearl Harbor in 1941, by the summer of 2000 the onetime Army Air Forces gunnery training field was home to the Air Force's 11th and 15th Reconnaissance Squadrons, the Air Combat Command units that flew Predators. For Swanson, however, Indian Springs was only a temporary home.

That spring, encouraged by Major Brian Raduenz and others who worked with Swanson during the WILD Predator experiment in the Balkans the year before, Big Safari Director Bill Grimes had asked the former special operations helicopter pilot if he'd like a green door assignment as the technology shop's chief Predator operator. The job would mean transferring from the 11th RS in Nevada to Big Safari's operating location at the General Atomics plant in Rancho Bernardo, California, just north of San Diego. *Single guy, San Diego, doing more of this neat stuff?* Swanson had asked himself. *Sure.* Swanson was still at Indian Springs only because his official orders to move to California had yet to take effect, which was why Snake Clark was calling from the Pentagon.

Clark wanted to know if Swanson could put together—without attracting attention—a briefing on the Predator and a flight demonstration for "a bunch of people in suits" who would be visiting Indian Springs in a few days. Bill Grimes would be among them, as would senior people from the CIA, the NSC, and other intelligence and military agencies. Clark and Grimes wanted Swanson to show the visitors what the Predator could do if used for a special mission in what Clark said was "a rugged part of the world." Clark was vague about what kind of mission, but Swanson read intelligence briefings. He could guess.

The dozen or so "high political rollers," as Swanson viewed them, spent a couple of hours at Indian Springs on the afternoon of July 12. Swanson briefed his visitors on the Predator's capabilities, showed them how it operated, and gave them a tour of the GCS. Then he answered their questions, some of which seemed to confirm his suspicions. By the time the members of the traveling party climbed back into their air-conditioned bus and drove away, Swanson was pretty sure he knew what kind of special mission the government officials had in mind.

A few days later, Swanson learned that Grimes and the rest of the delegation must have liked his briefing. The Predator was going to Afghanistan to hunt Osama bin Laden, and Scott Swanson would be the operation's chief pilot. Swanson thought that was neat stuff indeed.

Those planning the operation needed to solve a number of tricky problems. First, where could the Air Force put the ground control station?

This was a major issue, for although the Predator was flown largely through the Ku-band satellite dish in its nose, taking off or landing via satellite link wasn't recommended. To be relayed through a satellite in geostationary orbit, signals from the GCS to the Predator, and vice versa, had to travel about 25,000 miles into space and 25,000 miles back to Earth. The signals also had to be processed on each end by equipment that added milliseconds to their trip. Even with the signals traveling at 186,000 miles per second, there was enough delay between a pilot's commands and the aircraft's response, and the pilot's reaction to that response, and the pilot's next move, to make takeoffs and landings risky. Once in flight, the Predator flew largely on autopilot, so the roughly one-second signal latency caused by the satellite connection was less problematic. But for takeoffs and landings, crews always used the line-of-sight C-band link; they switched to Ku-band once the drone was airborne to extend the Predator's range over the horizon and switched back to land. This was why the Predator couldn't fly much farther than four hundred or five hundred miles from its landing point if it was going to loiter over a target area for the optimum seventeen to twenty-two hours.

Which posed a problem. Draw a circle with a five-hundred-mile radius on a map of Afghanistan and the center of the circle located at Tarnak Farms—a rundown agricultural complex near Kandahar where the Taliban had settled bin Laden and his wives and children in 1997— and the circumference will run through Iran, Pakistan, Tajikistan, Turkmenistan, and Uzbekistan. Even if any of the friendly countries on that list granted the United States permission to base Predators on its soil, there was no way to bring in all the equipment and personnel needed and still keep the operation covert. Besides a GCS, the operators would need a satellite earth terminal with a large antenna, a shelter where the aircraft could be kept and serviced, accommodation for several dozen people— you might as well put up a billboard.

Which raised a question. How remote from the Predator could the drone's controls be located? Could the three key elements of the system— the aircraft, the GCS, and the satellite earth terminal—be split up? What if the drone were launched somewhere near Afghanistan by a crew using the usual line-of-sight C-band link, then switched to the usual Ku-band satellite link, but then simultaneously taken over by a different crew in a full-up GCS that was far distant but somewhere within satellite range? The crew flying the Ku-band segment could perform the mission, then hand the Predator back to the first crew, who could land it using the C-band link. If the drone's flight were split up this way, the GCS and satellite terminal needn't be located with the Predator near Afghanistan; instead, they could be located someplace unobtrusive—at a U.S. air base in Europe, say, where security would be good and no one would pay much attention to a freight container or one more satellite dish.

Was something like that possible? That was the question Bill Grimes put to Werner that spring, as the Afghan Eyes proposal was being debated at higher reaches of the U.S. government's national security apparatus. Others within the Air Force and the intelligence community had tried to answer the same question but had come away stumped. Werner, however, reported back after a quick review of technical issues that "split operations," as he suggested they call the concept, could be done—just not easily.

Providing a stripped-down pilot console that could be located with a small maintenance facility at a base in Central Asia and used to take off and land the drone via C-band link wouldn't be particularly difficult. But finding a satellite that covered much of Afghanistan would be a challenge, since the typical satellite beam creates a footprint—usually amoeba-shaped—only five hundred to a thousand miles in diameter. It would be an even greater challenge to find a satellite that not only covered Afghanistan but also had an antenna able to communicate with the Predator. The Predator's Ku-band transmitter was so weak that it "whispered" to a satellite, as Werner put it, and the drone's Ku-band dish was so small it could barely "hear" what a satellite transmitted back. Beyond those problems, there weren't a lot of satellites in geostationary orbit whose footprint covered Afghanistan—because, as Werner observed, "satellite operators realized that not many goat herders and mountain dwellers were equipped with satellite receivers." The only candidate he could find, in fact, was a Dutch satellite aimed at India whose roughly circular footprint offered marginal coverage of Afghanistan.

Given those limitations, Werner later mused that "no satellite engineer in his right mind" would try to operate the Predator over Afghanistan using this method. Even so, he saw a way to make it work. The Air Force could fly the drone using New Skies Satellites' NSS-703. But the service would also need to put an earth terminal with an enormous dish antenna—an ear big enough to pick up the Predator's whispers—somewhere in Europe. Werner researched that, too, and found that the Air Force had only three terminals that were both large enough to do the job and sufficiently mobile to be packed into cargo aircraft and flown to Europe. Two were untouchable. The third was a terminal with an antenna dish eleven meters (more than thirty-six feet) in diameter called the Transportable Medium Earth Terminal, or TMET (pronounced "TEE-met"). The TMET was located in southern Virginia, at Langley Air Force Base. It belonged to Air Combat Command.

When Bill Grimes heard it was ACC's, he couldn't help but grin.

One day in early August, a crew of about twenty contractors showed up at Langley Air Force Base with a couple of big trucks, a heavy crane, a satellite earth terminal with a 6.2-meter dish, and a set of special, classified orders. After unloading the terminal they'd brought along, they dismantled ACC's TMET and its 11-meter dish, packed it on pallets, and set up the smaller 6.2-meter dish in its place. Then they loaded their trucks and drove away with the TMET.

The next morning, Werner got a call from the same ACC chief master sergeant who had ordered the laser designators taken off the WILD Predators the previous year. He was irate. Where was his satellite terminal? he demanded.

Werner looked at his watch. "Right now, it's at Dover Air Force Base in Delaware," he said, adding that the TMET was waiting to be picked up by a huge C-5 Galaxy cargo plane. The C-5 was going to take the terminal to a location he wasn't at liberty to divulge, but Big Safari had brought ACC a replacement satellite terminal with a 6.2-meter dish, Werner pointed out.

"After explaining that none of his satellite services were being interrupted or even diminished," Werner recalled years later, "I seemed to unclaw him from the ceiling just a bit."

A couple of weeks after the July 12 Predator demonstration at Indian Springs, Captain Scott Swanson threw most of his clothes in the backseat of his gold 1995 Lexus ES 300. Then he headed southwest on I-15 for his new assignment to Big Safari's office in the General Atomics Predator plant near San Diego. Along the way, Swanson took a side trip to the General Atomics flight control center at El Mirage to see a test of Werner's new split operations concept. Now refined, the plan was for a pilot assigned to a small "launch-and-recovery element" to put the Predator into the air using its C-band antenna, then hand the drone off to a crew in a ground control station elsewhere to fly the actual mission via the Ku-band satellite link. At mission's end, the GCS crew would fly the Predator by satellite to within the C-band antenna's roughly hundred-mile range, where the launch-and-recovery crew would once again take control and land the drone.

Before leaving for California, Swanson had been fully briefed about what Richard Clarke called Afghan Eyes and Big Safari was calling the Summer Project: the plan to hunt Osama bin Laden using the Predator. A CIA-led launch-and-recovery element employing just two contractor pilots and a couple of mechanics would take off, land, and service the Predators in Uzbekistan, one of three former Soviet republics bordering Afghanistan on the north. Uzbek President Islam Karimov, an authoritarian strongman and Taliban opponent, had agreed to let the drones fly from a small, rugged military airfield on his nation's soil. But since both the host country and the U.S. government wanted the American presence kept small enough to escape public notice, members of the CIA team would work in a heavy-duty cloth hangar and live in a tent.

Swanson and others flying the actual missions via Ku-band satellite would have it easier. Eight days after he moved into his new apartment in San Diego, Swanson was on his way to Ramstein Air Base, a U.S. Air Force facility in southwestern Germany. Ramstein was the headquarters of U.S. Air Forces Europe, a command known by the acronym USAFE (pronounced "you-SAY-fee"). Shortly before Swanson's arrival, the Air Force had created an ad hoc unit to conduct the Summer Project. To preserve secrecy, the 32nd Expeditionary Air Intelligence Squadron was formed by verbal rather than written orders, which were issued retroactively five months later. The unit's handpicked members would include Swanson, Big Safari sensor operator Master Sergeant Jeff Guay, and Major Brian Raduenz of the Big Safari detachment at General Atomics. A pilot and sensor operator borrowed from one of ACC's Predator squadrons, plus a dozen officers, enlisted personnel, and civilians from USAFE intelligence and communications squadrons, would work the CIA missions as well.

USAFE's director of intelligence, Colonel Edward J. Boyle, a Long Island native who had joined the Air Force in 1974 and worked with Big Safari often during his twenty-six years in uniform, was the ad hoc squadron's commander.

"If anything goes wrong, you're going to be kicked out of Germany," USAFE's commander, General Gregory S. "Speedy" Martin, told Boyle with a laugh. "But don't worry about it, you'll get a good job."

To plan and execute the Predator missions, Boyle recruited Major Mark A. Cooter, an intelligence officer recently transferred to the Pentagon from the Predator-flying 11th Reconnaissance Squadron. A thirty-six-year-old Tennessean popular with subordinates and superiors alike, Cooter had worked on Predator operations from the time his service took over the drone program from the Army in 1997. He had deployed to Taszár, Hungary, then Tuzla, Bosnia; he had also served as operations director at 11th RS headquarters in Nevada.

Boyle also brought Captain Ginger Wallace and a couple of other USAFE intelligence officers into the squadron. When Boyle told Wallace that she was going to help Big Safari and the CIA try to find terrorist training camps in Afghanistan and even Osama bin Laden himself using Predator drones launched in Uzbekistan but flown via satellite from Germany, Wallace thought her jaw would hit the floor.

"We're going to do *what*?" the cheery 1990 Air Force Academy graduate blurted in her Kentucky accent. "Really? We can *do* that?"

"We can," Boyle said. "And we're going to."

By the time Swanson arrived at Ramstein, the squadron's equipment was already in place. At one end of a runway, positioned next to another large satellite antenna, sat what members of the team quickly dubbed the Big Ass Dish—the TMET satellite earth terminal that Big Safari had commandeered from ACC. Nearby, on a fenced-off concrete pad nestled next to some pine trees, sat a Predator ground control station painted green-and-black camouflage. Ten feet from the GCS was a green-and-black camouflage tent roughly thirty feet square; outside the tent stood a couple of porta-potties. The tent would serve as an operations center, or "ops cell." Inside, tables and desks were crammed with computers and big display screens so those working in the ops cell could easily see what the Predator's sensors were seeing.

The Air Force communications crew, advised by Werner, had set up a data link via a fiber-optic cable that ran beneath the Atlantic to CIA headquarters at Langley, Virginia. The data link would stream video shot by the Predator from the GCS at Ramstein roughly four thousand miles, to a new flight operations center on the sixth floor of CIA headquarters, just down the hall from Charlie Allen's office. Computer terminals lined the walls and filled an island in the middle of the CIA's operations center; wide video screens were mounted high on the walls. Here, CTC analysts and others would be able to see what the Predator saw with a delay of less than a second.

Among those watching around the clock, in shifts, would be thirty-one imagery analysts Allen had borrowed from the National Imagery and Mapping Agency, which specialized in analyzing photo reconnaissance. Intelligence officers in the ops cell tent at Ramstein would relay information and orders from the CTC at Langley to the Predator crew in the GCS. The ops cell had secure computer chat rooms and phones that allowed the Air Force team at Ramstein to talk directly to CIA headquarters. Those in the ops cell could also communicate with the drone operators in the GCS via a separate chat room or over an intercom piped into the crew's headsets.

Members of the Air Force team at Ramstein were ordered to keep their mouths shut about their mission. To stress the importance of secrecy, USAFE commander Martin called a meeting with the unit's leaders: Boyle, Cooter, Wallace, communications specialist Captain Paul Welch, and Raduenz of Big Safari, who was there to help with logistics and personnel. Martin told them he was going to have the U.S. Air Force Office of Special Investigations test the special Predator unit's operational security, or, in military parlance, its OPSEC (pronounced "OPP-seck").

"I'm not going to tell them what you're doing, but I *am* going to give them access to your phones, your garbage cans, where you're located, and I'm going to have them try to find *out* what you're doing," the general said. "And if they do, I'm going to kill all of you. So if you think you can gibber about this at the snack bar or you can talk on the phone about anything, I'm telling you, your phones are tapped. And if I catch anybody leaking any of this stuff, you're dead."

The extraordinary security was mainly to keep Al Qaeda from finding out what was being done at Ramstein, but also to keep the mission secret from the German government. Someone well above the Summer Project team's pay grade had decided that although Germany was a NATO ally and Chancellor Gerhard Schroeder was friendly with President Clinton, it might be better to ask forgiveness rather than permission for using German soil to hunt a major terrorist. Why risk getting *nein* for an answer?

They found their quarry on live video a month into the operation—on Wednesday, September 27, 2000—during their seventh flight. Swanson was at the controls, and Big Safari sensor operator Jeff Guay was aiming the Predator's camera as the drone circled near Tarnak Farms, following instructions from the ops cell in the tent outside their GCS at Ramstein.

By now, Swanson and others on the Summer Project team were pretty familiar with the former agricultural complex the Taliban had provided bin Laden for his family and followers. The Predator had loitered over it several times during the previous six flights. To Swanson, the place looked like a typical Afghan village. Mud-brick buildings of various sizes sat behind walls so numerous that from fifteen thousand or more feet up they looked like a maze. The CIA had provided a written description of the compound and annotated satellite photos showing a building thought to be bin Laden's primary residence, a couple of other houses for his wives, and a meetinghouse of some sort used for prayer, though it didn't appear to be a mosque. The CIA also had a schedule of prayer times at Tarnak Farms, and on September 27 Swanson was directed to circle the Predator where Guay could keep both bin Laden's house and the meetinghouse in view around the time the Muslims might convene for prayers.

Just before noon, a tall man in white robes came out of the house believed to be bin Laden's and was met by a group of smaller figures in dark garb who had gathered in a courtyard. Nearby, the Predator team could see three vehicles, an SUV and a couple of trucks, which suggested a security detail. As the tall man in white emerged from the building, the group of shorter men rushed to him. As he began walking, they orbited the taller man as if to protect him, some bowing in an apparent show of obeisance. Having been briefed that bin Laden was six foot five, Swanson thought there was no question they had found their target.

"Yeah, that's definitely the dude," he told Guay.

Mission commander Cooter, watching on a screen in the ops cell tent, agreed.

Swanson kept the Predator circling, awaiting further orders and wondering how long it might take for the submarine or ship he and the others at Ramstein assumed was in range to get the word, spool up some Tomahawk cruise missiles, and take out this enemy who had declared war on America twice and begun waging it in earnest two years earlier. But as they continued to fly their unseen drone several miles above and away from what their cameras were pointed at below, Swanson realized that although their "customers" back at Langley seemed very excited, judging by what he was hearing over his headset, nothing was being said to suggest that cruise missiles would soon be on their way.

"Okay, guys, are they going to be inbound?" Swanson muttered under his breath.

Shortly after the tall man in white and his entourage went indoors, Cooter got word from a different intelligence source that an Afghan air force unit at Kandahar airport, just three and a quarter miles northeast of Tarnak Farms, had spotted something strange in the air and was preparing to investigate. Talking to his CIA counterpart through an Air Force liaison officer at Langley, Cooter said he was going to have Guay slew the Predator's camera toward the Kandahar airport to see what was happening. He met resistance: the CIA wanted to keep the Predator's camera on Tarnak Farms. Cooter could be a bull when certain he was right, and now, unable to get the CIA to agree with him, he decided that at the moment it was more important to preserve the Predator than to keep watching Tarnak Farms. As Swanson got up to take a break, giving the left-hand seat at the flight control console to a pilot from General Atomics, Cooter told Guay to point the Predator's camera toward the airport.

"Oops, guess they spotted us," Guay said, zooming in on a ground crew preparing a Russian-made MiG-21 fighter for takeoff. Minutes later, the Predator team watched the jet—one of five MiG-21s the Taliban's air force was still flying in those days—rise into the sky. Joined by Ed Boyle, who had arrived from his Ramstein office to see what was happening, the Summer Project team watched the jet make a climbing turn and head straight toward the Predator.

Everyone in the GCS and ops cell watched, transfixed, as the MiG silently flew toward them on the Predator's video screen. With Guay keeping the camera on the MiG, the General Atomics pilot—in his stocking feet, others would later recall—maneuvered the Predator to make the drone as difficult as possible for the Afghan pilot to spot. The MiG headed straight toward them, growing larger and larger, then simply zoomed past the Predator's lens. The MiG pilot launched no missile, fired no gun. *Man, that was close,* Swanson thought. Flying at several hundred miles an hour, the MiG pilot must have failed to see the tiny, slow-moving Predator, Swanson and others agreed.

The Predator team wondered how the Taliban had spotted the drone, which was circling several miles from the airport and roughly four miles high. They were sure the Predator was too high to be heard, too small to be seen flying at twenty thousand feet, and at less than a hundred knots too slow for Afghan radar operators to identify. The most likely possibility, the team decided, was that an alert hilltop lookout had seen sun glint off the Predator's wings. To ward off ice at Afghanistan's high altitudes, the wings had been modified to pump glycol de-icing fluid out of hundreds of tiny laser-drilled holes along their leading edges. The drone's "weeping wings" could keep ice from forming and adding so much weight the plane would crash, but the fluid coating gave the Predator's composite skin a brushed-aluminum look, which reflected sunlight.

The CIA's Charlie Allen saw the Predator video of the tall man presumed to be bin Laden only on tape, not live, partly because noon in Afghanistan was 4:30 a.m. Eastern Daylight Time in Washington. Someone called Allen at home a couple of hours after the sighting and said, "We found him—we think." Later, the National Imagery and Mapping Agency analysts brought to the Predator team by Allen analyzed the drone's video freeze-frame by freeze-frame and confirmed that the tall man was indeed bin Laden. Studying the video from the previous six Summer Project missions more closely, the analysts determined that the Predator's camera had actually captured bin Laden for the first time during the second mission flown, nearly a month earlier.

After the imagery analysts concluded that the man in white was indeed bin Laden, a CTC officer came to Allen's office with a tape and played it for the person who had pushed harder than anyone at the CIA for using the Predator.

"It's bin Laden! It's bin Laden!" Allen said excitedly. "And there are his lieutenants!"

Unlike the Summer Project team at Ramstein, Allen and others at the CIA knew that no cruise missiles would be launched. Before the idea of using the Predator to find bin Laden ever arose, Hank Crumpton, a clandestine operations officer and one of CTC director Cofer Black's three deputies, had advocated sending military and CIA commando teams to "work with our Afghan partners to target (bin Laden) with lethal force." Black told Crumpton there was "insufficient political will."

Back in August, after the committee of senior officials known as the Small Group had approved the Predator operation, Richard Clarke's deputy at the NSC, Roger Cressey, had sent National Security Adviser Sandy Berger a memo on how the intelligence the Afghan Eyes project gathered might be used. If the Predator found bin Laden, Cressey reasoned, emergency meetings of the NSC's Counterterrorism Security Group and the cabinet-level Principals Committee might be needed to decide what to do. Berger made it clear a mere sighting wasn't going to be enough to persuade President Clinton to authorize an attempt to kill bin Laden. Several hours would be needed for cruise missiles launched from the Indian Ocean to be programmed and to cover the distance to the target, and if the target moved after those missiles were fired, they couldn't be called back. Burned by the reaction to his 1998 cruise missile strikes against Al Qaeda, Clinton was wary of trying that option again. "I will want *more* than verified location: we will need, at least, data on *pattern* of movements to provide some assurance he will remain in place," Berger wrote in the margin of Cressey's memo, underlining *more* and *pattern* himself.

Clarke argued that a cruise missile shot would be worth a try even if bin Laden escaped; he saw no downside in blowing up the terrorist leader's house. Berger and Secretary of State Madeleine Albright, however, thought a miss would be a political victory for Al Qaeda.

Allen understood from the first that the Predator missions over Afghanistan were regarded as an experiment. Still, he felt vindicated when he showed what quickly became known as the "Tall Man in White" video to CIA chief Tenet and a handful of others in the director's conference room the morning after the Predator's camera shot it. Tenet was astonished by the clarity of the video, Allen could see.

"Whatever doubts he had about the Predator vanished," Allen later recalled.

Although the Summer Project team was elated to learn that they had indeed spotted Osama bin Laden, some were disillusioned when nothing happened as a result. Their orders were to acquire actionable intelligence, and after September 27 those at Ramstein figured they had accomplished that goal. Yet no action had been taken, nor did any seem to be in the cards.

Over the next several weeks, the team flew the Predator over other intelligence targets in Afghanistan, documenting Al Qaeda's presence and mapping Taliban military assets. Guided by intelligence from the CIA, the missions produced hours and hours of videotape revealing useful information. They even captured on video terrorist training being conducted at a camp at Garmabak Ghar. Those in the ops cell at Ramstein were amazed to see black-garbed young men firing weapons and scrambling through obstacle courses. Richard Clarke and Roger Cressey sometimes drove the eight miles from the White House to Langley around midnight to watch the drone's video live in the CTC flight operations center. Clarke was utterly fascinated by this technological magic trick—the ability to surreptitiously watch your enemies on the other side of the globe live and in color. "This sort of intelligence capability was something we had seen only in Hollywood movies," Clarke later wrote.

In the weeks following the bin Laden sighting, increasingly bad weather over Afghanistan rendered the Predator missions less productive. Icing conditions and high winds were annoyances, but the main problem was cloud cover, which often made it impossible to fly the drone low enough to loiter without being seen. Some days the team couldn't even consider flying.

Just as boredom began to set in at Ramstein, Al Qaeda struck again. On October 12, at 11:15 a.m. local time, a fiberglass fishing boat slowly pulled up alongside the USS *Cole*, an American destroyer at anchor in the Arabian Peninsula port of Aden, Yemen. The boat stopped in the water next to the warship. Two men in the little vessel rose, smiled, waved, and stood at attention—then vanished in the fireball of an explosion. The blast ripped a forty-by-forty-foot hole in the port side of the *Cole*'s steel hull, killing seventeen U.S. sailors, wounding thirty-seven, and nearly sinking the ship.

Bin Laden—who three months later was videotaped reading a poem that included a tribute to the *Cole* bombing—was so certain the United States would strike back that he sent his deputy, Ayman al-Zawahiri, to Kabul and ordered Al Qaeda military commander Mohammed Atef to a different location in Kandahar so the expected attack couldn't kill them all simultaneously. But Richard Clarke and others who favored a retaliatory strike in Afghanistan were unable to persuade military or civilian leaders to launch one, because neither the CIA nor the FBI could confirm that Al Qaeda was responsible for the *Cole* bombing. President Clinton later wrote that he came close to ordering a cruise missile strike at bin Laden after the *Cole* bombing but "the CIA recommended that we call it off at the last minute, believing that the evidence of his presence was insufficiently reliable."

After the *Cole* bombing, no one on the Summer Project team lacked moti-
vation; they were all livid. But soon Clarke and other Predator advocates
reluctantly agreed that the drone's flights over Afghanistan should cease,
at least for the winter. The difficulty of flying in bad weather, not to mention the risk of a crash that might expose the covert flights, left little
choice. The Summer Project officially ended on November 8.

Around the same time, Clarke, his deputy Cressey, and their ally Charlie Allen learned of an intriguing new development, an Air Force project
that had been stalled for weeks but just might offer a radical new option for
dealing with bin Laden. Seven months earlier, General John P. Jumper, an
innovative former fighter pilot who had taken over Air Combat Command
early in 2000, had ordered Big Safari and General Atomics to give the Predator a new capability. As Clarke later noted in a strategy paper about Al
Qaeda, "This new capability would permit a 'see it/shoot it' option."

Prior to taking over ACC, Jumper had commanded U.S. Air Forces
Europe for two years and two months, a period that included the air war
in Kosovo. Like other commanders, he had been frustrated with how
hard it was for allied pilots to find and hit mobile targets such as Serb
armored vehicles and antiaircraft missile batteries during that campaign. The Predator had shown in Kosovo that it could find targets with
its cameras and even carry a laser designator to pinpoint them so manned
aircraft could attack. But Jumper wanted the Predator to do more, and a
"see it/shoot it" option was exactly what he had in mind. He decided to
arm the drone.

The effect of putting weapons on the Predator would be nothing short
of revolutionary. Soon the drone would be much more than just a persistent eye in the sky. Armed, it would be a remote-control killing machine.

Jumper called it "the next logical step."

_____
=======

8

THE NEXT LOGICAL STEP

By the spring of 2000, General John Jumper had been in uniform thirty-four years and in the Air Force all his life. An Air Force brat, he was the son of fighter pilot Jimmy Jumper, who in the early 1970s was a two-star general on his way to three stars, until lung cancer cut him down. By then, Jimmy's son Johnny was a "shit hot" pilot in his own right, with two tours in Vietnam under his belt and forty flights as a "fast forward air controller," or Fast FAC. That meant zigzagging his beefy F-4D Phantom over hostile territory at high speed and low altitude, often dodging bright red streams of tracer fire, to find targets for other planes to attack. It was the same death-defying tactic pioneered in the 1960s by the Misty Fast FACs, whose number included Ronald Fogleman, the pilot who later became Air Force chief of staff and decided his service was the Predator's rightful home.

Five foot ten and barrel-chested, Johnny Jumper had a full head of thin brown hair, lively eyes, and exceptionally long arms. In a photo snapped in 1970 after he climbed out of his cockpit at Udorn Royal Thai Air Force Base, Thailand, Jumper's hands are draped over the shoulders of two squadron mates and dangle so far from his body that at first glance they appear fake. Wearing flight suits, parachutes, and insouciant grins as they celebrate a comrade's last combat mission, Jumper and his 555th Tactical Fighter Squadron buddies look fearless and fun-loving, and

Jumper certainly was. A "good stick" in the cockpit, on the ground he was a practical joker. He once poured a pool of oil under the engine of a fellow pilot's expensive new sports car so he could cackle at the proud owner's reaction. As a contributor to a magazine published by the Fighter Weapons School at Nellis Air Force Base, Nevada, where young Captain Jumper was a star instructor in the mid-1970s, he faked a cover showing Air Force pilots strafing a parachuting Soviet flier who had ejected from his plane. Then Jumper talked the wing commander—a colonel, three ranks above him—into slamming the sham cover down on the desk of Jumper's boss and telling the shaken lieutenant colonel that he could hit the street as soon as the outrageous cover on the magazine's three thousand copies did.

Stationed in England, Jumper flew unscheduled mock dogfights against Royal Air Force pilots, using air-to-air maneuvers he later admitted were "so dangerous it wasn't even fun. It was plain stupid." But he was serious about his profession, and a knack for devising novel tactics set the 1966 Virginia Military Institute graduate apart throughout his Air Force career. As a captain, he figured out how to extend the range of the "dive toss" method of bombing to reduce the risk to pilots. He also devised a way for two-ship fighter formations to fly at low levels without using radio calls, an innovation adopted by U.S. pilots around the world. Educated as an electrical engineer, Jumper was also unusually eager to adopt or adapt technology.

During the last of his two tours in Vietnam, he became a big fan of laser-guided weapons. One February day in 1970, Captain Jumper and his backseater, Lieutenant Dick Anderegg, were flying their F-4D on a Fast FAC mission over the Ho Chi Minh Trail, the Communist supply line that ran through Laos and Cambodia. Anderegg, later Air Force chief historian, described their introduction to the wonder of laser-guided weapons in his 2001 book, *Sierra Hotel: Flying Air Force Fighters in the Decade After Vietnam*. The Fast FAC tactic was to search at low altitude for enemy trucks, troops, or supply caches, climb to rendezvous with fighters carrying bombs, lead them to the targets and fire white phosphorous rockets to mark where they should strike, then get out of the way. It was hazardous duty: two months earlier, Jumper and

Anderegg's squadron mate Lieutenant Richard Honey had bled to death in the cockpit after a .50-caliber bullet hit him in the chest as his F-4's pilot jinked over the same dirt road they were searching that day in Laos.

After a couple of hours in the danger zone, Jumper took their Phantom roaring to safer altitudes while Anderegg tuned to the radio frequency used by a flight of F-4s who were waiting to pounce and using the call sign "Buick." When the Buick flight leader asked if Jumper and Anderegg had any targets for his planes to hit, Jumper suggested an enemy storage area they had found. Surprisingly, the Buick leader said that wouldn't be a good target for the ordnance they were carrying. He wanted "a small, pinpoint target." Jumper suggested a single thirty-seven-millimeter gun "that's been shooting at us pretty good," to which Buick replied, "That's perfect."

Jumper and Anderegg led the other fighters to the target, dove to mark it with a white phosphorous rocket, and climbed out of the way. They were then puzzled to watch the Buick flight leader circle in a lazy left-hand turn while his wingman rolled in from well above normal bombing altitude. The wingman was so high that Jumper and Anderegg were sure his bomb would miss. "Bomb gone," they heard him say over the radio—then they watched in amazement as the attack scored a direct hit. They later learned that the circling F-4 had been shining a laser designator's beam on the target for the other Phantom's new laser-guided bomb.

The phenomenal accuracy of bombs able to home in on the sparkle created by a pulsing laser beam would soon save time, money, and the lives of both American air crews and innocent civilians near their targets. On April 27, 1972, for example, F-4s used laser-guided bombs to drop one end of the Thanh Hoa Bridge, a strategic link in the Ho Chi Minh Trail that U.S. aircraft had tried to cut 871 times since 1965 without success, and at painful cost. By some calculations, 104 American pilots were lost in unsuccessful missions against the Dragon's Jaw, as the structure was known.

Laser guidance "was an epiphany for us," Anderegg recalled more than four decades later. "It was like, 'Holy smokes! If we can do that, just think of what else we can do!'"

Jumper was eager to push the envelope his whole career. In 1999, as the four-star commander of U.S. Air Forces Europe, he strongly supported putting a laser designator on the Predator to help fighter pilots find targets in Kosovo. After that experiment ended, he concluded that it had worked well—and was furious when he took over ACC the next year and learned that his new command had made Big Safari strip the laser designators off the WILD Predators it had modified.

"Why on earth would we do that?" Jumper asked his subordinates.

"Well, because they're not part of the program" was the answer he got.

Jumper would soon see about that.

Big doors swing on small hinges, as the saying goes. Shortly after discovering that his new command had directed Big Safari to remove the laser designators, Jumper came up with an even more ambitious idea for how to make the Predator more useful. The broad concept wasn't new, but in the year 2000 the innovation that Jumper proposed was both technically possible and politically timely. The door to it hinged on an unexpected spring thunderstorm.

On March 15, 2000, Jumper spoke at a black-tie dinner at the Hilton Sandestin Beach Resort and Spa in Destin, Florida, the sumptuous setting for a three-day, military-industrial get-together styled as a high-level deep-think event by its two-star-general host. Major General Michael C. Kostelnik, head of the Air Armament Center at nearby Eglin Air Force Base, billed his Air Armament Summit 2000 as a venue for top Air Force and industry leaders—"company presidents, directors of research, or major division chiefs"—to discuss what sorts of bombs and missiles the service might need over the coming quarter century. Fighter pilot Kostelnik also wanted to use the summit to promote his pet project, the development of a 250-pound, GPS-guided "Small Smart Bomb" he thought the Air Force needed for its stealth fighters. Kostelnik had been promoting the experimental weapon for more than a year but was finding that few others in the Air Force wanted to fund a bantamweight bomb with money they could spend on airplanes instead. Kostelnik could see he needed a new sales strategy, and the air war in Kosovo led him to one. Maybe, he reasoned, his Small Smart Bomb could piggyback, literally and politically, on the increasingly successful Predator.

At the Air Armament Summit, Kostelnik's deputy, Brigadier General Kevin Sullivan, was due to present a proposal that industry join the Air Force in funding and conducting a two-year "Weaponized UAV Demonstration," in which a Predator would be modified to drop a Small Smart Bomb just to test the concept of arming a drone. Jumper was scheduled to leave before Sullivan's presentation, but one of Florida's frequent thunderstorms grounded the ACC chief's plane the morning after his speech. Seizing the chance, Kostelnik asked if Sullivan could give Jumper his presentation privately, and Jumper readily agreed.

Jumper frequently interrupted with questions as Sullivan cited events during the air war in Kosovo as evidence that, politically as well as technologically, the time had come to start arming UAVs. A PowerPoint slide titled "The Rules Have Changed" showed a photo of a Serb soldier standing triumphantly over the shredded windshield of the F-117 stealth fighter plane shot down over Kosovo in March 1999. Another photo showed Serbia's Grdelica railroad bridge, where two TV-guided missiles fired by an F-15E Strike Eagle fighter-bomber in April 1999 inadvertently hit a passenger train, killing more than ten civilians and wounding many others. A Predator armed with a Small Smart Bomb, Sullivan suggested, could reduce the risks to pilots, and to innocent civilians as well, in future conflicts. Then he laid out a plan to involve nine Air Force agencies, the three other military services, DARPA, the Pentagon's Ballistic Missile Defense Organization, General Atomics, and aerospace giants Lockheed Martin Corporation and Boeing Company in a two-year collaboration. The goal would be to drop a live Small Smart Bomb from a Predator by May 2001 and start producing some kind of "weaponized UAV" between 2004 and 2006.

When Sullivan finished, Jumper told Kostelnik he was welcome to pursue the idea, as long as he did so within the Air Armament Center's existing budget. With that, Jumper left. But over the next six weeks, the new ACC commander kept thinking about what he had heard that morning in Florida. Putting a weapon on the Predator wasn't just a good idea, Jumper reflected—it was a *great* idea. Carrying a laser designator, as in

Kosovo, the Predator might find targets with its sensors and lase them for strike aircraft, but those other planes might be miles away, and their pilots had to be talked onto targets the drone found, which gave mobile targets time to escape. Jumper could also imagine situations where a Predator might find a "high-value target" with no strike aircraft available to attack. So why not just go ahead and arm the Predator itself so it could strike targets on its own, not just find them for others? Why not turn this unmanned scout into an unmanned killer scout?

On May 1, Jumper sent an announcement to the Air Force chief of staff, the secretary of the Air Force, and other top service leaders. "Chief, ACC has internalized the Predator lessons learned from Operation Allied Force and is changing the direction for the Predator program," Jumper's message began. "The original construct of the Predator as just a reconnaissance surveillance target acquisition asset no longer applies. ACC will employ Predator as a FAC-like resource, with look-out, target identification, and target acquisition roles." Using military jargon, the announcement added that the Predator would be getting a new laser designator. Then Jumper dropped a bureaucratic bombshell. ACC, his message concluded, was "moving out on the next logical step for USAF UAVs using Predator—weaponizing UAVs."

Contrary to later accounts, Jumper's initiative to arm the Predator originally had nothing to do with the CIA's covert operations against Osama bin Laden and Al Qaeda. Nor was Jumper's project secret, though defense trade publications were the only media paying attention. The well-sourced newsletter *Inside the Air Force* revealed Jumper's decision on May 26, 2000, just over three weeks after he made it, and continued to report on the project for months. At the time, though, few outside the service and the Pentagon or readers of *Inside the Air Force* took any apparent notice of Jumper's initiative, or had much reason to care if they did.

When Jumper announced his intent to arm the Predator, using the unarmed version of the drone to look for Osama bin Laden was still no more than an idea the NSC's Richard Clarke and the CIA's Charlie Allen were urging on their reluctant bosses. The Afghan Eyes/Summer Project had yet to be approved, and would be a tightly held secret once it was. Hardly anyone outside the military even knew what a Predator was, and many insiders were unimpressed by this fragile little reconnaissance drone, which in Bosnia had proved vulnerable to bad weather and relatively easy for the enemy to shoot down. Some regarded the Predator as an oddity of dubious value that owed its survival to the strange circumstances of its birth. "This $600 million program has so many combat limitations that its long-term viability remains in question," Air Force Colonel Thomas P. Ehrhard wrote in a PhD dissertation on drones published the same month Jumper made his decision. Ehrhard did allow, however, that "despite its meandering path to Air Force adoption," the Predator "seems to have found a home."

Even so, the Air Force owned only sixteen Predator air vehicles at the time, and the service would have had even fewer if Representative Jerry Lewis of California hadn't added another twenty million dollars to the program in that year's defense appropriations bill. The Air Force was planning to buy a total of only forty-eight Predators in all by the end of 2003. Interest in the drone was still uneven, its future uncertain. By arming the Predator, Jumper was simply trying to make the drone more useful in fighting wars. "All I wanted to do was to be able to cure the problem that we had in Kosovo," Jumper recalled a decade later, "and that is, the Predator is sitting there looking at the target. Why can't you put something on there that allows you to do something about it, instead of just looking at it?"

For technical, legal, and cultural reasons, the next logical step was a giant one. Since the Kettering Bug, World War I's never-used "aerial torpedo," the U.S. military had tried putting explosives or bombs or missiles on drones several times, but the results were never satisfactory. The closest brush with success came in the 1970s, when the Air Force and Teledyne Ryan put the TV-guided Maverick missile and later a TV-guided glide bomb on some Firebee target drones like the ones Big Safari modified to fly unmanned reconnaissance missions in Vietnam. By firing a Maverick from a modified Firebee on December 14, 1971, at Edwards Air Force Base in California, the Air Force's 6514th Test Squadron claimed a place in aviation history—the first launch of an air-to-ground missile from a remotely piloted aircraft. None was put into operation, though, and with the end of U.S. involvement in Vietnam, Air Force interest in drones evaporated. The Navy, meanwhile, cancelled the most extensive armed UAV program in U.S. history the same year the armed Firebee was tested, retiring its QH-50 DASH drone helicopter, which carried torpedoes and even nuclear depth bombs that were never used in combat.

Over the three decades since those experiments, the idea of weaponizing UAVs had been pursued by a number of people, including Abe Karem with one concept for his Amber, and Neal and Linden Blue with the first General Atomics kit plane Predator in the 1980s. But after 1987 the very legality of arming drones became questionable, at least for the United States and the Soviet Union. On December 8 of that year, President Ronald Reagan and Soviet leader Mikhail Gorbachev signed the Intermediate-Range Nuclear Forces Treaty, which required both nations to eliminate ground-launched ballistic and cruise missiles with ranges between 500 and 5,500 kilometers (300 to 3,300 miles). Missiles launched from the sea or air were outside the pact, which defined a ground-launched cruise missile as "an unmanned, self-propelled vehicle that sustains flight through the use of aerodynamic lift over most of its flight path" and "a weapon-delivery vehicle." The INF Treaty, as it is known, prompted Congress to give the Navy-run Unmanned Aerial Vehicle Joint Program Office authority solely over "nonlethal" drones.

By 1996, the Soviet Union had met its demise, but the INF Treaty between Washington and Moscow remained in force. The Predator's success in Bosnia, however, was sparking new thinking about drones. For some, it was more exciting to imagine the technical possibilities than the possible legal limits. That year, U.S. Representative Curt Weldon, a Pennsylvania Republican influential on defense issues, got ten million dollars included in the House version of the annual defense authorization bill to demonstrate "air-to-surface precision guided munitions employment using a Predator, Hunter, or Pioneer unmanned aerial vehicle and a nondevelopmental laser target designator." But the Pentagon, as Weldon later wrote, saw "UAVs solely as a reconnaissance asset" and "aggressively opposed" his legislation. Consequently, a House-Senate conference committee ultimately stripped it from the defense bill. The idea of arming the Predator lay dormant until the spring of 2000, when a Florida thunderstorm helped revive it.

No one was more excited about Jumper's decision than Kostelnik, who saw it as an opportunity to advance his Small Smart Bomb. He wanted to run Jumper's project, but Big Safari Director Bill Grimes thought it rightfully belonged to his outfit, which after all was the Predator's official System Program Office. Lieutenant General Robert F. Raggio, a three-star Grimes and Kostelnik both answered to, sided with Grimes. In early June 2000, Raggio told Kostelnik to stand down and directed Big Safari to figure out the smartest way to meet Jumper's goal.

Grimes gave the assignment to a trio of majors on his staff—Brian Raduenz, Raymond Pry, and Mark "Spoon" Mattoon—who came up with three options. The Air Force, they found, owned no weapons light enough for a Predator to carry and had only two experimental ones in the works, the Small Smart Bomb and a lightweight air-launched cruise missile that was still just a concept. The Army, however, had a missile that Big Safari thought showed promise. It weighed a mere ninety-eight pounds but packed enough punch to kill a tank. Army helicopters had first fired it in combat nine years earlier, during the 1991 Gulf War, so it was proven. The Army had more than eleven thousand in stock, and the Navy and Marine Corps had some, too. Best of all, this Army missile was a "smart" weapon; it homed in on its targets by seeking the sparkle of a laser designator. The missile's official designation was AGM-114, with AGM standing for "anti-tank guided missile." Its official name was Heliborne-Launched Fire-and-Forget Missile. But to those familiar with it, the missile was known by an acronym describing what it delivered—Hellfire.

Air Combat Command headquarters resides in a two-story, redbrick building at Langley Air Force Base in coastal Virginia's Hampton Roads region, near Norfolk. On June 21, Jumper got a briefing there from Colonel Robert E. Dehnert Jr., director of reconnaissance programs for the Aeronautical Systems Center at Wright-Patterson Air Force Base in Dayton, on the three options Big Safari had come up with. The two Air Force weapons that might work, Jumper was told, would not be available in any useful quantities for several years. The Army's Hellfire was available immediately and could be integrated with the Predator—made to fit under the drone's wing and be launched from it—for as little as $485,000, a pittance to the Pentagon. The one major technical risk was that no one knew how launching a Hellfire would affect the aerodynamically delicate Predator.

There were also two legal hurdles to the project, no matter what weapon Jumper chose.

First, to modify the Predator this drastically, the Air Force might need to ask key members of Congress to approve a so-called New Start Notification, a legal requirement for significant and unanticipated changes in defense programs made between annual appropriations bills. Air Force leaders were especially sensitive to this issue in 2000 because members of Congress and the news media had severely criticized them in 1999 for ignoring that legal requirement with respect to other programs.

The second legal issue was the 1987 INF Treaty, which was still in effect. A committee of government lawyers would have to decide whether an armed Predator fit the INF Treaty's definition of a ground-launched cruise missile. If it did, Jumper's "next logical step" could be a violation of a major international agreement.

Jumper couldn't resolve the legal issues, but he knew a good military idea when he saw one. At the conclusion of Dehnert's briefing, he directed his staff to work with Big Safari to come up with a detailed plan for arming the Predator with the Hellfire.

Just over three weeks later, on July 14, Dehnert returned to Jumper's headquarters with the three Big Safari majors who had prepared the presentation that the ACC commander was about to receive. The conference room was packed with more than forty Air Force officers, senior enlisted experts, and officials and engineers from General Atomics and other companies, all crowded around a long table or seated in chairs against the walls. Standing beside a screen at one end of the conference room, Dehnert went through a series of slides that outlined two possible plans for arming the Predator with the Hellfire.

"The immediate objective is to fire a Hellfire missile from a Predator and hit something," one of the first slides said. The first option Dehnert described would take nine months, cost an estimated $1.3 million, and offer "medium technical risk." The second option was a twelve-week "Accelerated Demo" expected to cost $1.5 million and disrupt all other Predator projects. This quicker option would also come with "high technical risk," for it would be done the Big Safari way: with the least possible government regulation and paperwork.

Three-quarters of the way through Dehnert's briefing, Jumper turned to Tom Cassidy of General Atomics, who was seated next to him, and quietly asked, "What do you think about all this?"

"Let's go in your office," Cassidy suggested.

The general and the former admiral excused themselves and left the room, leaving the others exchanging puzzled looks and curious whispers. Once they were alone, Cassidy told Jumper, "You give us two million bucks and two months and it'll be a done deal."

"Done," Jumper replied.

Cassidy went back to the meeting, leaving Jumper in his office. The ACC commander didn't return to the conference room for some time; when he did, he told the gathering he had just phoned General Michael E. Ryan, the Air Force chief of staff, and General William J. Begert, assistant vice chief of staff. Then Jumper gave those attending the briefing a surprise. Big Safari, he said, would get three million dollars to arm the Predator with the Hellfire—about double the cost of either option Dehnert had outlined, and two hundred thousand dollars more than the two combined. He also directed Big Safari to execute both the accelerated demonstration and the more cautious one.

Ryan would find the funding. Begert would get the required congressional approval. Big Safari and General Atomics were to arm the Predator and get it tested in flight as quickly as possible. Wrinkles could be ironed out later. The Air Force, Jumper explained, "wants to make rapid progress on weaponizing UAVs."

In his private conversation with Jumper, Cassidy made it sound easy, but marrying the Hellfire to the Predator was no simple matter. A week after getting Jumper's order, Big Safari Director Grimes hosted a meeting at his tightly secured headquarters in Dayton to discuss technical and other issues with representatives from the Hellfire program office at the Army's Redstone Arsenal, engineers from General Atomics and other companies, and various Air Force experts.

"My first question is can I fire your missile off Predator without knocking it out of the sky?" Grimes asked the Army contingent.

No one was entirely sure. Whether the thrust from the Hellfire's launch would throw the Predator into a spin when fired, or whether the missile's plume—1,050 degrees Fahrenheit at its hottest—would damage the aircraft's composite wings, tail, or fuselage, were questions that required engineering analysis, the team decided.

General Atomics already knew the wings needed to be beefed up to withstand the strain of carrying missiles. "Hardpoints" in the current wings could carry payloads of up to one hundred pounds, but each Hellfire would need a launcher—a metal rack with a rail to carry and fire it from—and electrical equipment to make it function. The Army experts said their Hellfire launchers were in short supply, so Big Safari might have to borrow a couple from the Navy and modify them to carry only one instead of the usual four missiles per launcher used by helicopters. The engineering team would also have to find a way to reduce the thrust needed to trigger a release spring on the rail whose function was to hold a missile in place until fired. The spring's standard 600 pounds of resistance would have to be cut to about 235 pounds, or else a launch might rip the wing right off the aircraft.

The Hellfire's software would have to be modified, too, to launch the missile properly from the Predator's normal operating altitude of about fifteen thousand feet, for the AGM-114 was designed to be launched at tanks by helicopters flying two thousand feet or less above the ground. Test firings—first from the ground, then in the air—would be necessary. New tactics for launching Hellfires from the Predator would have to be devised, too.

Beyond all that, the engineers would have to integrate the missile's circuitry and software with the Predator's flight control computer and a new sensor turret, or "modified Kosovo ball," which Raytheon Corporation was developing. The new turret would add the daylight camera lacking in the laser ball used in Kosovo.

On July 28, Big Safari received formal approval from Headquarters Air Force to do what Jumper wanted, but the instruction said no Predators were to be modified until the service got both congressional approval and a ruling that arming the drone was acceptable under the INF Treaty. Under the circumstances, the Big Safari team did as much analysis and made as many modifications as they could.

Engineers at Wright-Patterson Air Force Base analyzed the Hellfire's rocket plume and came up with encouraging results. Because the Hellfire would get away from the Predator so fast—it would be sixteen feet past the drone's nose within 250 milliseconds—and its rocket plume was so compact, the aircraft's tail would only "see" (in engineering jargon) a high temperature of 440 degrees Fahrenheit as the missile departed, and that only briefly. The wing and fuselage would see only 170 degrees, and the air pressure change around the plume would present no problems.

General Atomics, meanwhile, conducted analyses showing that a Hellfire could indeed be launched from a Predator without breaking the aircraft apart or throwing it into a spin. Engineers at the General Atomics factory in California began writing the software needed to wed the Hellfire to the Predator. They also designed new ribs and cross brackets to go inside the Predator's wings at their hardpoints, allowing them to carry a single-rail launcher derived from a multi-rail launcher that Big Safari had quickly gotten from the Navy. The engineers were still barred, though, from making any changes to the aircraft chosen to become the first armed Predator, tail number 97-3034. Predator 3034 had been built the previous year but flown only seven times, always at El Mirage, for a total of thirteen hours.

On August 11, *Inside the Air Force* reported that the Predator "will rain Hellfire this fall" upon the practice bombing areas at Nellis Air Force Base, a sprawling installation north of Las Vegas. Lieutenant Colonel Dan Novak, ACC's weapons requirements branch chief, told the publication that the Air Force first wanted to "see if it is feasible for a Predator to do this." The article noted that the Air Force "may have to inform Congress of a new start because the test will add a new capability to the UAV." According to the newsletter, the Air Force expected to fire a test missile at Nellis for the first time later that year, probably in October or November.

Less than three weeks after the article appeared, the schedule Novak had described to *Inside the Air Force* fell apart. On August 30, Air Force lawyers issued a legal opinion forbidding all "touch labor" to arm the Predator prior to getting approval from Congress. Now the team working on Jumper's project was barred from modifying not only Predator 3034 but any of the other equipment needed for the project. All they could to do was look and analyze, not act. It was frustrating.

Eight days after the Hellfire project came to a halt, the Summer Project team at Ramstein Air Base in Germany began flying an unarmed Predator over Afghanistan via satellite in the CIA's secret search for Osama bin Laden. Soon they would learn that all anyone was going to do when they found the terrorist leader was look and analyze, not act. It was more than frustrating—it was infuriating.

In early October, visitors to the General Atomics flight test facility at El Mirage were treated to a strange sight. Parked on the painted concrete floor of an aluminum hangar, the rubber wheels of its three-legged landing gear locked in bright yellow chocks, was Predator 3034, looking like a patient in the midst of drastic surgery. The drone's wings were missing. Amidships was the familiar U.S. Air Force star and bar insignia; just forward of the Predator's distinctive inverted-V tail was a short string of black numerals: 97-3034. A dozen feet to either side, sitting atop aluminum wing stands—trestles akin to sawhorses—were the Predator's unattached wings.

Midway along the underside of one wing hung a single rail cut from what once was a four-rail M299 Hellfire launcher. Hung from the rail was a sinister-looking black Hellfire. In fact, the missile was what Big Safari called a House Mouse, a term the team learned from the Army. Not only did this Hellfire carry no propellant to create thrust and make it fly, but it also lacked the shaped explosive charge a live missile would carry, a charge that could generate a jet of heat and pressure powerful enough to drill through a heavy tank's armor on impact. This mock Hellfire, however, held all the same electronics as a live one. Running from the launcher where the House Mouse hung on the unattached wing to the socket where the wing was meant to fit into Predator 3034's fuselage was a collection of gray wires. Stretched to their limit, the wires measured twenty-six feet.

This unorthodox sight had resulted from a phone call received by the Big Safari office at General Atomics on September 21, a call that brought good news and bad. The Air Force had secured congressional approval to spend money arming the Predator, meaning that touch labor would now be allowed. But the State Department general counsel's "initial opinion," as a senior Air Force procurement officer reported in an e-mail to Jumper and others, was that a "weaponized Predator constitutes a cruise missile, hence an INF Treaty problem." Lieutenant General Stephen Plummer added that the Defense Department's general counsel was "working with them to change that opinion." But until the issue was resolved, no missile could be mounted on a Predator able to fly.

Jumper was irate. "Chief, we should not allow this opinion to stand or to ripen for any length of time," the ACC commander e-mailed Chief of Staff Mike Ryan. "With your permission I would like to put together a briefing (case study) from Kosovo that explains what we are after and engage the lawyers," Jumper added, signing the e-mail, "Your Junk Yard Dog (and happy to do it). John."

Big Safari's solution, meanwhile, was to put the missile launcher on a detached wing and then wire it to the flight control computer in the Predator's fuselage to check whether the systems would work together once the wing was reinstalled. The tactic was legal, for a Predator unable to fly was clearly outside the INF Treaty definition of a cruise missile as "an unmanned, self-propelled vehicle that sustains flight." It was also classic Big Safari. Being creative within the rules was part of the organization's culture, as suggested by the sign Bill Grimes had posted on Big Safari's door at Wright-Patterson Air Force Base: "Those who say it cannot be done should not get in the way of those doing it."

On September 27, a week after the Big Safari office at Rancho Bernardo got the message that inspired the wing stand solution, the Summer Project team in Germany spotted bin Laden for the first time. Colonel Ed Boyle, the Summer Project commander for the Air Force, was just as surprised as Predator pilot Scott Swanson when they found their terrorist target and no cruise missiles were fired. A couple of hours after the sighting, with the Predator on its way back to Uzbekistan, Boyle had the ops cell make a videotape of bin Laden at Tarnak Farms, then jumped in his car with it and drove the three-quarters of a mile to the office of the USAFE commander, General Gregory "Speedy" Martin. After Martin watched the video, they had the imagery streamed to General Jumper at his ACC office at Langley. Then Martin phoned Jumper to talk about the video.

Boyle wasn't privy to their conversation, but he knew Jumper pretty well. Not only had Boyle been Jumper's director of intelligence when Jumper commanded USAFE, they had known each other since Jumper was a lieutenant colonel and Boyle was a captain. Boyle figured Jumper would climb the walls when he learned that the Summer Project team had found bin Laden and nothing was being done about it. Boyle also knew Jumper had a project under way to arm the Predator, for Boyle had been among the many officers in the June 21 meeting at Langley when Jumper chose the Hellfire. Boyle hoped the video of bin Laden that his old boss had just seen would speed that project up.

It didn't—even after the *Cole* bombing two weeks later. The wheels of government grind slowly at any time, and as the end of Bill Clinton's second term in the White House approached, decisions were hard to come by. By October 17 the members of the Big Safari team working to arm the Predator had done all the work they could pending a resolution of the treaty issue. They were also waiting for Raytheon to deliver the new sensor ball combining a laser designator with a daylight camera. For the moment, the two most important Predator projects were in limbo.

That same month, Summer Project operations director Major Mark Cooter and Captain Scott Swanson happened to see the flag-draped caskets of some USS *Cole* sailors being removed from a cargo plane at Ramstein Air Base in Germany, a stopover on the way to the Air Force Mortuary Affairs Operations Center at Dover Air Force Base in Delaware.

Cooter and Swanson got out of their car, stood at attention, and saluted as the caskets were unloaded. The sight made them sad—and angry. Over the next few days, Cooter loudly and bitterly complained about the U.S. failure to strike back, living up to a fiery reputation that had led an Air Force security officer to call the burly intelligence officer a "cowboy" for bridling at computer restrictions Cooter thought were slowing operations. When Cooter turned thirty-seven on October 20, eight days after the *Cole* bombing, his team threw him a party and gave him a pair of cavalry spurs and a big white Stetson. Cooter laughed but resisted their demands that he try the gag gifts on for size. Instead, he put a magnetic clip on the brim of the Stetson and hung the cowboy hat and spurs from a metal equipment rack at the back of the Predator ground control station. He would wear them, Cooter told the team, when Washington worked up enough gumption to take some action against Osama bin Laden and Al Qaeda.

By the following month, Cooter's feelings were only stronger. On November 14, he sent a scathing letter to Boyle, Snake Clark and Cooter's opposite number at the CIA, arguing that if actionable intelligence produced by the Predator flights were going to lead to no action, the missions should be stopped and new options considered. Cooter was so angry, in fact, that he originally drafted his protest under the file name "resignationletter." After talking it over with a lieutenant colonel he was close to, he deleted a sentence declaring that he was going to resign, but he didn't mince words when expressing his frustration with the failure of those in power to act against terrorists clearly determined to kill as many Americans as possible. The Air Force team had proven they could find bin Laden with the Predator, but such operations were high in risk and low in return, Cooter argued. In a dozen missions that fall, the Predator had spotted bin Laden twice for sure and possibly a third time. In Cooter's view, the Predator team should stop flying over Afghanistan until those with the power to decide figured out what they really wanted to do about Osama bin Laden.

Summer Project commander Boyle was angry, too. Boyle's gut told him that bin Laden and his lieutenants were finalizing their plans for the *Cole* bombing when the Predator's cameras saw the Al Qaeda chief at

Tarnak Farms on September 27. He figured the sailors killed on the *Cole* might still be alive if a cruise missile had hit bin Laden's meeting that day. He fervently hoped the Predator would soon be armed; when it was, he also hoped the team he had led in the Summer Project could go hunting for bin Laden again. Boyle wanted to rain Hellfire on him.

9

HELLFIRE AND HESITATION

Now Predator 3034 resembled a prisoner more than it did a patient. On January 23, 2001, wings and nose restored but tires missing, 3034 was chained by its landing gear struts to a concrete pad atop a barren hilltop overlooking a shallow desert valley. The dry swale below the hill was on a test range at California's landlocked China Lake Naval Air Weapons Station, whose 1.1 million acres make it 50 percent larger than Rhode Island, and whose 17,000 square miles of restricted airspace make it ideal for trying out military weapons. Here, on Pad J54 at Test Site G-6, Predator 3034 would be put through a "static ground launch" of a Hellfire to see, before trying it in the air, what a missile rocketing off the drone's wing would do to the aircraft. Under each of 3034's shiny new white wings—attached to the fuselage three weeks earlier after months of resting on metal stands—hung a sixty-four-inch-long Hellfire incapable of living up to its name. There was no explosive inside.

Only one of these "inert" Hellfires would be launched in this test, but each had white stripes along its menacing black skin, the better to help high-speed film and video cameras see the missile's aerodynamics in flight. The stresses on the drone from the heat and thrust of the Hellfire's rocket plume would be measured by thermal, strain, and pressure gauges, and by temperature-sensitive crayons applied to the laser ball, tails, and leading edge of the wings. The rocket's effects would also be visible in the flapping of strips of tape attached to 3034's composite skin, whose inverted-V tail now sported the Scotch plaid colors of the 11th Reconnaissance Squadron, plus Big Safari's black-and-gold African shield with crossed spears.

General John Jumper's project to arm the Predator had been released at last from its bureaucratic limbo a month earlier, on December 21, when government treaty experts abruptly decided that a lethal drone was permissible under the 1987 Intermediate-Range Nuclear Forces Treaty. The decision took months to reach, but the logic was simple—especially after NSC counterterrorism chief and armed Predator advocate Richard Clarke weighed in. Clarke, who had been deputy assistant secretary of state for intelligence when the INF treaty was negotiated and served as assistant secretary of state for politico-military affairs before going to work at the NSC, pointed out that, by definition, a cruise missile had a warhead and the Predator didn't. The Predator was merely a platform, an unmanned aerial vehicle that had landing gear and was designed to return to base after a mission.

On January 2, Predator 3034 got its wings back in the General Atomics hangar at El Mirage. The company's Hellfire project manager, Christopher Dusseault, thirty-three, a former Air Force engineer with three master's degrees to his credit, happily supervised as the brand-new beefed-up wings were fastened into their fuselage slots and all the right wires were connected. Each wing held a single gray launch rail, and each rail angled downward five degrees from its wing's leading edge. With the wings in place, a small group of engineers and technicians fitted 3034 with a Forty-Four ball, the same laser designator turret used on the WILD Predators flown over Kosovo in 1999. Then, after three weeks of ground and flight tests of various kinds, the team trucked 3034, a ground control station, and other equipment ninety miles north to the test range at China Lake to start shooting missiles.

Chained to its test pad four hundred feet above sea level, 3034 sat with its nose pointed northwest and upward nine degrees. Behind the drone and its Hellfires was a second hill forty feet higher, with two big antennas on its summit, one to stream the Predator's video, one to communicate with a ground-based laser designator sitting beside a control

van a couple of miles downrange. A crew manning this second laser designator would shine a laser beam to guide the inert Hellfire to a mock
target, a dusty, defunct green tank sitting in the desert three miles
straight ahead of the Predator.

Shielded from the test pad by the hill holding the antennas was a concrete bunker full of test gear and engineers, including General Atomics
project manager Dusseault and Major Spoon Mattoon, a weapons testing
expert and Big Safari's project manager. Behind the bunker sat the Predator's ground control station, looming up from the desert floor like a lost
freight container, its big, black tires powdered with desert sand, its dull
metal skin painted black, tan, and beige desert camouflage.

At 10:39 a.m., with the Predator's engine running and its small pusher
propeller gently turning, Mattoon decided it was time to launch a missile.

"Four . . . three . . . two . . . one . . . fire!" a China Lake test director
ordered over an intercom piped into the GCS and other locations. After
a split-second pause, a jet of flame as long as the missile spurted from the
rear of the Hellfire under the Predator's right wing. As recorded by a
high-speed camera sitting off to the side of 3034, the mock weapon's
rocket plume reflected yellow on the underside of the white wing but
vanished in milliseconds.

"Item away, item away," the test director intoned as the missile zoomed
off in a low parabola toward a distant mountain. A forward-facing camera recorded the Hellfire and its rocket plume disappearing from view.

"Plus five . . . plus ten . . . plus fifteen . . . plus twenty," the test director reported as the missile flew. Reaching Mach 1.3 in the flight's first
two and a half seconds—around a thousand miles an hour at this altitude and temperature—and slowing to about four hundred miles per
hour as it traveled, the Hellfire slammed into the side of the target tank's
turret, right where a nearby camera able to detect laser light showed the
beam's sparkle flickering. The aluminum test missile burst into ragged
black chunks.

"We have impact," the test director reported unemotionally. "End
of test."

Mattoon, Dusseault, and their team reacted like the NASA engineers
in Houston when astronaut Neil Armstrong set mankind's first foot on

the moon: giving high fives all around, jumping up and down, patting one another on the back.

The Predator team spent the rest of the day analyzing video of the Hellfire launch and the missile smashing into the right side of the tank, studying the test from every angle at actual speed, in slow motion, and in super slow motion. They analyzed the data from thermal gauges on the wing and tail, the flapping of the tape strips attached to the drone, the flutter of the wings. Then they adjourned to a restaurant in nearby Ridgecrest, California, and after a nice dinner enjoyed a proud and rowdy night at the bar. Now the question was whether the Predator could repeat its new trick in flight.

Chona Hawes feared her husband might be having a seizure. She came upstairs at dusk one evening at their north Las Vegas house to find Air Force Captain Curt Hawes flat on his back in bed. The lights were off, the curtains closed, and her husband was clad only in underwear and a tee-shirt. Eyes shut, knees bent, his bare feet moved up and down in a dance with no rhythm. Hands flitting back and forth in the air, his index fingers poked and pressed while his thumbs turned and twitched.

"Curt?"

No answer.

"Curt!" his wife demanded, turning on a light. Curt stopped gyrating and sat up with a start. He looked at Chona wide-eyed, then reached to his ears with both hands and removed yellow foam plugs.

"What's happening?" she asked worriedly.

Sorry, Curt replied with a sheepish smile, but it was hard to get to sleep this early, even wearing earplugs, when you knew you had to get to the park-and-ride by 3:45 a.m. to catch the bus to Indian Springs airfield for a 4:30 a.m. briefing. As a Predator pilot, the possibility of missing or arriving late for a preflight briefing was one of Curt's worst fears, and the briefing he would help conduct the morning of Friday, February 16, 2001, was one of the most exciting and important in his twenty-year career. That day, Hawes, thirty-eight, a Minnesota farm boy who dreamt of being a military pilot but missed the minimum five-foot-four height requirement by a quarter inch, was to make aviation history. He would become the first person ever to launch a Hellfire missile from a Predator in flight, a privilege Hawes felt blessed by God to have been granted.

By regulation, a pilot was supposed to get eight hours of uninterrupted sleep before reporting for a flight. Whatever the rules, Hawes wanted to be rested and ready to make history, so he had plugged his ears to help get to sleep. Then, worried the plugs might make him miss his wakeup alarm, he set three clocks to go off simultaneously. Still too nervous to sleep, he began visualizing and practicing the moves he would make at the console in the ground control station when he flew the Predator the next day. His feet were moving the rudder pedals; his hands were manipulating the keyboard, the mouse, the throttle, and joystick on the Predator control console. Military pilots often do a "chair fly" before a mission; Curt just happened to be doing a "bed fly" when Chona interrupted him.

Hawes wanted to do everything precisely right the next day, especially the most important move he would make. At the end of a countdown, with a ground-based laser designator shining its beam at a target tank on a test range at nearby Nellis Air Force Base, Hawes would depress and hold down a black thumb button on his throttle, activating the trigger on his joystick, then squeeze the trigger to launch an inert Hellfire at that tank from an altitude of two thousand feet. Whatever he did, Hawes had to make sure he put his left thumb on the correct button. The missile launch button on the throttle, whose original purpose was to deploy an emergency parachute, was positioned on the joystick just a quarter inch from another button that, if pressed and held, would kill the Predator's engine, yet another emergency mechanism.

There were other reasons to be cautious, for the Predator's controls— its human-machine interface, in the language of engineers—were complex and at times confusing. The previous September, another pilot at Indian Springs who thought he had the complicated drop-down menus of the ground control station computer memorized got into the wrong menu, commanded the equivalent of a system shutdown, and crashed Predator 3023 at Nellis. The purpose of that flight was to test the laser designator carried in one of the three remaining Forty-Four balls; as a result of the crash, the Air Force now had only two Forty-Four balls left.

Hawes wasn't likely to make that kind of mistake. He had learned to fly the Predator in 1996 as a Naval Reserve officer on loan to the Air Force, and had flown multiple missions over Bosnia and Iraq. During a break in his military service, he'd flown the Predator for General Atomics. Now, having severed his Navy ties and joined the Air Force, Hawes was an Air Combat Command UAV test pilot, a "plank holder" in a new unit of the 53rd Test and Evaluation Group that was less than a month old. ACC commander Jumper, intent on standardizing how the Air Force handled the Predator, had ordered the test unit created. Thus far, the detachment was just three men strong. Hawes was its pilot; Major Kenneth "2K" Kilmurray, the detachment commander, and Master Sergeant Leo Glovka, a veteran of Predator operations since 1995, were the unit's sensor operators. Test-launching the Hellfire from Predator 3034 was the detachment's first major assignment.

Certain the test would be covered by CNN, Hawes told his parents back in Minnesota to watch for him. The first Hellfire launch from a Predator in flight would indeed be historic, and the test was no secret. The Air Force and General Atomics would issue news releases about it, prompting *Inside the Air Force* and the Las Vegas *Review-Journal* to write articles about the project. As it turned out, however, the event was of far less interest to CNN than to the CIA and the NSC.

Charlie Allen of the CIA and Richard Clarke of the NSC had been wowed by the Predator video of bin Laden produced by the Summer Project. Motivated by both the USS *Cole* bombing and intelligence indicating that Al Qaeda was planning further attacks on U.S. interests, they were also keenly interested in the Air Force project to arm the Predator. Clarke had already recommended sending armed Predators to Afghanistan, in a paper titled "Strategy for Eliminating the Threat from the Jihadist Networks of al Qida: Status and Prospects," which he had finished on December 29, just over a week after Big Safari got word the INF Treaty roadblock had been lifted. On January 25, two days after the test ground launch of a Hellfire from Predator 3034 and five days after President George W. Bush was inaugurated, Clarke sent the new national security adviser, Condoleezza Rice, another memo with his Al Qaeda strategy paper attached. In this memo, Clarke told Rice, "We *urgently* need . . . a

Principals level review on the al Qida network." By that, the NSC counterterrorism chief meant that key players at the highest levels of
government—including the new president—needed to have a discussion
of what Clarke saw as the increasing threat posed by Osama bin Laden
and Al Qaeda. The Islamic terrorist group, he noted, was trying "to drive
the US out of the Muslim world" and "replace moderate, modern, Western regime [sic] in Muslim countries with theocracies modeled along
the lines of the Taliban."

As Clarke soon learned, getting the Bush administration to focus on
Al Qaeda, much less *do* something about it, would be no easy task. But
Clarke; his deputy, Roger Cressey; the CIA's Allen; and other senior officials were watching closely as the Air Force began conducting airborne
test launches of Hellfires from Predator 3034 that February.

Curt Hawes and most others on the test team were oblivious to the interest in what they were doing at the NSC and the CIA. Big Safari's Hellfire
test director Spoon Mattoon, however, knew who the armed Predator's
first customer was likely to be once the team he was leading proved it
ready for operations. The day after the new test detachment was established, the Summer Project team, including Big Safari's designated Predator crew, Scott Swanson and Gunny Guay, had gathered in a large,
windowless conference room on the sixth floor of CIA headquarters in
Langley, Virginia, for a "hot wash"—a detailed review—of the previous
fall's Predator flights over Afghanistan. For three full days, the Air Force
team and their CIA Counterterrorist Center partners discussed and
debated the pros and cons, accomplishments and failures, lessons learned
and ideas generated by the fifteen missions they had conducted. Besides
spotting bin Laden as many as three times, they had gotten video of terrorist training in progress, discovered training sites previously
unknown, mapped Taliban air defenses, and charted other military
assets. The intelligence gathered was impressive.

On the second day of the hot wash, CIA Director George Tenet and
CTC Director Cofer Black came by to congratulate and thank the participants. Black gave each a "challenge coin," a medallion the size of a silver

dollar, as a token of appreciation. On one side, the coins bore the initials CTC on a red, white, and blue background. "DCI Counterterrorist Center" and "Central Intelligence Agency" in brass-colored lettering trimmed the coin's border on that side. The flip side displayed the CIA seal: an American bald eagle's head, a compass with sixteen radiating spokes, and a white shield, bordered by "Central Intelligence Agency" and "United States of America" in gold.

The coins were nice, but many in the Air Force contingent were frustrated, and they found their CIA colleagues divided. Some at the hot wash agreed with Clarke and Allen that Predator reconnaissance flights alone were valuable enough to resume. Others, including Summer Project operations director Major Mark Cooter, wanted to wait and send the Predator back only when it was armed rather than risk discovery with more unarmed flights. On the CIA side, some opposed using an armed Predator against bin Laden or his lieutenants even if the Air Force perfected it. Revelations in the 1970s of CIA assassination plots against Cuban dictator Fidel Castro and other foreign leaders had led to searing Senate hearings that stained the agency's reputation. In 1976, President Gerald Ford signed an executive order banning any U.S. employee from engaging in, or conspiring to engage in, "political assassination," an order President Jimmy Carter renewed and President Ronald Reagan broadened by removing the word *political*. After the African embassy bombings in 1998, President Clinton signed a secret order giving the CIA authority to kill bin Laden in certain circumstances, but sending an armed drone to stalk the terrorist leader hadn't been contemplated then. For many at the CIA, there was ample reason to think twice before agreeing to such an operation, which could go badly wrong in many ways and would be controversial even if it succeeded. With the technology still being tested, the Bush administration still getting under way, the Al Qaeda threat still seemingly distant, and major legal and political issues still unresolved, the way forward was murky at best.

Soon these uncertainties would vanish. But as 2001 began, those pondering whether to send Hellfire-armed Predators on a big safari for Osama bin Laden and his top disciples were not so different from Captain Curt Hawes when his wife walked into their bedroom on that

February evening. They were groping in the dark, anxious about pulling the trigger.

Curt Hawes made it on time to his 4:30 a.m. briefing on February 16, which was held in the 15th Reconnaissance Squadron's auditorium at Indian Springs. At the briefing, Big Safari's Mattoon went through the plan for the first test shot of a Hellfire from a Predator in flight. The Air Force contingent wore green flight suits or camouflage fatigues; the rest of the twenty-two-member team, all civilians, were dressed in work pants or jeans, and most wore sweaters and jackets against the early morning desert chill. Everyone in the auditorium was tired but excited: since February 5, when General Atomics trucked Predator 3034 from El Mirage to Indian Springs, the team had worked almost nonstop to prepare for the test.

As the briefing ended, Hawes stood up and faced the motley crew. "We have come too far and all worked too hard for this to be anything but successful," he declared. "Let's go out and kick some ass!"

A few minutes later, a contractor crew using a ground control station at Indian Springs launched 3034 and flew the Predator northeast into Nellis Air Force Base's vast test and exercise ranges. After the drone was beyond some hills that made C-band line-of-sight control impossible, Hawes and sensor operator Leo Glovka took control of 3034 from a second ground control station parked on the Nellis test range, also using a C-band antenna. Under the crawl-walk-run philosophy of testing, the first Hellfires would be launched with the Predator under line-of-sight control, thus avoiding the risk of losing link to the drone when flying via satellite.

With 3034 carrying an inert, instrumented Hellfire (a missile fitted with sensors to gather and transmit data in flight), Hawes did some dry runs toward the target, an old tank parked in the desert. Glovka would go through the motions of a launch, putting the crosshairs of the Forty-Four ball's heat-detecting infrared sensor on the tank. To reduce the chances of a miss, though, a ground-based laser designator team would shine the beam used to guide the Hellfire to its target.

Finally satisfied they were ready, Hawes used the nose camera to line the Predator up on the tank at an altitude of two thousand feet, then flew toward a predetermined "engagement zone." Once 3034 entered the zone, Hawes depressed and held the black launch button on the throttle with his left thumb, then squeezed the trigger on the front of the joystick with his right forefinger. With a flash of heat and light that momentarily turned Glovka's infrared screen a milky white, the Hellfire rocketed off the drone's left wing and instantly disappeared.

The unarmed missile traveled three miles downrange and struck the tank about six inches to the right of dead center. As Major Ray Pry of Big Safari put it in an Air Force news release, the Hellfire "made a big, gray dent in the turret—just beautiful." Best of all, as instruments aboard the drone showed, the Predator barely shook.

After the test was finished, Hawes was struck by how anticlimactic the experience was. From the earthbound cockpit he was using to fly the Predator, he heard and felt nothing as the Hellfire left the wing and completed its flight in less than thirty seconds. The shot Hawes had anticipated for weeks seemed to be over almost before it began.

Five days later, the team repeated the performance twice. This time, though, Glovka used Predator 3034's Forty-Four ball to lase the target tank, and the second of the Hellfires they shot was live. Hawes launched the first shot while flying via C-band link, and the second while flying via Ku-band satellite control. Some on the team were nervous about the second shot, which they knew was being streamed live into the Pentagon so that several generals, including Jumper, could watch. To help ensure that Glovka could find the cold tank with the Forty-Four ball's heat-sensing infrared sensor—the Forty-Four lacked a daylight camera—some of the Army members of the team, Hellfire experts from Redstone Arsenal in Huntsville, Alabama, poured bags of Kingsford charcoal into the defunct tank's empty ammunition box, doused it with lighter fluid, and put a match to it. Because the desert sun had warmed the earth, they also drove a Chevy Suburban onto the sand in front of the tank and carved some donuts to churn up cooler soil, striving to provide even more contrast for the infrared camera.

Both Hellfire shots hit the target. That afternoon, Hawes and Glovka posed for a triumphant photo next to the tank they had hit, each still in his green flight suit, each standing with one dusty boot on a broken wheel their live missile had blasted loose. Hawes had found these Hell-fire shots far more exciting; he kept expecting a CNN crew to show up and ask to talk to the man who had fired the "shot heard around the world," though he later chastised himself for possibly being prideful. But technological revolutions often arrive quietly, and for the moment at least, Hawes and Glovka had to settle for a few high fives and pats on the back from their teammates.

A couple of weeks after the Hellfire test shots in Nevada, Snake Clark brought a small group of top managers and engineers from the Army Hellfire program office at Redstone Arsenal to CIA headquarters. Jumper and his fellow generals had been far from the only ones interested when Curt Hawes and Leo Glovka hit that tank in the desert with a live Hell-fire. When Richard Clarke, Charlie Allen, and others at the NSC and CIA learned that arming the Predator was proving feasible, they began press-ing to get this new weapon operational—ready to hunt Osama bin Laden and his top Al Qaeda lieutenants. Others within the "black world" of intelligence operations were also becoming far more interested in Jump-er's project to arm the Predator. Before they could decide whether to try using it against Al Qaeda, though, a number of difficult issues needed to be resolved. Snake Clark had brought the Army Hellfire experts to the CIA to help sort through some of the remaining technical challenges.

Greeted by Counterterrorist Center and Directorate of Operations representatives, the Army experts, civilians all, were given a tour of the sixth-floor CTC operations center created to command the unarmed Predator flights over Afghanistan the previous September. Their CIA hosts then took them to a conference room and showed the visitors something that made their eyes bulge: the "Tall Man in White" footage of Osama bin Laden crossing a courtyard at Tarnak Farms, his disciples orbiting their hero like planets about a sun. The CTC officials also showed the Army experts color video of other Al Qaeda figures cap-tured by the Predator's camera before the operation was suspended.

Then the CIA officials told their visitors something even more surprising: the CIA wanted to kill the people in those videos. They wanted to kill them with Hellfire missiles launched from Predators, and they wanted the Army experts to help make sure this experimental weapon could get the job done. The Air Force, General Atomics, Forty-Four ball maker Raytheon Corporation, and the Army Hellfire office had fired a couple of missiles off a Predator from two thousand feet above the ground and hit a big tank parked in the desert. The CIA wanted to know whether a Hellfire shot from a Predator flying at ten thousand or fifteen thousand feet could accurately strike a man walking in the open, or riding on a horse, or seated in a vehicle, or sheltering in a mud-brick building.

Terry McLean, a defense contractor engineer working for the Hellfire office, saw his Army colleagues blanch as the CIA men unabashedly used the word *kill*. During a discussion that lasted a good two hours, they seemed to sprinkle it into every sentence. It was jarring, to say the least; in those days, most members of the military-industrial complex would do verbal backflips to avoid the word *kill*, preferring euphemisms such as *kinetic action*. The Hellfire was an antitank missile, a weapon built to destroy machines. People might be inside those machines, but nobody ever talked about that.

The Hellfire was a "tank killer"—could it kill people who weren't inside tanks, where the missile's explosion was contained and intensified? Probably, the Army experts told the CIA officials, but not with the C-model Hellfire launched in the Nevada tests, a variant designed to be fired from helicopters flying two thousand feet or less above the ground. Nor could the Hellfire do what the CIA wanted with the Forty-Four ball's laser designator, whose range was far less than the five miles or more needed to lase a target from the altitudes where the Predator loitered. Engineering fixes for those problems could probably be found, the experts allowed. A newer K-model Hellfire, whose digital guidance was better than the C model's analog mechanism, might work. But the antitank Hellfire's lethality against "soft targets," as the engineers preferred to put it, would have to be tested. The missile was designed to penetrate armor with a jet of molten molybdenum formed by a precursor explosion on impact. The molten molybdenum would burn a hole through steel, providing entry for a high-explosive warhead weighing less than twenty pounds but whose detonation, contained by the metal walls of a tank, would incinerate anything inside. If fired at a soft target, the missile might go right through it and explode in the ground.

That was appalling, one of the Army experts gasped as the group drove away from the CIA. A long-standing executive order made it illegal for federal government employees to take part in assassinations, he reminded his colleagues. Just helping the CIA devise a weapon to use this way might get them all in trouble. In any event, this was no job for the Hellfire program office. The Army Hellfire program existed to provide combat weapons for the military, not the CIA.

Soon Terry McLean, an Auburn University engineering graduate and Huntsville native—his engineer father had worked on the space program—found himself in a strange situation. The Army program office unofficially left it to McLean, a contractor, to lead a half dozen Army engineers assigned to help Big Safari and the CIA adapt the helicopter-launched, antitank Hellfire to be fired from the Predator in targeted killings.

About the time McLean and his colleagues visited Langley, and at the urging of Richard Clarke, National Security Adviser Condoleezza Rice asked the CIA to draft an order for President Bush to sign authorizing covert operations in Afghanistan that might include lethal action. On March 14, General Jumper convened a meeting about the Predator at Air Combat Command, and then issued a series of orders governing Air Force use of the drone. One of his orders directed Big Safari to get a new laser ball on the Predator and modify the Hellfire to work from altitude. And he wanted it done ASAP.

They were packed into the ground control station like sardines, roughly twenty of them, mostly engineers, all but one male, making enough involuntary skin contact to feed phobias. But as they squeezed into the crowded confines of this eight-by-eight-by-twenty-four-foot metal box crammed with computer work stations and humming electronics, no one was griping. On April 4, 2001, everyone on the team developing the Hellfire Predator, as insiders had begun calling it, wanted to be in the GCS at El Mirage to see how a new sensor turret would perform in its first test flight aboard the Predator. Especially eager was William M. Casey, forty-seven, chief engineer for Raytheon Corporation's new Multi-Spectral Targeting System, known to the Hellfire Predator team as the MTS ball.

A derivative of Raytheon's Forty-Four ball, the battleship gray MTS looked much the same on the outside. The first MTS, in fact, was partially fabricated from salvaged remains of the Forty-Four ball crushed in the first Wartime Integrated Laser Designator Predator test at Indian Springs, on May 4, 1999, when the drone's composite nose gear collapsed on landing and the aircraft slid to a stop on its sensor turret. Like the Forty-Four ball, the MTS was nineteen inches tall, but the glass apertures in the MTS ball's aluminum skin were different sizes and shapes. The MTS's camera aperture was squarish instead of round, with a lens window that angled down and in at its top, slanting toward the small, round laser designator aperture on the other side of the turret's face. The effect (viewed with imagination) was a mechanical squint, lending the MTS the look of a robot taking aim. With a circumference of 17.8 inches, the MTS was only an inch or so fatter than the Forty-Four ball, but at 124 pounds, it was more than ten pounds heavier. In addition to an infrared sensor and a laser designator with nearly twice the range of the one in the Forty-Four ball, the MTS held a daylight video camera. Carrying the MTS, the Predator would be able to beam back not just black-and-white infrared images but also color video of what it saw. The new ball's laser designator could also paint a target from five miles or more away.

Big Safari, viewing the WILD Predator as a successful experiment despite its limited use, had advocated development of the MTS in late 1999, after Kosovo. General Jumper had kick-started it in early 2000, after taking over Air Combat Command and learning that ACC had taken the Forty-Four balls off the three WILD Predators sent to Kosovo. Raytheon's Casey persuaded the Air Force and Navy to make the MTS a joint project, and they pooled their money with the company's to design, develop, and fabricate three prototypes incorporating major improvements over the Forty-Four ball. Thanks to newly available semiconductors, the MTS would carry one of the first-ever "staring" infrared sensors, a device able to detect heat within its field of view the way a camera senses light, rather than producing an image by the less advanced scanning method used in the Forty-Four ball. The more advanced MTS infrared sensor also provided a far sharper black-and-white image at far greater distances.

Originally, Big Safari was to get one MTS prototype for Jumper's project to arm the Predator, and the Navy was to get two for testing. In late March 2001, however, after the cadre of officials eager to use the Predator to hunt bin Laden got excited by the missile tests at Nellis, and after Jumper ordered the project sped up, all three MTS prototypes went to the Hellfire project. Now, on April 4, the engineers were jammed into a ground control station at El Mirage to see how the MTS worked.

Years later, General Atomics project manager Chris Dusseault offered a dry assessment of the results: "Many issues were discovered during the testing." Two General Atomics pilots who were at the controls in the GCS for the initial test flight described their response much more vividly.

"Man, this color sucks," Raytheon's Casey heard one of them say early on, complaining about the color balance in the daylight TV camera.

"What did he say?" someone at the back of the GCS asked.

"Color sucks!" someone replied.

As one of the General Atomics crew tried to use an autotracker feature to lock on a target with the laser designator, Casey heard him say, "The tracker sucks."

"What?" someone in back asked.

"Tracker sucks!" someone replied.

Then Casey heard another comment: "Focus sucks."

"What?"

"Focus *sucks!*"

The MTS ball's black-and-white infrared imagery was about the only feature of the new sensor turret spared complaints. As the test flight went on, snorts were heard and sharp glances exchanged in the increasingly claustrophobic GCS.

Casey and two Raytheon engineers with him weren't surprised by the performance of the MTS, which they knew was immature. They were a bit dispirited, though, to realize how much work needed to be done before the technology would be ready for operational use. Casey figured they needed to do something to dispel that cloud.

At the project team's daily briefing the next morning, Casey stood in the El Mirage hangar and told the group the GCS had been so crowded the day before that it was "hard to hear the evaluations at the back." So in order to "enhance and facilitate communications," and to ensure that "everybody has access to the information," he and Raytheon engineer Willie Norman had fabricated some communication aids for use in the GCS during the next test. Made from six-by-six-inch squares of poster board glued to wooden tongue depressors, the aids were signs bearing messages Casey and Norman had written out by hand with felt markers. Some were intended for use by the Predator flight crew, Casey explained, and he and Norman would use a couple of others. Then Casey held them up so everyone could see what they said:

"Color sucks."

"Tracker sucks."

"Focus sucks."

As laughter echoed through the hangar, Casey held up a message that he and Norman might use:

"Bite me."

The tension from the previous day's failures evaporated.

Many changes would have to be made before this new sensor ball could be used either for reconnaissance or for guiding a Hellfire from a Predator to a target, and both tasks would prove challenging. All through April, the team flew the MTS on Predator 3034, first at El Mirage, then at nearby Edwards Air Force Base, where on isolated test ranges they could shine the invisible but potentially blinding laser beam.

Among many other problems, the Predator team discovered that it was difficult to keep the invisible laser designator beam "bore-sighted"— precisely linked to the aim point visible in graphic overlays on the monitors of the daylight and infrared cameras of the MTS. With the laser beam accurately bore-sighted, the sensor operator could guide a Hellfire to a precise aim point by keeping the crosshairs of either camera, daylight or infrared, on the exact spot the missile was meant to hit. But as the April flights continued, it proved impossible to keep the laser beam bore-sighted after the Predator was airborne. While using the drone's cameras to aim the laser beam at the center of a black-and-white grid on a sixteen-by-sixteen-foot plywood "target board" and viewing its sparkle through a special camera on the ground, the team observed consistent aim point variances of several feet between the MTS's designator and its cameras. A variance of that size would mean nothing if the weapon following the laser were a five-hundred-pound bomb, but with the Hellfire's tiny twenty-pound warhead, and against targets as small as a man, a miss of a few feet would be as good as a mile. Unless the Predator team could correct it, the inability to bore-sight accurately was a potentially showstopping flaw.

Given that and lesser problems, Bill Casey reluctantly sent the MTS back to Raytheon's factory in McKinney, Texas, where they could take it apart, diagnose the sources of its problems, and perform major surgery. Casey and his team then spent the last week of April and the first week of May rehabilitating the MTS. They replaced the ball's laser transmitter, upgraded its software, and made other fixes. On May 10 they sent the ball back to El Mirage.

During the two-week pause, Raytheon's engineers also came up with a solution for the bore-sighting problem. After puzzling over its cause for some time, Casey concluded that after the Predator left the hot desert floor and climbed into the below-freezing temperatures at fifteen thousand feet or more, some piece of metal in the MTS must be contracting more than other pieces and skewing the laser beam. But isolating that piece of metal might prove impossible, so Casey and his engineers came up with a different bore-sighting method. From now on, the Predator's operators would launch the drone and climb to the median altitude planned for its mission, then aim the camera crosshairs at the center of the target board on the ground and shine the laser beam. Someone looking at the target board through the special camera able to see laser light would check the divergence between the MTS laser designator and its camera aim points and then tell the sensor operator, say, "You're six feet left and four feet high." The sensor operator would type that information into the keyboard on the flight control console in the GCS and transmit it to the MTS ball, whose internal steering mechanisms would adjust the laser beam and cameras accordingly.

The Predator team got mixed results in more Hellfire tests on the China Lake range from May 22 through May 31. Flying 3034 at various altitudes and shooting a number of missiles at target tanks, they found that although the latest fixes helped, this jury-rigged weapon performed awkwardly at best. The hybrid system—a featherweight drone originally designed to carry sensors but not weapons; a missile originally designed to attack tanks from low altitude, not people from several miles up and away; a prototype sensor ball drafted into service before its creators deemed it ready—was very much a work in progress.

The team also discovered a new problem. Terry McLean and his engineers had been correct in saying that the antitank K model of the Hellfire could be launched from far greater altitudes than its standard two-thousand-foot ceiling, but to do that they had to overcome the missile's inherent "pitch bias." The standard Hellfire was programmed to climb when fired so a helicopter could launch it from behind a tree or hilltop. McLean had General Atomics alter electronic signals sent to the missile from the Predator before launch, essentially tricking the Hellfire's autopilot into thinking it was being launched nose up so it would veer downward as severely as possible. That fix helped, but even so, four out of nine shots they took at China Lake tanks over the last nine days of May missed. Once, the Ku-band satellite link was lost just as the missile was launched. Once, the missile malfunctioned. Once, the electronic signal used to fool the missile's autopilot was too weak and the missile went off at the wrong angle. Another time, the bright, hot plume from the Hellfire's rocket blinded the laser designator and the device lost the target.

Getting the Hellfire Predator ready to hunt Osama bin Laden was taking a lot longer, and proving much more difficult, than those who wanted to use it that way had expected.

So was getting a decision on whether to use it. Six days after the MTS ball went back to Raytheon, Richard Clarke finally got a semblance of what he had been urging since President Bush took office: high-level attention to the Al Qaeda threat. On April 30, the NSC's Deputies Committee met to review terrorism policy for the first time under Bush. By then, Clarke was increasingly frustrated with the new administration's approach to what, in his judgment, was the most serious and immediate threat facing the United States.

Earlier that spring, Condoleezza Rice, the new national security adviser, had decided to downgrade Clarke's position. She cut him out of meetings he had formerly attended of the Principals Committee, meaning the NSC's five statutory members (the president, the vice president, and the secretaries of state, defense, and treasury) and other legally designated advisers. She also decided that Clarke's interagency Counterterrorism Security Group would no longer report to the Principals Committee directly, as it had done under Clinton. Rice asked Clarke to stay on at the NSC, but she and her deputy, Stephen Hadley, wanted a new, more comprehensive approach to combatting terrorism, as opposed to what she regarded as "tit-for-tat" responses exemplified by President Clinton's cruise missile strikes on targets in Afghanistan and Sudan after Al Qaeda's bombings of U.S. embassies in Africa in 1998.

Clarke began the April 30 Deputies Committee session by arguing that "we need to target Bin Laden and his leadership by reinitiating flights of the Predator." As Clarke later wrote, Paul Wolfowitz, the deputy defense secretary, was puzzled by this focus on one man. Instead, Wolfowitz wanted to talk about the terrorist threat posed by dictator Saddam Hussein of Iraq, a threat for which Clarke and Deputy CIA Director John McLaughlin told Wolfowitz they saw no evidence.

Leaders of the CIA agreed that Al Qaeda was a major threat, but the agency was divided on what to do about using the Predator against bin Laden. In meetings at CIA headquarters that spring, Clarke ally Charlie Allen pushed their view that the unarmed Predator should be sent back to Afghanistan as soon as weather permitted, and the armed version as soon as the Air Force had it ready. Allen ran into a wall of opposition.

Cofer Black, the CIA Counterterrorist Center director, argued against sending the unarmed Predator back for fear the Taliban would shoot one down. The Taliban had scrambled MiG fighter jets to go after the drone half a dozen times the previous fall, after all. "I do not believe the possible recon value outweighs the risk of possible program termination when the stakes are raised by the Taliban parading a charred Predator in front of CNN," Black wrote in a memo to Clarke dated January 25, the same day Clarke sent his first memos on Al Qaeda to Rice. CIA Director George Tenet, meanwhile, was leery of using an armed Predator if his agency was to be responsible for pulling the trigger. He questioned whether the CIA director had legal authority to use such a weapon. He questioned whether a civilian intelligence agency should even be given such a mission.

Others at the CIA questioned how effective the Hellfire might be against soft targets, a doubt that led to a construction project whose nature, in later years, would become a media myth.

Within days of the Deputies Committee meeting, Big Safari's Spoon Mattoon got word that the CIA wanted to know what the Hellfire would do to a mud-and-wattle building of the sort found in Afghanistan, and to any people inside. Cofer Black wanted the Air Force to prove that if a Hellfire hit Osama bin Laden's residence at Tarnak Farms it could kill the terrorist leader. The answer was unknown, for what a Hellfire's lethal radius in a mud-brick house would be, or what collateral damage it might cause, had never been tested. The CIA wanted Big Safari to find out.

The CIA officer who brought the request to Mattoon had already hired a contractor in Tucson, Arizona, to erect an imitation Afghan building on a desert range at China Lake. The CIA officer also sent Mattoon the substantial bill—$170,000, which Mattoon had to pay from the $3.1 million the Air Force had budgeted for the entire Hellfire project. The Tucson contractor began work at China Lake around the time Mattoon's team began test launches from Predator 3034 at tanks using the MTS ball. Though the Hellfire Predator was still little more than a technological experiment, Mattoon and his team were under rising pressure to make it work, and fast. Snake Clark was calling every day to get updates for the Air Force brass, the CIA, and others. So on Friday, June 1, despite the mixed results of the missile launch tests thus far, the Predator team moved its testing to the building in the desert at China Lake erected at the CIA's behest.

When Mattoon, project manager Chris Dusseault of General Atomics, and Army Hellfire expert Terry McLean went to see the structure, they were flabbergasted. "A hundred and seventy thousand dollars for this?" Mattoon sputtered. The edifice Mattoon and his colleagues observed that day would be described in an article published in 2002 in the *Washington Post* as a "stone-for-stone replica" of a "four-room villa" outside Kandahar where Osama bin Laden had once lived. In 2006, *U.S. News & World Report* called the building "a replica of the home that bin Laden lived in at Tarnak Farms, a square, squat building whose structure and density the technicians approximated with satellite imagery provided by the National Geospatial-Intelligence Agency."

In fact, it was nothing of the sort. The target building at China Lake resembled neither a villa, nor the housing at Tarnak Farms, nor indeed any structure typical of those found in Afghanistan. Instead, it was straight out of Southwest America, an adobe brick rectangle whose exterior walls stood a little over thirteen feet tall and were forty-eight feet long by about nineteen feet wide. The four walls rested on a four-inch concrete slab and held up an adobe brick roof resting on forty-nine rough-cut four-by-twelve Douglas fir timbers. Inside the building, two eight-inch-thick adobe brick walls divided the "villa" into three rooms. The bricks of the exterior walls were mostly eighteen inches long, nine inches wide, and six inches thick, and the walls themselves were two brick lengths thick. Besides an empty doorway, the structure had four big, empty windows. When McLean stuck his arm into one of them and reached in as far as he could, he found the walls were as thick as the distance from his armpit to his fingertips—thirty-eight inches.

Mattoon was outraged at what the contractor had built—by misreading the specifications the CIA had provided, apparently. The thickness of the walls, the strength of the foundation and roof, plus the yawning windows and doorway were going to make it tough to extrapolate the results of Hellfire test shots here to any structure in Afghanistan. When Mattoon walked around the south end of the adobe building, though, he got a surprise that brightened his mood. A China Lake surveyor had draped a big white tarp along the top edge of the pinkish structure that bore a cheerful sign. It read: "Hellfire Tacos," with "Hellfire" written in red and "Tacos" in green. In a red circle above and to the right of those words, the sign maker had advertised "3/99¢." The Predator team immediately dubbed the building Taco Bell.

When the team fired a K-model Hellfire at Taco Bell that Friday night, however, Mattoon's mood again turned sour. The rocket plume blinded the MTS laser designator, and the missile missed the building by such a wide margin that it flew into the side of a distant mountain. Afterward, the usually jaunty Mattoon came to Casey wearing a scowl.

"Bill, we've got to fix this," he said grimly.

Casey and his Raytheon team worked through the weekend, and by early the next week they had come up with a way to deal with the blinding of the laser designator by the heat and light of the missile's rocket plume. Part of the problem was that the MTS ball's autotracker, the feature that allowed a sensor operator to lock the laser designator onto a target, worked by analyzing the Predator's video and using a computer algorithm to keep the laser beam aimed at the target. But when the Hellfire launched and its rocket fired, the video became nothing but a wavy heat mirage. Their solution was to program the autotracker to turn off automatically when the Predator's pilot pulled the trigger—there was an interval of one second before the missile actually launched—and to come back on four seconds later. By then, the missile was away and its rocket engine's three-second burn was over.

Five days after the first shot failed, the Predator team was ready to fire another K-model Hellfire at Taco Bell. To help answer the question of whether the Hellfire would kill bin Laden indoors, air pressure and temperature gauges were placed inside the hut. Chris Dusseault of General Atomics added another wrinkle after consulting a Redstone Arsenal expert on lethality against soft targets. As Dusseault learned from the expert—a five-foot-five blonde named Edith Crow and known to teasing colleagues as Lady Death or the Black Widow—small-arms lethality tests usually used special manikins filled with ballistic gelatin to mimic human flesh. Lethality tests of military weapons such as grenades and missiles, on the other hand, usually used "witness panels" of Sheetrock and plywood to imitate the ways battle dress uniforms, other gear carried by troops, and bone protect internal organs from penetration by shrapnel. Lacking time and money for such scientific methods, the Big Safari team cut human silhouettes out of plywood and propped them up inside Taco Bell. At Crow's suggestion, Dusseault also drove a pickup truck to a nearby grocery and bought fifty watermelons. The rind of a watermelon, Lady Death had explained, was imperfect for the purpose, but in a weapons test it could serve as a relatively good equivalent of human skin. If a piece of metal punctured a watermelon rind, it was also likely to go through skin, which is thinner but tougher.

The team propped the watermelons throughout the interior of Taco Bell, setting some on the floor to simulate someone sitting or sleeping, and using stacks of bricks to arrange them at heights where enemies might logically be caught standing. Then, with Captain Scott Swanson and Master Sergeant Jeff Guay of Big Safari operating Predator 3034, they fired a live K-model Hellfire into the hut's south wall. Aided by the autotracker, Guay guided the missile into the wall only a few feet below the "Hellfire Tacos 3/99¢" sign.

The missile's precursor charge—the explosive designed to punch a hole through armor by creating a jet of molten molybdenum—left a fairly small hole in the exterior of Taco Bell's thick adobe walls. But when the main warhead detonated milliseconds after the precursor charge, the high explosive blasted a circular chunk of bricks about six feet in diameter into the hut. Inspecting the interior afterward, the team found bits of brick and metal a bit larger than BBs in the plywood silhouettes and multiple holes in the rinds of the watermelons. The watermelons closest to the explosion had been split open by the concussion. The plywood silhouettes had been knocked over. Temperature and pressure gauges that had been standing lay on the floor, covered with loose bricks. There was also a fist-size hole in the sand, created as the molten molybdenum cooled nearly instantly and formed a solid metal rod that buried itself dozens of feet into the ground.

The next day, June 7, the team fired an M-model Hellfire into their Taco Bell, a newer "blast fragmentation" variant of the missile introduced the previous year and designed for use against boats and small ships, which are softer targets than tanks. As planned, Guay guided the missile straight through the roof, but the warhead exploded as it hit, failing to penetrate deeply enough into the room to spray it with shrapnel. Terry McLean had his doubts about the utility of the M model in any event, for it had a tendency to "dud" if it struck a target at the wrong angle.

Asked to gauge the Hellfire's effectiveness against other targets as well, the Predator team fired an M-model Hellfire at a white Chevy Suburban parked in the desert. Osama bin Laden was known to drive a Mitsubishi Pajero Mini SUV, sold in the United States as the Montero. To gauge lethality, the testers put a watermelon in the driver's seat of the Suburban. Just for fun, they also taped an eight-by-ten glossy photo of Snake Clark to the melon and tossed pictures of him, Mattoon, and Dusseault onto the front seat. This time, though, Guay tried so hard to keep the crosshairs on the target that he must have moved them slightly as the missile was in flight. The Hellfire exploded in the sand several feet to the side of the vehicle.

With that, the test shots ended for the time being. On June 8, Swanson and a General Atomics pilot ferried Predator 3034 from China Lake back to El Mirage. After thirteen missile tests at China Lake, the team concluded that a building as sturdy as their Taco Bell wasn't going to collapse if hit by a Hellfire K, though it would do a lot of damage and almost certainly kill most or all the people inside who happened to be close to the explosion. If a Hellfire M was used—and went off—people inside might survive, though anyone left standing was going to have a mean headache and a lot of trouble hearing for a good while. Of the thirteen test shots, six had missed their mark; given the experimental nature of the weapon, the team considered this an acceptable batting average. On June 9, Big Safari reported to Washington that the Hellfire Predator was ready to deploy.

When their report got back to Washington, the CIA sent two of its officers to Redstone Arsenal in Huntsville to talk about how they might make the Hellfire a better weapon for killing people outside tanks. Redstone assigned the problem to an expert on urban warfare, who immediately began figuring out how to make the missile more deadly to enemies caught out in the open or sheltering in their mud-and-wattle homes.

When Chris Dusseault submitted his expense report for the month, he included a request for reimbursement for more than two hundred dollars for watermelons. His boss at General Atomics, Brad Clark, was furious. Dusseault was thirty-three years old and known to enjoy a party.

"What are you guys doing out there," Clark demanded angrily, "having a kegger?"

No, Dusseault explained, just improvising.

They were improvising in Washington, too. Throughout the spring, the number and credibility of terrorist threats against the United States reported to and by the CIA and the FBI had been rising dramatically. Richard Clarke had begun the April 30 NSC Deputies Committee meeting by describing CIA warnings about Al Qaeda; in early May, a "walk-in" informant told the FBI that Al Qaeda was making plans for attacks on London, Boston, and New York. On May 16, a tip phoned in to a U.S. embassy warned that bin Laden allies were planning an attack in the United States using "high explosives." As a government report would later phrase it, the "system was blinking red."

On May 29, Clarke wrote a memo to Condoleezza Rice and her deputy, Stephen Hadley, discussing the potential threats and warning that "When these attacks occur, as they likely will, we will wonder what more we could have done to stop them." The CIA was getting worried, too. Cofer Black told Rice in May that on a scale of one to ten he judged the terrorist threat level to be at seven.

With the risk of an attack by Al Qaeda increasing and Big Safari reporting the Hellfire Predator tested enough to deploy, the CIA got down to discussing the nuts and bolts of how a mission to kill bin Laden with an armed drone might be conducted. Sometime in late June, Air Force Lieutenant General John "Soup" Campbell, who as associate director of central intelligence for military support was chief liaison between Langley and the Joint Chiefs of Staff, scheduled two "tabletop" exercises to help wring out the issues. A soft-spoken, gentlemanly fighter pilot from Kentucky, Campbell had gravitated into intelligence work after a stint on the Joint Staff in the 1990s and had arrived at the CIA the previous June. Now, in windowless conference rooms at the CIA, he led what amounted to a couple of "chair flies" of the first Predator drone strike ever contemplated. The first was attended by a large group of officials, action officers, and experts. Campbell wanted every agency that had skin in the game, including the NSA and what was then the National Imagery and Mapping Agency, to be part of the deliberations. The second tabletop, in the seventh-floor director's conference room, was an executive session for top CIA officials only.

At the first such session, about twenty people were at the table, including Charlie Allen, who was seated next to Richard Clarke's deputy, Roger Cressey. A number of CIA, NSC, and Defense Department lawyers were present; lining the room's walls were twenty or so Counterterrorist Center officials, Air Force officers, and what are known in government as SMEs, for "subject matter experts." After inviting participants to shed their jackets and loosen their ties, Campbell asked a former Army officer hired by the CTC for his deep experience in counterterrorism to present what the CIA knew about bin Laden from other sources as of September 27, 2000, when the Predator's camera shot the "Tall Man in White" video.

That took about an hour, and then the briefer presented a specific scenario. Let's say HUMINT tells us that bin Laden is going to be at Tarnak Farms, the former Army officer said, so we decide to launch the armed Predator. Then Campbell screened the "Tall Man in White" video, which many in the room had never seen. When it ended, Campbell asked who would be willing to fire a Hellfire missile from a Predator at the man in the video, and who feared that doing so might be a mistake, and why. The response was unanimous: everyone in the room said they would support a decision to fire a missile at the man on the screen. The total intelligence picture—not just the Predator video—left the group feeling certain that the man in the video was in fact Osama bin Laden, that the admirers surrounding him must also be extremists, and that there were no women or children at risk of being hurt by a Hellfire explosion.

Then the briefer offered a second scenario. In this one, no HUMINT or other supplementary intelligence was available. All the group had to go on when deciding whether to fire was another video, this time one that showed scenes the Predator's camera had captured during the Summer Project while flying over a suspected Al Qaeda training camp. Suddenly a tall man in white robes was on the screen, walking along the outside wall of the terrorist training compound with a group of other men fanned out as if in a security cordon. The appearance of the tall man and the behavior of those around him suggested he was bin Laden, but the imagery alone left room for doubt, and there was no corroborating intelligence from CIA agents or tribal allies to offer positive identification.

Once again Campbell asked the room: who would be willing to fire a missile at the man and who would pass on doing so? This time there was disagreement. Some argued that the video justified taking a shot; if the man was indeed bin Laden, it might eliminate a great threat to America, and in any event it would take out some Al Qaeda terrorists. Others argued that without supporting intelligence, there was too much room for error. Campbell found this encouraging. If this new weapon was going to be used, he wanted to be sure that those using it would be discriminating, not just say, "We'll shoot anything that moves."

After the group had worked through the two scenarios, Campbell led a discussion of other issues. What rules should be adopted to avoid collateral damage, especially that which killed or hurt women and children? And how would the CIA and the rest of the government deal with the aftermath of a drone strike that killed bin Laden? "Okay, we're going to shoot," he posited. "What comes next? What do we do the next day?"

Campbell and his Army officer briefer later held a smaller tabletop for more senior CIA officials and encountered much greater division. Despite the existence of secret presidential orders, findings, and other directives relating to bin Laden and Al Qaeda, Director Tenet was sure his agency lacked the legal authority to kill someone by firing a missile from a drone, a worry others shared. Some in the smaller meeting also expressed concern about what might happen if the CIA's hand in a drone strike became known.

Other meetings about the Predator were held that summer at both the CIA and the White House. In one, Richard Shiffrin, deputy general counsel for intelligence at the Pentagon, raised an issue that set the Hellfire Predator project back weeks. Under a Status of Forces Agreement between the United States and Germany (a pact delineating what U.S. troops and forces could legally do on German soil), the United States might risk major legal and diplomatic problems, Shiffrin warned, if a crew in a ground control station at Ramstein Air Base, where the GCS had been located during the Summer Project, fired missiles from a Predator. Charlie Allen thought Shiffrin's argument specious—the missile would be fired in Afghanistan, not Germany—but the Pentagon lawyer was adamant. Either the German government would have to officially agree to the presence on its soil of a crew controlling the Predator and launching the drone's Hellfires, in which case the Americans could surely forget keeping the operation covert for very long, or the GCS would have to be located somewhere else.

But where? Even with the system blinking red, even with the Hellfire Predator working well enough to deploy, there seemed many reasons to hesitate.

10

READY OR NOT

"What if I could figure out a way to operate the Predators from a location in the United States?"

That question, posed with unusual trepidation for him, was asked by Werner, the technoscientist on contract to Big Safari. In 1995, Werner had streamed Predator video into the Pentagon for the first time ever. In 1999 he had created a way to cue fighter pilots over Kosovo to what the Predator's cameras were seeing. In 2000 he had devised a unique satellite setup that allowed the Air Force to fly the unarmed version of the Predator over Afghanistan for the CIA from a ground control station in Germany. Now, during a meeting in the latter part of July 2001 at the CIA that included more than a hundred military and intelligence experts, Werner gingerly raised his hand to suggest he could solve a problem that had stumped everyone else in the room. Until he spoke up, the group seemed about ready to abandon the idea of sending an armed Predator to hunt Osama bin Laden.

The room fell silent, though Werner could hear some quiet chuckles and, from the corner of his eye, glimpse some shaking heads.

"Do you really think you can do this?" asked the leader of the meeting, Counterterrorist Center Deputy Director Alec B., his voice betraying a mixture of incredulity and hope. (Alec B. has never been willing to allow his full name to be published.)

All through June, reports that Al Qaeda was planning major attacks continued to flow in from various sources to the CIA, the FBI, and other arms of government. During the first week of July, Richard Clarke convened the NSC's Counterterrorism Security Group and asked the various federal agency members to go on "full alert" against terrorist attacks. On July 11 the deputy national security adviser, Stephen Hadley, hoping to hurry along the Hellfire Predator project, sent a memo to CIA Deputy Director John McLaughlin, Deputy Defense Secretary Paul Wolfowitz, and Air Force General Richard Myers, vice chairman of the Joint Chiefs of Staff, telling them that by September 1 the White House wanted to deploy Predators "capable of being armed." The same day, the Air Force legislative liaison office sent ten key members of Congress letters that Snake Clark's staff had prepared reporting that $2.275 million was being transferred from other programs "to complete the Hellfire demonstration." The money would be used, the letters said, "to modify two more Predator aircraft to develop useable tactics, techniques and procedures for weapons delivery from UAVs."

By this point, senior officials had concluded that firing missiles off a drone controlled from German soil was legally and politically impossible unless they asked Berlin's permission, and no one wanted to risk that. Attempts to find another country in Europe where the GCS could be based had failed. Werner and Air Force Major Mark Cooter, who had served as operations director for the Summer Project flights of the Predator over Afghanistan and would reprise that role if such flights resumed, had studied twelve different alternatives to Ramstein, from putting the ground control station on a ship to placing it in Scotland. For various technical and political reasons, none of the satellite and communications experts in the meeting at the CIA could identify a suitable new location anywhere abroad, and no one except Werner thought it possible to effectively control a Predator and fire its missiles from the United States. The curvature of the earth made it impossible to communicate from U.S. soil to a Predator over Afghanistan through a single satellite relay, and every expert but Werner believed that any other setup would introduce too much latency—delay in the signal due to travel time—to allow a sensor operator to reliably hold the laser designator's beam on a target, especially in the case of a moving target. Even when the GCS was located in Germany there had been nearly a full second of latency for the pilot controlling the Predator over Afghanistan, and slightly more than a full second's delay in the video from Afghanistan reaching Washington via Ramstein. But Werner had been studying the idea of operating Predators from the United States for quite a while, and he thought he saw a way to overcome the extra latency. He would do it by adding a new wrinkle to split operations, the scheme he had devised for the Summer Project.

Under split operations, a flight crew in Uzbekistan equipped with a C-band line-of-sight data link and minimal controls had launched and recovered the Predator while a flight crew in a GCS at Ramstein used the Ku-band satellite link to fly the drone on its missions over Afghanistan. Since then, Werner had studied the idea of moving the mission crew to Indian Springs Air Force Auxiliary Field, where the two Air Force Predator squadrons were based. He had even mused about the possibility of having Predator operators fly missions from a permanent building with pilot and sensor operator consoles built into comfortable, soundproofed rooms like those of a television station, instead of in a freestanding equivalent of a freight container. The pilots could fly their missions during the day, then go home to their families for dinner in the evening and sleep in their own beds. Some found the idea nothing short of absurd: a couple of years earlier, Werner had proposed this notion during an Air Combat Command meeting at Indian Springs, and those present told him he was dreaming. "We will never operate that way," he was assured. So Werner filed the idea away in the back of his mind—until the July 2001 meeting of experts at CIA headquarters.

Based on his extensive knowledge of the satellite system and unofficial technical inquiries he had made of experts at satellite manufacturers and elsewhere, Werner declared that flying the Predator from U.S. soil "should be possible." It could be done, he thought, by deconstructing a black box in the Predator system's satellite earth terminal, which contained both a multiplexer—a device that combined the various data signals from the GCS into a single digital stream—and a modem, which converted the digital stream from the multiplexer into an analog radio signal for uplink to the satellite. The modem performed the opposite function when the Predator's data signal came back from the satellite, converting that analog radio signal into a digital signal for return to the GCS.

Werner's idea was to put several thousand miles in between the multiplexer and the modem by locating them on either side of an existing fiber-optic network that crossed the Atlantic Ocean. He would move the multiplexer with the ground control station to the United States and leave the modem with the satellite earth terminal in Germany. If the Defense Department fiber-optic network were chosen carefully, Werner calculated that he could hold the round-trip latency on the fiber network between Ramstein and the United States to less than two-tenths of a second. This would make the round-trip latency between the GCS at Langley and the Predator over Afghanistan—the amount of time that would elapse between a pilot sending the drone a control input and receiving return signals showing the results—less than 1.3 seconds in all.

After describing his idea to those attending the CIA meeting, Werner added that "I should hasten to point out that this has never actually been done before, so there may be a part of the architecture somewhere that might preclude it."

Hearing this caution, Alec B. asked how much confidence Werner had in his scheme.

"I would give it an eighty percent chance of succeeding," the Big Safari scientist replied. Then he added a final word: "Although these odds significantly favor success, they're not the odds I would want to go into heart surgery with. It all depends on how desperate you are to do the operation."

"How about we let you know tomorrow?" Alec B. responded.

The next afternoon, Alec B. phoned to ask how long Werner thought it would take to create and test the system he envisioned. With enough money and people, Werner told him, maybe three months.

"We have six weeks," replied the CIA man. Given how early winter weather set in over Afghanistan, he noted, they had to start flying sometime in September, even if they couldn't be ready by September 1, as the NSC had wanted. Alec B. said he would call Big Safari Director Bill Grimes to make sure Werner got what he needed.

Over the next few days, Werner did deeper research on what it would take to put in place what he was now thinking of as remote split operations, in which the satellite earth terminal and GCS would be separated by an ocean. On August 1, Werner met at the Pentagon with Brigadier General Scott Gration, the Joint Staff's deputy director for operations, who more than a year earlier had first suggested the CIA use the Predator to search for Osama bin Laden. The Deputies Committee of the National Security Council was meeting that same day to discuss, for a second time, Richard Clarke's proposal to kill Osama bin Laden with the armed Predator. Now deeply involved in the Hellfire Predator project, Gration told Werner that Clarke hoped by August 7 to get the Principals Committee of the NSC to agree to use the armed Predator in Afghanistan. Clarke wanted the CIA and Air Force to be ready to start flying no later than September 25. Could Werner get his remote split operations scheme working in time to make that happen?

Werner promised to get back to Gration with an answer as soon as possible.

The next day, after a discussion with a vice president of L-3 Communications, a Salt Lake City company that had been providing communications technology for the Predator since the drone's birth, Werner told Gration they could meet the September 25 target date.

At the time, even Werner failed to grasp the technological revolution that would follow if he found a way to make remote split operations of the Hellfire Predator work. For the first time in history, it would be possible to target and kill an enemy much the way a sniper does—from ambush, and with precision—but from the other side of the world. Science fiction would become science fact.

CIA headquarters covers 258 acres carved out of verdant woods on the Virginia side of the Potomac River, eight miles and eighteen minutes northwest of the White House by car, in an unincorporated area known as Langley. The well-marked main entrance is on the south end of the property, just off Dolley Madison Boulevard. Leafy woods shield the rest of the grounds from public view, and even most visitors allowed to travel past the front gate see little of the CIA compound. Once they and their vehicles pass inspection by an armed guard, they motor nearly half a mile down a curving, tree-lined drive along the easternmost edge of the property, then park in front of the 1960s-vintage Old Headquarters Building. The east front of that seven-story structure faces the Potomac, and the capital beyond; the west side connects to two six-story office towers completed in 1991. Behind those towers, parking lots fan out in several directions and service roads snake into the tree-covered southern end of the compound. This part of the campus is home to an ad hoc scattering of storage sheds, utility buildings, power generators, and a large, white water tank tucked into some thick woods not far from the CIA day care center.

In the summer of 2001, the trees directly south of that water tank had been cleared for a couple of dozen yards to either side, creating a secluded glade where a construction crew was storing equipment and supplies. One unusually pleasant morning—the Washington region is normally insufferably muggy in August—this glade was the first of several planned stops on a tour of the CIA campus being conducted for Cofer Black, the no-nonsense director of the intelligence agency's Counterterrorist Center. Major Mark Cooter and Black's deputy Alec B. had set out that morning to show Black and about twenty other officials and experts various spots on the CIA campus that might make suitable locations for a Predator ground control station and a mobile home that an Air Force team could use as an operations cell, if President Bush and his National Security Council ultimately decided to send the armed drone in search of Osama bin Laden.

"Major," Black barked as the group stood in the glade.

"Yes, sir," replied Cooter, the only military officer in the group.

"Where do *you* think we should put the equipment?"

"Right here, sir."

"I agree," Black said, then turned and started walking back to the CIA headquarters building. Tour over.

Colonel Ed Boyle, who as intelligence director for U.S. Air Forces Europe had been the Summer Project's commander at Ramstein and would reprise his role if new Predator flights over Afghanistan were ordered, had wanted to put the ground control station at another Langley this time: Langley Air Force Base, near Hampton Roads, Virginia. The latter Langley was home to Air Combat Command, where Boyle had transferred in April, requested by General Jumper to be ACC's director of intelligence, a prestigious assignment. The CIA, however, wanted tighter control over the operation than an Air Force base could provide, especially now that the Predator could fire missiles. Higher-ups had decided to put the drone's operators at the CIA's Langley.

With that decision, Boyle thought of embedding the Air Force contingent in the Global Response Center on the sixth floor of CIA headquarters. No one liked working in a cramped, chilly, and often smelly Predator GCS, and members of the Air Force team assigned to the operations cell tent next to the GCS at Ramstein during the so-called Summer Project had complained of the damp and cold of Germany's autumn, which featured much rain and not a little snow. The tent was so poorly heated that they often had to work in gloves and field jackets to stay warm, and when it rained the tent leaked. Captain Ginger Wallace, the only woman officer on the Summer Project, especially disliked having to share a porta-potty with a football team's worth of men during the Ramstein operation.

Boyle thought his people would be happier indoors, but the CIA rejected that idea and insisted that the Predator team set up its operation away from the main building. The agency wanted as few Air Force people as possible working in its headquarters; besides, with roughly three hundred employees, the twenty-four-hour CTC operations center was crowded already. Their CIA hosts also wanted to keep the Predator operation as inconspicuous as possible, so Air Force participants were instructed to wear civilian clothes only, and the unit's little base in the glade near the water tower would be made to look as much as possible like a construction site. The CIA campus at Langley was a favorite photographic subject for foreign spy satellites—and, for that matter, users of Google Earth.

"You've got to be kidding me, right?" Wallace blurted out when Cooter called her at Ramstein to tell her about the move to Langley. She and Captain Paul Welch, a communications officer at Ramstein, had worked for the past six months to get ready for more Predator flights over Afghanistan conducted from Germany. They already had a semipermanent building on the spot at Ramstein where the ops tent and the huge satellite earth terminal required for split operations of the Predator were located. The building was only a two-story metal shelter akin to one GCS stacked atop another, but it had tile floors, windows with glass in them, reliable heat, good lighting, and comfortable work spaces. It also had an indoor toilet.

Cooter assured Wallace that things wouldn't be so bad at Langley. There would be no building like the one she and Welch had set up at Ramstein, but there would also be no tent. The ops cell would be in a double-wide mobile home, which the CIA rented and parked in the glade not long after the site was chosen.

"Okay, I don't care what our setup is, but we *will* have a bathroom in that trailer," Wallace told Cooter. "I will *not* spend ninety more days going to the bathroom in a porta-potty."

On July 11, the day Stephen Hadley told the CIA and Joint Chiefs of Staff to get ready to deploy armed Predators in September and the Air Force told Congress it would fund the completion of the Hellfire project, Big Safari gave General Atomics a new contract. It directed the company to modify two more existing Predators to carry MTS balls and Hellfires, to make software changes so all three Hellfire Predators could "engage moving targets," and to "conduct live fire flight demonstrations" at China Lake. General Atomics was also to paint Predator 3034 and the two other Hellfire Predators "air superiority gray," the color used on Air Force warplanes to make them hard for enemies to see. Cooter had insisted on the color scheme. Remembering the Taliban MiGs that had come looking for the Summer Project's unarmed Predators the year before, he wanted to take every step possible to preserve the element of surprise as they stalked Osama bin Laden.

Air Force policy nominally stipulated four Predator air vehicles per ground control station, but aside from the one MTS ball on Predator 3034, only two other prototypes existed. For that matter, there weren't that many Predators around, even seven years after the drone's birth. At the beginning of 2001, the entire fleet numbered just sixteen, for despite all the sudden interest in the Hellfire Predator, drones were still extremely low on the Air Force's list of priorities. The service was buying so few, in fact, that in August of that year, General Atomics' Frank Pace told Tom Cassidy they might have to lay off about ten employees.

As General Atomics prepared the two additional Hellfire Predators, the Big Safari team began working out how to use them most effectively against Al Qaeda. Cooter pushed Major Spoon Mattoon of Big Safari, the project's test director, to conduct more flight tests. Cooter wanted to see if the Hellfires and their electronic components worked as well after twenty hours of flying in the cold air of high altitude as they did within an hour or so of taking off from the warm desert floor. By August 22, Scott Swanson and Jeff Guay of Big Safari, with two General Atomics pilots, were flying practice missions lasting hours at China Lake, devising and testing flight patterns they might use to find Osama bin Laden with the MTS ball, follow him without being detected, and possibly launch Hellfires at him. To make the exercises more productive, and help the team pass the time, Cooter and Mattoon devised some scenarios requiring members of the Hellfire Predator team to play the roles of "terrorists" and "civilians" by moving around a China Lake range at night in trucks and SUVs. The Predator crew had to find them in the desert using the MTS ball's sensors, and then decide whether they were targets worth following.

Werner arrived at China Lake on August 23, still working on aspects of his remote split operations scheme. When he heard about the nighttime exercises in the desert, he couldn't resist getting involved. Werner was once commissioned by an intelligence agency other than the CIA to write a scenario for an exercise focused on defending against a possible attack on the U.S. communications infrastructure; his scenario was so realistic and worrisome that the agency immediately classified his work. Intrigued by what the Big Safari team was doing at China Lake, Werner sat down and wrote a couple of scenarios more elaborate than Cooter and Mattoon's—six-hour plays, in effect, in which almost all the nearly two dozen members of the Hellfire Predator team had roles to play.

In one scenario, a dozen or more of the team members were divided into small squads and sent out into the black desert night in various directions and in multiple vehicles. At certain times and places, staggered for the different squads taking part, they were to stop, get out of their vehicles, and post guards. One of the men in one of the vehicles was "Dr. Zhukov," a nefarious character whose purpose was to meet up with a vehicle carrying people who would hand him a suitcase containing a small nuclear bomb—fictional, of course. Another character was a "Western intelligence agency plant"—a spy. The Predator crew's assignment was to use their drone to find the various squads and, by observing their behavior, discern which man was Dr. Zhukov and which was the Western spy. The Western spy would be distinguished by the way he walked around outside his squad's vehicle during stops while posing as a guard. While the others would meander in circles during stops to ease the burden of being on their feet, as guards usually do, the Western spy would occasionally walk in a short, straight line, then turn at a sharp right angle and walk in a longer straight line, describing a capital L.

For Hellfire engineer Terry McLean and Raytheon engineers Bill Casey and Willie Norman, acting out roles in Werner's scenarios—or playing "Rescue Rangers," as they called it—made them feel a little silly, but the games gave them a way to have a bit of fun and blow off some steam after a summer of difficult work in the blazing desert. It also led to some comical experiences.

On their first night of playacting, McLean was cast as the spy and Casey and Norman as terrorists traveling with him. After a couple of stops in the desert, his companions were to discover McLean walking his L, then shoot him down. The Predator crew's assignment was to catch the drama on video. Having done that scene, McLean, Casey, and Norman had some time to kill in the desert before the next act, so they pulled some cheap folding chairs they had bought for that purpose out of their SUV and sat down to relax. Sitting in the pitch black of the desert, their eyes were naturally drawn up to the glorious sight of the Milky Way, made all the more mesmerizing by the absence of any nearby man-made light. After they had been staring at the stars for a while, they heard a coyote howl in the distance, just like in a Hollywood Western.

"Oh, that's pretty cool," McLean said. Then another coyote howled, but this time from much closer. Turning on a flashlight and pointing it in the direction of the second howl, McLean saw red eyes glowing back at him from only about fifty feet away. Swinging their flashlights around in a circle, the three engineers got a surprise that sent chills up their spines. Perhaps thirty sets of red eyes peered at them: they were surrounded by an entire pack of coyotes. "You've never seen three middle-aged men jump in an SUV as fast," McLean recalled. "We left the chairs and hauled ass."

The next night, Casey realized at a certain point during Werner's second scenario that they were getting a little giddy from the long hours. This time, to show the Predator crew that they had spotted the drone overhead, Casey, McLean, and Norman offered the MTS ball's sensors an ad hoc rendition, in song and arm signals, of the Village People disco classic "Y.M.C.A." That's when Werner, watching from the GCS, knew they were having entirely too much fun.

Werner came up with another scenario that was played out that month, but this one was for real. After telling Gration of the Joint Staff that he could make remote split operations work in time to have Predators controlled from Langley over Afghanistan by September 25, Werner discovered they would need a new satellite earth terminal at Ramstein to do that. They could still use the eleven-meter TMET—the "Big Ass Dish"—to receive signals from the Predator, but the Dutch communications satellite used during the Summer Project for transmitting the drone's signals was no longer available, for its capacity had been leased to another customer. Werner found an alternative: a Russian-built, French-operated satellite known as SESAT (an acronym derived from "Siberia-Europe satellite"), but its only unleased capacity would require transmitting GCS data from the earth terminal to the SESAT at a lower frequency than the TMET could provide.

With a bit of research, Werner found a company in Catania, Sicily, that was offering for lease a satellite earth terminal with a four-meter antenna that could transmit in the 13.75- to 14-gigahertz range the SESAT required. The company seemed a bit desperate for business, and after negotiating a price Werner thought a bargain, he added an unusual condition. For operational security, he insisted that the Sicilian company deliver the satellite terminal to a location in Germany he would disclose to them at a time of his choosing and hand it over without being told where the equipment was going. The Sicilians agreed, and Werner choreographed a clandestine exchange that unfolded one night a few miles east of the Rhine River.

As instructed, the Italian company transported their terminal to Germany on a flatbed trailer, with the representative who negotiated the deal with Werner following in a passenger car. Exactly one hour after Werner called the Sicilian's cell phone and told him where to take the terminal, the Italians pulled into a rest stop on the A5 Autobahn near Offenburg, a city about two hours south of Ramstein Air Base by car. Three Air Force contractors sent by Werner met the Italians there and carefully inspected the flatbed and the satellite terminal. They even scanned both the truck and the terminal with a "radio frequency sniffer" to check for hidden transmitters. The handoff made, the Sicilians left the rest stop in their passenger car, leaving the flatbed and satellite terminal to the Americans.

As the team Werner sent to meet the Italians drove north in the flatbed with the terminal, a pair of cars driven by two other Air Force contractors assigned to the operation fell in behind the satellite dish. Continually varying their distances to disguise their purpose, they watched for other cars that might be following the satellite terminal to its destination. Yet another car, driven by an American contractor, followed the Italians to make sure they didn't double back. Werner's team detected nothing suspicious, and when the flatbed reached Ramstein a couple of hours later, it was met and set up by the engineers permanently assigned to the air base to take care of the TMET.

A few days later, the rest of the equipment needed for remote split operation of the Predator was in place at CIA headquarters. Now all Werner had to do was find out whether his jury-rigged system would work.

As the three Hellfire Predators and the remote split operations scheme for using them to go after Osama bin Laden neared readiness, Scott Swanson and Jeff Guay were assigned to test yet another bit of technology. Designed by Big Safari and installed in a GCS at China Lake, the new device was a little red toggle switch under a clear plastic cover. The switch assembly, fastened to a short wooden plank, was connected by a long black cable to the Predator flight control console. The function of this tethered remote switch was to supplant the joystick trigger a Predator pilot had to pull to launch a Hellfire. Lifting the plastic cover and flipping the red switch attached to the board would potentially become the final step in the launch sequence. Its purpose was to let someone other than a military pilot fire the missile—presumably someone from the CIA—and thus take legal responsibility for the act. Chronically cynical Gunny Guay immediately dubbed it the Monkey Switch. Even a monkey could work it, Guay told Swanson, so that must be what the bosses had in mind.

Guay was just being Guay, but he was right about the origins of the Monkey Switch. It was a product of the indecision and anguish gripping top CIA officials and military leaders as they approached the prospect of using an armed drone to stalk and kill a man. The NSC Deputies Committee had decided at its August 1 meeting that the CIA could legally use the Hellfire Predator to kill bin Laden or one of his deputies without violating Executive Order 12333, the long-standing ban on assassination. That order, signed by President Ronald Reagan on December 4, 1981, and carrying the force of law, was a detailed codification of intelligence community authorities and limits, but one section, "Prohibition on Assassination," was unadorned. Section 2.11 stated simply, "No person employed by or acting on behalf of the United States Government shall engage in, or conspire to engage in, assassination." Section 2.12, "Indirect Participation," added, "No agency of the Intelligence Community shall participate in or request any person to undertake activities forbidden by this Order."

Beyond those two statements, Executive Order 12333 offered no specifics on how to define *assassination* or how to interpret or apply the ban on U.S. employees engaging in it. The Deputies Committee decided drone strikes against Al Qaeda leaders would be acts of self-defense, not assassinations, but the deputies could only offer their opinion on such a complex legal issue. The NSC Principals Committee would have to decide whether they were right. The principals would also have to decide who would authorize any drone strikes conducted, who would foot the bill for the Hellfire Predators, and whether an officer of the military or of the CIA would actually pull the trigger.

John McLaughlin, a career intelligence analyst who became CIA deputy director exactly a week after the USS *Cole* bombing, agreed with the decision at the August 1 meeting but still harbored reservations. McLaughlin was enthusiastic about the idea of using the Predator to go after bin Laden, who between the African embassy bombings and the *Cole* had a lot of American blood on his hands. The Predator's persistence— its ability to keep its eye on a location for more than twenty-four hours— and the fact that Al Qaeda would have no way of anticipating such a weapon made the happenstance of the Air Force project to arm the drone manna from heaven in McLaughlin's view. But he and other long-time Langley veterans were still traumatized by scandals over CIA assassination schemes that had been revealed in the mid-1970s and had led to curbs on the Agency's activities. McLaughlin told the meeting that the Agency needed to be sure that all those involved would be willing to share the responsibility if the Predator were used to kill bin Laden.

McLaughlin worried about how the public and politicians might react to newspaper headlines about the CIA assassinating a terrorist in Afghanistan. McLaughlin's fear, a common one at Langley, was that the politicians were likely to run for cover and let the CIA take the blame if an attempt to kill bin Laden with the Predator went awry, especially if there was collateral damage. Among the items discussed at Langley was how to avoid killing or wounding innocent civilians. Predator video from the Summer Project included imagery of women and children near the homes of Taliban leader Mullah Omar, bin Laden, and the Al Qaeda leader's deputies in Afghanistan. If a drone strike ended up killing children, it wasn't hard to imagine Washington politicians lining up to get in front of TV cameras to do their best imitations of Captain Louis Renault, the cynical French police inspector in the film *Casablanca* who declares that he is "shocked, shocked to find that gambling is going on in here" just as a croupier hands him money he's won in the casino he's shutting down.

Charlie Allen was one of the few CIA old-timers ready from the first to hunt bin Laden with the armed version of the Predator; at one of that year's meetings, he had appalled Director George Tenet by declaring that he was even willing to pull the trigger himself. Tenet remained wary even after the Deputies Committee decided the CIA could legally kill a terrorist who had openly declared war on America and whose organization had killed Americans. The CIA director was also still skeptical that an intelligence agency could legally fire a military weapon. The head of the CIA's clandestine activities branch, meanwhile, Deputy Director for Operations James Pavitt, was even more opposed to using the Hellfire Predator than he had been to deploying the unarmed version. The lives of his operatives around the world would be at risk if the Agency used such a weapon and the fact got out, Pavitt argued. CIA people would become targets themselves.

But the military was equally opposed to having *its* people pull the trigger—hence the Monkey Switch. "There was concern that you couldn't have a military officer actually pulling the trigger in a situation that wasn't declared war, was part of a covert action," the CIA's liaison to the military at the time, Lieutenant General Soup Campbell, explained years later. "So the idea was that maybe we would actually put a trigger or switch in there and a CIA guy who was covered under the [presidential] finding would push it."

To prepare for that possibility, the CIA sent a couple of its officers to China Lake that summer so Swanson and Guay could train them in using the Monkey Switch. Mark Cooter came out to China Lake to supervise, and on the day of the training Cooter had Swanson stop at a grocery store on his way to work. After each of the CIA officers had, as instructed, stood to the side of the flight control console, held the wooden plank in both hands, and toggled the switch a time or two, Cooter asked Swanson, "Well, are they good?"

"Yes," Swanson replied in his cheery Minnesota lilt. "They can do it!"

Reaching up into the dimly lit top of the flight control console, Cooter plucked two bananas off the bunch Swanson had bought that morning as instructed and handed the CIA men one each. Then they all laughed.

The Monkey Switch was never used again.

When the question of who would pull the trigger finally reached the people with the power to decide such issues, they punted. On September 4, 2001, the NSC Principals Committee held its first meeting on Al Qaeda since President Bush's election—a meeting Richard Clarke had been begging for since four days after Bush's inauguration. Among those gathered in the White House Situation Room that day were NSC principals President Bush, Vice President Dick Cheney, Secretary of State Colin Powell, Deputy Defense Secretary Paul Wolfowitz (sitting in for Secretary Donald Rumsfeld), and Treasury Secretary Paul O'Neill, with statutory advisers Tenet and Joint Chiefs vice chairman Richard Myers, who was a few days away from succeeding Army General Hugh Shelton as Joint Chiefs chairman. After a brief discussion, the committee approved the expanded authorities for a broad campaign against Al Qaeda as outlined in a classified memo that National Security Adviser Condoleezza Rice had asked the CIA to draw up earlier in the year. The memo laid out a more aggressive new U.S. policy whose goal would be to eliminate Osama bin Laden and Al Qaeda both, in part by having the CIA funnel money and military equipment and supplies to Afghanistan's Northern Alliance, the main insurgent force trying to overthrow bin Laden's hosts, the ruling Taliban.

Next, those at the NSC meeting discussed the armed Predator. Neither the CIA nor the military wanted to take responsibility for pulling the trigger, and neither wanted to pay for the program—issues that led to heated discussion. Rice's deputy, Stephen Hadley, told the leaders that the Predator might be useful in the effort to gather more intelligence on Al Qaeda. But he offered a far more conservative view than Big Safari's of how ready the armed version of the drone was to deploy, saying the Hellfire Predator might not be suitable for immediate use. Rice suggested the spring of 2002 might a better time to deploy it. Powell, a former Army general who had been chairman of the Joint Chiefs of Staff when President Bush's father was president, was in favor of using the armed Predator but doubted that bin Laden would be easy to target.

Tenet, who had been briefed in detail on the Hellfire test shots conducted between May 22 and June 7, knew that although the missile was highly accurate, the reliability and thus the lethality of the weapon was iffy. He contended that the probability of taking bin Laden out with a Hellfire was low, and Rice concurred. Tenet also said it would be a terrible mistake for the CIA director to decide when to fire a weapon like this. Others assured Tenet that the decision to fire would be the president's to make. As for who would actually pull the trigger, the military or the CIA, that question was left unresolved, though Myers said that if a strike were launched covertly the CIA would have to do it.

In the end, the principals decided against trying to kill bin Laden with the Predator, at least for the time being, but agreed the military should consider it among other options. They left it to Tenet to decide whether the CIA would use the Predator for more unarmed reconnaissance missions but agreed it was a good idea. Tenet later directed the CIA to go ahead with the plan under way to deploy the Hellfire Predators to Uzbekistan in late September, but he told them to prepare to fly the drones, controlled from the Langley campus, for intelligence gathering only.

Richard Clarke left the meeting feeling more frustrated than ever. Before the session, Clarke had sent Rice a personal note urging her to press the "real question" the principals should focus on—"are we serious about dealing with the al Qida threat?"—rather than leaving it to the lower-level Counterterrorism Security Group he chaired. In his note, he added a passionate, and prescient, prediction:

"Decision makers should imagine themselves on a future day when the CSG has not succeeded in stopping al Qida attacks and hundreds of Americans lay dead in several countries, including the US. What would those decision makers wish that they had done earlier? That future day could happen at any time."

Even as the National Security Council principals hesitated to use the new Hellfire Predator, the Air Force team was making final preparations to give them the option. On August 26 and 27, the Big Safari and General Atomics flight crews flew Predator 3034 in a twenty-four-hour test culminating in a Hellfire launch at a China Lake target. Then they ferried 3034 back to El Mirage to get its air superiority gray paint job. On August 30 they began testing Predator 3037 and Predator 3038, the two other drones modified to carry the prototype MTS ball and Hellfire missiles under the July 11 contract Big Safari had given General Atomics. Those tests, which included missile shots, would continue at China Lake through the Labor Day weekend.

Mark Cooter and his CIA Counterterrorist Center opposite number Alec B., meanwhile, spent Labor Day weekend performing an unusual task. On Friday night, the Predator ground control station the Summer Project team had used in Germany arrived from Ramstein Air Base, where it had been in storage all year. Cooter and a Big Safari communications technician, Master Sergeant Cliff Gross, met and inspected the GCS at Andrews Air Force Base. When Cooter turned the GCS's meat-locker-style door handle and walked inside, he was surprised, and pleased, to find the white Stetson and cavalry spurs the Summer Project crew had given him for his birthday the previous October. They were still hanging from the equipment rack at the back of the GCS, where he had sworn to leave them until they were allowed to take some action against Al Qaeda.

The GCS was trucked to a warehouse on a CIA property in northern Virginia that night; the next day, Cooter, Gross, and Alec B., along with a CIA security officer and a logistics expert from the Counterterrorist Center, met at the warehouse wearing jeans and T-shirts. The logistician brought along two Wagner Power Painters, a collection of paintbrushes, rollers, and trays, and a couple of hundred gallons of flat white industrial paint he had purchased at the Home Depot.

The five men set to work, and though they ran the power painters so hard the machines broke, forcing them to finish the job with rollers on extension poles, by nightfall they were done. The CIA wanted the ground control station that would be parked on its campus to look like any old freight container, perhaps one used for storage by the construction crew that had been using the space that way earlier that year, but the GCS had arrived from Ramstein with its metal skin painted black, brown, and green camouflage. Now its exterior was a scruffy white. "The requirement isn't that it's pretty," Cooter reminded the others as they stood back to admire their work and wipe their paint-smeared brows. "The requirement is that it's not camouflage." Nothing about the white metal box suggested the technological revolution it would unleash.

That August, Ginger Wallace was transferred to Colonel Ed Boyle's ACC intelligence staff at Langley Air Force Base. She also received orders to report for ninety days of temporary duty at the other Langley, CIA headquarters, commencing the Monday after Labor Day. Though she'd been irritated when Cooter called to tell her they would be operating out of a double-wide trailer at CIA headquarters instead of the base she and Paul Welch had prepared at Ramstein, Wallace was eager to get started. Cooter had also asked for Welch; he wanted him at CIA headquarters that summer to make sure Werner's scheme for remote split operations was correctly set up. Cooter also knew Welch could get the Air Force team connected to all the military intelligence sources and resources needed to guarantee success once they started flying again.

Wallace and Welch were due to meet Cooter at CIA headquarters on Monday, September 10, to prepare for the planned arrival on Tuesday of a full team of Air Force intelligence analysts. Everyone would need to get an ID badge, find their way to the double-wide, and begin to prepare to operate Predators over Afghanistan again. A CIA-led launch-and-recovery team was in Uzbekistan already, preparing a hangar for the drones.

On Sunday, September 9, Werner flew from his East Coast home to Palmdale, California, where Big Safari had a detachment at the Skunk Works, the famed Lockheed Martin Corporation facility where secret and exotic aircraft such as the Mach 3 SR-71 spy plane were built. Monday, September 10, would be the first of three planned days of flight tests of remote split operations, which L-3 Communications and Air Force engineers had put together during August according to Werner's specifications.

That same Sunday, Colonel Ed Boyle was preparing to fly to Arizona. He planned to take a few days off to see Army Brigadier General James A. "Spider" Marks, an old friend, take command of the U.S. Army Intelligence Center at Fort Huachuca—by coincidence, the base where the Predator had flown its first operational tests just six and a half years earlier. The change-of-command ceremony was scheduled for Tuesday; Boyle would attend with another friend, Air Force Colonel Rich Gibaldi, then fly back home to Langley Air Force Base. When he got back, Boyle planned to put in his retirement papers. His mentor, General John Jumper, who on Thursday had taken over as Air Force chief of staff, had phoned Boyle that Sunday with some mortifying news. Jumper had just found out that, for reasons he couldn't explain, a promotions board choosing new brigadier generals had just passed over Boyle.

"We'll work on fixing this next year," Jumper promised.

Boyle believed him. At the moment, though, he was just too angry and hurt to care.

Eleven months after Al Qaeda suicide bombers blew a hole in the side of his ship and killed seventeen of his sailors, the captain of the USS *Cole* paid his first visit ever to CIA headquarters. At 6:30 a.m. on Tuesday, September 11, Commander Kirk S. Lippold arrived at Langley and spent a few minutes waiting in the lobby for his escort. While he waited, Lippold admired the big inlaid granite CIA seal in the shiny floor. He also pondered rows of gold stars embedded in the lobby's north wall to commemorate, anonymously, CIA men and women killed in the line of duty.

Earlier in his Navy career, Lippold had served on the guided-missile cruiser USS *Shiloh*, as executive officer. The vessel's skipper, Captain John Russack, had since retired from the Navy and gone to work at the CIA as Charlie Allen's deputy. Lippold himself was now working at the Pentagon, in the Strategic Plans and Policy Division of the Office of the Chairman of the Joint Chiefs of Staff, and Allen had told Russack to ask Lippold to visit them at Langley. Allen wanted to tell Lippold some of what the CIA knew about Osama bin Laden and how Al Qaeda had carried out the bombing of the *Cole*. The CIA veteran felt terrible about the bombing, about the intelligence community's failure to detect the plot in advance, and about the government's failure—under both President Bill Clinton and President George W. Bush—to retaliate after the attack was tied to Al Qaeda.

Russack soon arrived in the lobby and took Lippold to Allen's sixth-floor office, where at 7:00 a.m. sharp Allen invited them in for bagels, coffee, and orange juice. For the next hour and a half, Allen told Lippold the story of the largely secret war with Al Qaeda; he also explained how and why he had been obsessed with Osama bin Laden ever since the African embassy bombings of 1998. Given Lippold's lack of certain clearances, there was much that Allen couldn't tell him, but Lippold was grateful nonetheless. As the conversation ended, the naval officer shook the older man's hand and thanked him.

"It means an awful lot for me to understand what our country is doing to catch this guy," Lippold said. "But I don't think America understands. I believe it is going to take a seminal event, probably in this country, where hundreds, if not thousands, are going to have to die before Americans realize that we're at war with this guy."

Lippold thought Allen seemed surprised. "Well, hopefully that'll never happen," Allen said. "I hope we'll be able to head that off before it does."

Russack and Lippold then left Allen. Russack wanted to take his former shipmate and subordinate to meet some other people at the agency and see some satellite imagery of Al Qaeda's training camps.

About ten minutes before nine, as they were walking through an office in another part of the building from Allen's, a news bulletin on a television there caught their attention. Black smoke and fire were pouring from a hole near the top of the North Tower of the World Trade Center in New York; the broadcast anchor was casting doubt on an earlier report that a small plane had hit the tower. Russack and Lippold continued their tour, making their way to the office of Cofer Black, the Counterterrorist Center director. As they waited for Black to finish a phone call, they watched the drama in New York play out on TV—and at 9:03 a.m. saw an airliner fly straight into the World Trade Center's South Tower.

"In that instant, it was clear the United States was under attack," Lippold recalled in his memoir, *Front Burner: Al Qaeda's Attack on the USS Cole.* "The office became a ferocious beehive of activity, with people running in and out of Black's office. We slipped in, were quickly introduced, and just as quickly slipped out."

As Russack and Lippold were leaving, an office assistant with a phone to her ear told them that Allen wanted to see the two of them in his office immediately. When they arrived, Allen came out from behind his desk and put his arm around Lippold's shoulders.

"Kirk, I can't believe you said what you did this morning," Allen said. "I think the seminal event has just happened."

11

WILDFIRE

When Al Qaeda hijackers slammed an American Airlines plane into the World Trade Center at 8:46 a.m., Eastern Standard Time, Colonel Ed Boyle, director of intelligence for Air Combat Command, was in Arizona, driving south on State Highway 90 in a rented Mercury Grand Marquis sedan. Boyle had spent part of the summer of 2001 organizing an expanded "expeditionary intelligence squadron" to fly Predators for the CIA over Afghanistan. Those missions were set to begin on September 25, but for the moment Boyle had time for some other business. He and Colonel Rich Gibaldi, another senior intelligence officer at Langley Air Force Base, flew to Davis-Monthan Air Force Base, near Tucson, and spent Monday, September 10, in meetings with the commander of 12th Air Force and his staff. On Tuesday, Boyle and Gibaldi, native New Yorkers who had been friends since high school, were driving the roughly hour and a half south from Tucson to Fort Huachuca, home of the U.S. Army Intelligence Center. An Army intelligence officer friend, Brigadier General James "Spider" Marks, was scheduled to take command of the base that day, in a ceremony that promised to be inspiring, followed by a reception that promised to be a good time.

Boyle and Gibaldi had been on the road less than an hour when Fox News Radio reported that the North Tower of the World Trade Center in New York had been hit by what was thought to be a small airplane. Boyle was immediately suspicious. "No planes are allowed on that side of Manhattan," he remarked. Imperfect eyesight had prevented Boyle from becoming a pilot in the Air Force, but when he was a youth a family friend taught him to fly on Long Island, and he knew New York's air traffic rules.

"Yeah, it must be really bad weather," Gibaldi said. But then a radio reporter described the brilliantly blue skies over Manhattan on that crisp, late summer morning, and soon the men heard that a second plane had hit the trade center's South Tower.

Boyle and Gibaldi gave each other a look. "We've got a problem," Boyle said. Gibaldi stepped on the gas.

Within half an hour, they were at the Fort Huachuca gate. They were still reaching for their military IDs to show the guards when Boyle's cell phone rang.

"Where are you?" asked the acting commander of Air Combat Command, Lieutenant General Donald Cook, calling from ACC headquarters at Langley Air Force Base, Virginia. Boyle explained that he and Gibaldi were about to see General Marks take command at Fort Huachuca. Cook told Boyle to get back to Langley Air Force Base as soon as possible—but first, the general ordered, "Call me from a secure phone."

By the time Boyle and Gibaldi found Spider Marks, a third hijacked plane had hit the Pentagon and people at Fort Huachuca were too busy for a change-of-command ceremony. Marks offered to let Boyle use the secure phone in his new residence, but when they got there, they realized the phone needed a new "seed key" to activate it, which incoming commander Marks had yet to receive. The friends shook hands, and Boyle and Gibaldi headed back to Davis-Monthan.

As they drove, Boyle called Cook to explain why it would take a while before he could call back from a secure phone.

"You need to get your butt back here," Cook told him. "Jumper wants to know when you can be operational and flying."

There was no need to be more specific.

When the attacks began, General Jumper was in the Air Force Operations Center in the basement of the Pentagon, presiding over his first staff meeting since being confirmed by the Senate the previous Thursday as the seventeenth chief of staff of the Air Force. Seated at a curved table in the ops center briefing room, with senior officers to either side and subordinates occupying a couple of rows of tiered theater seating behind them, Jumper was listening to a daily intelligence briefing. The briefing officer was using imagery and other displays on a large screen facing the audience.

Just before 9:00 a.m., another officer entered and spoke quietly to the briefer, who then announced they were switching the screen to live coverage from CNN because a plane had crashed into one of the World Trade Center towers in Manhattan. As the broadcast came up, the CNN anchor was reporting speculation that the plane had strayed off course from LaGuardia Airport, whose runways were just over eight miles from the towers. With bright blue sky behind the black smoke pouring from the North Tower, Jumper and every other pilot in the room knew there was no way bad navigation was at fault. Then they watched, dumbstruck, as United Airlines Flight 175 banked into the trade center's South Tower. Now they knew this was a terrorist attack.

Within minutes, a report came in that air traffic controllers at Dulles International Airport, to the west of Washington, had spotted a plane with its transponder shut off headed in the general direction of the Pentagon. Officers of all ranks rushed upstairs to get people out of the E Ring, the five-sided Pentagon's exterior set of office buildings. The E Ring, with its windows on the outside world, is reserved for the most senior officers and officials of the Defense Department and their staffs.

After hearing the report, Jumper wanted to get Air Force Secretary James Roche out of his fourth-floor E Ring office and down to the safer operations center. He found Roche, and as they headed to the operations center together, people began running down the halls, some screaming. American Airlines Flight 77, a Boeing 757 with sixty-four passengers and crew and five Al Qaeda hijackers aboard, had flown into the west side of the Pentagon even as Jumper was on his way to fetch Roche. In the world's largest office building, whose interior courtyard covers five acres, the distance from where the plane hit to the Air Force secretary's suite was so great that neither Jumper nor Roche had realized the building was struck—until they saw people running from the smoke and smelled the stench of aviation fuel now seeping through the corridors.

Big Safari Director Bill Grimes was at his desk in Building 557 at Wright-Patterson Air Force Base, in Dayton, Ohio, that morning when someone stuck their head in his door and said, "Hey, an airplane just crashed into the World Trade Center." Grimes joined others around the television in the conference room next door. He remembered that a B-25 bomber had hit the Empire State Building by accident in 1945, so the initial reports that something similar had happened at the North Tower didn't seem implausible. But then the second plane hit the South Tower.

Within a few minutes, Grimes was called back to his office to take a phone call. Snake Clark's deputy, Lieutenant Colonel Kenneth Johns, was calling from Air Force headquarters. He wanted to know what needed to be done to get the three Hellfire Predators and whatever else was needed to fly them in the airspace over Afghanistan ready to go. They had just started discussing the matter when Johns said he'd have to call back: the Pentagon was being evacuated. Grimes promised to have answers when they talked again.

His first call was to Major Spoon Mattoon, the Big Safari officer who had been running the Hellfire Predator testing at China Lake.

Captain Ginger Wallace, wearing jeans and a light sweater, was watching television in the Counterterrorist Center at CIA headquarters when the planes hit the World Trade Center. She and Captain Paul Welch had met Major Mark Cooter there early that morning to start organizing the planned new round of Predator reconnaissance flights over Afghanistan. Wallace was a specialist in intelligence collection; Welch, the son of a former Air Force chief of staff, was a communications specialist who had worked on the Summer Project at Ramstein. Welch had also helped Big Safari scientist Werner set up the communications structure for the new Predator operations base in the glade near the CIA's day care center. As with the Summer Project, Cooter was to serve as Air Force operations director for the Predator team, working with his counterpart Alec B. of the Counterterrorist Center in running the CIA reconnaissance missions. Cooter, Wallace, and Welch had expected to spend September 11 preparing for the arrival of the Air Force intelligence analysts selected to work in the double-wide trailer when Predator flights resumed. Now, with the World Trade Center in flames, Wallace wasn't sure what the Predator team would be told to do.

After the Pentagon was hit, Wallace and Welch left Cooter at the CTC and went out to the double-wide to watch news coverage on a television there and make preparations for the others who would work there. The picture quality on the TV in the trailer was poor, but at 9:59 they watched in rapt horror as the South Tower collapsed, and then, twenty-nine minutes later, the North Tower fell. They also saw reports that a fourth hijacked plane was in the air.

After a couple of hours in the trailer, Wallace and Welch walked back to the headquarters building and found it nearly empty. CIA Director George Tenet had ordered the headquarters complex evacuated in case it, too, was on Al Qaeda's target list. Nonessential personnel were sent home, while critical staff went to the CIA printing plant, a small building with a basement elsewhere on the campus. At Director Cofer Black's insistence, the CTC was still occupied and at work, and Cooter was among those there, talking almost constantly on a secure phone. Several of his calls were with Ed Boyle, who by midmorning Arizona time had made it back to Davis-Monthan Air Force Base and found a secure phone.

Boyle's first call was to ACC commander Cook. The White House, Cook told him, wanted to know how soon the Air Force could get those three Hellfire Predators over Afghanistan—with missiles under their wings.

The telephone in his San Diego apartment woke Scott Swanson that morning just before 6:30 a.m., Pacific time. "They just hit the World Trade Center," said Jeff Guay, the other half of Big Safari's sole Predator crew. "Turn on your TV."

Swanson jumped out of bed and started watching the news. Like others on the Hellfire Predator team, he assumed that the burning towers were the work of Al Qaeda. Rubbing shoulders with CIA officers during the Hellfire Predator tests that summer, Swanson had gotten a sense of why the project seemed so urgent, at least to some at high levels. But like most people paying attention to Al Qaeda, Swanson had figured that if the terrorist group struck again, the target would be somewhere overseas.

The previous Friday night, Swanson had spent two hours in a ground control station at China Lake with a General Atomics crew assigned to the anticipated CIA missions. They put Predator 3038 into the air, bore-sighted its MTS ball, and launched Hellfires at target tanks. On Saturday, all the team members were sent home to get rested and ready to deploy. Some would be moving to the ad hoc base at Langley, some to Central Asia to man the launch-and-recovery element, which would take off and land the Predators from a scruffy little airfield in Uzbekistan. Some members of the LRE had flown to Tashkent, Uzbekistan, on August 28, and then traveled to the airfield to erect a portable hangar.

After driving home to San Diego from China Lake, Swanson spent Sunday relaxing, the first real break he'd had in weeks. On Monday, he had taken his car to a garage for minor repairs and left it while the shop got in some parts. Now, after Guay's wakeup call and the horrific reports on TV, he decided he'd better stay near the phone. Swanson had known he would soon be heading to the white GCS and the double-wide trailer on the western edge of the CIA grounds to fly more Predator missions, but he wasn't due to fly east for a week or so.

Not long after the third hijacked plane hit the Pentagon, Swanson got another call, this time from Big Safari headquarters in Dayton, Ohio. "Pack your bags," the caller said, "you're going to deploy early."

Werner had arrived in Palmdale, California, on September 9 to conduct flight tests of his new remote split operations scheme from Big Safari's office in the Lockheed Martin facility there. On September 11 he was shaving in his hotel room with the television on when the second hijacked plane struck the South Tower of the World Trade Center. He happened to see it live.

A few hours later, Grimes called.

"How are things going with your new toy out there?" Grimes asked.

"Well, pretty good so far," Werner said. "I've got two more days of tests scheduled."

"Well, you're done with your testing," Grimes told him. "As of right now, your system's been declared operational."

"But it's just a prototype," Werner protested.

"We understand that, but we need it," Grimes replied, telling Werner to get ready to travel because "you're going to have an airplane picking you up."

No airplane would be picking up Ed Boyle and Rich Gibaldi, who were now desperate to get back from Arizona to their assignments at Langley Air Force Base in Virginia. But the only military aircraft flying after Al Qaeda struck were fighter planes on patrol, tankers in the air to refuel them, and Airborne Warning and Control System—abbreviated AWACS and pronounced "A-wax"—radar and communications planes to detect threats and direct the fighters. Just after the South Tower was hit, the Federal Aviation Administration issued an unprecedented ban on all takeoffs of nonemergency aircraft.

That afternoon, Boyle and Gibaldi drove about 450 miles to Kirtland Air Force Base, near Albuquerque, New Mexico, hoping to find "space available" seats on a military flight. No transports were flying, so they caught a few hours of sleep in a motel, rose early on Wednesday, and went back to Kirtland to try again. Still no flights were available; after a while, they gave up and started driving east as fast as they could. Nearly two thousand miles of highway separated them from Langley Air Force Base.

Stopping as little as possible, they made about a thousand miles, then pulled into Little Rock Air Force Base in Arkansas to try once more to find a flight. Stymied again, they spent the night and then lit out Thursday morning for Virginia. They were making good time—Boyle was doing about ninety miles an hour on Interstate 40—when they passed a tractor trailer truck poking along at seventy or so just east of Forrest City, Arkansas. A white Chevrolet Camaro in front of the truck caught Gibaldi's eye.

"You know, Ed, I think that was a state trooper," Gibaldi said. He was soon proved right by a flashing blue light.

Boyle and Gibaldi were glad to see the officer's military-style haircut as he got out of his car and put on his hat. They figured he might be a marine, and sympathetic. They were half right: Trooper Mike Kennedy, twenty-seven at the time, had never served in the armed forces, but he was on the Arkansas State Police Special Weapons and Tactics Team (SWAT) and had military bearing. He was also happy to let the two colonels in uniform off the hook when they told him they were rushing to Virginia to get ready for war with Al Qaeda.

"I've already called you in, so I have to give you this warning ticket," the trooper said apologetically, quickly filling out a pale green Arkansas State Police Warning of Violation citation and handing it to Boyle. "Sir, go kill the bastards," Kennedy added. "Between you and me and the border, there's no more state troopers."

Boyle and Gibaldi pulled into Langley Air Force Base just after midnight and went straight to their two-story, redbrick houses there. Boyle's wife, Bev, met him at the door. She had some bags with fresh clothes already packed for him, in case he needed to leave again right away, but Boyle had to see Lieutenant General Cook in the morning. Then he would get in his car, drive three hours north to the other Langley—CIA headquarters—and take command of the special Air Force cadre now assembling to fly the Hellfire Predator over Afghanistan. This time, Boyle hoped the newly armed drone would let them do exactly what Arkansas State Trooper Mike Kennedy had urged: go kill the bastards.

Not long after Boyle arrived home that night, an Air Force C-17 Globemaster III cargo plane roared out of the dark, empty skies over Washington, D.C., and landed with a screech of its tires at Andrews Air Force Base, roughly a dozen miles southeast of the capital. As the squat gray transport parked on a taxiway and its jet engines whined to a stop, a ground crew swarmed the aircraft. Soon a portly man in slacks and a polo shirt stepped from the shadows and walked to the C-17's side door.

Snake Clark, who until May 1 had worn the blue uniform and silver eagles of an Air Force colonel, was now a civilian, though he was still technical director, simulation and integration, Office of the Assistant Vice Chief of Staff, Headquarters U.S. Air Force. He was also still the Predator's Wizard of Oz in the Pentagon, the man behind the curtain who pulled strings and twisted knobs, or in Clark's case twisted arms. And once again he had worked his magic: with no civilian and few military planes in the air, and even senior officers unable to hitch a ride on those flying, Clark—with a little help from the CIA—had arranged for this huge Air Force cargo jet to cross the United States on a trip begun barely twenty-four hours after the attacks of 9/11. Now, in the wee hours of Friday, September 14, he wanted to see for himself the C-17's unusual cargo.

Strapped to the deck of the transport's eighty-eight-foot-long hold were three tan, fiberglass-reinforced, polyester-plastic "coffins," each twenty-seven feet long; four feet, five inches wide; and two feet tall. Each held a disassembled Hellfire Predator, tail numbers 3034, 3037, and 3038. Crates nearby held a stripped-down flight control console and a portable C-band radio antenna, which a small team of experts could use to get the three Hellfire Predators in and out of the air from almost any airfield on earth. Also in the hold was a pallet cradling about a dozen tarp-covered black-and-yellow AGM-114K Hellfire missiles.

All this equipment, plus the small team of experts needed to handle it, would remain aboard when the C-17 departed. The rest of the C-17's passengers, though, were getting off at Andrews. Barely more than a dozen in number, they were the initial cadre who would fly the Hellfire Predators from the white GCS parked next to the double-wide trailer on the CIA grounds in Langley, Virginia. They included Spoon Mattoon, Scott Swanson, Jeff Guay, and Werner; three Predator pilots (one a woman) and six sensor operators from the Air Force's 11th and 15th Reconnaissance Squadrons at Indian Springs; two General Atomics pilots, some avionics experts, and a handful of engineers from their company and L-3 Communications.

Mattoon had boarded the C-17 at China Lake on Wednesday, the day after the twin towers fell, bringing aboard—at the loadmaster's suggestion—a rented Jeep Cherokee he'd had no time to return. (Clark would cackle about that bit of chutzpah for years to come.) From China Lake, the cargo plane flew to Palmdale, where Werner, Swanson, Guay, the other Air Force drone operators, and the contractors were waiting in the Big Safari office at Lockheed Martin. The Globemaster took off again at 7:00 p.m., almost precisely sunset. Sitting in a cockpit jump seat so he could chat with the crew and get a view as they flew, Swanson found it the eeriest flight of his life. No other aircraft were visible in the sky, and the C-17 provided the only light between the ground and the stars. Their first stop, after a bit more than four hours, was the Army's Redstone Arsenal, in Huntsville, Alabama. The previous day, only hours after the attacks in New York and Washington, Mattoon had telephoned Hellfire engineer Terry McLean, who had flown home to Huntsville the previous weekend, exhausted after their summer of round-the-clock Predator tests in the desert.

"We're making our way down your way," Mattoon said cryptically. "We want to pick up some jalapeños." Speaking over an unsecure phone line, he used a nickname for Hellfires they had cooked up while testing the missile against "Taco Bell" at China Lake that summer. McLean knew exactly what Mattoon meant, and told him whom he should call. When the C-17 landed at Huntsville, the pallet of Hellfires was waiting.

From there, the Globemaster flew to Charleston Air Force Base, in South Carolina, arriving at 4:00 a.m. Thursday. To the surprise and frustration of some of the plane's passengers, their ride remained on the ground there for the next twenty hours. The C-17's three-member crew was required to stop flying and rest; beyond that, the airplane needed inspection, maintenance, and fuel, and a new crew had to be found to take the Globemaster on the rest of its long journey to Uzbekistan. The C-17 was wheels up out of Charleston at midnight.

At Andrews, where they arrived at 1:30 a.m. on Friday, Swanson and the other pilots and sensor operators, plus a couple of contractors assigned to work with them at the CIA, were met by not only Snake Clark, but also Major Darran Jergensen, a Predator pilot most of them knew who had recently transferred to Air Combat Command. Jergensen had a white bus waiting to take them to the Marriott Residence Inn at Tysons Corner, a sprawl of shopping malls and office buildings just off the Washington Beltway in Virginia and a five-minute drive from CIA headquarters. The night of September 11, Ed Boyle had ordered a subordinate at ACC to book almost all of the Marriott's roughly one hundred rooms indefinitely. In addition to the small Predator flight crew cadre, Boyle figured three daily shifts of as many as thirty Air Force intelligence analysts would be needed to digest the drone's video and perform other tasks. Though the Predator carried no pilot, it might need fifteen to twenty people at a time in the GCS and the double-wide to monitor and assess the products of its video camera and other sensors during round-the-clock missions.

Recruited that summer for the Predator missions the CIA was planning, Jergensen had been summoned to the Pentagon on September 11 a few hours after the attacks on New York and Washington. A former special operations navigator, he would share mission commander duties with Mark Cooter, directing the flight crews in the GCS and, when useful, helping them fly their Predators. As Jergensen's charges boarded the bus, he invited them to take a beer from a case he had brought along; then, after asking the driver to step outside and away from the bus, he briefed the group on what they would be doing after they got oriented at CIA headquarters.

Jergensen told the group they would use the ground control station there to fly the Hellfire Predators over Afghanistan, picking the drones up via Ku-band satellite link after an LRE in Central Asia got them into the air with their portable C-band antenna. If the CIA's sources in Afghanistan could tip them to the whereabouts of Osama bin Laden or his lieutenants, they might launch a Hellfire strike, buddy-lase for warplanes with laser-guided bombs, or simply talk them onto the target. Their first priority, however, would be to use the Predator's cameras and other sensors to hunt bin Laden and other Al Qaeda and Taliban leaders; at the same time, they would scout out targets that regular U.S. and allied military forces could attack if President Bush decided, as seemed increasingly likely, to go to war.

"Any questions?" Jergensen asked when he finished.

"Yeah, I have a question," said a General Atomics pilot. "Who are you?"

Like everyone else, Jergensen was wearing civilian clothes.

When Mattoon turned in his rented Jeep Cherokee at Washington National Airport, the car company agent was befuddled. Mattoon had rented the vehicle in California, more than two thousand miles away. But according to the odometer, the Jeep had been driven only two hundred miles. How was that possible?

Someone must have made a mistake, Mattoon said with a shrug.

The armed Predator's call sign—the way the cadre would identify themselves to other military units by radio—would be Wildfire. The WILD Predators flown over Kosovo by Big Safari had carried a laser designator; these added Hellfire missiles. Someone did the obvious math: WILD + Hellfire = Wildfire.

By the weekend of September 15, the handful of technicians and engineers in the CIA-led LRE was fully in place at a secret, isolated airfield in Uzbekistan near the Afghan border. To cloak their presence as much as possible, LRE members were barred from going into the tiny border town nearby and told to avoid contact with locals. Living in a tent, working in an inflatable hangar, their duty would be to maintain, service, and operate the three Hellfire Predators at the start and finish of their missions over Afghanistan using the portable flight control console they had brought with them. After takeoff, the pilot was to fly the Predator to mission altitude, where a technician would bore-sight the MTS ball; next, the pilot would put the Predator into an orbit, at which point the mission crew in the GCS at CIA headquarters would take control using the Ku-band satellite link. The timing was worked out so precisely that no conversation or messaging was necessary.

After a couple of "functional flight checks"—test drives—over their host nation during the weekend of September 15–16, the first armed

Predator entered Afghan airspace on Tuesday, September 18. The hunt for Osama bin Laden and his lieutenants that Charlie Allen, Richard Clarke, and the other Predator advocates had long been working for was at last under way—a week to the day after Al Qaeda's devastating attacks on New York and Washington.

Four days after the operation began, the Predator team suffered a major setback. A contractor pilot, radio call sign "Big," was flying Predator 3038 over Afghanistan on September 22 when the screens in the GCS showing the video imagery and the airspeed, altitude, and other constantly changing numbers suddenly froze. "Crap," Big muttered.

The Ku-band satellite link had been lost. In such a circumstance, Predator 3038 was programmed to return to base, but for these missions, only after loitering at about twenty-five thousand feet for fifteen hours. The long loiter time was meant to make sure the Predator crossed the border after dark; Uzbekistan's authoritarian leader wanted to do everything possible to prevent the Taliban and restive Islamists on his side of the border from finding out about the Predator operation. Fifteen hours after losing link, Predator 3038 was still missing. The team was soon certain that it had crashed.

A year earlier, the Summer Project had suffered a crash as well, losing Predator 3050 on the runway in Uzbekistan because of a malfunction of some sort. That accident caused a lengthy argument between the CIA and the Air Force over who would pay the roughly $1.5 million needed to replace the aircraft. When Predator 3038 crashed, no one was arguing over money anymore. As a satellite reconnaissance photo later confirmed, 3038 went down near Mazar-i-Sharif, an area held by the U.S.-allied Northern Alliance, so the Taliban, as far as U.S. officials knew, remained ignorant of the armed version of the Predator. But the crash left the Wildfire team with only two armed Predators, just at the moment when the Bush administration's former qualms about using such a weapon evaporated.

The day before the Predator team's hunt for bin Laden began, President Bush visited the Pentagon for a briefing on special operations and was asked by a reporter, "Do you want bin Laden dead?"

Bush replied, "There's an old poster out West that I recall that said, 'Wanted Dead or Alive.'" Later that day, Monday, September 17, he signed a CIA Memorandum of Notification modifying the ban on assassinations in Executive Order 12333 and authorizing lethal covert action to disrupt Al Qaeda. The memorandum specifically empowered the CIA to use the armed Predator for that purpose.

Also on September 17, Colonel Ed Boyle officially assumed command of the Air Combat Command Expeditionary Air Intelligence Squadron—the unit that would be hunting bin Laden from the "Trailer Park," as insiders quickly took to calling the double-wide and GCS on the CIA campus. As he did, Boyle was told by Air Force lawyers that he would be the officer authorized to issue the actual order to launch a Hellfire from the Predator, empowered to do so by the laws of war and Title 10 of the U.S. Code. First, however, CIA Director George Tenet or his designee would have to authorize Boyle or *his* designee to order the trigger pulled.

Soon, the question of who should decide when to launch the Predator's missiles would prove much more complex than that, and the way that question was answered would mark a new chapter in the history of the CIA.

On September 28, President Bush chaired a National Security Council meeting at the White House to set rules of engagement for attacking Al Qaeda and the Taliban in Afghanistan. Ten days earlier, the president had signed a bill titled "Authorization for Use of Military Force against Terrorists," which had been approved by Congress on September 14; Bush now had the legal right to wage war in Afghanistan. The United States and its allies expected the conflict to be mainly an air war, with small units of CIA paramilitaries and special operations troops on the ground to direct bomb and missile strikes. But Bush was particularly worried about collateral damage, especially damage to mosques. At the NSC meeting, he and the other principals agreed that Army General Tommy Franks, commander of U.S. Central Command and commander in chief for the coming conflict, would have to obtain the president's approval to attack targets where "moderate or high collateral damage" was a risk. If the Air Force unit flying armed Predators for the CIA could find bin Laden or other Al Qaeda leaders, however, Bush's okay would not be necessary: Tenet or his designee could authorize a Hellfire shot. But the CIA was to coordinate with Franks before launching Hellfires in situations where other U.S. and allied military forces were involved.

The Predator cadre at the Trailer Park was already working hard to give Tenet a chance to approve a shot. Three pilots per shift, with one or two sensor operators available at all times, were flying two twelve-hour shifts a day, changing shifts at 1:00 p.m. and 1:00 a.m. None would stay "in the seat" more than a couple of hours at a time, for flying and manipulating sensors by remote control was often a mind-numbing job that required keen concentration. At first, Big Safari's Swanson and Guay—the only Air Force pilot and sensor operator taking part in the operation who had ever launched a Hellfire from a Predator—were scheduled to overlap with the other crews during the meat of each mission, in case a chance to take a shot arose. One of the two General Atomics pilots, who had far more time flying the Predator than even Swanson, would sit or stand behind the military pilots, coaching them through any tricky situations. The General Atomics pilots and the other Air Force crews would fly the Predator on the roughly six-hour "ferry flights" necessary to get the drone to and from its base in Uzbekistan to the skies above the Taliban stronghold of Kandahar and other areas of interest in southern Afghanistan.

Summer Project veteran Cooter and Major Darran Jergensen, meanwhile, were swapping out each twelve-hour shift as mission commander, spending much of their time in the ground control station or the double-wide at the Trailer Park. From there, they would talk on a headset with the Counterterrorist Center in the "Big House," as the Air Force contingent had begun calling the CIA headquarters building. As operations director for the Air Force cadre, Cooter also spent a lot of time in the CIA Global Response Center working with his counterpart there, Alec B.

Finding and killing Osama bin Laden and other Al Qaeda leaders was the Predator team's primary goal, but keeping track of the Taliban's leader, Mullah Mohammed Omar, was also among the cadre's assignments. Omar, a former mujahedeen insurgent and reputed sharpshooter with rocket-propelled grenades, had by 1996 become "Head of the Supreme Council and Commander of the Faithful" within the Taliban, and thus de facto ruler of Afghanistan. Fanatically fundamentalist in his Muslim beliefs, Omar became Osama bin Laden's chief ally, providing the wealthy Saudi extremist a haven and training camps for Al Qaeda. Omar claimed Allah had appeared to him in a dream as an ordinary man and called him to lead the faithful, yet he was described as a "political hermit" whose lack of ambition was one reason the Taliban revered him. He was said never to have ventured much farther from Kandahar than Kabul, the official capital of Afghanistan, yet his goal was to impose his strict brand of Islam on the world.

During the last two weeks of September and the first week of October 2001, a Predator occasionally circled Omar's modest town house in downtown Kandahar and a walled hundred-acre compound northwest of the city that included a palatial residence bin Laden had built for Omar after a truck bomb exploded near the Taliban leader's home in 1999. Two hundred yards from that compound, Omar added a T-shaped bunker forty feet beneath the ground that had electricity and running water. By the time Bush decided irrevocably for war, bin Laden's whereabouts remained a mystery, but the CIA knew where to look for his ally and protector Mullah Mohammed Omar.

On Sunday, October 7, at 1:00 p.m., Eastern Daylight Time (9:30 p.m. in Afghanistan), President Bush addressed the nation and the world from the Treaty Room of the White House. "On my orders, the United States military has begun strikes against Al Qaeda terrorist training camps and military installations of the Taliban regime in Afghanistan," the president declared. The initial strikes had begun a half hour before Bush spoke, with fifty Tomahawk cruise missiles launched from ships and submarines in the North Arabian Sea and attacks by Air Force bombers against preplanned, fixed targets, mainly Taliban air defenses and military headquarters. The purpose of Operation Enduring Freedom, Bush said in his speech, would be "to disrupt the use of Afghanistan as a terrorist base of operations, and to attack the military capability of the Taliban regime."

Bush's address, delivered on a sunny Sunday afternoon in Washington, lasted just six minutes and thirty seconds. By then, on a clear, starry night in Afghanistan, Predator 3034, call sign Wildfire 34, carrying two

K-model Hellfires, was flying past Kabul en route to Kandahar, and by midnight was circling within camera range of Taliban leader Mullah Mohammed Omar's compound northwest of the city. Forty minutes later, the drone's cameras saw a bright flash above the Taliban leader's nearby bunker—perhaps a gunshot, perhaps an explosion, but in any event, nothing dropped or launched by U.S. forces. U.S. planners had decided against bombing Omar's compound for fear of killing innocents.

An hour and fifteen minutes after the flash at the compound was recorded, a convoy of three vehicles departed, heading southeast toward Kandahar. The Predator followed, for those in command were sure one of those vehicles had the Taliban leader inside. Swanson and Guay were in the pilot and sensor operator seats in the GCS, controlling Predator 3034 from the CIA campus, seven thousand miles away from what their cameras were showing. Four F/A-18 fighter-bombers were also loitering in the vicinity of Kandahar, with a KC-10 aerial refueling tanker nearby to keep them from running out of gas. The fighter-bombers were waiting for the Predator to follow the Taliban leader to a spot where they could bomb and kill him.

Memories are fallible, especially memories formed in the infamous fog of war. Absent public release of whatever documentation still exists of what at the time was a highly classified operation, however, the memories of those participants willing to talk (including one who kept contemporaneous notes) provide the best evidence available to describe the drama that unfolded that night in Afghanistan. What can be said with certainty is that at the highest levels of the military, keen attention was being paid to the pursuit of Mullah Omar as seen in infrared Predator video.

Predator 3034's video was being viewed by General Tommy Franks on a screen at U.S. Central Command headquarters at MacDill Air Force Base, in Tampa, Florida; with him were several subordinates, including his chief legal officer: his judge advocate general, or JAG. In Washington, the CIA Predator's video was being watched in a basement office of the Pentagon by General John Jumper, with Snake Clark and the Air Force intelligence director, Major General Glen Shaffer, by his side, and with the chairman of the Joint Chiefs of Staff, General Dick Myers, joining them from time to time. The drone's video was also being fed to Prince

Sultan Air Base, a lonely batch of beige buildings in the desert about seventy miles southwest of Saudi Arabia's capital, Riyadh. Prince Sultan was home to the headquarters of the allied air war, the Combined Air Operations Center. From the main CAOC building—a big, hangar-shaped structure furnished with dozens of desks, phones, computers, and four theater-size screens to project imagery on two large walls—Air Force Lieutenant General Charles F. "Chuck" Wald was to run the air war.

Wald, a former North Dakota State University wide receiver selected by the Atlanta Falcons in the National Football League draft of 1970, was the Combined Forces Air Component Commander. While directing the air war, Wald would be joined in the main building by Major General David Deptula, the director of the CAOC; Colonel James Poss, Wald's intelligence director; and Major Peter Gersten, Wald's aide-de-camp. The four men would be sitting on an elevated platform known as the Crow's Nest, a cockpit formed by three modular office tables littered with computers, telephones, radios, and coffeepots and cups; here they could see all the imagery on the CAOC screens, which would help them command and control air operations. As the war began, however, no one in the main CAOC building—not even Wald or any of the other men in the Crow's Nest—could see the video from the CIA's armed Predator. The operation at Langley was regarded as so secret and sensitive that the screen receiving the Predator's feed was installed in a smaller building next door, the better to prevent French and Saudi officers at desks a few feet in front of the Crow's Nest from finding out about America's new weapon.

 Swanson and Guay were still at the controls of Wildfire 34 as Omar's convoy entered Kandahar at 1:10 a.m., local time, on October 8. The small convoy consisted of an SUV (a Toyota Land Cruiser or similar model) followed by a white dual-cab and another pickup truck with armed men crammed into its cargo bed. "Vehicles joined by motorcycles at Kandahar," an officer sitting near Wald and keeping notes at the CAOC in Saudi Arabia wrote forty-five minutes later. "Get the fighters up there ASAP."

A few minutes later, the vehicles stopped in front of a compound in downtown Kandahar and some of the occupants went inside. At 2:12

a.m., Kandahar time, General Deptula told subordinates to get a direct line from the Crow's Nest to Colonel Ed Boyle at the CIA. A new set of F/A-18 fighter-bombers, recorded the officer taking notes, would arrive over this "time sensitive target" at about 3:10 a.m., Afghan time. As the planes flew, Deptula was amazed to hear that Franks planned to decide himself whether they should bomb the building they believed Omar was inside, or whether the risk of collateral damage was too high. Deptula thought such tactical decisions rightly belonged not to the strategic commander, the officer highest in the chain of command, but to the air commander and his staff.

Air commander Wald, however, was not surprised. He knew Bush and Defense Secretary Donald Rumsfeld had made clear to Franks before the war that they regarded collateral damage in Afghanistan as a strategic issue. Their view was that killing civilians or damaging mosques could make it appear that the United States and its allies were waging war on the Afghan people and Muslims in general, as Al Qaeda and the Taliban were saying, and thus turn potential friends into enemies.

Franks would later write that, with his JAG telling him that the convoy now parked at the compound in Kandahar was a "valid target for Hellfire," he directed Langley to have the Predator launch a missile, then waited as the drone lined up for the shot. For reasons unexplained in his book, neither Franks nor anyone else at U.S. Central Command—or the CIA, apparently—told those in the CAOC in Saudi Arabia that Franks had told the CIA to launch a Hellfire.

Unable to see the Predator's video, Wald, Deptula, and the two other officers in the Crow's Nest were also unable to see the convoy or the compound in Kandahar. Nor could they talk directly to the Predator's operators at the CIA. Communications about what Predator 3034 was doing were instead being relayed to the Crow's Nest by a CIA liaison officer in the building next door, who was fielding phone calls and reading computer chat room messages from Langley aloud into a Crow's Nest phone that Major Gersten had set to "speaker." Wald, meanwhile, was talking and listening the same way to an AWACS communications and surveillance plane as it relayed his instructions to the leader of the Navy F/A-18s by radio. Suddenly, from one of the Crow's Nest phones on speaker, a disembodied voice no one recognized said blandly, "Cleared to fire."

"Where'd that come from?" Wald demanded as he and the others in the Crow's Nest swiveled their heads in confusion. "Stop!" he ordered the AWACS, assuming the clearance to fire was being given by someone in the surveillance plane to the fighter-bombers. "Knock it off!" Wald ordered. "You're not cleared to fire! Don't do anything!"

After a flurry of phone calls, Wald was incensed to learn that the order to fire was a command to the Predator from someone elsewhere, not the AWACS. When he realized that fact, Wald decided it was time for Operation Enduring Freedom's air commander to get direct access to the CIA Predator's screen, too. "Get it here now," Wald ordered a senior officer in charge of CAOC communications.

"Sir, we can't," the officer said. "It's a classified system on a classified net." The Predator screen was supposed to remain in the smaller building next door, which housed the CAOC's Sensitive Compartmented Information Facility, a secured room with controlled access known as a "skiff" for its initials, SCIF.

"I don't give shit. Do it," Wald said. "I need the system on the deck so I can make operational decisions. Bring it in."

By 2:32 a.m., Afghan time, a boxy white TV monitor with a filter screen on its front sat on the table at Gersten's position toward the back of the Crow's Nest. A thin, black cable ran through a hole in the table, down the Crow's Nest steps, across the rear of the CAOC, under a door leading out into the Saudi sun, and across the sand to the SCIF in the building next door, where the Predator feed arrived from Langley. Wald and his key subordinates were asked to sign letters acknowledging that the air commander had ordered the CIA Predator screen be brought out of the SCIF. Although a computer showing chat rooms that those at Langley were using had to remain in the smaller building, Wald and his crew could now watch the silent infrared video the Predator was producing.

The vehicles in Mullah Omar's convoy had begun moving before the Predator was in a position to take the shot Franks wanted in Kandahar, Franks wrote in a memoir published three years later. By the time the Predator screen was set up in the Crow's Nest at the CAOC in Saudi

Arabia, the three vehicles had arrived at another destination after a journey of about thirty minutes.

Kandahar's winding streets made it tough for Guay to keep the infrared camera on the SUV and the two trucks as they made their way through the urban maze. But Guay managed, and as the convoy reached the countryside the Predator followed. Uncertain they could hit a moving vehicle with a Hellfire launched from the Predator, which had been tested so far only against stationary targets, Cooter told Swanson and Guay simply to follow Omar and his men, who finally pulled into a mud-walled compound about southwest of Kandahar. This compound featured two fairly large, one-story rectangular buildings oriented north–south; though situated parallel to each other, they were separated by a courtyard perhaps as big as a soccer field. On the north end of the compound was another, smaller building whose purpose, as with the other structures, was hard to discern in an infrared image shot at night.

Omar's convoy pulled into the compound from the west, crossing a small bridge over a creek or gully. One truck stopped just beyond the bridge, and a couple of armed men got out and began pacing. The other two vehicles turned south, drove around the first building, and parked in the courtyard on the other side. There, several men got out of the vehicles and stood next to the big building on the west side of the courtyard, fuzzy white figures on the Predator video screen. The infrared image, created by detecting and displaying contrasts in heat, provided no way to discern the features of the men below or guess which one, if any, might be Omar. But having followed the three-vehicle convoy from Omar's compound to this one, those secretly watching from thousands of miles away were all but certain that the Predator had the Taliban leader and his inner circle in its sights.

"I've got the shot," Predator mission commander Cooter told the CIA Global Response Center, certain Swanson and Guay could put a Hellfire into the men as they stood there next to their vehicles.

Cooter was told to sit tight for a while. Someone at Central Command believed the small building at the north end of the compound might be a mosque. Talking over a speaker phone in the GCS, Cooter conversed with his counterparts on the sixth floor of CIA headquarters and described precisely how he would direct his crew to fly the Predator so that even if the Hellfire's twenty-pound warhead missed the Taliban leaders, there would be no risk of hitting the small building. As the higher-ups debated what to do, though, the potential targets entered the large rectangular building, disappearing from view. Cooter was furious.

Adrenaline was flowing at the CAOC in Saudi Arabia, too, where Wald, Deptula, and Gersten had clustered their chairs at one end of the Crow's Nest to watch the silent infrared drama playing out on the TV monitor now feeding them the Predator's video. Wald was distracted, still seething that someone had been ready to launch a missile at a building in Kandahar without even giving the air commander a heads-up. Deptula and Gersten had their blood up. Only hours into the war, the Predator had handed the air commander and his team an opportunity to take out the Taliban's leader and perhaps his most senior subordinates—a strategic blow of incalculable proportions. Knocking out the Taliban leadership would leave the enemy in disarray, strip bin Laden of his protectors, and possibly lead others to turn on the Al Qaeda leader and serve him up to the United States.

While awaiting a decision from Central Command, Deptula instructed two Navy F-14C Tomcats carrying thousand-pound bombs to go into a holding pattern twenty miles south of Omar's latest stop. The Predator, with its tiny engine and pusher propeller, could circle above the Taliban's heads unnoticed, but a loitering F-14's roar might be heard for miles. Deptula wanted the two fighter planes far enough away to keep anyone in the compound below from hearing them, but ready to strike as soon as Franks gave the okay.

At CIA headquarters, Boyle walked outside and hurried to the GCS. If a shot was taken, he was required to order it. Swanson and Guay, with contractor pilot Big standing behind them, kept the Predator circling with its infrared camera on the compound as they waited to hear from Cooter what they were to do. A Hellfire's relatively small warhead would be useless against the large building Omar, or the man they presumed to be Omar, had entered, but now the Taliban leader was in a place that could be obliterated with ease by warplanes. The excitement in the GCS was palpable. The war was on. The Predator team had in their sights a target they knew was important. Fighter-bombers were on hand, just waiting for the Predator crew to lead them to the target.

Thirty minutes passed. Swanson kept Predator 3034 circling. Guay kept its infrared camera on the building they were sure Omar had entered. The others in the GCS kept watching. A half hour stretched into an hour. One hour stretched toward two. The men outside the truck parked near the bridge at the entrance of the compound in Afghanistan split up, came back together, and meandered in circles. The F-14s were long gone, thirsty for fuel, but two new F/A-18s had been summoned and were close enough to kill the Taliban's leader. Yet from the sixth floor of the CIA, from the CAOC in Saudi Arabia, from U.S. Central Command in Tampa, no orders came down.

"What are they *waiting* on?" Guay grumbled.

12

CLEARED TO FIRE

General John Jumper, watching the pursuit of Mullah Omar unfold live but silently on a Predator screen in the Pentagon, was asking the same question as Master Sergeant Jeff Guay: *What are they waiting on?* As Air Force chief of staff, Jumper was both the most senior officer in his service and a member of the Joint Chiefs of Staff. His job, however, was to work with the secretary of the Air Force to manage the service—to "recruit, organize, supply, equip, train, service, mobilize, demobilize, administer and maintain"—not command units in combat. Jumper was free to offer his advice on military matters, including combat operations, to the chairman of the Joint Chiefs, who as principal military adviser to the president could share that advice with the commander in chief. But when it came to operations, the members of the Joint Chiefs were legally outside the chain of command, which ran from the president to the secretary of defense to the combatant commander—in this case, Army General Tommy Franks. Which was why Jumper—watching the war with Snake Clark and several others outside the chain of command—was increasingly puzzled by the failure to strike first at the Taliban leader's convoy and later at the buildings Omar was thought to be inside.

"We'd gone to all this trouble to set this up and get this architecture," Jumper recalled years later, "and I thought we were exactly where we needed to be to make the right decision."

Omar's convoy (or, more correctly, the convoy believed to contain the Taliban chief) was the very definition of a "fleeting target," the elusive sort that had led Jumper to decide to arm the Predator less than a year and a half earlier. Jumper had watched with anticipation as the little convoy went from Omar's house in Kandahar to the walled compound in the countryside. When the new chairman of the Joint Chiefs, Air Force General Dick Myers, walked into the SCIF in the Pentagon where Jumper was watching the Predator video, Jumper told Myers he had thought the drone was going to launch a Hellfire at Omar's convoy.

"We didn't shoot, and I don't know why," Jumper said.

More than an hour later, the Predator was still circling the compound southwest of Kandahar while Franks, his legal officer, and others at U.S. Central Command in Tampa argued with the CIA about whether one of the buildings in the compound—either the larger one they thought Omar was in or the smaller one to the north—was a mosque. Neither structure had a minaret, but not all mosques do. The CIA and the leaders of the Combined Air Operations Center in Saudi Arabia wanted fighters to drop bombs on the building they believed Omar had entered, the large one on the west side of the courtyard. CIA experts were sure that that building was just a meeting hall and the smaller one perhaps a kitchen.

"As I watched, I remembered my final conversation with President Bush," Franks wrote in a memoir three years later. "The President had reminded me that the enemy was al Qaeda and the Taliban, not the Afghan people. 'And this is not about religion,' he'd said. 'If you see bin Laden go into a mosque, wait until he comes out to kill him.' *Wait till they come out*, I thought."

At the CAOC, Lieutenant General Chuck Wald, air commander for Operation Enduring Freedom, was talking to Franks by phone from time to time and sharing what he heard with those in the Crow's Nest with him: Major General David Deptula, Colonel James Poss, and Major Peter Gersten. Deptula was confident that, whatever the smaller building might be, it was distant enough from the one they wanted to bomb to rule out any significant risk of collateral damage. "CINC not hitting building because of collateral damage," a CAOC officer keeping notes wrote, using the acronym for commander in chief to mean Franks. "Amazing. We could get Omar but the CINC's worried about collateral damage."

At the Trailer Park tucked into the glade on the CIA campus, Predator pilot Captain Scott Swanson, sensor operator Guay, and others in the ground control station and the operations cell kept asking, or wondering, why nothing was happening. "They're not going to drop because they think it's too close to a mosque," Major Mark Cooter, the mission commander in the GCS, finally told them after getting the explanation from an Air Force liaison officer in the CIA Global Response Center.

Then, suddenly, the situation changed. Cooter was told by the liaison officer that higher-ups wanted the Predator operators to launch a Hellfire into a vehicle parked at the bridge leading into the compound, where dismounted armed guards kept gathering. Swanson thought the "guys upstairs" at the CIA had finally lost their patience with the hesitation at Centcom, as U.S. Central Command was known. But according to Franks's memoir, that wasn't the case at all. After being told the Predator had only enough fuel to stay above the compound less than an hour more, Franks wrote, he decided to have the drone's operators put a Hellfire into one of the vehicles "parked near the wall," an apparent reference to the truck parked near the bridge at the gate to the walled compound. That gate was on the west side of the larger building, which Franks believed was a mosque. "Maybe that will persuade the people to leave the mosque and give us a shot at the principals," Franks recalled saying.

Some thought the order simply dumb, given the odds against figuring out who the principals might be in a fuzzy infrared video. But the idea of taking a shot to flush Omar out had been discussed between Centcom and the CAOC in Saudi Arabia earlier, judging by the notes one officer took at the time. "The CINC is directing Predator to shoot two Hellfire with 30-pound warheads when we have F-18s with GBU-12s on station," the officer wrote at 3:15 a.m., Afghan time, erring ten pounds on the high side in describing the Hellfire warhead. "Hellfires will bounce off the building," the officer added in a bit of hyperbole, misunderstanding which target Franks had picked. The note taker added that Deptula had asked Wald to "call the CINC and tell him." The notes added Centcom's logic: *"Perhaps"*—with "perhaps" double underlined—"use Hellfires to scare them out to go to another hold site and then hit them."

Swanson needed a few minutes to get the Predator in position to fire. Based on the Hellfire's projected flight path, he would have to pull the trigger when the Predator was within a "sweet spot" of half a kilometer or less to make sure the missile hit where Guay was aiming the crosshairs of the laser designator. Precision flying was required, and then a countdown to the moment to fire, to be sure Guay had the beam on target when Swanson pulled the trigger.

As the time to begin the launch sequence approached, contractor pilot Big looked back at Cooter and nodded toward the white cowboy hat hanging on a metal rack above Cooter's head. When the Summer Project crew gave him the hat for his birthday a year earlier, Cooter swore never to wear it until they were taking action against Al Qaeda. Now he looked up at the hat, looked back at Big and gave him a grin, then reached up and grabbed the white Stetson and put it on his head. This was the moment Cooter had been itching for ever since he and Swanson saw the caskets of USS *Cole* sailors being unloaded in Germany. "Okay," Cooter told Swanson and Guay. "Cleared to fire."

"Ten, nine, eight," Swanson announced, pacing his count with the Predator's closure rate while pressing and holding the "arm" button on the throttle with his left thumb. As he finished—"two, one, launch"—he pulled the trigger on his joystick. A second later, the GCS video screens went wavy for a moment as the bright light of the Hellfire's rocket plume disrupted the infrared sensor. Then the missile vanished. "Weapon away," Swanson said calmly.

For the next twenty seconds, sensor operator Guay took center stage. For the missile to hit its target, Guay had to lock the laser designator crosshairs on the truck near the bridge no matter how the air might buffet the Predator. Swanson focused on keeping the aircraft steady as the missile streaked unseen toward the men below. Then a bloom of bright light silently flashed on their video screens, and a glowing object of some kind somersaulted into the air and fell to the ground.

"We've got a *flip-pah*," Guay declared in a mock thick Maine accent as the object spun in the air and disappeared in the infrared glow from the now-flaming truck. The "flipper" was one of the guards who had been standing next to the vehicle the Hellfire hit.

As the bright blossom of the initial explosion cleared, Swanson could see a couple of glowing bodies on the ground. Luminous figures poured out of the buildings in the compound and began running in all directions, many clearly carrying weapons and searching for the source of the munition that had hit the truck. None of them seemed to be looking up. Swanson thought the men below reacted as if they had been mortared or hit from across the road with a rocket-propelled grenade. He and Guay traded high fives with each other and with contractor pilot Big behind them. Cheers from the double-wide trailer echoed in their headsets.

The moment was historic. The Hellfire Predator was no longer just a concept. A new way of waging war had been inaugurated, a new way of killing enemies proven. Remote-control war and remote-control killing were no longer remote ideas: they were realities. One of the intelligence analysts in the double-wide printed a freeze frame of Predator 3034's video at the moment the truck hit by the Hellfire exploded; annotated the photo with the date, location, and other data; and taped it to a wall in the trailer, a record of the world's first intercontinental drone strike. Soon there would be more such pictures on the double-wide's walls—many more.

Those at the CAOC in Saudi Arabia reacted far differently from the high-fiving crew in the GCS at Langley. Wald and Deptula, seated side by side, had turned their chairs to watch the Predator screen now sitting on the table at the back of the Crow's Nest. Wald had been leaning back in his chair, occasionally putting a Styrofoam coffee cup to his lips to catch the shells of sunflower seeds he was chewing. When the silent infrared picture suddenly flared in the familiar white blossom of an explosion, the three-star general sat bolt upright.

"Who the fuck did *that*?" Wald and Deptula blurted in unison, staring at each other in wide-eyed shock as men poured out of the building they had wanted to bomb and dashed around the courtyard of the compound in Afghanistan.

"It's like an anthill down there," Deptula muttered.

Wald and Deptula watched as dozens of men filled the courtyard; there were too many to count. Some jumped in vehicles and drove away. The Predator's infrared camera followed one vehicle that had been part of Omar's convoy.

Wald phoned Franks and then told the others what the CINC had told him.

"Predator fired one Hellfire at the vehicles," the officer taking notes recorded. "CINC did not know—we did not know: Who issued the fire order?" Franks, according to this officer's contemporaneous notes, told Wald he didn't know who had ordered the Hellfire shot—contrary to what Franks later wrote in his memoir.

"Looks like we gave up—forfeited—an opportunity to take out the entire Taliban leadership because CIA or Intel controlling Predator," the officer at the CAOC taking notes wrote. "We were not notified Hellfire would be shot. CINC did not know, either. Who gave the fire order? Wald on the phone to CINC ten minutes after fire of Hellfire. Did not know."

Wald's next phone call was to Lieutenant General Soup Campbell, the CIA's military liaison and a fellow Air Force fighter pilot. They had known each other for years.

"What the fuck, over?" Wald began.

Campbell was chagrined. He thought Franks and the CINC's intelligence director at Centcom were in direct touch with Colonel Ed Boyle at the CIA and Wald both. In any event, Campbell told Wald, he thought Boyle had issued the specific order to fire.

Fourteen minutes after his call to Campbell, Wald called the Centcom operations director, Major General Gene Renuart, another fellow Air Force officer Wald knew well. "If you were me, what do you think I'd want to know?" Wald said. Then he answered the question himself: *"Who the fuck is running what?"*

Next Wald called Boyle, another officer he had known for nearly twenty years. Wald reached Boyle in the double-wide trailer at the CIA.

"Eddie, first of all, I'm going to kill you, and then I'm going to have you go to jail for this," Wald loudly threatened, apparently with no humor intended. Wald knew Boyle was one of John Jumper's favorites. He also knew Jumper was unhappy that the armed Predator hadn't been used earlier during the Omar chase. Myers, the Joint Chiefs chairman, had called Wald and said so. But Jumper was outside the chain of command.

"You're working for Johnny Jumper," Wald accused.

Boyle denied the accusation.

"You're lying through your teeth," Wald said.

Boyle nearly exploded. "Hey, boss, to be all honest with you, go fuck yourself!" he snarled. Those nearby whipped their heads around. Boyle was pale and trembling. "I don't give a shit what you try to do to me tonight," he loudly added.

For the next few minutes, Boyle and Wald argued about how the Hellfire shot had come about. Their heated conversation ended only after Boyle assured Wald, as the CIA's military liaison Campbell had done earlier, that Wald or his staff would be told in advance before the Predator took any other Hellfire shots.

Twenty minutes later, Deptula telephoned Boyle. "Hey, Ed, calm down," urged the CAOC director, who had worked with Boyle off and on since the 1991 Gulf War.

"Dave, in all honesty, the boss called me a fuckin' liar," Boyle fumed. "Franks and his staff didn't have the courtesy to read Wald in, and you're blaming me?"

"You'll get over it," Deptula soothed.

The officer taking notes wrote later that night that the "actual fire order" for the first Hellfire launch by a Predator in combat was issued by Franks to the Centcom director of intelligence, Army Brigadier General Jeff Kimmons, who relayed it to an Army lieutenant colonel serving as Centcom's liaison in the CIA Global Response Center, who relayed it to a CIA official, who relayed it to Boyle, who then gave the order to fire to the crew in the ground control station.

By now—5:17 a.m. on Monday, October 8, in Afghanistan—the Predator was circling a building half a mile south of the compound where the

Hellfire shot had been taken. The drone's cameras had followed some people who fled there in one of the vehicles from Mullah Omar's former convoy. Now officers at Centcom and analysts from the National Imagery and Mapping Agency were debating whether *that* building was a mosque, with the intelligence analysts sure that it was. "Picture up," the officer at the CAOC taking notes wrote. "Boyle watching mosque area. Centcom guys have no idea what's going on. Argument between Centcom and NIMA over mosque. No coordination at all."

In his memoir, Franks wrote that he was in the Fusion Cell at Centcom headquarters in Tampa, as the SCIF where his Predator screen was located was called. He saw the building the Predator was watching as a "large, multistory house behind a fortress-like wall" and figured that those inside were Taliban leaders. By his account, some F/A-18s (planes that the officer taking notes in the CAOC recorded as F-14s) were within striking distance. Franks ordered the CAOC to direct the fighters to the scene while he called Defense Secretary Donald Rumsfeld to request clearance to bomb the building "as a high collateral damage target." Rumsfeld said he would call Bush and get back in touch as soon as possible.

"Within five minutes, President Bush had approved the target for immediate strike," Franks wrote, but when he got back to the Fusion Cell, an officer calling from CIA headquarters was on the phone with a member of Franks's staff. "Don't shoot," the officer said. "We think this building is a mosque." According to his memoir, Franks, with his legal officer concurring, called Wald and ordered him to have the fighters drop their bombs anyway.

In the GCS, contractor pilot Big raised the fighters on the Predator's unsecured radio and talked them onto the target building. With Wald's okay, Deptula had a colonel on the CAOC floor pass approval through the AWACS for the planes to drop their bombs. "Two on one building, two on the second building," the officer taking notes wrote. The target, Franks wrote in his book, "disappeared in a cloud of dust and smoke."

Soon afterward, Wald was surprised—and annoyed—to get a call from Jumper. The Air Force chief of staff said he realized this was Wald's turf, but he wanted to be sure Wald knew that the people thought to be

Taliban leaders had fled those buildings before the bombs hit. Jumper had seen them go on the Predator's video.

"Chief, are you watching this in real time?" Wald demanded, clearly suggesting Jumper shouldn't be. *Who else has got a Predator feed?* Wald wondered. *Mullah Omar?*

As the buildings fell, the time was 5:48 a.m., Monday, in Afghanistan. The Predator had thirty minutes left before its dwindling fuel would require flying back to its base, a trip of about six hours, given the drone's slow cruising speed. Contractor pilot Big, who had taken over for Swanson, turned the drone north for home.

As the Predator poked along, Big was instructed to fly over Kandahar's airport, which was on the way. U.S. bombers had hit the airfield earlier that night, but three concrete buildings Osama bin Laden was known to have visited in the past were still standing. Boyle got CIA higher-ups to approve putting the Predator's remaining Hellfire into the middle one of those three buildings. Getting rid of the second missile would reduce the Predator's aerodynamic drag, making it easier for the drone to get home, and the airfield was a valid target in any event. Guay had given up the sensor operator's seat to another Air Force enlisted man, who after Big pulled the trigger kept the laser designator on the structure and scored a direct hit. How much damage the strike did, or whether anyone was inside the little building, was impossible to tell, but the Predator's camera showed debris blowing out of the structure's back wall.

A few minutes later, Boyle's phone rang.

"What the fuck, over?" Wald demanded. "You'll get no more fighters from us."

Wald then called Franks, told him about Jumper's call, and complained about the "screwed up command and control of the Predator." Franks agreed with Wald. The CIA's armed Predator should be part of the CAOC's daily Air Tasking Order, a document listing every allied aircraft flying in the theater of operations by radio call sign, aircraft type, and mission. The CIA's Predator operators should coordinate with the CAOC, not just fly around independently, even if their primary mission *was* to hunt "high-value targets" such as Osama bin Laden.

As soon as they were off the phone, Wald called Centcom operations director Renuart again and told him about Jumper's call. "Who is in control?" Wald fumed. "I'm ready to fold up and come home."

In his memoir, Franks also reported getting a call about Jumper's observations on Omar's escape. "Within an hour, Dick Myers called on the STU-III," Franks wrote, referring to a secure telephone. "'Tom,' he said, 'John Jumper has been watching the Predator scene at Air Force ops here in the Pentagon, and he tells me that the principals left the house before the bombs went in. He knows this is your business, says he's just trying to be helpful.'"

After calling Rumsfeld to thank him for his and Bush's quick reaction to his request to bomb what others thought was a mosque, Franks wrote, he called Myers back and complained about what he viewed as Jumper's meddling. Franks then quotes himself as telling Myers, "I'd appreciate it if you would remove the fucking Predator downlink from the Building."

The next day, the Predator video feed into the Pentagon was cut off. A Predator video feed to the White House, though, remained in place, and had an avid viewer: President Bush. As Bob Woodward reported in his book *Bush at War*, on October 10, 2001, three days after the Afghan campaign began, Bush brought up the Predator during a National Security Council meeting in the White House Situation Room. "Why can't we fly more than one Predator at a time?" Bush asked, remarking on how impressed he was with the drone.

"We're going to try to get two simultaneously," offered CIA Director George Tenet, alluding to a plan his agency and the Air Force were working on to add a second ground control station to the Trailer Park and get more Hellfire Predators to the base in Uzbekistan.

"We ought to have 50 of these things," Bush said.

Later that day, Bush attended a news conference at FBI headquarters to announce a new list of the twenty-two "Most Wanted Terrorists." Led by bin Laden, the list included his top two deputies, Egyptians Ayman al-Zawahiri and Mohammed Atef, the Al Qaeda military commander, whose daughter was married to bin Laden's son. "Bush took a classified version for himself that had photos, brief biographies and personality sketches of the 22 men," Woodward reported. "When he returned to his desk in the Oval Office, he slipped the list of names and faces into a drawer, ready at hand, his own personal scorecard for the war."

In the early days of the war, firing missiles was only a small part of what the Hellfire Predators did over Afghanistan. With 3034 and 3037 the only two remaining Predators modified to carry the missiles, with only a dozen or so Hellfire Ks left at their operating base in Uzbekistan after the first night of the war, with only one Air Force pilot experienced in firing them, and with bin Laden, Omar, and other Al Qaeda and Taliban leaders gone to ground, U.S. commanders had as much or greater need of the Predator's cameras and other sensors as for its weapons.

The first night of the war, before the botched pursuit of Mullah Omar began, the Wildfire team had flown 3034 undetected near Taliban anti-aircraft missile batteries and helped B-2 stealth bombers flying from Missouri bypass that threat. Rather than go through the CAOC in Saudi Arabia, however, the Wildfire team communicated with the B-2s through a special data distribution system. Following the first night's confusion over command and control during the Omar chase, Wald and Franks insisted the CIA-controlled Hellfire Predators be part of the CAOC's daily Air Tasking Order. After that, and for the next four or five days, the Hellfire Predators divided their time between searching for Al Qaeda and Taliban leaders—with help from CIA paramilitaries, tribal allies, and other agents on the ground—while also helping manned air-craft hit targets selected by the military. If the manned aircraft carried GPS-guided bombs, the Predator crew would provide a target's geo-graphic coordinates; if it carried laser-guided bombs, the Predator crew would provide a laser spot or talk the attacking planes onto their targets.

The number of fixed targets U.S. commanders wanted to hit, though, diminished quickly. The first night of the war, U.S. and British warplanes and ships firing cruise missiles hit thirty-one Taliban airfields, air defenses, communications facilities, Al Qaeda terrorist training camps, and related sites. The second day, they struck only thirteen such targets. "We're not running out of targets, Afghanistan is," Defense Secretary Rumsfeld cracked on the third day of the war at his daily Pentagon news briefing with Joint Chiefs Chairman Myers. But targets worth striking were "emerging as we continue," Rumsfeld noted, meaning Al Qaeda and Taliban forces were being hit whenever they could be found.

The Hellfire Predator was proving useful in both finding and striking targets. A given Predator mission typically lasted twenty to twenty-four hours, with four to six hours on each end needed for transit time. At the CAOC's behest, the Wildfire crew would sometimes watch a particular location for evidence of Al Qaeda or Taliban fighters for hours; every couple of hours, pilots and sensor operators in the GCS would shift in and out of the seat. When a bomb strike was ordered, the Predator crew would guide manned aircraft onto the targets. One Predator operator at the Trailer Park, a former F-15E Strike Eagle pilot, had dropped a lot of bombs on Serb targets in Kosovo two years earlier and was especially good as a virtual forward air controller, which required knowing how to conduct a "Nine-line Brief." In a nine-line, a forward air controller talks a pilot onto a target by providing instructions and descriptions in nine standard steps, starting with "initial point," meaning where to begin the bomb or missile run, and ending with "egress direction," meaning which way the attacking pilot should depart the scene of a strike.

During the first weeks of the war, the Wildfire crews used the Predator's cameras and laser designator to help F/A-18, F-14, F-15, and F-16 strike aircraft, plus B-1B, B-2, and B-52 bombers find and hit targets ranging from Taliban helicopters found on the ground by the drone to groups of Taliban or Al Qaeda fighters detected by its cameras. With the enemy on the run, the Wildfire team worked frequently with AC-130U "Spooky" and AC-130H "Spectre" gunships—fearsome special operations ground attack aircraft equipped with side-firing 40 millimeter and 105 millimeter cannons and a Gatling gun. The gunships were called in several times after the Predator, lurking high above for hours, tracked men in trucks or SUVs to compounds or buildings clearly under guard by enemy fighters.

Sometimes, after a bomb strike on such a target, the Predator would help track and attack what the Wildfire crews took to calling "squirters" and those in the CAOC usually called "spitters"—survivors running from the scene of a strike. Sometimes, the Predator crew would be directed to launch a Hellfire at squirters as they climbed into a truck or SUV or some other vehicle to flee, or simply ran for cover. For CAOC commanders, the Predator's cameras were vital to maintaining the so-called chain of custody—the proof that their targets were indeed people positively identified as enemy fighters—required to attack.

Despite their initial frustration and Wald's anger over the CIA and Franks controlling the Hellfire Predator without consulting him, commanders at the CAOC found the drone extremely valuable in corroborating intelligence tips from other sources about activity on the ground. One officer recalled that CIA paramilitaries or other intelligence sources might report, "There's a meeting at such and such a location at such and such a time. So the Predator would go there and look. And sure enough, there'd be a group of people entering. You'd watch them enter, you'd loiter, you'd wait till the meeting came out. Then you'd watch the vehicles go away and then you'd assign an AC-130 to go take out those vehicles. We did that multiple times. You've got bad guys meeting, you don't take out the building with large-scale weapons because you've got potential for collateral damage."

Defense Secretary Rumsfeld quickly became a Predator enthusiast. "In those first days of combat in Afghanistan, the Predator and other unmanned aerial vehicles (UAV) conclusively proved their value to our military and intelligence personnel," Rumsfeld wrote in his memoir *Known and Unknown*—though the Predator was actually the only UAV in use in Afghanistan during the first month of the war. Rumsfeld added in a note that "with coalition operations underway in Afghanistan, George Tenet and I began to sort out Defense-CIA joint Predator operations. We came to an agreement over who owned and paid for the assets, where they would operate, and who would 'pull the trigger' on the very few UAVs that were armed at the time." Left unmentioned by Rumsfeld was that after the escape of Mullah Omar the first night of the war, the CIA often coordinated with Centcom but never again deferred to Franks before taking a shot at a high-value target.

In early October 2001, Rumsfeld and other officials were saying little in public about the Predator. But in the October 22 issue of *The New Yorker* magazine, journalist Seymour Hersh revealed that the CIA was controlling an armed version of the drone that had tracked Mullah

Omar the first night of the war and had been refused permission to fire on him by Franks. Tom Ricks of the *Washington Post* quickly followed up with a front-page article calling the armed Predator "a revolutionary step in the conduct of warfare." Even so, months would pass before many others began to grasp just how revolutionary a step the Predator was.

On the drone revolution's ramparts—in the ground control station or the double-wide trailer on the CIA campus—the initial cadre of revolutionaries knew they were players in a real-life drama. In bull sessions, the Wildfire team joked about which Hollywood actors should play them in the movie about their operation. But as the initial adrenaline rush of waging war by remote control ebbed, some began to feel they had entered the Twilight Zone, where a twelve-hour shift might consist of either mind-numbing tedium or nerve-wracking tension. Improvisation and on-the-job training were essential to their success. At first, Big Safari's Swanson, the only Air Force pilot on the team who had fired any Hellfires before the war, was the only Air Force pilot to launch missiles over Afghanistan. Contractor Big had fired them in tests, too. Later, other operators began taking shots but, in their case, without ever firing a missile at a practice target. With only two Predators modified to carry Hellfires in those early days of the war, there was no way for the pilots and sensor operators to fully rehearse their lethal act before going onstage, although taking a couple of dry runs at a real target before firing was useful and usual.

The more they fired, the more they noticed peculiar things about using this new weapon. Unlike pilots or other crew in strike aircraft or big bombers, the Predator's operators could watch their targets for hours, see their missiles strike, and continue to watch the aftermath long after the smoke had cleared. Often—but not always, for some of their targets were inside vehicles or buildings—they could see the people they were about to attack, although never well enough to discern their faces, just enough to distinguish them from others. They also saw bodies flip, or disappear, or lie lifeless on the ground; sometimes, severely wounded, the men they had targeted would try to crawl away. Operating the Predator was less like flying an attack aircraft than like being a sniper lying in ambush, which for some made the act of killing somehow seem more personal.

Yet the Predator crews, communicating over their headsets with the mission commander seated toward the back of the ground control station, or with intelligence analysts in the double-wide, rarely had any idea whom they were stalking and killing. This was true even in the case of so-called high-value targets. Rather than keeping a scorecard, operations director Mark Cooter and mission commander Darran Jergensen concentrated on making sure their crews could deliver what their CIA controllers wanted the Predator to do. Ed Boyle and Air Force liaison officers who routinely spent time in the CIA Global Response Center might know more about individual targets, but there was no reason to pass such information on to the flight crews. Picking targets was the CIA's business. Besides, CIA culture focused to the point of obsession on "compartmentalizing" information—keeping it secret from all but those with a clear need to know. The Counterterrorist Center mission managers on Langley's sixth floor seemed particularly wary of sharing information that might reveal sources and methods of identifying Al Qaeda or Taliban members the CIA wanted to target.

"Generally, we would have some kind of target or area to look at, and that was based on some other type of cross intel," one crew member recalled. "If there was something there that caught the attention of the guys up in the CTC, we might linger for hours or days. At some point, they would go, 'Hey, this is a valid target.' Our mission commander, the guy sitting in the back of the GCS, would be in [computer] chat and perhaps on a direct phone line to the guys upstairs, passing that information back and forth, and eventually it would come down, 'Yes, put a round on target. I want you to put a round through the building; take out those people; take out that car.'" For the Predator crews, the names of those in the crosshairs were unknown and unimportant, just as a fighter or bomber pilot, or a soldier in combat on the ground, almost never knows anything personal about the enemy. All the Wildfire crews knew was that they were killing "bad guys."

One name the Predator crews did know was Lucky. He was the dog who regularly wandered into the picture on the Predator screen just as they were about to launch a missile, a glowing, four-legged apparition who continually tempted fate. There were often dogs in the mud-brick compounds common to Afghanistan, which usually contained a house or two behind a tall outer wall and heavy iron gates. The wall provided security and privacy for extended families, allowing women to go unveiled and children, chickens, and goats to wander freely. Al Qaeda and Taliban fighters sometimes took refuge in such compounds, and when the Predator crews launched Hellfires at them, any dogs in proximity invariably bolted several seconds before the missile hit, alerted by their keen sense of hearing, the Wildfire team supposed. Humans never ran. A human might hear a shrill shriek during the final subsonic portion of the Hellfire's flight, but the shriek lasted only a split second, and by then it was too late. Early on in the war, someone at the Trailer Park—inveterate cut-up Guay, most likely—started calling every canine that appeared just as a strike was being launched Lucky, and the joke caught on. "There goes Lucky," someone would say as a dog fled an incoming Hellfire.

Guay was a reliable source of humor, and perhaps because of the Predator team's somewhat strange circumstances, his sarcastic outlook became contagious. By late October or early November, the crews had spent weeks working in the chilly GCS or the drafty double-wide for twelve hours on, twelve hours off, seven days a week, with infrequent trips to the Big House for food, and most toilet breaks taken in a thin-walled bathroom in one corner of the trailer or in one of three porta-potties outdoors. At smoke breaks in the glade, over beers at the Tysons Corner Marriott or Mr. Smith's, a favorite bar nearby, gripes were nursed about spending days and nights hidden away in the woods. They would joke that they were so close to the edge of the CIA campus they might as well be in West Virginia, which was actually fifty miles or so away.

Then one of the CIA people made a crack about the Predator crews being "trailer trash"—just about the time, as it happened, that Ginger Wallace and other women on the team were complaining to Boyle about a broken toilet in the double-wide. No one at the Big House seemed to care about getting the toilet repaired, so Guay and some of the others decided to send the CIA a message. "We're trailer trash, so we might as well look that way," one declared. They took the malfunctioning toilet out of the double-wide, plopped it on the ground outside, and stuck a pot of flowers in its bowl. "All we need now is a sofa out front, a broken-down truck on cement blocks, and pink flamingos," someone said, and though they couldn't manage the sofa and truck, someone came up with four plastic pink flamingos, which they stuck in the ground around their "redneck flower pot."

CIA officials came out to the Trailer Park from time to time for various reasons, and one or two who saw the pink flamingos and toilet bowl on their grounds suffered shock and awe. Some told Boyle he had to get rid of that junk, if not for operational security then for aesthetic reasons. When CIA Director Tenet saw the hillbilly tableau, he chuckled, then chuckled some more. He also promised to get the toilet fixed, and did. But the flamingos stayed.

Tenet, gregarious by nature, occasionally made the fifteen-minute trip from his office to the double-wide on his way home at night to let the Air Force team know how much he appreciated what they were doing. Some weekends, he would come out to the Trailer Park in blue jeans, plop down in a chair with an unlit Cohiba cigar in his mouth, and shoot the breeze for twenty or thirty minutes with whoever happened to be there. Tenet also lingered in the Global Response Center on the sixth floor and watched operations unfold when the Predator was on an important target; sometimes he himself issued the approval to launch the Hellfires. Before 9/11, he had been skeptical and cautious about the CIA using the armed Predator, but after Al Qaeda's attacks on America, and after seeing what the drone could do in the first days of the war, Tenet became a "disciple," as one official close to him put it.

One of those employing this new technology was a remarkable young woman—remarkable even before she made history by becoming the first of her sex to launch a lethal drone strike. Among the first female fighter pilots in U.S. history, she was an F-15E Strike Eagle flier who logged combat hours over Iraq, Bosnia, and Kosovo before becoming a Predator operator. Even out of the cockpit, she stood out. Tall, blond, athletic, and bold, she was a self-described tomboy—the only sister of four brothers—whose sole observable fear was being taken less seriously because she was female. She liked to drink, and when she drank too much, she tended to get into fights—wrestling bouts, really, and always with men. She and her husband had first gotten acquainted when they started wrestling and rolling on the floor at a Christmas party where there was alcohol to drink and cake to shove in each other's faces.

Her tough-girl tendencies also inspired her radio call sign "Ghengis" (which she spelled that way). Her first F-15E squadron chose her call sign, and while stationed overseas later, she lived up to the moniker during a crowded apartment party. She was sitting on the floor with her back against the front of a sofa and a drink in her hand when a weapon systems officer (a "backseater," in military slang) slid onto the seat behind her. When he rested his legs on her shoulders, let out a sigh, and loudly declared, "Now that's what women are good for," Ghengis knocked him over the back of the sofa. He got up with a bloody lip.

Ghengis—at her stipulation, the only way she will be identified in this account—was an Air Force brat. Her father was an officer, and one of her brothers was a fighter pilot. Yet she chose her career on a whim. One day at the start of her sophomore year at a junior college, she was driving down the road with her arm out the window, letting her hand play in the wind like an airplane wing. As she put it years later, "Just out of the blue, I decided I wanted to go to the Air Force Academy." She also wanted to fly fighters, and was lucky in her timing. About the time she got her Air Force commission, the Clinton administration decided women should be allowed to pilot combat planes.

Another male weapon systems officer—a job also known as a Wizzo, after the abbreviation WSO—learned in a different way not to mess with Ghengis. Her greatest difficulty piloting F-15Es over Iraq wasn't the occasional antiaircraft missile she had to dodge but the duration of the missions, which could last ten hours—a long time to go without emptying your bladder. Males could urinate in flight into a piddle pack, a small vinyl bag lined with compressed sponges. But at the time, no such device existed for female fighter pilots. Ghengis griped about this aloud, and one day, while flying over Iraq, the male WSO in her F-15E's backseat began gleefully reporting each time he used his piddle pack. About the third time she heard him say, "Ahhh, yeahhh, peein' now," she jerked back on the control stick, throwing the plane into a sharp vertical climb that caused the WSO to wizz all over himself. No WSO ever teased Ghengis about the piddle pack problem again.

Months later, it was Ghengis's turn to fume. Her squadron commander told her that the instructor pilot billet she had requested as her next assignment wasn't available; instead, the Air Force was sending her to Indian Springs, Nevada, to fly the Predator. This wasn't punishment, he assured her, just dues she had to pay for the great three-year assignment she was finishing up.

Her shoulders fell. "Predator?" Ghengis asked in disbelief. "Seriously?"

No fighter pilot volunteered for life at "One G," as two F-16 jockeys assigned to the Predator called it in a rap video lament that found its way onto the Internet. Even by the summer of 2000, Indian Springs was still known as "the Land of Misfit Toys," among other unflattering nicknames. "What did you screw up to get here?" asked a fellow fighter pilot who reported for Predator training with Ghengis after damaging his back in a hard landing. Fourteen months later, in October 2001, Ghengis found herself flying combat missions again, only this time from the ground control station at the Trailer Park at the CIA. On October 24, three weeks into the war in Afghanistan, she became the first woman ever to fire a missile from a drone in combat.

Over the previous five weeks, Ghengis had flown Predators 3034 and 3037 over Afghanistan more than sixty-two hours, recording her flight time in a small diary she kept. She also noted specifics of her workouts at a local gym—"weights, sit-ups, X-trainer 30 min"—how far she jogged, and visits to Washington by her parents and friends. Unlike Swanson, who had flown many of the Hellfire tests at China Lake before the war, Ghengis launched her first missile at a target with people inside. She had no idea who they were. The mission commander simply told her to "take out that truck." She and a sensor operator did, with a K-model Hellfire.

Now her little diary entries recorded acts of war as well. On October 24 she wrote, "Notify Gold's Gym if here past 25 Nov (or if leaving)—7.5 miles—FLY 3.5—1 x K truck."

As time went on, the former fighter-bomber pilot found it a strange form of combat. Dropping bombs in Kosovo, she'd known she might be killing people, but it was rare to spot people on the ground or see what happened after the bombs hit. Her view of the strikes she made from her F-15E came from brief glimpses of infrared video, but then she'd quickly fly away. Flying the Predator, Ghengis watched people for long periods of time—hours in some cases—and after firing missiles at them or directing other aircraft to attack them, she usually kept the drone loitering and saw the aftermath. She would have preferred to forget some of the scenes she witnessed. "I'd say it was more difficult in Predator," she mused years later.

A few days before Ghengis launched her first Hellfire, the Wildfire team took on a new type of mission: using the Hellfire Predator's sensors to help troops on the ground. The first U.S. troops into Afghanistan were two Special Forces teams that infiltrated the country the night of October 19–20, flying in on MH-47E Chinook helicopters. One twelve-man detachment, Operational Detachment Alpha (ODA) 595, landed in the mountains fifty miles south of Mazar-i-Sharif. The other, ODA 555, deployed in mountains farther northeast, above the Panjshir Valley. One of their missions was to call in air strikes on enemy troops, and on the radio, ODA 555 was "Tiger Zero One." ODA 595 was "Tiger Zero Two." Years later, Scott Swanson vividly remembered one radio call he had with a soldier from ODA 595 after the CAOC directed the Predator to help find some Taliban who had the Special Forces unit under fire near a former Soviet airfield at Bagram, just north of Kabul.

"Tiger Zero Two, this is Wildfire three four. Understand you need help," Swanson said over the radio that day in early November 2001.

"Wildfire, I don't see you guys on my list. What are you?" the soldier replied.

"Cyclops," Swanson explained, using radio code for a UAV.

"Oh, okay," the soldier said. "So if you're not in the airplane, where are you?"

"The Land of the Big BX," Swanson said, using a military nickname for the United States—in other words, the "land of the big Base Exchange," where all the comforts of home can be found.

"Well, have a cold beer on me," the soldier said, a sip of scorn in his voice.

The soldier's tone changed dramatically when the Predator's camera found the Taliban and put a laser spot on the target, allowing the intelligence analysts in the double-wide to pinpoint the enemy's geographic coordinates and pass them to a B-52 bomber. The B-52 dropped bombs, and the Taliban shooting stopped. There were no apparent survivors.

"I don't care if you guys are sitting at home drinking beer and playing video games or not," the soldier told Swanson after the mission ended. "You can support us *any* day."

13

NEVER MIND . . . WE'LL DO IT OURSELVES

He was an extraordinary enemy, perhaps more directly responsible than even Osama bin Laden for the American blood their Islamic fundamentalist followers shed in the final decade of the twentieth century. Born in 1944, according to most sources, Mohammed Atef (also known as Abu Hafs al-Masri, among many aliases) was a tall, thin-faced, heavily bearded, quietly imposing Egyptian. Atef went to Afghanistan in the 1980s to wage jihad against the Soviet Union with bin Laden and other Arab volunteers, and as the Soviets began leaving that country in 1988, he was among half a dozen jihadists who, with bin Laden, founded Al Qaeda. In the early 1990s, Atef traveled to Somalia to instigate and train fundamentalists there to fight U.S. troops, and in 1998 he was said to have masterminded the U.S. embassy bombings in Kenya and Tanzania. He preceded those attacks by publicizing, with other Al Qaeda members, a fatwa declaring it the duty of all Muslims to wage holy war on the United States and drive all Americans, military or civilian, out of the Persian Gulf region.

Three months after the embassy bombings, a federal grand jury in New York issued a 319-count indictment charging Atef, along with bin Laden and various others, with felonies that included "conspiracy to murder, bomb, and maim" and "conspiracy to use weapons of mass destruction against nationals of the United States." The same day the indictment was made public, November 4, 1998, the State Department offered a five-million-dollar reward for information leading to the arrest or conviction anywhere in the world of either bin Laden or Atef for their roles in the bombings.

Following the success of his operations in Africa, Atef joined with Al Qaeda's second-ranking leader, fellow Egyptian and physician Ayman al-Zawahiri, in arguing that they should try to acquire biological and chemical weapons to use against the "enemies of Islam" rather than seeking the nuclear bombs bin Laden favored. In November 1999, Atef joined bin Laden and the later infamous Khalid Sheikh Mohammed in picking targets for "the planes operation," as they called the plot to have suicide teams hijack airliners and crash them into U.S. military and civilian buildings. The next year, Atef publicly took credit for the bombing of the USS *Cole*, explaining that Al Qaeda had hoped the attack would provoke the United States into invading Afghanistan, where the jihadists could wage holy war against Americans just as they had against the Soviets.

Although Atef was the third most important member of Al Qaeda, he may have ranked higher in bin Laden's heart. Journalists who interviewed bin Laden in 1998, after the U.S. cruise missile strikes on Al Qaeda training camps, said Atef personally searched them. Two and a half years later, in January 2001, bin Laden and Atef arranged the marriage of Atef's fourteen-year-old daughter to bin Laden's seventeen-year-old son. At the videotaped wedding, bin Laden and Atef sat side by side, and bin Laden read a poem celebrating the bombing of the *Cole*.

With the exception of bin Laden and Zawahiri, Mohammed Atef was the highest of high-value targets for the United States. And with the United States waging war in Afghanistan, he was on the run.

On Thursday, November 15, after several days of intense U.S. air strikes in Afghanistan, reports that Mohammed Atef had been killed began filtering out of the country. The next day, when Defense Secretary Rumsfeld visited the naval training center at Great Lakes, Illinois, he was asked if he could confirm those reports.

"I have seen those reports," Rumsfeld said. "Do I know for a fact that that's the case? I don't. I suspect—the reports I've received seem authoritative."

Later that Friday, a Defense Department spokesman added a wrinkle. Rear Admiral John Stufflebeem said U.S. forces had hit a "series of targets" in Afghanistan over the past week that were thought to be Taliban or Al Qaeda "command and control." After one such strike "a couple of days ago," he said, "intelligence reports picking up discussions" indicated that Atef had been killed, but "we haven't been able to confirm that."

On November 17, the day after Stufflebeem's comments, Taliban spokesman Mullah Najibullah, speaking from a town near Kandahar, told the Associated Press that Atef and seven other Al Qaeda members had been killed in a U.S. air strike three days earlier, though he refused to say where, and there was no guarantee he was telling the truth. Later that Saturday, quoting "U.S. officials," CNN reported that after a bomb strike "south of Kabul"—no date was specified—the "United States intercepted communications from people sifting through the bombed wreckage who made frantic statements saying Atef had been killed."

In succeeding days, and over succeeding years, various accounts of how Mohammed Atef died would emerge. The accounts often contradicted one another on fundamental facts, from the exact date of his death, to the precise place he died, to the aircraft and weapon or weapons used to kill him. Some accounts said Atef was killed in Kabul; some said in Gardez. Some said he was found by a Predator and killed by bombs from a fighter plane; some said a Hellfire missile launched by a Predator killed him; some reports included no mention of the Predator at all. The date Atef died has been reported to be anywhere from November 12 to November 16.

The nature and pace of military operations and the number of air strikes U.S. forces conducted in Afghanistan during October and November 2001 likely make it impossible—especially without access to relevant classified information that still exists—to verify any account of Atef's death beyond the shadow of a doubt. But a number of former senior officers who were in the U.S. military chain of command at the time, and who have never before disclosed their recollections of this event, retain distinct and vivid memories of how they believe Atef died—and all of them agree that the role played by the Predator was central. What they believe about how Atef died, however, cannot be considered proven fact, for as one explained, "We didn't control the site, we didn't recover the body or anything. It's been confirmed by the process of elimination."

As with the escape of Taliban leader Mullah Omar, the recollections of participants or others who witnessed via Predator video the action believed to have eliminated Al Qaeda's chief planner of terrorist and military operations disagree on some points. Taken together and carefully weighed, though, they shed new light on what at the time was the most important blow U.S. forces had ever dealt Al Qaeda's leadership, and still ranks as perhaps the second most important, behind only the killing of bin Laden himself. The Predator made it possible—the Predator and a trip to RadioShack.

By Monday, November 12, 2001, there were two ground control stations in the glade on the CIA campus and, as Director George Tenet had promised President Bush, the Wildfire team was flying two Predators at a time. That afternoon, Washington time, Major Darran Jergensen was in the Trailer Park's original GCS, commanding Predator 3037; sitting in the pilot's seat was Ghengis, the former fighter pilot. It was nine and a half hours later in Afghanistan and already dark when the drone's infrared camera began following three vehicles heading toward Kabul, Afghanistan's capital. CIA paramilitaries on the ground had passed Langley a tip that the little convoy was carrying high-value targets, possibly one or more senior Al Qaeda figures.

Exactly who rode inside the vehicles was unclear; nor could the Predator's cameras help figure that out. Popular misconceptions aside, there was no way at the time to recognize a face at the resolution provided by a Predator's daylight TV camera, and its infrared sensor was unable to detect facial features at all. Depending on how the infrared sensor was set, a person simply showed up as "white hot" or "black hot." The convoy's signature, however, seemed to confirm the tip. One vehicle was an SUV, one was a pickup truck with armed men in back, and they were moving toward Kabul at night—despite a Taliban curfew imposed as the war began that was still in effect five weeks later. As the convoy neared Kabul, moreover, the Predator was able to provide some supporting intelligence, for while its "eyes" were unable to detect who was in the vehicles, the drone also carried electronic "ears."

More than a year before the war, during the Summer Project of 2000, Major Mark Cooter had been concerned when Taliban MiG-21 fighter planes came looking for what to them was an unidentified flying object circling over Tarnak Farms: the unarmed Predator. As the Summer Project team made plans before 9/11 to resume reconnaissance flights over Afghanistan in 2001, Cooter decided they needed a better way to receive warnings of MiG launches or other threats, so he asked Big Safari to put a standard, unsecure, multiband military radio on the Predator. When Bill Grimes, Big Safari's director, questioned the need for such a radio on a drone flying a covert mission, Cooter replied, "Mr. Grimes, I don't want to *talk* to the good guys, I want to *listen* to the bad guys."

Cooter next asked one of the Summer Project's communications specialists, Master Sergeant Cliff Gross, to figure out how to feed what the radio's antenna picked up over Afghanistan to linguists able to understand Pashtun, Arabic, and other relevant languages. Gross went through a carton of cigarettes and a two-liter bottle of Coke studying the matter, then came back to Cooter and said, "If you want this operational, I need twelve dollars and ninety-five cents." Cooter gave him a twenty.

Gross paid a visit to RadioShack and returned with a headset for a home phone. He soldered it to the inside wall of the ground control station, next to a speaker for the drone's radio, and plugged the headset jack into a secure telephone. Now language specialists at other locations could call in to that phone before a Predator mission, have the GCS crew leave the receiver off the hook, and listen to what the radio was picking up over Afghanistan on known "bad guy frequencies."

On November 12, linguists were listening to Predator 3037's multiband radio as the drone flew above the three-vehicle convoy headed toward Kabul. As the vehicles approached the city, the eavesdroppers picked up a conversation between someone in the convoy and a man elsewhere who said something like "we're waiting for you at the traffic circle." The Predator crew had already seen a vehicle parked at one of Kabul's several large traffic circles, and precisely as the intercepted call suggested, the convoy soon rendezvoused with that vehicle and followed it into the city. The Predator followed.

The suspected Al Qaeda convoy finally stopped in front of a house in Kabul's diplomatic quarter, Wazir Akbar Khan, a neighborhood of mostly two-story villas dating from the 1950s. After emerging from their vehicles, the convoy's occupants stood outside in the dark for a few minutes, then entered the house. Recollections vary on precisely how much time went by, but as the Predator orbited, keeping its electronic eyes on the building, Director Tenet showed up in the CIA's Global Response Center. His military liaison, Air Force Lieutenant General Soup Campbell, was also there.

Soon mission commander Jergensen was told by an Air Force liaison in the Global Response Center that his crew should watch the house in Kabul and get ready to talk fighter-bombers onto the target, which the building had now become. The Wildfire team now included a former F-15E weapon systems officer, radio call sign "Dewey," who had arrived soon after the war began and who, like former F-15E pilot Ghengis, was skilled at talking planes onto targets. Now Dewey was summoned from the double-wide to the GCS. As the Predator continued its orbit, Dewey sat between Ghengis and the sensor operator, studying maps and freeze-frame images of the house and its neighborhood. He was putting together the data he would need to conduct a modified nine-line brief and lead incoming fighters to the target.

After a considerable wait, Dewey got instructions to contact the lead aircraft in a two-ship F-15E flight flying under the radio call sign "Crockett." When he radioed the lead plane, the F-15 pilot replied, "Dewey, is that you?" Both the Strike Eagle's pilot, call sign "Slokes," and his WSO, call sign "Snitch," had been squadron mates of Dewey's when he flew in

F-15Es. Slokes and Snitch and the crew of the second F-15E (pilot "Spear" and WSO "Buzzer") were with the Air Force's 391st Fighter Squadron and had taken off hours earlier from Al Jaber Air Base in Kuwait. When launched, each plane had carried nine laser-guided, five-hundred-pound GBU-12 bombs.

Their route had taken the Strike Eagles southeast over the Persian Gulf and then out to the Gulf of Oman, where they rendezvoused with an aerial refueling tanker. Next they turned north to cross Pakistan and took up station over Afghanistan, ready to bomb whatever targets an AWACS communications plane instructed. Over the next few hours, the two F-15Es were directed to bomb two houses in Kabul and a Taliban roadblock south of the city; they were then told to head home. On their way back to Kuwait—while flying over Pakistan and using "finger lights" on the tips of their gloves to eat cold cheeseburgers in their darkened cockpits—Slokes got a call from the AWACS asking if they had enough bombs left to turn back and hit an extremely high-priority target in Kabul. Slokes said they had the bombs and could go back, but they would "need a waiver on the crew duty day, because we're going to land past twelve hours."

After a brief pause, the AWACS controller came back and said, "You're cleared north."

"Call Mom and let her know we'll be home late," replied Slokes. He and Spear then banked their F-15s back toward Afghanistan.

The order to return came from newly promoted Lieutenant General T. Michael "Buzz" Moseley, an F-15 pilot himself and former commander of the F-15 division of his service's elite Fighter Weapons School. Just five days earlier, Moseley had taken over as Combined Forces Air Component Commander from Lieutenant General Chuck Wald, a long-scheduled move that put Moseley in charge of the air war in Afghanistan. After two years running U.S. Central Command air forces, Wald was rising to deputy chief of staff of the Air Force for air and space operations.

Moseley, a Grand Prairie, Texas, native who learned to fly before he could legally drive a car, had earned two degrees from Texas A&M University before entering the Air Force. Beloved by subordinates, whom he called "my babies," Buzz Moseley was serenely confident, even for a fighter pilot, and took pride in his Texas roots. He wore cowboy boots when out of uniform, rode horses when he could, and tended to speak his mind bluntly, in a natural twang. "It's a whole lot like listenin' to a cow pee on a flat rock," he once told a Pentagon news briefing, providing his view of retired generals critiquing war plans on TV.

Moseley had been meeting with Wald in the Pentagon when American Airlines Flight 77 crashed into the building on 9/11, killing more than three hundred people, and he was eager to strike back at Al Qaeda. Before taking over the air war, he had met with combatant commander General Tommy Franks and Central Command's operations director, Air Force Major General Gene Renuart, to discuss how the CAOC and Centcom could be more agile in striking emerging targets. In Moseley's view, U.S. forces were missing opportunities because of what he saw as "dicked-up" rules of engagement modeled on peacetime enforcement of no-fly zones over Iraq. Getting approval for a strike shouldn't have to take hours, in Moseley's view, and before he assumed command at the CAOC he made a proposal to Franks. If the combatant commander gave authority for approving air strikes back to the air commander, Moseley would create strict new procedures at the CAOC to ensure careful review of potential collateral damage before targets were struck. After taking the issue to Rumsfeld, Franks agreed, and when the CIA Global Response Center passed word on November 12 that a Predator had followed some high-value targets to a three-story house in Kabul, a first test of the new procedure was at hand.

After learning about the convoy, Moseley immediately convened a meeting over a map table in a new part of the CAOC called the Battle Cab, a glass-enclosed balcony overlooking the operations center floor that had replaced the Crow's Nest. Below were U.S., British, French, and Saudi officers at long rows of tables, working amid a cacophony of ringing phones and conversations beneath the facility's theater-size imagery screens. Outside the Battle Cab—where CAOC commanders had moved after the first few days of the Afghan war—there were armed guards; inside was the CIA Predator screen that Wald had angrily moved to the Crow's Nest the first night of the war.

As intelligence officers watching the Predator video plotted geographic coordinates for the target house in Kabul's diplomatic quarter and talked to Langley via secure computer chat rooms, Moseley prepared a strike. "Find out who's airborne," he ordered. "Find out how much gas they've got. Find out where a tanker is."

Moseley also wanted to know more about the target: in such a densely populated, internationally sensitive area, he wanted to take great care to make sure the fighters hit the right structure and avoided collateral damage. "Get a hold of Centcom and let's find out what they know, what they think they know and let's fill in any blanks," Moseley told his subordinates.

After studying the house in Kabul, CAOC targeteers decided that the two F-15Es with their laser-guided bombs should make the attack.

"This is Wildfire. Ready to copy nine-line?" Dewey asked, talking over the Predator's radio from the GCS at the Trailer Park to the backseaters in the F-15Es now circling in the night sky about twenty thousand feet over Kabul. On their way to the Afghan capital, lead pilot Slokes had decided that his wingman plane, flown by Spear with backseater Buzzer, would strike first because they had more bombs left than he and Snitch did.

"Crockett Five Two, ready to copy," Buzzer replied to Wildfire.

"Crockett Five One, ready to copy," Snitch confirmed.

Using the Predator's video, Dewey studied the area around the target house and then began an abbreviated nine-line tailored to the situation. He skipped the first three steps—where to start the bombing approach, what heading to fly en route to the target, what distance that should be. The fighter crews could decide or figure out those elements of the strike for themselves.

"Line four," he began, then read the target's elevation above sea level in feet. "Five niner zero six."

Target description came next. "Line five. A building with a small square on the roof." Then Dewey provided geographic coordinates. "Line six," he said. "North thirty-four, thirty-two, zero one, decimal niner three. East sixty-nine, eleven, zero three, decimal thirty-four."

Buzzer read the details back, concluding with "Copy all." Then, after Snitch added his own confirmation, the two WSOs cued their laser targeting pods to the house and said in turn, "Captured. Ready for talk-on."

"There's a baseball diamond southwest of the target," Dewey began, directing their eyes to a playing field, which in the Predator's infrared imagery resembled a ballpark. "Call 'captured,' " Dewey added, instructing them to tell him when they saw the field.

"Captured," the backseaters reported in turn as their pilots "arced the target," lining up for a bomb run that Crockett 52 would lead.

Dewey continued talking the backseaters onto the target by describing prominent features of the area around the target house, ending with "There's a building across the street shaped like Utah with the small end pointing across the street to your target."

When Snitch saw the Utah-shaped building, he knew without a doubt they had the target. "Captured," he said.

"Captured," Buzzer echoed.

"You're cleared hot," Dewey said, relaying approval from the CAOC to strike the house.

"Stand by," Buzzer replied as he and Snitch put the crosshairs of their targeting pods onto the house.

The Predator crew waited, watching their silent infrared video until a voice over the radio reported that the bombs had been released. "Off hot," the voice said. "T impact, twenty seconds." A second or two passed; then Buzzer reported, "Laser on." Then, as witnesses at Langley, in the CAOC, and other locations with a Predator screen watched, two five-hundred-pound bombs ripped across the infrared image and hit near the roof at the front of the house. "Impact," Buzzer reported.

As black smoke rolled skyward from the house, cheers from the double-wide roared over the headsets of the Predator crew, who kept the drone circling the site. When the infrared bloom of the explosion cleared, though, only the back of the house was gone. The structure was still standing.

"Shit hot, it's over," Moseley heard someone say over the CAOC's connection to the AWACS. "Whoever they are, we got 'em."

A subordinate asked if the CAOC should tell the F-15Es to "safe up"—turn off their targeting pods and go home. Moseley shook his head. "No," he said. "The structure's still intact." With most of the building still standing, Moseley wasn't satisfied the strike had killed the high-value targets the CIA said were inside. He ordered a second strike.

"Sir, are you sure you want to do that?" asked one officer accustomed to Centcom's habit of erring on the side of caution when it came to collateral damage.

"Prosecute the target," Moseley commanded.

Slokes and Snitch, flying about five hundred miles an hour, had been trailing well behind Spear and Buzzer. Perhaps four minutes after the first strike, just in time to release their bombs on that run, they heard Dewey say, "Cleared hot."

"Off hot," Slokes reported over the radio, then banked the F-15 while Snitch kept his laser crosshairs on the roof of the target house to guide the bombs to their mark.

Moments later, Moseley and others in the Battle Cab watched their silent Predator screen as the bombs streaked down straight through the top of the house in Kabul. The fuses of the bombs, set by ground crews in Kuwait before takeoff, must have been timed to explode ten milliseconds or so later than the first bombs dropped, Moseley figured, taking them deep enough into the house to hit some propane tanks in the basement. What remained of the house disappeared in black clouds of smoke that mushroomed upward while a bright white flame flashed a good thirty yards or more out of the front of the house. The huge heat bloom lingered for some time.

Despite the direct hit, six or seven "squirters" emerged within seconds and began rapidly walking away from the structure whose destruction they had somehow survived. "Clearly there was a lot of adrenaline pumping," one senior official who saw the Predator video recalled years later. "They walked and walked and walked."

The Predator followed, its camera watching as those fleeing entered a small one-story house in a compound well away from the building the long-gone F-15Es had hit. Four or five of the survivors went inside the little house, but a couple of them remained on a porch. As they stood there, the CIA Global Response Center told mission commander

Jergensen to have the Predator crew put a Hellfire into the house, which was small enough to make a suitable target for the missile.

Years later, memories were clouded on which pilot and sensor operator took the shot. But Swanson, who was in the GCS at the time, was struck by how much the target resembled, if only in size and shape, the sturdy adobe "Taco Bell" the Big Safari team had perforated with Hellfires at China Lake the previous summer. Though at China Lake, no human beings stood in the missile's path.

When the infrared blossom of the Hellfire's explosion cleared from the Predator screen, the men who had been on the porch were gone. And this time no one saw any squirters.

The F-15Es landed back in Kuwait fifteen and a half hours after takeoff, the longest mission on record for a Strike Eagle. They called it the "Kabul-ki Dance."

Earlier that same evening, BBC correspondent William Reeve was being interviewed live from Kabul by fellow correspondent Lyse Doucet of BBC News 24 in London when he got the fright of his life. Dressed in casual slacks and a blue shirt under an Afghan-style vest and seated at his desk at BBC House, a two-story stone villa in Kabul's diplomatic quarter where he and another correspondent lived and worked, Reeve was telling Doucet about the war's effect on average Afghans. "There's not much people can do," he said, looking into a camera that was on a tripod to the right side of his desk, his back to a large, dark BBC banner hung over a big window a few feet behind him. "Where can they go?" Reeve said of the Afghans. "All they can do is stay at home and hope for the best."

As Reeve paused for the next question, viewers heard a whoosh grow into a roar followed by a muffled blast and the sound of crashing glass. As the BBC banner fell, Reeve flinched, fear on his face, and rolled out of his chair and to the floor. Then, from his knees, he looked back at the dust pouring into the room over the laptop and microphone on his desk.

"Jesus Christ!" his cameraman cried out.

"Go to the basement!" Reeve shouted. "Go to the basement!"

A few minutes later, shaken but uninjured, Reeve and his colleagues grabbed what equipment and possessions they could carry, jumped into two SUVs, and sped off into the darkened streets of Kabul, fearing more bombs might drop on their neighborhood. They decided to drive west, to the other side of the city and the presumed safety of the Intercontinental Hotel, which they believed U.S. and allied forces would spare for future use. At the hotel, Reeve called London to let his office know that he and the others were safe. Reeve then asked a Turkish cameraman he knew to call the bureau of Al Jazeera, an Arabic-language television network whose correspondent and about a dozen staff worked from a villa a few blocks from BBC House in Wazir Akbar Khan. Owned by the government of Qatar, Al Jazeera was famous for its access to Osama bin Laden and the Taliban; in fact, the network's Kabul correspondent Tayseer Allouni had interviewed bin Laden on October 11, just four days after the war began. But the BBC and other news organizations particularly valued Al Jazeera for its bureau's satellite uplink, which they and others often paid to use.

Reeve and an Afghan colleague returned early the next morning to BBC House to start covering the unfolding takeover of Kabul by the Northern Alliance. When he arrived, Reeve saw a huge gap in the street perhaps seventy-five yards from BBC House. Until the night before, the home of Taliban police chief Abdul Razak and two other houses had stood there. Reeve also soon learned that Al Jazeera's villa, several blocks away, had been destroyed later the same evening. Al Jazeera and other news organizations were reporting that the network's employees had left the villa shortly beforehand.

Two days after the strikes in Wazir Akbar Khan, Al Jazeera broadcast a telephone interview with its correspondent Allouni; the network said he had been missing for more than a day and was now reporting from Gardez, a city close to eighty miles south of Kabul. Allouni said that while fleeing the capital just before midnight on November 12 he had been beaten—he refused to say by whom—and had witnessed "scenes that, I'm sorry, I couldn't describe to anybody." Allouni added that he was in "deep psychological shock," and Al Jazeera reported that he was leaving Afghanistan for medical treatment.

The day before Allouni resurfaced, reports emerged that the Al

Jazeera bureau in Kabul had been struck by bombs or missiles. Responding to a question about those reports, a Pentagon spokesman told journalists at the State Department Foreign Press Center in Washington that "some weapons have failed and some human errors have been made, resulting in targets being struck that we did not intend to strike." Rear Admiral Craig Quigley added that if Al Jazeera's bureau had been hit in error, the Defense Department would "stand up and say so. We're not to that point yet. But if that would be the case, that is what you will hear from us."

Al Jazeera Washington bureau chief Hafez Al-Mirazi, meanwhile, wrote a letter to the Pentagon demanding an explanation. Victoria Clarke, assistant secretary of defense for public affairs, replied on December 6, writing that "the building we struck was a known al-Qaeda facility in central Kabul." She added that "there were no indications that this or any nearby facility was used by Al-Jazeera." A subsequent letter to Defense Secretary Rumsfeld from the executive director of the Committee to Protect Journalists, Ann Cooper, elicited a similar reply from Air Force General Dick Myers, chairman of the Joint Chiefs of Staff.

"Please be assured any decision to strike a target is made carefully," Myers wrote to Cooper. "As Assistant Secretary of Defense Clarke noted in her letter to Mr. Al-Mirazi-Osman, the building we struck was a known al-Qaeda facility in central Kabul."

Myers, like Clarke, offered no evidence to support the description of the house as an Al Qaeda facility, nor did he acknowledge that it was Al Jazeera's bureau—which it was, as BBC reporter Reeve confirmed years later. It was also the house visited by the convoy that was tracked by the Predator on the night of November 12, a fact confirmed by geographic coordinates and a review of videos of the bomb strike by the F-15Es flying under the radio call sign Crockett.

And there was more. Several days after the F-15Es leveled the Al Jazeera villa and the Predator launched a Hellfire at the survivors who fled, the fighter-bomber crews were told that higher-ups believed the strike on that house, the one they were called back to Kabul to conduct, had killed Mohammed Atef. But no one explained how that was known.

Others concede the possibility that Atef died (if indeed he was killed that night) when the Predator's Hellfire hit the smaller house shortly after the villa was bombed. Unless a credible witness or more evidence comes forward, the absolute truth simply cannot be known. But retired four-star general Renuart, who was Centcom operations director at the time, said years later that he believed Atef was killed in the bomb strike on what turned out to be Al Jazeera's villa—a fact unknown at the time to those who conducted the bombing.

"The reality is we'll never know for certain," Renuart acknowledged. But Atef died around the time of the strike, and as Renuart said, "I think everybody felt pretty confident, listening to what we listened to on the radios subsequent to that, that that was a successful strike, and that was the one that got him."

Sometime after the news of Atef's death reached Langley, CIA military liaison Soup Campbell went to Director Tenet's office and suggested they visit the Trailer Park to congratulate the Predator team. As he waited for Tenet, Campbell asked the director's secretary for the key to the executive dining room liquor cabinet. Campbell took out a bottle of Scotch and handed the whisky to Tenet as they headed to the Trailer Park. Why not offer the Predator team a drink to celebrate? Campbell suggested.

When they arrived at the double-wide, everyone who could be spared from the two GCSs was waiting, crowded around a center island of tables laden with computers, video screens, phones, and other gear. Tenet shook people's hands, and then spoke. No one took down the director's words, but he offered congratulations on the great work they had been doing. He ended by holding up the Scotch and announcing: "This is for the team when we get him." Then he turned and placed the unopened bottle on a shelf that ran along one of the double-wide's walls, a trophy in waiting for the day they bagged the biggest high-value target of all, Osama bin Laden.

A week after the Taliban confirmed Atef's death, the *New York Times* revealed the important role the Predator was playing in the war in an article headlined, "Ugly Duckling Turns Out to Be Formidable in the

Air." Among other things, the article revealed that the Predator "was used to coordinate the surgical strike" that killed Al Qaeda military commander Atef. It also reported that after the escape of Mullah Omar, the CIA had been given "authority to strike beyond a narrow range of counterterrorism targets."

At the Trailer Park, the Wildfire team decided to create a souvenir to commemorate the revolutionary role they and their unorthodox weapon had carved out in a scant two months of operations and six weeks of war. They designed a "challenge coin"—a popular form of military memento—and had a batch minted. Paid for from their squadron snack fund, the coin they created was designed by the team, just as everything they had done was as a team.

On one side of the coin, against a brass background, the words "United States of America" and "Operation Enduring Freedom" encircled a relief of the World Trade Center towers against an American flag in the shape of the Pentagon, with the numerals 9 and 11 on either side. The coin's flip side was more distinctive, and unique. At its top was a representation of a double-wide mobile home constructed around a Predator, with the drone's nose, wings, and inverted-V tail protruding from the trailer's sides. Under the wings were Hellfire missiles. Below the Predator were head-on reliefs of an AC-130 gunship, B-1B and B-2 bombers, and F/A-18 and A-10 attack aircraft. Between the fighters, one front paw raised in the classic pose, was a hunting dog, pointing. Everyone knew the dog was the Hellfire-dodging Lucky, but no name was on the coin. The only writing on that side was a motto the team had adopted as their CIA controllers grew more and more willing to pull the Predator's trigger without Centcom agreement. Embossed in capital letters at the top and bottom of the coin, the motto declared, "Never Mind . . . We'll Do It Ourselves."

Sometime that November, President Bush took his "Most Wanted Terrorists" scorecard out of his desk drawer in the Oval Office and drew a large X through the photo of Mohammed Atef. On December 11, about a month after Atef's death, Bush traveled to Charleston, South Carolina, to speak at the Citadel, the state military academy, where he told the corps of cadets that a new age in warfare was dawning, an age in which "innovative doctrine in high-tech weaponry" was the key to defeating "shadowy, entrenched enemies." Bush didn't mention the killing of Atef, but he told his audience that "Afghanistan has been a proving ground" for what defense professionals called "military transformation," a policy relying on high technology rather than manpower to fight and win wars. "The Predator is a good example," Bush said. "This unmanned aerial vehicle is able to circle over enemy forces, gather intelligence, transmit information instantly back to commanders, then fire on targets with extreme accuracy. Before the war, the Predator had skeptics because it did not fit the old ways. Now it is clear: The military does not have enough unmanned vehicles."

Major decisions are often made, and millions are often spent or invested, based on far weaker presidential endorsements of a program or a product. Those few sentences sent a powerful signal to the military-industrial complex and the traditional defense establishment, which for decades had largely ignored not just the Predator but any unmanned aircraft. Lots of different drones had been built, and several had occasionally been used in combat, but remote-control aircraft had remained a niche technology. Now all that would change, and the old ways would soon start to disappear. A new era in aviation had begun.

The day after Bush spoke, U.S. Central Command issued a Combat Mission Needs Statement requesting that all Air Force Predators be fitted with laser designators and Hellfire missiles. The new armed Predators would be designated MQ-1 rather than RQ-1, as the unarmed version was designated—R standing for reconnaissance, M for multimission, and Q for drone. Even before the Atef operation, the Air Force, under inveterate innovator John Jumper and like-minded Secretary James Roche, had decided to double the number of Predators it would buy in the coming year to about two a month. They had also decided to spend ten million dollars for two prototypes of a larger "Predator B," which had recently been produced by General Atomics. Tom Cassidy, ever an aggressive salesman for the company and its products, had been pushing the bigger, more capable aircraft on the Air Force for months. Not long before Bush spoke at the Citadel, Jumper had told those gathered at a Capitol Hill breakfast that the original Predator was his service's "workhorse" unmanned aerial vehicle, but that the bigger, turboprop Predator B would offer "a little bit longer endurance and greater carrying capacity." Left unmentioned by Jumper was the fact that the Predator B would carry bombs as well as Hellfire missiles.

The Predator's missiles, the wide distribution of its live streaming video, and the remarkable ability to fly the drone by remote control on the other side of the planet were the gee-whiz features that caught the world's attention. Yet the novel feature that made the Predator a dramatic departure from the drones of the past was its phenomenal flight endurance, and that capability was what made it uniquely valuable to the military. Mark Cooter liked to say that the Predator's Hellfires, with their puny twenty-pound warheads, were just "two silver bullets" that might be expended during ten minutes of a mission lasting a total of twenty hours. Over that mission's duration, though, the unblinking, unseen Predator could lurk in the sky, find enemy targets for manned fighters and bombers, allow them to, as Cooter put it, "rain down lots of iron on bad guys," and then keep loitering to help manned aircraft do the same thing again and again.

Necessity being the mother of invention, and war being the mother of necessity, Big Safari would soon be working to improve the Predator and make its video much more widely available. For now, though, the drone revolution was only dawning, and many had yet to see the light. Two weeks before the death of Mohammed Atef, the Pentagon's director of operational test and evaluation, Thomas Christie, issued a report declaring that the Predator was "not operationally effective or suitable" for combat.

Cooter printed a one-page summary of the report and posted it in the original GCS at the Trailer Park. He figured others on the Predator team could also use a laugh.

EPILOGUE

When Scott Swanson and Jeff Guay used Predator 3034 to kill some of Mullah Omar's security detail on the opening night of the war in Afghanistan, a new way of waging war was born. When the Predator tracked and led attacks by other aircraft on U.S. enemies such as Mohammed Atef, this new kind of killer scout opened eyes and gained many more advocates among military commanders and senior intelligence agency officials. When President George W. Bush declared in December 2001 that the Predator had proven that more unmanned aerial vehicles were needed, the military-industrial complex got busy providing them. But the drone revolution truly began, members of the Wildfire team believe, on March 4, 2002, when a couple of dozen U.S. troops endured a nightmare of a day atop a snowcapped peak in the mountains of Afghanistan called Takur Ghar, later known as Roberts Ridge.

For those at the Trailer Park, the drama began on the evening of March 3, when Ghengis and a sensor operator named Andy, flying Predator 3037 from the original GCS, spotted a flash in the dark Afghan sky roughly twenty miles away from their aircraft. A few moments later, the Predator's camera recorded the crash of a big tandem-rotor helicopter on Takur Ghar. It was 6:10 a.m. on Monday, March 4, in Afghanistan; what the Wildfire team knew was that U.S. forces were conducting Operation Anaconda, a campaign to kill or capture Al Qaeda forces who had taken refuge in the mountains. What the team didn't know was that this was in fact the third Chinook to be riddled with gunfire that day by Al Qaeda fighters dug in on the peak where the helicopter had crashed.

Three hours and twenty minutes earlier, a Navy SEAL, Petty Officer First Class Neil Roberts, had fallen from the back ramp of a Chinook that was attempting to drop off a seven-man SEAL reconnaissance team on Takur Ghar. Al Qaeda fighters, hidden in a trench and log-lined bunkers, put a rocket-propelled grenade into the Chinook as it was trying to land; Roberts was lost as the pilot lifted back up to escape the enemy fire. The wounded Chinook lurched over the side of the mountain and plunged through the air toward a valley below, but the pilot somehow avoided a fatal crash.

As would later emerge, Roberts was soon dead, slain by an Al Qaeda bullet to the head. But a little more than two hours after he fell from the helicopter, the six others in his SEAL team returned in another MH-47 to try to rescue him. Though this Chinook, too, came under fire as it descended, it successfully dropped the SEALs on the ridge before flying away with serious damage. The SEAL team immediately got into a firefight with the Al Qaeda fighters; outnumbered and outgunned, the SEALs were soon forced to retreat down the side of the mountain with one of their number killed and three wounded.

Just over an hour later, a third Chinook—the helicopter that had caught the eye of the Predator team at Langley—descended toward the ridge in a second attempt to retrieve Roberts. Manned by a crew of seven, this Army MH-47E had flown Captain Nate Self, eight other Army Rangers, four Air Force Special Tactics men, and an Army medic to the mountain on the rescue mission. But because of command, control, and communications failures, Self and his Ranger-led quick reaction force were also ambushed the moment they arrived; under heavy enemy fire, their Chinook crashed, injuring some of Self's team when it hit the ground. Then, as its crippled rotors whined to a stop, the aircraft was perforated by small arms and RPG fire from multiple directions. Four men were dead before Self and other survivors could get out of the helicopter and fight back.

At the Trailer Park, contractor pilot Big saw the Chinook crash from the second ground control station, which had a video feed from the original GCS. Big, piloting a second Predator, was just handing over his own drone to the launch-and-recovery element in Central Asia to land. Already due to relieve Ghengis after that handoff, Big immediately walked over to the original GCS. There, Ghengis told him she had radioed an AWACS that was controlling the airspace to ask permission to take up station above the mountain where the Chinook was down and see if the Predator could help. She had been denied permission because a third Predator—this one unarmed—was there already, but she was trying to make the AWACS controllers understand that her Predator was armed. Finally, minutes after Big relieved Ghengis and took the controls of Predator 3037, the AWACS cleared him to put the drone into an orbit above Takur Ghar. The AWACS also gave him the Ranger team's radio call sign, Slick Zero One, which was being used by Air Force Staff Sergeant Gabe Brown, an enlisted tactical air controller, to call in close air support for the Rangers.

Over the rest of that Monday, the Wildfire team put all the Predator's powers to work for the troops battling for their lives on Takur Ghar. The Predator's video, fed to the U.S. Joint Special Operations Command on Masirah Island, near Oman, and a tactical operations center at Bagram Airfield in Afghanistan, provided a live view of the battle, which for some commanders was a revelation. In the end, though, Predator 3037's Hellfire missiles played an even more important role as the firefight raged near the fallen Chinook.

After the Rangers scuttled away from their disabled helicopter, they took cover behind some rocks a few feet to one side of the aircraft. Their redoubt was only about seventy-five yards from an enemy bunker under what Self and Brown quickly dubbed the "bonsai" tree; the Rangers were taking fire from both the bunker and Al Qaeda positions farther up the ridge. Soon after the Rangers asked the AWACS for air support, two F-15E Strike Eagles and two F-16C Fighting Falcons streaked over the mountain several times firing 20-millimeter cannons, but the fighter planes' strafing runs failed to take out the Al Qaeda positions. The Rangers tried to assault the hilltop themselves, even though only five of the men who had landed on the Chinook were still able to pull a trigger. Self ordered a retreat when he realized the enemy had a heavy machine gun in a bunker shielded by thick logs.

When the Rangers got back down the ridge and behind the rocks again, they came under mortar fire. Self had Brown call on an F-16C to try to hit the enemy position under the bonsai tree with a five-hundred-pound bomb; the target was so close to Self's men that the pilot asked Brown for Self's initials so he could later prove that Self had approved the strike. Three bombs missed, and the last rained gravel on his men, leading Self to decide that the risk was too great. Then, shortly after calling off the bombing, the Ranger captain heard Brown talking to the Predator. Worried about enemy movement, Brown was asking Big to tell him what the Predator's camera was seeing to the east.

"Find out if it's armed," Self told Brown.

"What do you mean?" Brown said.

"Just find out if it's armed," Self replied. "Some of the Predators have Hellfires." Self had picked up this bit of highly classified information during planning sessions for Operation Anaconda.

A couple of minutes later, after learning that the Predator circling nearby was indeed armed, Self told Brown to have the drone put a Hellfire in the bunker beneath the bonsai tree. The first missile launched by Big and a sensor operator named Will landed well short of the bunker; years later, participants disagreed on why. But the second Hellfire shot was perfect. As war correspondent Sean Naylor wrote in *Not a Good Day to Die*, a book about Operation Anaconda, "Rocks, dirt and branches flew over the Rangers' heads. They cheered. When the smoke had cleared from the top of Takur Ghar, the bunker had collapsed and part of the tree was missing. They took no more fire from there."

As the day went on, the Rangers continued to take mortar fire and fight off assaults by groups of Al Qaeda fighting from a second bunker beyond the bonsai tree. The crews flying Predator 3037, now out of Hellfires, used the drone's cameras to help spot enemy movements and warn the ground troops. At one point the enemy began a major assault from the second bunker, and the Predator team buddy-lased two bomb strikes by two French Mirage 2000D fighter planes dispatched by the AWACS. The first bomb hit the bunker, but some of the Al Qaeda fighters survived and scrambled down the mountainside, taking cover under a tree. The Predator spotted them, and in short order buddy-lased another strike by the Mirages that apparently killed all the enemy hiding beneath the tree.

Late that afternoon, Self and his men—several wounded, one dying—waited anxiously for rescuers, but commanders refused to send help until after dark. By now, Scott Swanson was flying the Predator and Jeff Guay was operating its sensors; both were listening over the radio as the Rangers repeatedly asked to be picked up before more of their comrades died. Years later, Swanson was still haunted by the memory of the Rangers' pleas over the radio.

As darkness fell in Afghanistan, Guay began using a new Predator feature to help calm the desperate Rangers. The drone's MTS ball now included not only a laser designator but a laser illuminator—an infrared flashlight, in essence—whose beam expanded into an ever-larger cone as it traveled, and whose light could be seen through night vision goggles worn by the Rangers and by Air Force air controller Brown.

"Every time he'd get a little nervous, I'd illuminate the ground in front of him," Guay told a Big Safari reunion later that year, describing how he used the laser light to reassure the trapped Rangers that he was watching out for them. Even more important, Guay said, he later shined the laser illuminator on a spot designated by the troops on the ground and thus helped guide two Chinooks to a safe landing when they finally flew onto the ridge after dark. The helicopters picked up all the Americans on the mountain, including Roberts and the six others killed.

Within military circles, word of what the Predator had done that day spread like wildfire.

"Roberts Ridge was our coming-out party," Ed Boyle proudly recalled some years later. "That night, it was more than an experiment; it was saving American lives. We were a sideshow up until that point in time. People were talking about us, but not as something that was going to be a long-lasting thing. After that, Predator became what it is today. Nobody ever doubted us again."

After genesis came the flood.

The arming of the Predator and its rigging for global remote control transformed a slow evolution toward wider military use of unmanned aerial vehicles into an outright revolution. In less than a decade, military drone technology proliferated to an extent that even its most ardent advocates never imagined, and an explosion in civilian drone technology followed. Given advances in the underlying technologies— lightweight composite material, smaller and more sophisticated cameras, digital communications, GPS, laser-guided weapons—UAVs would almost certainly have become more than a niche technology in time. But by radically changing the way people thought about drones, the Predator changed the military overnight.

As 2001 began, the U.S. military owned just 82 unmanned aerial vehicles and had three types in use: the Predator and two small reconnaissance drones, the Navy/Marine Corps Pioneer and the Army's Hunter. An April 2001 Defense Department study—after noting that the U.S. military had "a long and continuous history of involvement with UAVs" going back to 1917—estimated that by 2010 the armed services might own 290 in all, but the study predicted that there would still be only three types.

In fact, when 2010 arrived, the military owned nearly 8,000 UAVs of fourteen different types. Six thousand of these were camera-carrying drones the size of model airplanes, but the Air Force had 165 armed Predators, more than three times the 48 unarmed RQ-1s the service had planned to buy before 9/11. And the Air Force owned 73 armed MQ-9 Reapers (the official name for the Predator B introduced by General Atomics nine years earlier). Each Reaper could carry four instead of the Predator's two Hellfires, plus two laser-guided five-hundred-pound bombs. And as was suggested by the crash in Iran in 2011 of a previously secret unarmed drone designated the RQ-170 Sentinel, the U.S. military and intelligence agencies were surely using or developing other unmanned aircraft covertly.

In the decade following the development of the first armed drone,

Predators and Reapers flew hundreds of missions during the wars in Afghanistan and Iraq, and in antiterrorist operations in Asia, the Middle East, and Africa. By 2013 those two types of drones alone had logged more than two million flight hours. The Department of Homeland Security, meanwhile, was flying unarmed Predators along U.S. borders to detect smugglers and other threats. And the FBI was using mini-drones to help agents track criminals and gather intelligence at crime scenes.

The drone revolution was fueled in part by innovations Big Safari and others continued to devise for the Predator. In November 2001, Big Safari asked technoscientist Werner to devise a way for Air Force AC-130U Spooky gunship crews to receive video in flight from a Predator already over their target. This allowed the Spooky crews to line up their cannons before Al Qaeda and Taliban militants could hear the big plane coming, a new tactic that proved devastating to the enemy. A few weeks later, in early 2002, Werner designed and Big Safari built a device dubbed ROVER (for Remotely Operated Video Enhanced Receiver) that made it possible for ground troops to view live Predator video on a shoe box–size device they could carry in the field.

As the Predator evolved, so did the nature of warfare. In the decade following 9/11, the CIA and U.S. political leaders ordered an ever larger number of targeted killings of known or suspected terrorists. Before long, this new kind of intercontinental sniper rifle—and the nature of the conflict that helped spawn it—changed the character of America's spy agency as well, turning its focus from espionage to paramilitary operations.

The drone revolution also reshaped the military, whose UAVs were increasingly flown by a rapidly expanding force of "remotely piloted aircraft" operators specifically recruited and trained for the task. In August 2009 the Air Force stunned experts by announcing that over the coming year it would train more pilots to fly unmanned aerial vehicles than conventional aircraft. The same month, an Air Force study predicted that its fleet would one day include a wide range of unmanned aircraft, from moth-size nano-drones that would be able to flit through windows and spy inside buildings to largely autonomous bombers and fighters. This study—"Unmanned Aircraft Systems Flight Plan, 2009–2047"—even forecast that by the one hundredth anniversary of the independent Air

Force in 2047, the service would have armed drones automated with artificial intelligence capable of deciding on their own when and whether to attack a target. The report admitted, however, that the development of such a capability would be "contingent upon political and military leaders resolving legal and ethical questions" about such "lethal autonomy," and the Air Force later backed away from the concept.

The other U.S. armed services also invested heavily in unmanned aircraft. By 2010 the Army was flying its own armed derivative of the Predator, the General Atomics MQ-1C Gray Eagle; the Navy and Marine Corps, meanwhile, were flying drone helicopters. The Navy was also developing its own version of Northrop Grumman's high-flying RQ-4 Global Hawk reconnaissance drone.

The Predator's success also changed the defense aviation industry, whose interest in drones largely reflected the attitudes of its military customers. Northrop and Boeing began investing heavily in drones and related technologies. In 2009 Boeing, one of the largest manufacturers of military and civilian aircraft in the world, created a new Unmanned Airborne Systems unit within the Unmanned Systems Division it had created in 2001 and began buying or teaming with smaller companies to make UAVs of all types and sizes. By 2014, major defense industry players Lockheed Martin, Raytheon, Textron, and more than fifty other U.S. companies, universities, and government agencies were developing, selling, buying, or flying more than one hundred and fifty types of drones ranging in size from forty to forty thousand pounds. At least fifty other countries were also making or buying drones and, in some cases, arming them.

But not all drones were being built for military purposes. If wars and antiterrorist operations had fomented the drone revolution, by a decade after the armed Predator's debut something far larger was happening. Enabled by ever more accessible and affordable component technologies, a new generation of mini-drones quickly began gaining popularity. And just as it transformed the military and the CIA, the drone revolution also promises to reshape society, from the way our laws are enforced and how much privacy we enjoy, to the way our food is grown, our news is gathered, and our goods and services are bought, sold, and delivered.

Law enforcement, wildfire management, precision agriculture, news and entertainment media, search and rescue, environmental research, disaster response—the list of potential uses for drones providing a bird's-eye view of the world is nearly inexhaustible, the possibilities as boundless as the human imagination. For the moment, Federal Aviation Administration regulations limit the use of unmanned aircraft to hobbyists and government and academic entities granted a special certificate of authorization by the FAA. Commercial use of drones is banned. But in time those rules will surely change: a revolution in the civilian use of drones seems inevitable.

As with many revolutions, technological as well as political, the history of this one was written partly in blood, and targeted killings using drone strikes raised a set of profound moral, legal, political, and practical questions. About a year after such strikes began, the world beyond the military began waking up to the existence of the armed Predator and its capabilities. During the early months of the war in Afghanistan, Predator strikes went largely unnoticed, but when similar attacks were launched outside the war zone, the response changed. On November 3, 2002, a Hellfire strike on an SUV in Yemen made major news. Killed, along with five others, was Qaed Salim Sinan al-Harethi, an Al Qaeda leader partly responsible for the bombing of the USS *Cole*. Over the years that followed, the CIA's use of drones to kill people identified as terrorists would become one of the Agency's least secret covert programs ever.

The CIA itself refused to acknowledge the practice publicly, so exact numbers are impossible to come by, but the frequency of such strikes clearly grew after Al Qaeda leaders chased out of Afghanistan took refuge in lawless areas of Pakistan and Yemen. The New America Foundation, a think tank that began using open media and what it called "U.S. sources" to track drone strikes beginning in 2004, estimated that the CIA conducted about 50 strikes in Yemen and Pakistan under President George W. Bush and more than 400 during President Barack Obama's first term, launching 122 in 2010 alone. As many as thirty-three hundred Al Qaeda, Taliban, and other militants were killed as a result, the foundation estimated, including more than fifty senior terrorist leaders.

Initially, the CIA drone strikes raised little controversy in the United States, and public opinion polls showed that most Americans supported them. The reaction overseas was very different. Critics contended that drone strikes often killed innocent civilians, an allegation that U.S. officials denied. After a decade of tracking, the New America Foundation reported that unintended casualties from drone strikes had steadily declined over the years, but reliable numbers were unavailable. Pakistanis and Yemenis were angered by what they viewed as a violation of their national sovereignty, though their governments had agreed to many if not all the strikes, and had even requested some. The thought that unseen machines in the sky might rain down death at any moment clearly made many people in those countries anxious. Some argued that outrage over drone strikes was a source of recruitment for Al Qaeda.

The Obama administration defended targeted killings as necessary to prevent further attacks by Al Qaeda and its allies. "Very frankly, it's the only game in town in terms of confronting or trying to disrupt the Al Qaeda leadership," CIA Director Leon Panetta said in May 2009. But over the next couple of years, the debate over the legality and morality of drone strikes heated up and came home.

In 2010 the UN Special Rapporteur on Extrajudicial, Summary, or Arbitrary Executions denounced U.S. drone strikes and the secrecy surrounding their conduct as an "ill-defined license to kill without accountability." More Americans expressed misgivings the following year after a drone strike in Yemen killed U.S. citizen Anwar al-Awlaki, an Islamic militant said to have aided and abetted Al Qaeda operations, including attempts to explode bombs in airliners in flight. Critics questioned whether it was legal to kill a U.S. citizen in places such as Yemen, which was not at war with the United States, and without affording the person his or her constitutional rights.

When President Obama finally addressed the issue publicly, in a speech at the National Defense University, in Washington, D.C., on May 23, 2013, he acknowledged the legitimacy of the debate, saying, "This new technology raises profound questions—about who is targeted, and why;

about civilian casualties, and the risk of creating new enemies; about the legality of such strikes under U.S. and international law; about account-ability and morality." But he also defended the tactic, saying drone strikes were legal under America's "legitimate claim of self-defense" against Al Qaeda and other terrorists and were being conducted under "clear guidelines, oversight and accountability that is now codified in Presidential Policy Guidance that I signed yesterday." The new guidance on "Use of Force in Counterterrorism Operations" stipulated, among other things, that "lethal force" (drones strikes) would be used only when there was no alternative means of preventing a terrorist posing a "continu-ing, imminent threat" to "U.S. persons" and when there was a "near cer-tainty" that no "non-combatants" would be injured or killed. The process used to reach those conclusions, however, remains cloaked in government secrecy.

In the same speech, Obama declared that lethal force was necessary against terrorists because capturing them was often impractical, risked casualties among U.S. forces, and posed a greater risk to innocent bystanders than drone strikes did. "Conventional airpower or missiles are far less precise than drones, and are likely to cause more civilian casualties and more local outrage," he noted. "By narrowly targeting our action against those who want to kill us and not the people they hide among, we are choosing the course of action least likely to result in the loss of innocent life."

The debate is far from settled, but even CIA veterans are worried that the practice of conducting drone strikes to kill terrorists has helped transform the Agency from an intelligence service into a paramilitary organization—a concern that echoes former director George Tenet's reluctance before 9/11 to use a military weapon such as the armed Pred-ator. There is also growing sentiment in favor of returning all authority to "pull the trigger" back to where Tenet originally felt it belonged: at the Pentagon. The state of emergency that followed 9/11, after all, is over. Whether the CIA will return to its original purpose in the age of global terrorism, though, is another open question.

Just over a decade into the drone revolution, many questions remain. One is how much this new technology will really change things in the end. Will armed drones play important roles in future wars, or were the Predator and Reaper so prominent in Afghanistan and Iraq because they were used against enemies who lacked air defenses? Clearly the answer will depend on the nature of the war, the strength of the opponent, and the capabilities of future drones.

Will civilian drones someday crowd the skies, becoming reliable enough not just to deliver goods but also to carry passengers? Perhaps, though the limits of line-of-sight remote control and the expense of satellite data links seem to argue against the prospect of pizza and book delivery by quadcopter. Meanwhile, the fallibility of technology argues against the prospect of passengers entrusting their fate to an aircraft with no pilot on board.

Only two things about the drone revolution seem certain. First, the new UAV technology is here to stay. Second, society needs to figure out how to cope with its implications. When automobiles replaced horses, traffic laws and stoplights and roads were needed. When powered flight was invented, new laws and rules and airports and agencies to govern aviation had to be created. At the turn of the twenty-first century, a technology developed for military purposes began proliferating rapidly, and its implications are still being recognized. Drone technology has already changed the way people die; one day it may change the way people live.

Purely by coincidence, the Air Force created its third Predator unit four days after the firefight at Roberts Ridge, and on May 29, 2002, a detachment from the new 17th Reconnaissance Squadron took over at the Trailer Park on the CIA campus. The Air Combat Command Expeditionary Air Intelligence Squadron, which since its creation the previous fall had been led by Colonel Ed Boyle and Major Mark Cooter, was deactivated. With the armed Predator's utility proven, the regular Air Force, under General John Jumper, was preparing to expand its use of the UAV that so many had once disdained.

That June, Cooter was transferred to Nellis Air Force Base in Nevada, where he would put his special Predator experience to work. The Air Force had decided to establish new facilities at Nellis from which regular crews could fly armed Predators almost anywhere in the world, whether on military or CIA missions. They would do so using the remote split operations satellite communications architecture designed by Big Safari consultant Werner less than a year earlier.

Within three more years, the Air Force would also implement Werner's once-rejected grander vision of flying Predators overseas from brick-and-mortar buildings rather than faux freight containers. In 2005, global Predator operations moved to just such a facility at Indian Springs Auxiliary Airfield, which was renamed Creech Air Force Base. And the structure at Creech was only the first Predator ground control station with indoor plumbing: within half a dozen more years, variations on that facility were being used to fly Predators and Reapers overseas from nearly a dozen other bases in the United States as well. Now Predator and Reaper operators could wage war by day or night and go home to their families after their shift was done, an even stranger way to wage war than the Trailer Park imposed on the Wildfire team.

Colonel Ed Boyle left the Trailer Park before the 17th RS detachment took over there. On April 1, 2002, Boyle put in his retirement papers and moved back to Langley Air Force Base, Virginia, to serve out the last months of his twenty-eight-year career. By the time he left the CIA operation, one entire wall of the double-wide was filled with freeze-frames of Predator Hellfire shots. Between the first strike on Mullah Omar's security detail on the opening night of the war in Afghanistan and the time Boyle departed, the team had fired fifty-four Hellfires. Boyle could remember only two missiles that missed their targets, both for mechanical reasons.

One retired general acknowledged years later that mistakes were made in choosing the Predator's targets, but responsibility for those mistakes and for issuing orders to fire rested with CIA officials and senior military officers elsewhere, not with the Wildfire team. "Any tall guy in a white jacket became a high probability of being Osama bin Laden, and we clearly struck a bunch of vehicles and groups of people that we thought could be and turned out not to be," this former general said. "When you're really searching for something desperately, you can believe—you begin to build a case for what you think you have. The sophistication of our intelligence analysis today is way better than it was in 2001, but even today we've seen Predator strikes that probably didn't get who we thought we were getting. You can get captured by the eye candy and lose track of [the fact that] the real mission is to have a very high degree of certainty that what you're about to kill is a valid target and the real person you're trying to get."

The Wildfire team never earned the right to drink the bottle of Scotch placed on the shelf in the double-wide by CIA Director George Tenet for the day the Predator finally "got him." By the time Navy SEALs killed Osama bin Laden in Pakistan on May 2, 2011, the Trailer Park had been dismantled and the Scotch had disappeared, perhaps lost in the move to Nevada. But from time to time, beginning shortly after bin Laden's death, members of the Wildfire team and those in the Air Force, the CIA, or private companies who commanded or worked with the Hellfire Predator's initial operators got together for reunions, and someone nearly always brought along a bottle of Scotch to pass around. For many, the Predator missions were the highlight of their careers. The missiles they launched were not targeted killings; they were military operations undertaken on the orders of their commander in chief and in response to heinous acts of terrorism that killed nearly three thousand innocent Americans.

A number of the initial cadre who armed and used the Predator continued to work on or with the drone and its derivatives, whether as part of their continuing Air Force careers or after retiring from the service. By 2014, for example, nearly two decades after the Air Force chief of staff sent him to look into Predator operations in Hungary, Snake Clark was still the drone's promoter and protector in the Pentagon.

Others had moved on. Bill Grimes retired in December 2002, and when he wasn't fishing or hunting he wrote a history of Big Safari that was published in 2013.

Mark Cooter finished his Air Force career in 2013 as a colonel, a rank Ginger Wallace also achieved. Besides her role in the Summer Project and Trailer Park operations, Wallace made a bit of military history about a decade later. After the Obama administration's repeal in 2011 of the military's controversial Don't Ask, Don't Tell policy on homosexuality, she came out as a lesbian. Wallace had her partner pin on her silver eagles when Wallace became a colonel that December, and in January 2012 she sat in First Lady Michelle Obama's box at the president's State of the Union address to Congress, chosen to represent all gay and lesbian service members and veterans.

Scott Swanson worked for Big Safari on Predator projects for another two years after he left the Trailer Park. Perhaps the most exciting initiative after all those undertaken for the CIA was an experiment in which Big Safari put Stinger antiaircraft missiles, which are normally shoulder-fired, on a Predator in late 2002. The modification was an attempt to stop supersonic Iraqi MiG fighters that were hunting the drones as they flew surveillance of no-fly zones over Iraq. After several inconclusive engagements with Iraqi fighter planes over the no-fly zones, an Air Combat Command crew, with Swanson instructing them, lost in an exchange of missiles with an Iraqi MiG-25 Foxbat on December 23, 2002, the Predator's last air-to-air engagement. Two years after that, Swanson left Big Safari for another green door assignment, and in 2007 he retired from the Air Force.

By then, Guay was gone. The Big Safari sensor operator died of diabetes and liver damage on September 3, 2005, at age forty-five, in Hampton, Virginia, where he had moved after retiring from the Air Force on May 31. Wry to the end, Guay told his younger brother, Scott, that he was moving back to a suburban house he had bought years earlier, while stationed at Langley Air Force Base, to "be a gentleman farmer." The backyard had room for a small vegetable garden at best.

Guay's service record included a Bronze Star and nine oak leaf clusters for his work on the Predator. During the WILD Predator project, Guay had been the first sensor operator to lase targets for fighter aircraft from the drone. During the Summer Project, Guay had been at the controls of the Predator's cameras when they spotted Osama bin Laden. During the first night of the war in Afghanistan, he had aimed the laser designator in the armed Predator's first lethal strike near Kandahar. And at Roberts Ridge, he had used the Predator's laser illuminator to help the rescue helicopters land safely to pick up the stranded Rangers. At Big Safari's offices in San Diego, his friends dedicated a wall in a conference room to Guay, hanging his Bronze Star, framed under glass with its citation, next to another frame holding his many other ribbons.

On the evening of April 23, 2008, the Smithsonian National Air and Space Museum held an opening ceremony for a new Military Unmanned Aerial Vehicles exhibit. Installed at the west end of the museum's massive building on the National Mall in Washington, D.C., the display included six unmanned aircraft. Hung from the ceiling, they represented all four branches of the military. Included were the Navy's Pioneer and two other small tactical UAVs: the Army's Shadow 200 and the Marine Corps' Dragon Eye, a hand-launched drone small enough to fold up and carry in a backpack. Looming above those were three far larger aircraft. Two were experiments that had led short lives: DARPA's DarkStar, which was cancelled in 1999 after only seven flights by two prototypes, one of which crashed; and the X-45A, a technology demonstrator built by Boeing and Lockheed Martin for a joint program that included DARPA, the Air Force, and the Navy, and flew only in tests, which ended in 2005. The centerpiece of the exhibit—paid for by a donation from General Atomics Aeronautical Systems Inc.—was Predator 3034, slung from the ceiling at a slight banking angle, the better to display its Hellfire missiles. Also visible on its side was Big Safari's distinctive crossed spears and shield.

Those in the audience at the exhibition opening, which was followed by an open bar and elegant buffet dinner at the museum, included General John Jumper, Snake Clark, Spoon Mattoon, Ed Boyle, Mark Cooter, and Frank Pace, the software engineer Abe Karem had hired in the 1980s. Karem wasn't among the guests. But he would often proudly note to those who asked how he felt about the Predator's success that nearly every key department at General Atomics Aeronautical Systems was now run by one of the core group of engineers who joined Neal and Linden Blue's company with Karem after his own company, Leading Systems, went bankrupt. In 2010, Pace would succeed Tom Cassidy as president of the UAV affiliate of General Atomics.

Cassidy—the executive whose savvy on Capitol Hill had been so important to the development of the Predator, the Reaper, and other derivatives built by General Atomics—spoke at the UAV exhibit dedication. The keynote address, however, was delivered by the Air Force's deputy chief of staff for intelligence, surveillance, and reconnaissance, Lieutenant General David Deptula, who told his audience that it would be "difficult to overstate the growing role and importance of unmanned aircraft systems." Deptula said the exhibit was a testament to that role, but he added that the word *unmanned* tended to disguise the fact that "while no one physically sits in these aircraft . . . there are still men and women, U.S. combat veterans, skillfully and successfully piloting these aircraft."

Looking out over an audience that included members of the Air Force team that had flown Predator 3034 in Afghanistan back in 2001 and 2002, as well as others from Big Safari, General Atomics, Raytheon, L-3, and the CIA, Deptula thanked them for their work. Then he noted that Predator 3034 "brings with it a storied past and a distinguished history of combat service to our country." He added:

> This Predator was the first to test-fire the Hellfire—the brainchild of General John Jumper; it was the first U.S. aircraft over Afghanistan deploying on September 12th, 2001, courtesy of the efforts of Colonel Snake Clark; it was the first Predator to shoot a Hellfire in combat—as I witnessed on October 7, 2001, as the commander of the air operations center for Afghanistan, wondering just who issued the fire order, rapidly picking up the phone and asking Colonel Eddie Boyle 7,000 miles away if he knew—and the rest of the story I'll save for later.

By the time Predator 3034 was retired by the Air Force and shipped to the museum, the aircraft had flown 2,780 hours—2,338 of them over Afghanistan—at the hands of perhaps a dozen or more pilots. Snake Clark called 3034 the "Elvis of Predators." In his speech, Deptula called it "truly a piece of aviation history." Indeed it is, for like the *Spirit of St. Louis* and a couple of the other planes hanging from the museum's ceiling, this peculiar aircraft with its slender wings and bulging nose and upside-down tail did something extraordinary. It changed the world.

AUTHOR'S NOTE

The task of a narrative history is not to collect every fact on a subject but to find what in biography have been called the "fertile facts"—the facts that reveal character or, in a narrative history, the character of the story. This is a roundabout way of explaining why some facts that would be included if this were an academic history of the Predator are absent from this book. Expert readers may be surprised, for example, to find no discussion of the Defense Airborne Reconnaissance Office, a Pentagon entity that oversaw UAV programs from 1993 until its death in 1998. The reason for the omission is simple: while DARO was important bureaucratically, providing money to or withholding it from the Predator program each year it existed, it played no substantive role in developing or employing the aircraft.

Some may also wonder why the Predator's mission-type-series designations—RQ-1 and MQ-1—are mentioned only in this book's final chapter, while designations of some other aircraft are omitted altogether. Like DARO's role these are not fertile facts, though in cases of aircraft better known by their designations, such as F-15E and F-16, I have identified them that way.

Some readers may also find it annoying that this book unabashedly embraces the term *drone* to describe what many experts and advocates prefer to call *unmanned aerial vehicles, remotely piloted aircraft,* or *unmanned aircraft systems*, among other clunky constructions. Some argue that the only unmanned aircraft that can properly be called drones are those that are mere targets; others worry that in recent years, the word *drone* has taken on the connotation *robot killer aircraft*. In 2013, the Association of Unmanned Vehicle Systems International even made the password for Wi-Fi service in the media center of its annual conference "Don't say drones," an amusing but futile attempt to dissuade reporters from using the term. As I have written before—and said to AUVSI's genial and energetic leader, Michael Toscano—those in the drone business need to recognize that they long ago lost this debate and make the best of it. The word *drone* is not only handy, it is an easy and even elegant way to describe any aircraft with no pilot inside. In any event, it is here to stay, for by definition, revolutions change things—including definitions.

NOTES

1: THE GENIUS OF THE GENESIS

7 *From the time*: The account of Karem's childhood is based on author interviews with Abraham Karem and Dina Karem.

8 *as part of an exodus*: Reeva Spector Simon, Michael Menachem Laskier, and Sara Reguer, eds., *The Jews of the Middle East and North Africa in Modern Times* (New York: Columbia University Press, 2003), p. 348.

8 *socialist attitudes of collectivism*: Orit Rozin, *The Rise of the Individual in 1950s Israel: A Challenge to Collectivism* (Waltham, Mass.: Brandeis University Press, 2011), pp. xiii–xvi.

9 *three times won*: Abraham E. Karem career summary provided by Karem Aircraft Inc.

9 *he could get the Air Force commander*: Author interview with Shmuel Arbel, March 8, 2013.

10 *by the unorthodox means*: Shlomo Aloni, *Israeli A-4 Skyhawk Units in Combat* (New York: Osprey Publishing, 2009). An account of Dotan shooting down two MiG-17s on one mission can be found on the Israeli Air Force website, http://www.iaf.org.il/2540-30115-en/IAF.aspx, accessed March 11, 2013. Karem supplied the detail that the antitank rockets were Zunis.

11 *had cost Israel*: Lon O. Nordeen, *Air Warfare in the Missile Age* (Washington, D.C.: Smithsonian Institution Press, 2002), pp. 123–48.

11 *The SAMs had also inflicted*: Robert S. Bolia, "Overreliance on Technology in Warfare: The Yom Kippur War as a Case Study," *Parameters, the U.S. Army's Senior Professional Journal*, U.S. Army War College (Summer 2004): 46–56.

11 *nearly three times the speed of sound*: "Israeli Aircraft, Arab SAMS in Key Battle," *Aviation Week & Space Technology*, October 22, 1973, p. 14. According to *Aviation*

Week, the Soviet-supplied SA-6 "Gainful" antiaircraft missile, used in combat for the first time during the Yom Kippur War, reached a speed of Mach 2.98.

15 *used since the 1930s*: Laurence R. Newcome, *Unmanned Aviation: A Brief History of Unmanned Aerial Vehicles* (Reston, Va.: American Institute of Aeronautics and Astronautics, 2004), pp. 57–58.

16 *the winning aircraft is the one*: Fédération Aéronautique Internationale Sporting Code, Technical Regulations for Free Flight Contests, 2013, p. 9, http://www. google.com/search?hl=en&source=hp&q=F%C3%A9d%C3%A9ration+A%C3 %A9ronautique+Internationale+Sporting+Code%2C+Technical+Regulations+f or+Free+Flight+Contests%2C+2013&gbv=2&oq=F%C3%A9d%C3%A9ration+A %C3%A9ronautique+Internationale+Sporting+Code%2C+Technical+Regulatio ns+for+Free+Flight+Contests%2C+2013&gs_l=heirloom-hp.3 . . . 2262.2262.0 .3822.1.1.0.0.0.0.0.0..0.0. . . . 0 . . . 1ac..34.heirloom-hp..1.0.0.b0xGxN5Jl3M& rlz=1W1TSND_enUS413.

16 *he placed tenth*: "A/2 Glider Results, World Championships for Free Flight Models," *Aero Modeler*, October 1963, p. 510.

17 *cancelled the program after half*: The drone helicopter built by the U.S. Navy was the QH-50 DASH, an acronym for Drone Anti-Submarine Helicopter. Details can be found in Newcome, *Unmanned Aviation*, pp. 86–88.

19 *cancelled the project*: Newcome, *Unmanned Aviation*, pp. 23–30.

20 *Marilyn Monroe*: Ibid., p. 58; http://www.northrop grumman.com/Capabili ties/BQM74FAerialTarget/Documents/First-UCAVs.pdf, accessed March 6, 2013.

20 *code name Project Anvil*: Walter J. Boyne, "The Remote Control Bombers," *Air Force*, November 2010, pp. 86–88, provides an authoritative account of Project Aphrodite and Project Anvil. Some details about Kennedy's mission were taken from the Norfolk and Suffolk Aviation Museum website, http://www.aviation museum.net/Joe_Kennedy.htm, accessed March 6, 2013. The precise location where Kennedy's plane went down was provided in an e-mail to the author from Dr. Peggy Fraser of Denver, Colorado, whose mother was Lieutenant Willy's fiancée at the time of his death.

21 *was going to fly*: William Wagner, *Lightning Bugs and Other Reconnaissance Drones: The Can-Do Story of Ryan's Unmanned "Spy Planes"* (Fallbrook, Calif.: Aero Publishers Inc., 1982).

21 *Firebees, Fireflys, and Lightning Bugs*: Newcome, *Unmanned Aviation*, p. 83.

22 *They had to be launched*: Col. (Ret.) Jerry Knotts and Col. (Ret.) Patrick R. O'Malley, "The Big Safari Program Story . . . as Told by the Big Safari People," unpublished manuscript provided to the author.

22 *More than half*: Newcome, *Unmanned Aviation*, p. 86.

23 *seen as more promising*: Thomas P. Ehrhard, "Unmanned Aerial Vehicles in the United States Armed Services: A Comparative Study of Weapon System Innovation," Ph.D. dissertation, Johns Hopkins University, Washington, D.C., June 2000, pp. 120–25.

23 *less flies in it than swims*: Tina Baier, "Flattern über dem Himalaya," *Süddeutsche Zeitung*, July 18, 2009, p. 20.

24 *At weekly meetings*: Arbel interview.

25 *"We were DARPA's conduit"*: Author interview with Ira Kuhn.

25 *Robert Fossum figured*: Author interview with Robert Fossum, director, Defense Advanced Research Projects Agency, 1977–81.

26 *lunch each day*: Author interview with Hertenstein protégé Tim Just, August 12, 2013.

26 *thinking to himself*: Author interview with Jack Hertenstein, September 5, 2012.

27 *The pyrotechnics used*: Chronology provided by Karem Aircraft Inc.

2: THE BLUES

29 *the concept had been his*: Sources for the story of the *Yale Daily News* Asian Expedition include author interviews with Neal and Linden Blue in 2012 and 2013 and the articles that Neal Blue and his companions filed to the *New York Times* about their car trip from Paris to Calcutta, specifically: "U.S. Students Find Contrasts on Balkan Tour," July 4, 1955, p. 3; "U.S. Students See a Bustling Beirut," July 25, 1955, p. 6; "Risks Rule Trek from Damascus," August 3, 1955, p. 7; "Yale Party Visits Two More Lands," August 18, 1955, p. 25; "4 Yale Men Greeted by Afghans with Free Tea and Free Shave," September 28, 1955, p. 6.

29 *"He always had a plan"*: Author interview with Norman Augustine, August 7, 2009.

30 *posed for a news photographer*: "Yale Quartet Set for Global Goodwill Tour," June 3, 1955, International News Photos photograph and caption, accessed April 9, 2013, at http://www.corbisimages.com/stock-photo/rights-managed/U1284389INP/yale-students-studying-station-wagon.

32 *cars below moving faster*: Author interview with Linden Blue, September 26, 2012.

33 *"Presented with a fait accompli"*: "Denver Brothers, Students at Yale, to Tour Latin America in Small Plane," *Boston Globe*, May 21, 1956, p. 36.

33 *included a number of adventures*: "Flight of the 'Blue Bird,'" *Life*, April 8, 1957, pp. 82–93.

34 *Tacho liked wealth himself*: http://www.britannica.com/EBchecked/topic/554161/Anastasio-Somoza, accessed April 11, 2013.

35 *"Why don't you guys"*: The Anastasio Somoza García comment was remembered by Neal Blue.

35 *"Well, happy to have you here"*: The Anastasio Somoza Debayle comment was remembered by Linden Blue.

35 *cacao and banana plantation*: Di Freeze, "Linden Blue: From Disease-Resistant Bananas to UAVs," *Airport Journals*, October 2005, accessed Aug. 16, 2011, at http://www.airportjournals.com/Display.cfm?varID=0510013.

35 *also had a standing invitation*: Author interview with Neal Blue, April 1, 2013.

37 *his parents were working feverishly*: Ibid.

37 *both looking gaunt*: R. Hart Phillips, "Cuba Rejects U.S. Protest," *New York Times*, April 6, 1961, p. 2; and UPI, "Castro Releases 2 U.S. Prisoners," *New York Times*, April 5, 1961, p. 19.

37 *When he protested*: E-mail to the author from Linden Blue.

37 *nearly all 1,511 of them*: "C.I.A. Bares Its Bungling in Report on Bay of Pigs Invasion," *New York Times*, February 22, 1998; also http://www.foia.cia.gov/collection/bay-pigs-release, accessed May 6, 2013.

38 *they left the plantation*: Author interview with Linden Blue; and Freeze, "Linden Blue."

39 *a mere six million dollars*: Richard B. Collins, "Telluride's Tale of Eminent Domain, Home Rule, and Retroactivity," *Denver University Law Review* 86, no. 4 (2009): 1433, at http://www.law.du.edu/documents/denver-university-law-review/v86-4/Collins-final.pdf.

39 *hard-nosed tactics*: Barney Gimbel, "The Predator," *Fortune*, October 31, 2008, at http://money.cnn.com/2008/10/28/magazines/fortune/predator_gimbel.fortune/index.htm.

40 *president would allow*: Statement by Deputy Press Secretary Speakes on the Soviet Attack on a Korean Civilian Airliner, September 16, 1983.

41 *fleet of attack helicopters*: Stephen Kinzer, "Nicaraguan Says Soviet Ship Carried One or Two Military Copters," *New York Times*, November 9, 1984, p. A10.

41 *"You could launch them"*: Gimbel, "The Predator."

41 *report in the* Wall Street Journal: "Chevron Considering Sale of Certain Retail and Refining Assets," *Wall Street Journal*, July 18, 1985.

42 *When Neal heard about GA*: Author interview with Neal Blue, April 1, 2013.

42 *Founded in 1955*: General Atomics Aeronautical Media Information, "Neal Blue, Chairman & CEO, General Atomics," undated; and Freeze, "Linden Blue."

42 *revenue of $170 million*: Ken Wells, "Chevron Plans to Sell Wells of Low Volume—Streamlining Move Includes Buying Other Producing and Marketing Facilities," *Wall Street Journal*, December 13, 1985.

42 *The company's businesses included*: Matt Potter, "General Atomics: Color It Blue," *San Diego Weekly Reader*, July 12, 2001.

42 *Neal and Linden Blue were buying*: "Chevron Agrees to Sell GA Technologies Unit to 2 Denver Investors," *Wall Street Journal*, August 14, 1986.

44 *Cassidy thought*: Author interviews with Rear Adm. (Ret.) Thomas J. Cassidy Jr., USN, April 2013.

44 *"always buy straw hats"*: Gimbel, "The Predator."

46 *Neal Blue wanted to call*: Author interview with Neal Blue, April 1, 2013.

3: A STRAW HAT IN WINTER

48 *described the ambitious event*: Robert R. Ropelewski and Bruce A. Smith, "Soviet Presence, RPV Developments Mark Inaugural San Diego Air Show," *Aviation Week & Space Technology*, May 23, 1988, pp. 29–30.

48 *The show's opening day*: "Tom Blair" column, *San Diego Union-Tribune*, May 12, 1988, p. B1.

48 *spectators could circle out*: Leonard Bernstein, "S.D. Cancels 1990 Air Show at Brown Field after Audit," *Los Angeles Times*, February 9, 1989.

49 *another booth displaying a drone*: Author interviews with Neal Blue, Linden Blue, Karsten Blue, Michael Melnick, and Abraham Karem.

49 *"gigantic phallic symbol"*: E-mail to the author from former Leading Systems Inc. employee Stephen Waide, May 2, 2013.

51 *Lehman had seen the Mastiff*: Author interviews with former Navy Secretary John F. Lehman Jr., March and April 2013.

52 *Mastiff could stay airborne*: The Mastiff's capabilities are listed in Kenneth Munson, *World Unmanned Aircraft* (London: Jane's Publishing Company Ltd., 1988), p. 60.

53 *proving to be a turkey*: Robert A. Moore, "Unmanned Air Vehicles: A Prospectus," *Aerospace America*, February 1989, p. 26. See also "Aquila Remotely Piloted Vehicle, Recent Developments and Alternatives," U.S. General Accounting Office, January 1986, GAO/NSIAD—86-4-41BR; and "Aquila Remotely Piloted Vehicle, Its Potential Battlefield Contribution Still in Doubt," U.S. General Accounting Office, October 1987, GAO/NSIAD—88-19.

54 *"people who should make us humble"*: Abraham Karem interview, September 22, 2012.

55 *four such systems had been built*: Ibid.

57 *told* Aviation Week: John D. Morocco, "Navy Plans Operational Trials for Amber RPV in 1989," *Aviation Week & Space Technology*, December 14, 1987, p. 25.

57 *gave* Aviation Week *another rosy prognosis*: "RPVs & Drones; Long-Term Observation and Radio Relay Missions Play Vital Navy Role," *Aviation Week & Space Technology*, May 2, 1988, p. 70.

58 *boondoggle known as Aquila*: "Aquila Remotely Piloted Vehicle, Its Potential Battlefield Contribution Still in Doubt," United States General Accounting Office, October 1987, GAO/NSIAD—88-19.

58 *froze all spending on drones*: Department of Defense Appropriation Bill, 1988, Senate Report 100–235, 100th Cong., 1st Sess., p. 250.

60 *navigated to within*: Steve La Rue, "S.D. Firm's Unmanned Plane Tested," *San Diego Union*, December 1, 1988, p. C1.

61 *RPV master plan*: Ronald D. Murphy, "AMBER for Long Endurance," *Aerospace America*, February 1989, p. 32.

61 *"could prove fatal"*: Robert A. Moore, "Unmanned Air Vehicles: A Prospectus," *Aerospace America*, February 1989, p. 26.

61 *one of three bidders*: The other two bidders for the 1989 short-range UAV contract were McDonnell Douglas Corporation and a team consisting of TRW Inc. and Israel Aircraft Industries. The TRW-IAI team later won the right to produce a UAV called the Hunter.

62 *commissioned to build*: Brian Wanstall and Bill Sweetman, "Unmanned Aircraft Fit Tight Budgets," *Interavia Aerospace Review* (April 1990): 315.

62 *JPO also made it clear*: Naval Air Systems Command contract solicitation N00019-89-R-0003, pp. 12–15.

63 *seven had been built*: Author interview with Leading Systems pilot Tim Just.

63 *couldn't pay an overdue phone bill*: Leading Systems Inc. bankruptcy papers, U.S. Bankruptcy Court, Central District of California, Case No. SA-90-07057-JB (Chapter Eleven).

64 *wanted to help Abe*: Author interviews with Ira Kuhn.

64 *"You guys have been wanting"*: The dialogue was remembered similarly by Ira Kuhn and Linden Blue.

66 *the Blues paid $1,850,000*: "Summary of Debts and Property," dated October 22, 1990, Leading Systems Inc. bankruptcy papers.

4: PREDATOR REBORN

69 *about to initiate an operation*: Author interviews with R. James Woolsey, Abraham Karem, and Thomas Twetten.

69 *got front-page coverage*: Walter Pincus, "'2 Little Guys' with a Big Idea," *Washington Post*, August 13, 1981, p. A1.

71 *conduct surveillance for long periods*: Author interview with R. James Woolsey, March 29, 2012.

71 *meeting in his CIA headquarters office*: Frank Strickland, "The Early Evolution of the Predator Drone" (extracts), *Studies in Intelligence* 57, no. 1 (March 2013): 106. (CIA officer Strickland's article, while helpful in understanding the CIA's Gnat 750 program, contains inaccuracies, especially in describing the history of the Amber, the distinctions between the Amber and the Gnat 750, and how General Atomics acquired the assets of Leading Systems Inc.)

72 *exactly the concept*: Ibid.

73 *briefed him on the meeting*: Author interview with Rear Admiral (Ret.) Michael Cramer, June 10, 2013.

73 *"get us ground truth"*: Ibid.

73 *one single dumb-luck hit*: R. W. Apple Jr., "WAR IN THE GULF: Scud Attack; Scud Missile Hits a U.S. Barracks, Killing 27," *New York Times*, February 26, 1991.

74 *to preclude objections about the cost*: http://www.globalsecurity.org/military/ops/strike_930117.htm, accessed June 12, 2013; Patrick McLain, "Settling the Score with Saddam: Resolution 1441 and Parallel Justifications for the Use of Force against Iraq," *Duke Journal of Comparative and International Law* 13 (2003): 233–90.

75 *visiting the San Diego offices*: 1993 work diaries of Capt. Allan Rutherford, loaned to the author.

75 *he noted only*: Ibid.

76 *the military was woefully behind*: Author interview with John M. Deutch, June 7, 2013.

76 *began talking regularly*: Ibid.

77 *"Tell these fellows"*: Thomas Twetten's recollection of what he and John Deutch said.

77 *eyes glaze over*: Author interview with Thomas Twetten.

77 *hoped to stimulate their competitive*: Author interview with Deutch.

77 *might want to talk about*: Author interviews with Deutch and Neal Blue.

78 *What went through his mind*: Author interview with Neal Blue.

78 *got a second phone*: Author interview with Capt. (Ret.) Steve Jayjock, USN.

78 *Jayjock had been assigned*: Author interviews with Jayjock and Admiral (Ret.) William Studeman, deputy CIA director, 1993.

79 *two-page memo*: Under Secretary of Defense Memorandum for Assistant Secretary of the Navy for Research, Development & Acquisition, Subject: Endurance Unmanned Aerial Vehicle (UAV) Program, July 12, 1993.

81 *seething letter*: Copy of the Kohler letter in the author's possession.

81 *replied by letter*: Copy of the Wagner letter in the author's possession.

81 *required the CIA team to relay*: David A. Fulghum, "CIA to Fly Missions from Inside Croatia," *Aviation Week & Space Technology*, July 11, 1994, p. 20.

83 *Tier I was a cover*: David A. Fulghum, "USAF Stresses UAVs for Recon," *Aviation Week & Space Technology*, September 27, 1993, p. 44.

83 *the magazine reported that*: "Gnat Goes Splat," *Aviation Week & Space Technology*, November 1, 1993, p. 23.

83 *some in Congress were talking*: David A. Fulghum, "Tier 2 UAV Aborts First Test Flight," *Aviation Week & Space Technology*, July 11, 1994, p. 22.

84 *motor used in ultralight sport aircraft*: The manufacturer's plant in Austria also built snowmobile engines, giving rise to an oft-repeated myth that the Predator was powered by an "Austrian snowmobile engine." The Rotax 912 and other engines used in the Predator have all been specifically designed for use in aircraft.

86 *fourteen seconds*: Author interview with Frank Pace, November 3, 2010.

5: PREDATOR'S PROGRESS

92 *Stratakes called up*: Jay Stratakes, "Medium Altitude Endurance UAV Program Briefing," January 11, 1995, copy in the author's possession.

93 *astounded by what they were watching*: Author interviews with Allan Rutherford.

95 *intelligence analysts dismissed color video*: Author interviews with "Werner."

98 *set a new UAV endurance record*: "Tier II UAV Sets Endurance Record," *Aerospace Daily*, January 24, 1995, p. 109.

99 *boiling point in the Balkans*: Lon O. Nordeen, *Air Warfare in the Missile Age* (Washington, D.C.: Smithsonian Institution Press, 2002), pp. 241–46.

100 *O'Grady parachuted safely*: Department of Defense news briefing, Adm. William Owens, vice chairman, Joint Chiefs of Staff, June 9, 1995.

101 *first combat deployment*: Details of the arrival come from an author interview with former Mibli Predator pilot and retired Army Chief Warrant Officer Greg Foscue.

103   *all the Predator could do*: Author interview with Col. Scott Sanborn, commander of the Predator detachment at Gjader, Albania, July–October 1995.

105   *"We're at risk"*: The dialogue is as remembered by both Greg Gordy and Scott Sanborn.

106   *Tanjug reported*: "Army Shoots Down Two Croatian Aircraft," Belgrade Tanjug in English, August 12, 1995, Foreign Broadcast Information Service transcribed text.

107   Washington Post *reported*: Bradley Graham, "Pentagon Loses Two Unmanned Spy Planes over Bosnia," *Washington Post*, August 15, 1995, p. A10.

107   *cost only $1.5 million apiece*: On October 18, 1995, the deputy director of the Defense Airborne Reconnaissance Office sent a memo to the Pentagon's Budget and Finance Directorate authorizing Rutherford's office to pay three million dollars to replace the two Predators lost in Bosnia. A copy of the memo is in the author's possession.

108   *"You proved the inherent"*: "Bravo Zulu for a job well done. Admiral Smith sends," unclassified message dated November 20, 1995, copy in the author's possession.

108   *At the National Defense University*: "On Fogleman's Watch," *Aerospace Daily* 174, no. 55 (June 19, 1995): 435.

108   *A month later*: Stacey Evers, "Big Changes in Store for DOD Intelligence Collection," *Aerospace Daily* 175, no. 13 (July 21, 1995): 102.

108   *Misty Fast FAC*: Rick Newman and Don Shepperd, *Bury Us Upside Down: The Misty Pilots and the Secret Battle for the Ho Chi Minh Trail* (New York: Presidio Press, 2006). The figures on Misty Fast FAC losses come from *Bury Us Upside Down*.

109   *Most were rescued*: Author interview with Gen. (Ret.) Ronald Fogleman.

109   *last regular Air Force RF-4C flight*: Stacey Evers, "Big Changes in Store for DOD Intelligence Collection," *Aerospace Daily*, July 21, 1995.

109   *just voted to reactivate*: "SR-71 Blackbird Back in Business," U.S. Air Force Air Combat Command news release, January 24, 1997.

111   *Joint Chiefs committee recommended*: Joint Requirements Oversight Council, "Memorandum for the Secretary of Defense, JROCM 151–95, Subject: Assignment of Service Lead for Operation of the Predator Unmanned Aerial Vehicle (UAV)," December 16, 1995, copy in the author's possession.

111   *Perry agreed to give*: William J. Perry, secretary of defense, "Memorandum for Secretaries of the Military Departments, Chairman of the Joint Chiefs of Staff, Under Secretaries of Defense, Subject: Assignment of Service Lead for Operation of the Predator Unmanned Aerial Vehicle (UAV)," April 8, 1996, copy in the author's possession.

111   *held in a huge conference room*: Dr. James M. George, "Predator Comes to Air Combat Command (1994–2005)," Office of ACC History, Headquarters, Air Combat Command, Langley Air Force Base, Virginia, August 2006.

112   *pilots openly showed their contempt*: Author interviews with General (Ret.) Richard E. Hawley, Rutherford, and Capt. (Ret.) Steve Jayjock, USN.

113   *the drone's engine failed*: Author interview with Lt. Col. Eric Johnson, June 29, 2009.

113 *"message to the field"*: "Griffith: Predator Not Responsive to Tactical Command-ers in Bosnia," *Inside the Army*, February 24, 1997, p. 10.

114 *then provide top cover*: Author interview with Fogleman.

115 *forty locations in all*: Peter H. Wiedemann, "On the Use of the Predator (MAE-UAV) System in Bosnia," paper presented at the Unmanned Vehicle Conference, Paris, France, June 13, 1997.

115 *system was created*: The new video dissemination system, developed specifically to get Predator video to commanders, is described in Maj. Mark Biwer, "The Joint Broadcast Service Supporting Bosnia: Value to the Warrior and Lessons Learned," Air Command and Staff College research paper, March 1997.

115 *didn't fly its Predators in wet weather*: Author interviews with Lt. Col. (Ret.) Jon Box and Lt. Col. Eric Johnson.

116 *the rest were tests and check flights*: Jon L. S. Box, Pilot Logbook 1996–99, loaned to the author by Box.

118 *Clark wrote in a report*: Col. James G. Clark, "Memorandum for AF/CVA, CV, CSAF, April 28, 1997, Subject: Predator," copy in the author's possession.

118 *"After my report was done"*: James "Snake" Clark, "Predator: A Personal History," *U.S. Air Force*, Air Force Historical Association, Andrews Air Force Base, Mary-land, 2006.

6: WILD PREDATOR

119 *Seventeen crew members*: "Shoot-Down of a USAF C-130 by Soviet Aircraft on 2 September 1958," declassified National Security Agency report, accessed at http://www.nsa.gov/public_info/declass/c130_shootdown.shtml; and Bill Grimes, *The History of Big Safari* (Bloomington, Ind.: Archway, 2014), pp. 121–25.

120 *Big Safari's game*: Knotts and O'Malley, "The Big Safari Program Story . . . as Told by the Big Safari People."

121 *taken by surprise*: David A. Fulghum, "Quiet USAF Organization Fields Covert Spycraft," *Aviation Week & Space Technology*, July 24, 2000, p. 176.

122 *Of forty U.S. aircraft*: David A. Fulghum, "Creating the Plan to Crack Iraq's Anti-aircraft Defenses," *Aviation Week & Space Technology*, July 24, 2000, p. 177.

122 *Big Safari studied*: Author interviews with William D. W. Grimes.

123 *DarkStar crashed*: "DarkStar—High Altitude Endurance UAV," paper presented by Harry A. Berman, DARPA HAE UAV Program Office, Defense Advanced Research Projects Agency, at Unmanned Vehicles '87 Conference and Exhibi-tion, Paris, France, June 12–13, 1997.

124 *Meermans talked regularly*: Author interviews with former representative Jerry Lewis (R-Calif.) and Letitia White, Michael Meermans, and William D. W. Grimes.

125 *House Intelligence Committee's report*: The fiscal 1998 legislation also abolished the Defense Airborne Reconnaissance Office, an umbrella organization super-imposed in 1994 over the Navy Joint Program Office to handle funding for all UAV programs.

125 *committee's report*: House Permanent Select Committee on Intelligence, "Report of the Intelligence Authorization Act for Fiscal Year 1998," 105th Cong., 1st Sess., 1997, report 105–135, part 1, p. 30.

129 *directed to install laser designators*: "Point Paper on Predator Laser Designator," drafted by Maj. Mark Mattoon of Big Safari, April 19, 1999.

131 *pilots were soon having trouble*: Benjamin S. Lambeth, *NATO's Air War for Kosovo* (Santa Monica, Calif.: RAND Corp., 2001), pp. 21–22.

131 *Clark even had a TV*: Author interview with Gen. (Ret.) Wesley Clark, June 18, 2013.

132 *General Clark, who was peering*: Ibid.

132 *his immediate response*: Clark remembered the incident much as Short did, but with the key difference that Clark recalled being in Aviano at the time, while Short thought Clark placed the call from Supreme Allied Commander Europe (SACEUR) headquarters in Belgium.

133 *Short admitted*: The story as Short told it to the AFA was repeated in Maj. Todd P. Harmer, USAF, "Enhancing the Operational Art: The Influence of the Information Environment on the Command and Control of Airpower," master's thesis, School of Advanced Airpower Studies, Air University, Maxwell Air Force Base, Alabama, June 2000, p. 87; and again in Lt. Col. Michael W. Kometer, USAF, "Command in Air War: Centralized vs. Decentralized Control of Combat Airpower," doctoral dissertation for the degree of doctor of philosophy in technology, management, and policy, Massachusetts Institute of Technology, May 2005, p. 100n54.

133 *"Invent it"*: Author interviews with Col. (Ret.) James G. "Snake" Clark and Gen. (Ret.) Michael E. Ryan. The account of Ryan's phone call was recalled by Clark and was verified by Ryan.

134 *some in Congress had proposed*: H.R. 3230, National Defense Authorization Act for Fiscal Year 1997, as passed by the House; also letter from Rep. Curt Weldon to Lt. Col. Sean M. Frisbee, USAF, May 24, 2004, provided to the author by Frisbee.

135 *His 110-page master's thesis*: Capt. Brian Dean Raduenz, "Digital Signal Processing Using Lapped Transforms with Variable Parameter Windows and Orthonormal Base," thesis presented to the faculty of the School of Engineering of the Air Force Institute of Technology, Air University, Wright-Patterson Air Force Base, Ohio, in partial fulfillment of the requirements for the degree of master of science in electrical engineering, December 1992.

135 *Bahrain Hilton*: The date and hotel information were supplied by Raduenz from travel vouchers and airline boarding passes he kept.

137 *officer at Big Safari's headquarters*: Mattoon, "Point Paper on Predator Laser Designator."

137 *at a premium of roughly 40 percent*: Author interview with William Casey, the Raytheon Corp. engineer who managed the company's work on the projects to adapt the AN/AAS-44(V) and MTS laser balls for use on the Predator, November 8, 2013.

139 *commander refused to let his crews*: Grimes, *The History of Big Safari*, p. 331.

139 *"not my kind of warrior"*: Author interview with Grimes. The 11th Reconnaissance Squadron commander at the time, Lt. Col. Dana Richards, declined several requests for an interview, but in an e-mail exchange with the author replied that Grimes's "comment displays his ignorance in what authorities I had. Big Safari trained a select group to employ the WILD Predator. The software was different, the hardware was different. I did not have the authority to decide who could and could not fly the aircraft." Richards also suggested the chief of staff of the Air Force would have had to issue a waiver to permit a "conventional crew" from the 11th Reconnaissance Squadron to operate an aircraft using "red line" technical orders, meaning maintenance and crew manuals that have not been "validated and verified." Others involved in the WILD Predator deployment side with Grimes on the question.

139 *On May 4, 1999*: Details of the tests at Indian Springs come from an e-mail from Raytheon engineer William M. Casey sent to Air Force Lt. Col. Sean Frisbee on May 3, 2004, when Frisbee was working on a master's thesis about the Predator. Frisbee provided this e-mail from Casey and dozens of other documents related to his thesis. The author is deeply grateful.

139 *When the team later watched*: A copy of the nose camera video is in the author's possession.

141 *Snake Clark used his pull*: Author interview with Werner.

141 *Only on June 2*: The June 2 date comes from a Bronze Star justification narrative for Col. Stanley Shinkle. A document provided by Snake Clark pinpoints the date as June 4. Neither document, unfortunately, is definitive.

142 *never got closer to combat*: In a 2011 academic paper for the Mitchell Institute for Airpower Studies, the author incorrectly reported, based on documents that included Shinkle's Bronze Star medal citation and on interviews later determined to be misinterpreted or inaccurate, that the WILD Predator crew followed a tank or some other armored vehicle to the building bombed by the A-10 and buddy-lased the target. (Richard Whittle, "Predator's Big Safari," Mitchell Paper 7, Mitchell Institute for Airpower Studies, Mitchell Institute Press, August 2011, pp. 15 and 41n.) Subsequent interviews have established to my satisfaction that no actual enemy target was ever buddy-lased by the WILD Predator team, but an A-10 was directed to and bombed a derelict building in a proof-of-concept exercise. The author regrets the error in the Mitchell Institute paper.

142 *daily maintenance report for June*: "Operation Joint Forge WILD Predator in Action, Bosnia-Herzegovina European Resort Travel Provided by Big Safari Maintenance Report, Current as of 2 July 1999," copy in the author's possession.

7: THE SUMMER PROJECT

143 *killing 213 people*: Lawrence Wright, *The Looming Tower: Al-Qaeda and the Road to 9/11* (New York: Alfred A. Knopf, 2006), p. 308.

144 *CIA's Counterterrorist Center*: The original name of the CIA Counterterrorist Center, "counterterrorist" with a "t" on the end, was changed in 2005 to Counterterrorism Center, with an "m" on the end. See Mark Mazzetti, *The Way of the*

Knife: The CIA, a Secret Army, and a War at the Ends of the Earth (New York: Penguin, 2013), note on page "Principal Characters."

144 *No evidence*: Wright, *Looming Tower*, p. 308.

144 *killed twenty to thirty people*: National Commission on Terrorist Attacks upon the United States, *The 9/11 Commission Report*, authorized edition (New York: W. W. Norton, 2004), p. 117.

145 *decided against a strike*: Ibid., pp. 126–31.

145 *administration officials were wary*: Ibid., p. 141.

145 *In early April*: Author interview with Allen, who pinpointed the time as early April 2000.

145 *Gration had asked Fry*: 9/11 Commission Report, p. 189; author interviews and e-mails with Ambassador and Maj. Gen. (Ret.) Scott Gration.

147 *Pavitt also made it clear*: Author interview with Allen.

147 *"I want to try something else"*: Steve Coll, *Ghost Wars: The Secret History of the CIA, Afghanistan, and Bin Laden, from the Soviet Invasion to September 10, 2001* (New York: Penguin, 2004), p. 524.

147 *"I will take the message back"*: Author interview with Allen.

147 *Clarke had sent a memo*: 9/11 Commission Report, p. 187.

148 *killing dogs*: Wright, *The Looming Tower*, p. 343; also Peter L. Bergen, *The Longest War: The Enduring Conflict Between America and al-Qaeda* (New York: Free Press, 2011), p. 222.

149 *Four weeks later*: 9/11 Commission Report, p. 506, n. 113.

149 *imposed by the White House*: Ibid., p. 189.

154 *in Uzbekistan*: Bob Woodward, *Bush at War* (New York: Simon and Schuster, 2002), p. 77; author interviews with participants.

154 *issued retroactively*: Special Order GD-09, which officially created the 32nd Expeditionary Air Intelligence Squadron, was issued on behalf of the commander, U.S. Air Forces Europe, by Maj. Gen. Stephen Lorenz, director of plans and programs, on January 16, 2001, but made retroactive to August 1, 2000. "The verbal orders of the commander are confirmed, circumstances prevented written orders in advance," the document explained. Copy in the author's possession.

155 *"If anything goes wrong"*: Author interview with Col. (Ret.) Edward J. Boyle.

155 *Wallace thought*: Author interview with Col. Ginger Wallace.

156 *Computer terminals lined the walls*: Henry A. Crumpton, *The Art of Intelligence: Lessons from a Life in the CIA's Clandestine Service* (New York: Penguin, 2012), p. 152.

160 *Black told Crumpton*: Ibid., p. 153.

161 *Berger wrote*: 9/11 Commission Report, p. 189.

161 *he saw no downside*: Author interview with Richard A. Clarke.

162 *Clarke was utterly fascinated*: Richard A. Clarke, *Against All Enemies: Inside America's War on Terror* (New York: Free Press, 2004).

162 *killing seventeen*: Wright, *Looming Tower*, p. 361; Kirk S. Lippold, *Front Burner: Al Qaeda's Attack on the USS* Cole (New York: Public Affairs, 2012), p. xxi.

162   *certain the United States would strike*: 911 Commission Report, p. 191.

162   *neither the CIA nor the FBI*: Clarke, *Against All Enemies*, p. 223.

162   *President Clinton later wrote*: William J. Clinton, *My Life* (New York: Alfred A. Knopf, 2004), p. 925.

163   *Summer Project officially ended*: Author interview with Gration.

163   *strategy paper about Al Qaeda*: Richard A. Clarke, "Strategy for Eliminating the Threat from the Jihadist Networks of al Qida: Status and Prospects," p. 8, partially declassified in 2004, accessed at http://www2.gwu.edu/~nsarchiv/NSAEBB /NSAEBB147/clarke%20attachment.pdf, July 9, 2012.

8: THE NEXT LOGICAL STEP

165   *Then Jumper talked*: C. R. Anderegg, *Sierra Hotel: Flying Air Force Fighters in the Decade After Vietnam* (Washington, D.C.: Air Force History and Museums Program, 2001), p. 56.

165   *the wonder of laser guided weapons*: Anderegg, *Sierra Hotel*; and author interviews with C. R. Anderegg.

166   *On April 27, 1972*: Walter J. Boyne, *Beyond the Wild Blue: A History of the U.S. Air Force* (New York: St. Martin's, 1997), p. 489.

167   *he strongly supported*: Jumper's April 28, 1999, Combat Mission Needs Statement for the laser designator addition to the Predator is referenced in Capability Development Document for MQ-1 Predator Multi-Role Remotely Piloted Aircraft System, Increment 2, ACAT II, March 12, 2004, copy in the author's possession.

167   *billed his Air Armament Summit*: *Commerce Business Daily*, October 25, 1999, PSA #2461, and December 10, 1999, PSA #2493.

167   *Maybe, he reasoned*: Author interview with Maj. Gen. (Ret.) Michael C. Kostelnik, USAF, April 18, 2011.

168   *A PowerPoint slide*: Weaponized UAV Demonstration, PowerPoint presentation by Brig. Gen. Kevin Sullivan, Air Armament Center vice commander, March 16, 2000, Air Armament Summit 2000, copy in the author's possession.

169   *Jumper sent an announcement*: "Air Combat Command message to Headquarters USAF et al., Subj: RQ-1, Predator, Program Direction," May 1, 2000, copy in the author's possession.

169   *Contrary to later accounts*: P. W. Singer, *Wired for War: The Robotics Revolution and Conflict in the 21st Century* (New York: Penguin, 2009). In *Wired for War*, Singer asserts on page 35 that the "CIA armed its Predators and the Air Force decided that it couldn't be left behind." In Crumpton, *The Art of Intelligence*, pp. 156–57, the author writes that after being refused permission to send commandos into Afghanistan to capture or kill bin Laden, "I realized that arming the Predator was perhaps our only chance of achieving our lethal mission." He also writes that CIA officers chose the Hellfire, a choice made by Jumper based on briefings produced by Big Safari, according to Jumper, those who prepared the briefings, and the dates on the briefings.

169   *revealed Jumper's decision*: "Air Force Plans Demonstration of Predator's Ability to Drop Bombs," *Inside the Air Force*, May 26, 2000.

170   *"its long-term viability remains in question"*: Thomas P. Ehrhard, "Unmanned Aerial Vehicles in the United States Armed Services: A Comparative Study of Weapon System Innovation," PhD dissertation, Johns Hopkins University, Washington, D.C., 2000, p. 546.

170   *"All I wanted to do"*: Author interviews with Gen. (Ret.) John P. Jumper, USAF, April 2010.

170   *first launch*: Wagner, *Lightning Bugs and Other Reconnaissance Drones*, p. 184.

171   *The Navy, meanwhile, cancelled*: Newcome, *Unmanned Aviation*, pp. 86–88. Details on weapons tests using the QH-50 DASH can be found in "Summary of ARPA-ASO, TTO Aerial Platform Programs: Volume 11, Remotely Piloted Helicopters," Report No. A-4642-II, Task No. 44, Defense Advanced Research Projects Agency, Tactical Technology Office Contract No. DAAHOI-/2-C-0982, ARPA Order No. 2209, July 1975.

171   *Intermediate-Range Nuclear Forces Treaty*: "Treaty Between the United States of America and the Union of Soviet Socialist Republics on the Elimination of Their Intermediate-Range and Shorter-Range Missiles (INF Treaty)," accessed at http://www.state.gov/t/avc/trty/102360.htm#text.

171   *authority solely over "nonlethal" drones*: Department of Defense Appropriation Bill, 1988, Senate Report 100–235, 100th Cong., 1st Sess., p. 250.

171   *as Weldon later wrote*: Letter from Rep. Curt Weldon to Lt. Col. Sean M. Frisbee, USAF, May 24, 2004. Weldon wrote the letter when Frisbee was researching his 2004 master's thesis, "Weaponizing the Predator UAV: Toward a New Theory of Weapon System Innovation," School of Advanced Air and Space Studies, Air University, Maxwell AFB, Alabama, 2004.

172   *Raggio told Kostelnik*: More details on Raggio's decision can be found in Whittle, "Predator's Big Safari," pp. 15–19.

172   *two experimental ones*: The one-hundred-pound cruise missile was the Low Cost Autonomous Attack System (LOCAAS), which was being developed at the time by Lockheed Martin Corporation as an Air Force Research Laboratory project. The LOCAAS was later cancelled.

172   *Jumper got a briefing*: "Predator Weaponization Decision Brief," Col. Bob Dehnert, ASC/RA, June 21, 2000, copy in the author's possession.

173   *leaders were especially sensitive*: Tom McLemore, "New Start Notification," *American Society of Military Comptrollers* (Washington chapter newsletter), June 2000; and House Report of the Committee on Appropriations, July 20, 1999, report 106–244, p. 9.

174   *Jumper turned to Tom Cassidy*: Author interviews with Jumper and Cassidy.

174   *"wants to make rapid progress"*: Jumper's explanation comes from a memo Dehnert wrote the next day to his immediate superior, "Memo for AFMC/CC, Subject: Predator/Hellfire Demo, Baseline vs. Accelerated, Robert E. Dehnert Jr., Colonel, USAF, Director, Reconnaissance SPO," copy in the author's possession.

176 *On July 28*: "Predator UAV Program—HELLFIRE Monthly Acquisition Report," November 2000, copy in the author's possession.

176 *Because the Hellfire would get away*: Dr. [Lawrence J.] Delaney [SAF/AQ] Predator/Hellfire Demo Status Update, August 16, 2000, Col. Bob Dehnert.

176 *Predator 3034*: Predator MQ-1L 97-3034 flight records, on file at the National Air and Space Museum, Washington, D.C.

177 *lawyers issued a legal opinion*: Predator/Hellfire Demo Status Update briefing, Maj. Ray Pry, ASC/RAB, October 25, 2000.

178 *e-mail to Jumper and others*: E-mail from Lt. Gen. Stephen Plummer, principal deputy assistant secretary of the Air Force for acquisition, to Gen. John Jumper et al., "Subject: Predator Weaponization," September 23, 2000, copy provided to the author by Air Force Public Affairs.

178 *the ACC commander e-mailed*: E-mail from Gen. John Jumper to Gen. Michael Ryan, "Subject: Predator Weaponization," September 24, 2000, copy provided to the author by Air Force Public Affairs.

9: HELLFIRE AND HESITATION

182 *China Lake Naval Air Weapons Station*: China Lake fact sheet, Naval Air Warfare Center Weapons Division, accessed at http://www.navair.navy.mil/index. cfm?fuseaction=home.display&key=AB5BB400-266F-4410-8733 -7D90BCA793C1.

183 *Clarke . . . pointed out*: Author interview with Richard Clarke.

183 *on January 2*: Timeline of Predator 3034 modification and Hellfire testing provided to the author by General Atomics Aeronautical Systems.

184 *Reaching Mach 1.3*: The missile speed calculations were provided to the author by former Army Hellfire engineer Terry McLean.

186 *crashed Predator 3023 at Nellis*: "Predator UAV Destroyed by Crash During Testing at Nellis Last Week," *Inside the Air Force*, September 21, 2000; and author interview with Lt. Col. (Ret.) Ken Kilmurray.

187 *finished on December 29*: Clarke, "Strategy for Eliminating the Threat," was classified on December 29, 2000, eight days after Big Safari Director Bill Grimes was told that the conflict with the INF Treaty had been resolved and the Hellfire project could proceed. Clarke's memo was declassified in part on April 7, 2004.

187 *Clarke sent the new national security adviser*: Richard A. Clarke, "Information Memorandum for Condoleezza Rice, From: Richard A. Clarke, Subject: Presidential Policy Initiative/Review—The Al Qida Network," classified January 25, 2001, declassified in part April 7, 2004.

188 *For three full days*: Author interviews with participants.

191 *The unarmed missile traveled*: Christopher Dusseault, "Predator Hellfire Live Fire Demonstration," paper presented by General Atomics Aeronautical Systems Inc., engineer Christopher Dusseault, to the Association of Unmanned Vehicle Systems International, August 1, 2001.

194 *draft an order*: 9/11 Commission Report, p. 210.

195 *paint a target from five miles*: Author interviews with William M. Casey.

196 *offered a dry assessment*: Timeline of Predator 3034 modification and Hellfire testing provided to the author by General Atomics Aeronautical Systems.

200 *Clarke was increasingly frustrated*: Clarke, *Against All Enemies*, p. 231.

200 *a new, more comprehensive approach*: 9/11 Commission Report, p. 202

200 *April 30 Deputies Committee session*: Clarke, *Against All Enemies*, p. 231.

200 *"I do not believe"*: 9/11 Commission Report, pp. 211 and 513n238.

201 *Cofer Black wanted*: Coll, *Ghost Wars*, p. 544.

202 *The edifice Mattoon*: Barton Gellman, "A Strategy's Cautious Evolution; Before Sept. 11, the Bush Anti-Terror Effort Was Mostly Ambition," *Washington Post*, January 20, 2002; Chitra Ragavan, Carol Hook, Danielle Burton, and Stephanie Salmon, "Clinton, Bush, and the Hunt for bin Laden," *U.S. News & World Report*, September 29, 2006, accessed at http://www.usnews.com/usnews/news/articles /060929/29predator.htm.

202 *exterior walls stood*: The measurements and other details of "Taco Bell" are taken from plans for the building provided to the author.

206 *terrorist threats against the United States*: 9/11 Commission Report, p. 255.

206 *"system was blinking red"*: Ibid., p. 254.

207 *lining the room's walls*: Author interviews with participants.

208 *Campbell found this comforting*: Author interview with Lt. Gen. (Ret.) John Campbell.

10: READY OR NOT

210 *"What if I could figure out"*: Author interviews with Werner.

211 *All through June*: 9/11 Commission Report, pp. 255–59.

211 *Richard Clarke convened*: Clarke, *Against All Enemies*, p. 236.

211 *sent a memo to CIA Deputy Director*: 9/11 Commission Report, p. 211.

211 *sent ten key members*: The letters went to the chairmen and ranking minority members of the Senate and House Armed Services committees, the Senate and House Defense Appropriations subcommittees, and the House Permanent Select Committee on Intelligence. Copies in the author's possession.

214 *meeting that same day*: 9/11 Commission Report, pp. 211–12.

216 *CTC operations center was crowded*: Greg Miller, "Warning on Focus of Spy Agencies," *Washington Post*, March 21, 2013, p. 1.

217 *gave General Atomics a new contract*: Department of the Air Force, 645th Material Squadron (AFMC), "Statement of Work for General Atomics Aeronautical Systems Incorporated, Predator HELLFIRE Integration Phase III Program," Contract F33657-98-G-3110-0020-05, Predator Program, July 11, 2001, copy in the author's possession.

218 *Pace told Tom Cassidy*: Author interview with Frank Pace.

222 *NSC Deputies Committee had decided*: 9/11 Commission Report, p. 212.

222 *That order*: Executive Order 12333, United States intelligence activities, 46 FR 59941, 3 CFR, 1981 Comp., December 4, 1981, p. 200.

224 *also still skeptical*: George Tenet, *At the Center of the Storm: My Years at the CIA* (New York: HarperCollins, 2007), p. 160.

224 *was even more opposed*: Daniel Benjamin and Steven Simon, *The Age of Sacred Terror: Radical Islam's War Against America* (New York: Random House, 2002), p. 344. Clarke, who was present at the September 4, 2001, meeting, cites *The Age of Sacred Terror's* description in his own book on page 222.

225 *After a brief discussion*: 9/11 Commission Report, p. 213.

225 *memo laid out*: Coll, *Ghost Wars*, p. 573.

225 *led to heated discussion*: Clarke, *Against All Enemies*.

225 *Tenet, who had been briefed*: George Tenet, written statement to the National Commission on Terrorist Attacks upon the United States, March 24, 2004, accessed at http://www.msnbc.msn.com/id/4592866/ns/us_news-security/.

226 *He contended*: Author interview with attendees at the September 4, 2001, meeting; Tenet, *At the Center of the Storm*, p. 160. Tenet writes that "the Predator still wasn't ready" to fly "weaponized," though "the Hellfire missile system was slowly edging toward being ready for deployment." Tenet also writes, "There was a legitimate question about whether aircraft firing missiles at enemies of the United States should be the function of the military or the CIA. It was an important issue, or so it seemed at the time, and I was skeptical about whether a military weapon should be fired outside the military chain of command."

226 *agreed that was a good idea*: 9/11 Commission Report, p. 214.

228 *launch-and-recovery team*: Woodward, *Bush at War*, p. 110.

11: WILDFIRE

233 *When the attacks began*: Author interviews with Gen. (Ret.) John P. Jumper, 2011 and 2014.

235 *Johns said he'd have to call*: Author interviews with Col. (Ret.) William Grimes and Lt. Col. (Ret.) Kenneth Johns.

235 *set up the communications structure*: Welch's father, Gen. (Ret.) Larry D. Welch, was Air Force chief of staff from 1986 to 1990. In a September 8, 2004, oral history interview for the Institute for Defense Analysis, retired general Welch said of his son, Paul, "He was the leader of the technical team that put together the control communications and the control stuff to fly the Predator from Langley, Virginia. Many experts said it couldn't be done because of the latency problem. But combat comm people don't know 'can't' and his colonel made certain that they had every opportunity to make it work and they did. So they can fly the Predator over Afghanistan and Iraq from the 5th floor of a building in Langley, Virginia." General Welch was incorrect about the location of the Predator flight controls, which were in a stand-alone ground control station on the CIA campus, not on the "5th floor of a building." Military Operations Research Society Oral History Interview with General Larry D. Welch, September 8, 2004, Institute for Defense Analyses (IDA), Alexandria, Virginia, Jim Bexfield and Bob Sheldon, interviewers, published in *Military Operations Research* 9, no. 4 (2004).

237 *airfield in Uzbekistan*: Woodward, *Bush at War*, p. 110.

239 *happy to let the two colonels*: Author interview with Lt. Mike Kennedy, Arkansas State Police, December 17, 2013.

241 *took off again at 7:00 p.m.*: Arrival and departure times of the C-17 are taken from contemporaneous notes kept by one member of the Predator team.

244 *Bush replied*: "There's No Rules," CNN.com, http://edition.cnn.com/2001/US/09 /17/gen.bush.transcript.

245 *memorandum specifically empowered*: Woodward, *Bush at War*, p. 101.

245 *would have to obtain*: Ibid., p. 166.

247 *residence bin Laden had built*: Coll, *Ghost Wars*, p. 493. A description of the compound can also be found in Jon Lee Anderson, *The Lion's Grave: Dispatches from Afghanistan* (New York: Grove Press, 2002).

247 *Omar added a T-shaped bunker*: "U.S. Special Forces Using Former Taliban Base," Associated Press, February 1, 2007.

247 *The initial strikes*: Benjamin S. Lambeth, "Air Power Against Terror: America's Conduct of Operation Enduring Freedom," prepared for the U.S. Central Command Air Forces, RAND National Defense Research Institute, Santa Monica, Calif., 2005, pp. 78–79.

248 *fighter-bombers were waiting*: Contemporaneous notes taken by an officer in the Combined Air Operations Center on October 7, 2001, and shown to the author.

248 *best evidence available*: The only detailed written account authored by a participant in the drama surrounding the attempt to kill Mullah Omar appears in Gen. (Ret.) Tommy Franks's memoir, *American Soldier*, written with Malcolm McConnell (New York: HarperCollins, 2004). Blatant inaccuracies in Franks's account, however, call into question the credibility of the rest. Franks describes, for example, talking directly to the pilot of the Predator, which pilot Scott Swanson and others present at the CIA on October 7, 2001, say never happened and was never contemplated. The chain of communication ran from Franks to an Army lieutenant colonel at the CIA who was his liaison, then to the Air Force operations director, then to the Air Force mission manager, and then to the pilot. Other participants dispute many other aspects of Franks's account, which among other things misstates by five hours the time difference between Tampa and Kandahar. Through an assistant, Franks declined the author's e-mailed request for an interview.

250 *Their view*: Author interview with Gen. (Ret.) Victor E. "Gene" Renuart Jr., U.S. Central Command operations director as the Afghan war began.

250 *Franks would later write*: None of several Air Force members of the Predator team on duty that night could recall Franks ordering the initial Hellfire shot he describes in his book.

251 *Franks wrote in a memoir*: Franks, *American Soldier*.

12: CLEARED TO FIRE

256 *argued with the CIA*: Franks reports nothing about this debate in his memoir, *American Soldier*.

256 *"As I watched"*: Franks, *American Soldier*, p. 293.

264 *"We ought to have 50"*: Woodward, *Bush at War*, p. 223.

265 *The first night of the war*: Pentagon News Briefing, Secretary Donald Rumsfeld and Gen. Richard B. Myers, chairman of the Joint Chiefs of Staff, October 9, 2001, transcript available at www.defense.gov.

267 *the only UAV in use*: A Pentagon spokesman announced on November 2, 2001, that the RQ-4 Global Hawk—a high-altitude UAV that, like the Predator, began as an Advanced Concept Technology Demonstration but first flew in 1998— would deploy to Afghanistan. The only other UAVs available at the time were the RQ-2 Pioneer, used by the Marine Corps, and the RQ-5 Hunter and RQ-7 Shadow, used by the Army. All of those were small, offered little endurance, and had sparked no great interest in drones. The Hunter program, in fact, had been cancelled in 1996, but the Army still owned four systems of eight aircraft each. As neither the Marine Corps nor the Army deployed to Afghanistan in the early days of the war, none of these UAVs was in use there at the time Rumsfeld was describing. For more detail, see Office of the Secretary of Defense, "Unmanned Aerial Vehicles Roadmap 2002–2007," published and released December 2002.

267 *journalist Seymour Hersh revealed*: Seymour Hersh, "Annals of National Security, King's Ransom, How Vulnerable Are the Saudi Royals?" *New Yorker*, October 22, 2001, p. 35. Hersh's description of the armed Predator's use by the CIA in Afghanistan was a global scoop, though his description of the aircraft and his account of the Mullah Omar pursuit are incorrect in many details.

268 *quickly followed up*: Tom Ricks, "U.S. Arms Unmanned Aircraft; 'Revolution' in Sky Above Afghanistan," *Washington Post*, October 18, 2001, p. A1.

273 *One G*: "One G" can be seen at http://www.youtube.com/watch?v=K5YD3BZO7Ys.

274 *first U.S. troops into Afghanistan*: Charles H. Briscoe, Richard L. Kiper, James A. Schroder, and Kalev I. Sepp, *Weapon of Choice: U.S. Army Special Operations Forces in Afghanistan* (Fort Leavenworth, Kans.: Combat Studies Institute Press, 2003), p. 96.

13: NEVER MIND . . . WE'LL DO IT OURSELVES

276 *319-count indictment*: Indictment S(9) 98 Cr. 1023 (LBS), U.S. District Court, Southern District of New York, November 4, 1998.

277 *State Department offered*: "Reward Offer: Osama Bin Laden and Mohammad Atef," press statement by James P. Rubin, spokesman, U.S. Department of State, November 4, 1998.

277 *acquire biological and chemical weapons*: Wright, *Looming Tower*, p. 343.

277 *Atef publicly took credit*: Peter Bergen, *The Osama bin Laden I Know* (New York: Free Press, 2006), p. 255.

277 *Atef personally searched them*: Khaled Dawoud, "Mohammed Atef: Egyptian Militant Who Rose to the Top of the al-Qaida Hierarchy," *Guardian*, November 18, 2001.

278 *"I have seen those reports"*: Department of Defense news transcript, "Secretary Rumsfeld Media Availability at Great Lakes, Ill., Friday, November 16, 2001— 12:29 p.m. EST."

278 *Rear Admiral John Stufflebeem said*: Department of Defense news transcript, "Enduring Freedom Operational Update—Rear Adm. Stufflebeem, Joint Staff, November 16, 2001—12:00 PM EDT."

278 *told the Associated Press*: Associated Press, "Taliban Confirms Death of Osama bin Laden's Military Chief in U.S. Strike," November 17, 2001.

278 *CNN reported*: "Reports Suggest Al Qaeda Military Chief Killed," CNN.com/ World, November 17, 2001, posted 5:52 AM EST (1052 GMT), at http://edition. cnn.com/2001/WORLD/asiapcf/central/11/17/ret.atef.reports.

280 *known "bad guy frequencies"*: Intelligence experts and retired Air Force generals said describing this method of using the Predator's radio to eavesdrop in 2001 reveals no classified or sensitive information. As an Associated Press dispatch reported in early 2013, an Al Qaeda "tip sheet" for avoiding drone strikes, found by an AP reporter in Timbuktu, Mali, included a recommendation to "maintain complete silence of all wireless contacts."

287 *the "Kabul-ki Dance"*: Senior Airman Benjamin Sutton, "'Kabulki Dance' Air-craft Makes History, Becomes Permanent Historic Display," *Air Force Print News Today*, August 10, 2011.

288 *Allouni said that while fleeing*: Gene Mater, "BBC's Kabul News Bureau Damaged by Bomb During Live Broadcast," freedomforum.org, posted November 14, 2001, at http://www.freedomforum.org/templates/document.asp?documentID=15355.

290 *the* New York Times *revealed*: Judith Miller and Eric Schmitt, "Ugly Duckling Turns Out to Be Formidable in the Air," *New York Times*, November 23, 2001.

291 *drew a large X through*: Woodward, *Bush at War*, p. 316.

292 *armed Predators would be designated*: Dr. James M. George, "Predator Comes to Air Combat Command (1994–2005)," Office of ACC History, Headquarters, Air Combat Command, Langley Air Force Base, Virginia, August 2006, pp. 80–81.

293 *issued a report declaring*: Christopher J. Castelli, "Predator UAV Given Poor Review by Pentagon Testers," InsideDefense.com, October 30, 2001. The tests were conducted by the Air Force Operational Test and Evaluation Center and Air Combat Command with unarmed versions of the Predator, judging them against standards set in an official Operational Requirements Document. The testers said the Predator was "unable to provide reliable, effective communica-tions through the aircraft, as required, or meet the target location accuracy requirement under operational conditions."

EPILOGUE

297 *"What do you mean"*: Nate Self, *Two Wars: One Hero's Fight on Two Fronts— Abroad and Within* (Carol Stream, Ill.: Tyndale House Publishers, 2008), p. 194.

297 *Self had picked up*: Ibid.

297   *The first missile launched*: Self thought that the first Hellfire shot was simply a miss. Predator pilot Big said years later that he and Will were asked by Brown to fire a demonstration shot, as Sean Naylor reported in *Not a Good Day to Die: The Untold Story of Operation Anaconda* (New York: Penguin, 2005). Boyle said the Predator crew put the missile where Self asked but that Self was mistaken about where the Al Qaeda fighters were. Other written accounts also disagree on why the first Hellfire shot was wasted.

297   *"Rocks, dirt and branches flew"*: Naylor, *Not a Good Day to Die*, p. 357.

299   *An April 2001 Defense Department study*: "Unmanned Aerial Vehicles Roadmap, 2000–2025," Office of the Secretary of Defense.

300   *more than two million flight hours*: "RPAs Reach 2 Million Hours," Air Force News Service, October 23, 2013.

300   *changed the character of America's spy agency*: The effect of the Predator and the war with Al Qaeda and its allies on the CIA after 9/11 is closely examined in Mazzetti, *The Way of the Knife*.

302   *Killed, along with five others*: Al-Harethi's death is still often described, incorrectly, as the first drone strike.

302   *estimated that the CIA conducted*: "Drone Wars, Pakistan: Analysis," New America Foundation, http://natsec.newamerica.net/drones/pakistan/analysis.

303   *agreed to many if not all*: Mazzetti, *The Way of the Knife*, pp. 86–87 and 108–9.

303   *said to have aided and abetted*: Peter Finn, "Awlaki Directed Christmas 'Underwear Bomber' Plot, Justice Department Memo Says," *Washington Post*, February 10, 2012.

303   *Critics questioned*: Charlie Savage, "Relatives Sue Officials over U.S. Citizens Killed by Drone Strikes in Yemen," *New York Times*, July 19, 2012.

303   *Obama finally addressed the issue*: The White House, Office of the Press Secretary, May 23, 2013, news release, "Remarks by the President at the National Defense University."

304   *"Presidential Policy Guidance"*: The White House, Office of the Press Secretary, May 23, 2013, "Fact Sheet: U.S. Policy Standards and Procedures for the Use of Force in Counterterrorism Operations Outside the United States and Areas of Active Hostilities."

308   *Guay told his younger brother*: Author interview with Scott Guay, March 31, 2014.

SELECTED BIBLIOGRAPHY

Aloni, Shlomo. *Israeli A-4 Skyhawk Units in Combat.* New York: Osprey Publishing, 2009.

Anderegg, C. R. *Sierra Hotel: Flying Air Force Fighters in the Decade After Vietnam.* Washington, D.C.: Air Force History and Museums Program, 2001.

Atkinson, Rick. *In the Company of Soldiers.* New York: Henry Holt and Company, 2004.

Barzilai, Yaniv. *102 Days of War: How Osama bin Laden, Al Qaeda & the Taliban Survived 2001.* Washington, D.C.: Potomac Books, 2013.

Benjamin, Daniel, and Steven Simon. *The Age of Sacred Terror: Radical Islam's War Against America.* New York: Random House, 2002.

Bergen, Peter L. *The Osama bin Laden I Know.* New York: Free Press, 2006.

———. *The Longest War: The Enduring Conflict Between America and al-Qaeda.* New York: Free Press, 2011.

Briscoe, Charles H., Richard L. Kiper, James A. Schroder, and Kalev I. Sepp. *Weapon of Choice: U.S. Army Special Operations Forces in Afghanistan.* Fort Leavenworth, Kans.: Combat Studies Institute Press, 2003.

Ceruzzi, Paul E. *Computing: A Concise History.* Cambridge, Mass.: MIT Press, 2012.

Clarke, Arthur C. *2001: A Space Odyssey,* based on a screenplay by Stanley Kubrick and Arthur C. Clarke. New York: New American Library, 2000.

Clarke, Richard A. *Against All Enemies.* New York: Free Press, 2004.

Coll, Steve. *Ghost Wars: The Secret History of the CIA, Afghanistan, and Bin Laden, from the Soviet Invasion to September 10, 2001.* New York: Penguin, 2004.

Crumpton, Henry A. *The Art of Intelligence: Lessons from a Life in the CIA's Clandestine Service.* New York: Penguin, 2012.

Du Picq, Col. Ardant. *Battle Studies: Ancient and Modern Battle.* Harrisburg, Pa.: Military Service Publishing Company, 1947.

Ehrhard, Thomas P. "Unmanned Aerial Vehicles in the United States Armed Services: A Comparative Study of Weapon System Innovation." PhD dissertation, Johns Hopkins University, Washington, D.C., June 2000.

Ehrhard, Thomas P. *Air Force UAVs: The Secret History*. Arlington, Va.: Mitchell Institute for Airpower Studies, 2010.

Franks, Tommy, with Malcolm McConnell. *American Soldier*. New York: HarperCollins, 2004.

Geraghty, Col. Timothy J., USMC (Ret.). *Peacekeepers at War: Beirut 1983—The Marine Commander Tells His Story*. Washington, D.C.: Potomac Books, 2009.

Grossman, Lt. Col. Dave. *On Killing: The Psychological Cost of Learning to Kill in War and Society*, revised ed. New York: Back Bay Books/Little, Brown and Company, 2009.

Khan, Riaz Mohammad. *Afghanistan and Pakistan: Conflict, Extremism, and Resistance to Modernity*. Washington, D.C.: Woodrow Wilson Center Press, 2011.

Knotts, Col. (Ret.) Jerry, and Col. (Ret.) Patrick R. O'Malley. "The Big Safari Program Story . . . as Told by the Big Safari People." Unpublished manuscript provided to the author.

Lambeth, Benjamin S. "Air Power Against Terror: America's Conduct of Operation Enduring Freedom." Prepared for the United States Central Command Air Forces, RAND National Defense Research Institute, Santa Monica, Calif., 2005.

Lehman, John F., Jr. *Command of the Seas*. Annapolis, Md.: Naval Institute Press, 2008.

Lippold, Kirk S. *Front Burner: Al Qaeda's Attack on the USS* Cole. New York: Public Affairs, 2012.

MacPherson, Malcolm. *Roberts Ridge: A Story of Courage and Sacrific on Takur Ghar Mountain, Afghanistan*. New York: Bantam Dell, 2005.

Martin, Matt J., with Charles W. Sasser. *Predator: The Remote-Control Air War over Iraq and Afghanistan: A Pilot's Story*. Minneapolis, Minn.: Zenith Press, 2010.

Moskin, J. Robert. *The U.S. Marine Corps Story*. Old Saybrook, Conn.: Konecky & Konecky, 1992.

Munson, Kenneth. *World Unmanned Aircraft*. London: Jane's Publishing Company Ltd., 1988.

National Commission on Terrorist Attacks upon the United States (Philip Zelikow, Executive Director; Bonnie D. Jenkins, Counsel; Ernest R. May, Senior Advisor). *The 9/11 Commission Report*, authorized edition. New York: W. W. Norton, 2004.

Naylor, Sean. *Not a Good Day to Die: The Untold Story of Operation Anaconda*. New York: Penguin, 2005.

Neville, Leigh. *Takur Ghar: The SEALs and Rangers on Roberts Ridge, Afghanistan, 2002*. New York: Osprey Publishing, 2013.

Newcome, Laurence R. *Unmanned Aviation: A Brief History of Unmanned Aerial Vehicles*. Reston, Va.: American Institute of Aeronautics and Astronautics, 2004.

Newman, Rick, and Don Shepperd. *Bury Us Upside Down: The Misty Pilots and the Secret Battle for the Ho Chi Minh Trail*. New York: Presidio Press, 2006.

Nordeen, Lon O. *Air Warfare in the Missile Age.* Washington, D.C.: Smithsonian Institution Press, 2002.

Office of the Secretary of Defense. "Unmanned Aerial Vehicles Roadmap 2002–2007." Published and released December 2002.

Pater, Alan F. *United States Battleships: The History of America's Great Fighting Fleet.* Beverly Hills, Calif.: Monitor Book Company, 1968.

Rizzo, John. *Company Man: Thirty Years of Controversy and Crisis in the CIA.* New York: Scribner, 2014.

Rozin, Orit. *The Rise of the Individual in 1950s Israel: A Challenge to Collectivism.* Waltham, Mass.: Brandeis University Press, 2011.

Rumsfeld, Donald. *Known and Unknown: A Memoir.* New York: Sentinel, 2011.

Self, Nate. *Two Wars: One Hero's Fight on Two Fronts—Abroad and Within.* Carol Stream, Ill.: Tyndale House Publishers Inc., 2008.

Simon, Reeva Spector, Michael Menachem Laskier, and Sara Reguer, eds. *The Jews of the Middle East and North Africa in Modern Times.* New York: Columbia University Press, 2003.

Singer, P. W. *Wired for War: The Robotics Revolution and Conflict in the 21st Century.* New York: Penguin, 2009.

Tenet, George, with Bill Harlow. *At the Center of the Storm: My Years at the CIA.* New York: HarperCollins, 2007.

Thirtle, Michael R., Robert V. Johnson, and John L. Birkler. "The Predator ACTD: A Case Study for Transition Planning to the Formal Acquisition Process." Prepared for the Office of the Secretary of Defense, RAND National Defense Research Institute, Santa Monica, Calif., 1997.

Wagner, William. *Lightning Bugs and Other Reconnaissance Drones: The Can-Do Story of Ryan's Unmanned "Spy Planes."* Fallbrook, Calif.: Aero Publishers Inc., 1982.

Wilson, George. *Supercarrier.* New York: Macmillan, 1986.

Woodward, Bob. *Bush at War.* New York: Simon and Schuster, 2002.

Wright, Lawrence. *The Looming Tower: Al-Qaeda and the Road to 9/11.* New York: Alfred A. Knopf, 2006.

Yenne, Bill. *Attack of the Drones: A History of Unmanned Aerial Combat.* St. Paul, Minn.: Zenith Press, 2004.

ACKNOWLEDGMENTS

This book is the product of a journey of discovery that began five years ago and led me to a number of facts and stories that some institutions and officials have been reluctant to see revealed. It is therefore not merely difficult but impossible to thank by name all of the dozens of people who gave me the benefit of their time, knowledge, insights, documents, contacts, advice, or just encouragement. For various reasons, some who helped insist on remaining anonymous. You know who you are; I hope you know how grateful I am. I am equally grateful to a number of people who played roles in the rise of the Predator and generously helped me understand it, but whose names go unmentioned in this book. I hope they will understand that the demands of narrative rather than lack of gratitude are to blame for their anonymity.

It would have been impossible to write this book without the cooperation of its main characters, particularly the inimitable Abe Karem and the utterly different but equally inimitable Neal and Linden Blue. Each is among the most extraordinary people I have ever met in a career that has often put me in close proximity to extraordinary people. Each has been generous with his time and assistance, and I am grateful to all three for opening to me not only their own doors but also the doors of others.

Another who has been a great friend to this project is retired Air Force Lieutenant General David Deptula, one of those rare military officers who truly understands the media and who, as a result, earns the media's respect. Aside from sharing his own recollections with me, Dave spent many hours over the past five years helping me try to understand and deal with his beloved Air Force. For all these reasons, I will always be grateful to him.

I am deeply grateful to many others who played larger roles in the Predator story and whose names appear often in the narrative. Many granted me one or more lengthy interviews, followed by repeated phone calls and e-mails to verify facts. So many helped so much that to name them one by one and describe their contributions would require several pages. I hope it will suffice if here I simply say to them as well, you know who you are, and I hope you know how much I value all you have done for me and this book.

The list of those who played no role in the story but contributed greatly to my ability to tell it, and to whom I am also indebted, includes people at two prestigious Washington addresses where it has been my privilege to work on this project: the Woodrow Wilson International Center for Scholars and the Smithsonian Institution's National Air and Space Museum.

At the Wilson Center, rightly ranked as one of the top ten research institutions in the world, I thank Sam Wells for opening the door and Rob Litwak for inviting me in as a Public Policy Scholar in 2011. That opportunity marked a turning point in my research, and my work that year was greatly aided by my Wilson Center intern, the diligent Dylan Jones. My seven-month stay in 2011 turned into a continuing affiliation, and in 2013 I had the honor of being named a Wilson Center Global Fellow, for which I again thank Rob Litwak, as well as Mike Van Dusen and Jane Harman. Among the many benefits of being affiliated with such a respected think tank is the ability to lean on some of the world's best librarians, who include the Wilson Center's unfailingly helpful Janet Spikes and Michelle Kamalich. I owe them both greatly for going above and beyond the call of duty to assist me on many occasions.

I was able to finish this book as the Alfred V. Verville Fellow for 2013–14 at the National Air and Space Museum, where the benefits include not only financial support but also the privilege of having an office around the corner or down the hall from some of the best aerospace historians alive. At the NASM there are several people I want to thank for their support, advice, and help, as well as their collegiality. The list begins with my two primary advisers, Aeronautics Department Chairman Bob van der Linden and Space History Department Chairman Paul Ceruzzi. It includes fellowship committee chairman Dom Pisano, fellowship program coordinator Collette Williams, NASM director General (Ret.) John Dailey (USMC), Deputy Director Roger Launius, and Tom Paone. But above all I must thank the NASM's Roger Connor, my guru on drones, rotorcraft, and just about any other aerospace topic. Roger and I met as I worked on my previous book, *The Dream Machine: The Untold History of the Notorious V-22 Osprey*, and I have drawn on him regularly and relentlessly ever since as a reservoir of advice, information, and enjoyable conversation. On this book, Roger's counsel has been invaluable at every stage, from suggesting research materials and other sources as I was getting started, to helping me define my concept for the book, to encouraging my interest in the Verville Fellowship, to reading and commenting on my draft manuscript. Roger even scanned photos for me to include in the book. Without question, this is a better book because of his generous help. If there are errors in it, they of course are my responsibility.

Many others deserve thanks for lending their support in other ways as I researched and wrote this book. They include former Air Force Secretary F. Whitten Peters, Robert L. Hutchings of the University of Texas, William Warmbrodt of NASA Ames Research Center, Michael Hirschberg of the American Helicopter Society International, J. J. Gertler of the Congressional Research Service, and John Harrington, Amir Pasic, and Eliot Cohen of the Johns Hopkins University School of Advanced International Studies, where I was honored to be a visiting scholar in 2011–12. I also thank Rebecca Grant, former director of the Air Force Association's Mitchell Institute for Airpower Studies, for publishing my 2011 Mitchell Institute monograph, "Predator's Big Safari." I am grateful as well to Linda Shiner, editor of *Air & Space Smithsonian*, for giving me the opportunity in 2013 to profile Abraham Karem in her fine magazine.

Others who have written about the Predator deserve my thanks for sharing their insights and documents. I am grateful to David Fulghum, now retired but for many years one of the brightest stars at *Aviation Week & Space Technology*, for giving me a copy of an unpublished Big Safari history that was illuminating, as well as pointing me to groundbreaking articles he wrote about this obscure organization during his impressive career. I am also grateful to Air Force Colonel Sean Frisbee, who shared not only his thoughts and knowledge but also a trove of key documents he collected as he wrote his excellent 2004 Air University master's thesis, "Weaponizing the Predator UAV: Toward a New Theory of Weapon System Innovation."

The Air University is a natural starting point for any research on Air Force topics, and I thank Colonel John Davis of the Air Force Research Institute, who as a lieutenant colonel at the Air University in 2009 provided academic papers and Air Force contacts that helped me get this project off the ground. For more recent Air Force assistance, I thank Major Mary Danner-Jones of Air Force Public Affairs for patiently arranging important interviews and quickly reviewing documents for release as I raced toward the finish line. She is a true professional.

Few if any books are shaped by an author alone, and on this one, the influence of several people is invisible but has been invaluable. I am lucky to have the best literary agent in the business, Richard Abate, who kept me focused and resilient as this project turned from a sprint into a marathon. I am also indebted to my friend and literary mentor James Reston Jr., a master craftsman whose seventeen (going on eighteen) books include several renowned narrative histories, and whose advice shaped this one in important ways. I am also grateful to Jim for sharing his wisdom on how to deal with the many challenges of life as an author aside from writing.

This is my first book for Henry Holt and Company, where I have been honored and blessed to have as my editor another master craftsman, John Sterling. When Richard Abate told me that the editor of Rick Atkinson's acclaimed Liberation Trilogy on World War II was interested in my book about the Predator, I was excited. Now, having seen John strengthen and sharpen every page of my manuscript, I am elated. At Henry Holt, I also thank Emi Ikkanda, production editor Chris O'Connell, and copy editor Jenna Dolan for their important contributions to this work.

My first and toughest reader, as always, has been my gifted and giving wife, Faye Ross, who read and reread every chapter as I drafted and redrafted, serving as a one-woman focus group and doing her best to keep me focused on the narrative as well as the facts—a challenge, at times, for a recovering newspaper reporter. For this, and so much else, I love her more than I can say.

INDEX

ABOUT THE AUTHOR

RICHARD WHITTLE is author of *The Dream Machine: The Untold History of the Notorious V-22 Osprey*. A Global Fellow at the Woodrow Wilson Center and a 2013–14 Verville Fellow at the National Air and Space Museum, Whittle has covered the military for three decades, including twenty-two years as Pentagon correspondent for *The Dallas Morning News*. He lives in Chevy Chase, Maryland.